ISBN 978-1-331-43384-2
PIBN 10189635

This book is a reproduction of an important historical work. Forgotten Books uses
state-of-the-art technology to digitally reconstruct the work, preserving the original format
whilst repairing imperfections present in the aged copy. In rare cases, an imperfection in
the original, such as a blemish or missing page, may be replicated in our edition. We do,
however, repair the vast majority of imperfections successfully; any imperfections that
remain are intentionally left to preserve the state of such historical works.

1 MONTH OF
FREE
READING

at
www.ForgottenBooks.com

By purchasing this book you are eligible for one month membership to ForgottenBooks.com, giving you unlimited access to our entire collection of over 700,000 titles via our web site and mobile apps.

To claim your free month visit:
www.forgottenbooks.com/free189635

English
Français
Deutsche
Italiano
Español
Português

www.forgottenbooks.com

Mythology Photography **Fiction** Fishing Christianity **Art** Cooking Essays Buddhism Freemasonry Medicine **Biology** Music **Ancient Egypt** Evolution Carpentry Physics Dance Geology **Mathematics** Fitness Shakespeare **Folklore** Yoga Marketing **Confidence** Immortality Biographies Poetry **Psychology** Witchcraft Electronics Chemistry History **Law** Accounting **Philosophy** Anthropology Alchemy Drama Quantum Mechanics Atheism Sexual Health **Ancient History** **Entrepreneurship** Languages Sport Paleontology Needlework Islam **Metaphysics** Investment Archaeology Parenting Statistics Criminology **Motivational**

THE

JUDGES OF ENGLAND;

WITH

SKETCHES OF THEIR LIVES,

AND

MISCELLANEOUS NOTICES

CONNECTED WITH

THE COURTS AT WESTMINSTER,

FROM THE TIME OF THE CONQUEST.

BY EDWARD FOSS, F.S.A.

OF THE INNER TEMPLE.

VOL. VI.

CONTAINING THE REIGNS OF

JAMES I. AND CHARLES I.; AND THE INTERREGNUM.

1603 — 1660.

LONDON:

LONGMAN, BROWN, GREEN, LONGMANS, & ROBERTS.

1857.

LONDON :
Printed by SPOTTISWOODE & Co.
New-street Square.

CONTENTS

OF

THE SIXTH VOLUME.

JUDGES OF ENGLAND.

JAMES I.

Reigned 22 years and 3 days, from March 24, 1603, to March 27, 1625.

SURVEY OF THE REIGN.

KING JAMES was not content with merely resuming the practice adopted by some of his predecessors, of occasionally appearing in the Court of King's Bench, when the chief justice made way for him and sat at his feet [1]; but he even claimed and attempted to exercise a judicial power. This led to a very amusing discussion between his Majesty and the judges, in which Sir Edward Coke, having stated that it was not competent for the king to decide questions of law, the king said, " that he thought the law was founded upon reason, and that he and others had reason as well as the judges." To this Coke answered, " That true it was, that God had endowed his Majesty with excellent science and great endowments of nature, but his Majesty was not learned in the laws of his realm, and causes which concern the life, or inheritance, or goods, or fortunes of his subjects, they are not to be decided by natural reason, but by the artificial reason and judgment of law; which law is an act which requires long study and experience before that a man can

---

[1] State Trials, iii. 942.

attain to the cognizance of it; and that the law was the
golden mete-wand and measure to try the causes of the subjects; and which protected his Majesty in safety and peace."
The king, greatly offended, said, "That then he should be
under the law, which was treason to affirm : " wherewith Coke
replied, "Bracton saith, *Quod rex non debet esse sub homine,
sed sub Deo et lege*."[1]

Though the manly resistance of Sir Edward Coke in this
instance prevailed, the king could not altogether refrain from
interfering with the practice of the courts.   He enjoined Lord
Ellesmere to delay one suit for the convenience of a defendant, "because he had in the parliament house showed himself
forward in our service;" and to hasten the proceedings in
another, that he might be "freed from the continuall importunities " of the parties.[2]   His attempts to supersede law by
proclamations[3]; his calling the judges to account for judgments
they had given[4]; his "auricular taking of opinions " from
them, as Coke called it, with a view to future conviction[5];
and the reprimand he gave them for disobeying his mandate
not to proceed in a private cause till they had first consulted
him[6]; betray his unfortunate propensity to intermeddle.
Such a course could not but tend to degrade the judicial
character, and to withdraw from the bench that respect and
veneration which had hitherto been its invariable attendants :
and the advice given by Bacon "to make some example
against the presumption of a judge, whereby the whole body
of those magistrates may be contained in better awe,"[7] showed
too ready a disposition to assist the sovereign in destroying
the independence of the bench, and converting the judges
from being expounders of the law, to be mere instruments
for the execution of the royal mandates.   How far the direful

---

[1] 12 Coke's Reports, 65.   [2] Egerton Papers, 464. 483.
[3] 12 Reports, 74.   [4] Ibid. 51.   [5] Johnson's Life of Coke, i. 246.
[6] Bacon's Works (Montagu), vii. 307—338.   [7] Ibid. xii. 36.

events of the next reign are to be attributed to Bacon's counsels, must be a subject of serious reflection with those who consider that one of the principal causes which led to the discontent of the people, was the corruption of the law and the subservience of its administrators.

Coke's sturdiness had few imitators among his colleagues. That they succumbed and acknowledged their error is not to be wondered at, since it is more than probable that they had paid for their places. The general corruption of this reign, which notoriously pervaded almost every department of the state, extended itself to the courts of justice and those connected with them. The proceedings against Lord Chancellor Bacon show that bribery was common, though dignified with the title of presents and new year's gifts. An entry in the archives of the borough of Lyme Regis leaves "to the mayor's discretion *what gratuity* he will give to the lord chief baron and his men" at the assizes in 1620, when their charter was in question.[1] No place or dignity but had its price. Sir James Ley offered the Duke of Buckingham 10,000*l.* for the office of attorney-general; and Sir Henry Yelverton, though he would not condescend to barter for it, felt himself constrained by the common practice, when he was appointed, to present the sum of 4000*l.* into the hands of his Majesty. Even the dignity of the coif could not be obtained without a payment to the king or those about him of 600*l.*; and Sir George Croke, by his refusal to submit to the imposition, enhanced the respect with which his character was regarded.[2]

The question that had long been agitated between the courts of Common Law and the Chancery as to the jurisdiction of the latter over the decisions of the former was now

---

[1] Walter Yonge's Diary, 37.

[2] Judge Whitelocke's Diary, quoted in Montagu's Works of Bacon (Life), vol. xvi. p. cccix. note.

brought to a conclusion, principally in consequence of the violent proceedings of Sir Edward Coke. That great lawyer was dismissed; and the functions claimed by the chancellor were finally established.

The Great Seal during this reign was in the hands of three persons only. The first two were lawyers, who, after being intrusted with it with the title of lord keeper, were honoured with the higher designation of lord chancellor. The third, after an interval of more than fifty years, was again selected from churchmen, and bore the title of lord keeper only.

LORD CHANCELLORS AND KEEPERS.

SIR THOMAS EGERTON, in whose hands the Great Seal had been for the last seven years of Elizabeth's life, was continued in the office of lord keeper by King James; who on July 19, 1603, created him Lord Ellesmere, and on the 24th, constituted him lord chancellor.[1] On November 7, 1616, the title of Viscount Brackley was bestowed upon him; and on March 3, 1617, his infirmities obliged him to resign the Seal, which was given to

SIR FRANCIS BACON, the attorney-general, on March 7, with the title of lord keeper, which was exchanged on the fourth of the following January for that of lord chancellor.[2] He was successively created Lord Verulam on July 11, 1618, and Viscount St. Albans on January 27, 1621. The disgraceful exposure which took place after he had held the office for five years, obliged the king to resume the Seal on May 1, 1621, when a commission was issued to Sir Julius Cæsar, master of the Rolls, Baron Bromley, and Justices Winch, Doderidge, and Sutton, with the masters in Chancery, to hear causes in that court; with two other commissions, one authorising Chief Justice Sir James Ley to act in the House of Peers, and another to three lords, with power to

---

[1] Rot. Claus. 1 Jac. I., p 12.   [2] Ibid. 16 Jac. I., n. 13.

perform the other duties devolving on the lord chancellor. These commissions remained in force for about two months, when

JOHN WILLIAMS, Dean of Westminster, and bishop designate of Lincoln, was on July 10, 1621, constituted lord keeper[1]; which he continued to hold till the death of the king on March 27, 1625.

The allowances to the lord chancellor and lord keeper are detailed in various patents.   He was to receive " for his wages, diettes, robes, and liveries of himself and the masters of our Chancery "' from the keeper of the Hanaper 542*l.* 15*s.* sterling by the year; also 50*l.* for every term, and 300*l.* by the year for his attendance in the Star Chamber: from the chief butler, 60*l.* for twelve tuns of˙wine by the year, and from the keeper of the great wardrobe, 16*l.* for his wax.[2]   What his emoluments were beyond these allowances does not appear; but some idea of them may be formed from the detail subsequently given of the profits of the master of the Rolls and their sources.

Queen Elizabeth's Great Seal was used by King James for more than four months after his accession.   On July 19, 1603, at Hampton Court it was returned to the king, who first struck it with a mallet, and then Charles Anthony, the royal seal engraver, totally destroyed it.   Nothing is said as to the appropriation of the pieces as a perquisite to the lord keeper, to whom a new seal was then delivered.[3]   Within two years this was˙found to be defective; "the canape over the picture of our face is so lowe imbossed, that therby the same scale in that place therof doth easily bruse and take disgrace."   An authority was thereupon given to Charles Anthony " to imbosse and engrave the said canape over the picture of our face higher and deeper;" and this was accord-

---

[1] Claus. 19 Jac. I., p. 13. n. 1.   [2] Rymer, xvi. 541., xvii. 1. 55. 311.
[3] Rymer, xvi. 495.

ingly done in the chancellor's house on the 28th of June,
1605.[1]

Camden, in his annals of this reign, notices the " solemn
procession in mighty pomp" of Sir Francis Bacon, keeper of
the Great Seal, to Westminster on the first day of the term
after his appointment : —

1. Clerks and inferior officers in Chancery.
2. Students in law.
3. Gentlemen, servants to the keeper, serjeants-at-arms, and the seal
   bearer : — all on foot.
4. Himself, on horseback, in a gown of *purple satin*, between the
   treasurer and the keeper of the Privy Seal.
5. Earls, barons, privy councillors.
6. Noblemen of all ranks.
7. Judges, to whom the next place to the privy councillors was assigned.

That the custom, which has only been lately discontinued,
of the lord chancellor having a nosegay of aromatic herbs,
prevailed in this reign, is proved by the authority of Bacon,
who in one of his letters to the king, says " It is my lord
chancellor's fashion, especially towards the summer, to carry
a posy of wormwood.[2]

MASTERS OF THE ROLLS.

SIR THOMAS EGERTON, who during the seven years he had
been lord keeper to Queen Elizabeth had also held the office
of master of the Rolls, was allowed to retain it for nearly
two months after King James's accession.

EDWARD BRUCE, LORD KINLOSS, a senator of the College
of Justice in Scotland, was appointed on May 18, 1603.
After holding the office about seven years he died in it, and
was succeeded by

SIR EDWARD PHELLIPS, serjeant-at-law, on January 14,
1611. He had in 1608 procured a grant of it in reversion

---

[1] Egerton Papers, 402.   [2] Bacon's Works (Montagu), xii. 36.

on Lord Kinloss's death, with a proviso in the patent that the grant should not operate as a precedent; and yet no sooner was Kinloss dead than a similar reversionary grant, to take effect on the death of Sir Edward Phellips, which occurred on September 11, 1614, was made to

SIR JULIUS CÆSAR, chancellor and under treasurer of the Exchequer; who obtained a new patent. of the place on October 1, 1614, and retained it during the king's life.

The emoluments of the office of master of the Rolls, by an account of actual receipts in the four terms preserved among the Lansdowne MSS. vol. 161. No. 329., appear to have been in 1608-9, 1987*l.* 8*s.*; and in 1609-10, 2110*l.* 5*s.* 9*d.* In No. 334 of the same volume is a " General view of fees due to the master of the Rolls, 20 Sept., 1614, " which gives the following detail of the profits : —

" The moytie of the casual fynes payed by the Cursitors upon original writts, and nowe receaved by Whitby, the Lo. Chancellor's servant, and yerely accompted for by him to the M^r. of the Rolles   -   -   -   -   -   -   -   - 900^{li}.

" Fees due for Patents passed the Great Seale, payed and accompted for by the Clerk of the Hanaper at th' end of every terme, being ii^s for every xx^s payed for the seale of any Patent, and so pro rata   -   -   -   -   -   - CC^{li}.

" Fees due for several busynes in the Pettie bagg   -   ·· 400^{li}.

" Fees due out of the Offices of the six Clerks, for decrees, dismissions, exemplifications, and dedims potestatem upon Sheriff's patents, and Escheator's patents   -   -   -   - 300^{li}.

" Fees due from the Clerks of the Inrollments for deeds and recognizances inrolled, and for cancellacons   -   -   - 200^{li}.

" Fees due from the Clerks of the Chappell -   -   - 200^{li}.

A Fee allowed oute of the Exchequer yerelie for exacacon of extracted Rolles   -   -   -   -   -   -   - 10^{li}.

" The Rents of tenements and houses yerelie belonging to the M^r. of the Rolles   -   -   -   -   -   -   - 160^{li}.

" In toto p. computac.   -   - 2370^{li}."

This computation was made on the appointment of Sir Julius Cæsar, who, in 1631, subjoined the following note : —

"Thus the proverb is verified : He that accompts without his hoast must accompt againe : — This exceedeth truth by much; for I found it but at 2200 lib. or thereabouts, in my first yere ; and since abated by litle and litle, so that this last yere it amounted but to 1600 lib. or thereabouts, and no more ; and in Q. Elizabeth's time at 1500, or 1400, or 1300, or 1200, or 1100." [1]

MASTERS IN CHANCERY.

Sir Thomas Egerton, M. R.	1 Jac. I.
Edward Bruce, Lord Kinloss, M. R.	1 to 8 —
Sir Matthew Carew, LL. D.	1 to 16 —
Sir Richard Swale, LL. D.	1 to 6 —
Sir Edward Stanhope, LL. D.	1 to 5 —
Thomas Legge, LL. D.	1 to 5 —
John Hone, LL. D.	1 to 14 —
William or John Hunt, LL. D.	1 to 13 —
Sir John Amye, LL. D.	1 to 19 —
Sir John Tyndall [2]	1 to 14 —
George Carewe	1 to 10 —
Edward Grymstone	1 to ? —
Henry Hickman, LL. D.	1 to 13 —
Henry Thoresbye	5 to 13 —
Sir John Bennet, LL. D.	5 to 19 —
Sir Thomas Crompton, LL. D.	6 -
Sir Thomas Ridley, LL. D.	6 to 17 —
Sir Edward Phellips, M. R.	8 to 12 —
Gregory-Bonhault	10 to 12 —
Sir Julius Cæsar, M. R.	12 to 23 —
Francis James, LL. D.	12 to 23 —
John Wolveridge	13 to 22 —
Sir Charles Cæsar, LL. D.	13 to 23 —
Richard More	13 to 23 —
Sir John Hayward, LL. D.	14 to 23 —
Ewball Thelwall	14 to 23 —

[1] Lodge's Life of Sir Julius Cæsar, 1810, p. 31.

[2] Sir John Tyndall was shot on Nov. 12, 1616, by Mr. Barham, a disappointed suitor, who afterwards hanged himself in prison. Diary of Walter Yonge, p. 28.

Robert Rich	-	-	-	-	-	16 to 23 Jac. I.
John Michell	-	-	-	-	-	17 to 23 —
Edward Salter	-	-	-	-	-	19 to 23 —
Edward Leech	-	-	-	-	-	19 to 23 —
Sir William Birde, LL. D.	-	-	-	19 to 22 —
Sir Peter Mutton	-	-	-	-	22 to 23 —
Edward Clarke	-	-	-	-	-	22 to 23 —

The offices of the Six Clerks in Chancery Lane were burned down on December 19, 1621 [1]; and the Rolls in their custody having been consumed, a proclamation was immediately issued for the relief of those who had suffered by the loss, and to remedy the inconvenience thereby occasioned.[2]

In the first year of his reign, King James thought proper to add another judge to the four who sat in each of the courts of King's Bench and Common Pleas; giving as his reason for doing so, that " many times in cases of great difficulty the judges being equally divided in opinion in either court, the matter depended long undecided." Sir David Williams was accordingly added to the Court of King's Bench, and Sir William Daniel to the Common Pleas; his majesty saying that " Numero Deus impare gaudet."[3] It is to be presumed that the alteration did not answer his expectation, for the odd number was discontinued after the eleventh year.

The salaries paid to the judges from the Exchequer in the time of Sir Edward Coke, were, to the chief justice of the King's Bench 224l. 19s. 4d., to the chief justice of the Common Pleas, 161l. 13s. 4d., and to each of the judges of those courts, 154l. 19s. 8d. They all received, in addition, 33l. 6s. 8d. a year for their circuits, together with their diet and travelling expenses. The chief baron was paid the same as the puisne judges, and the other barons had only 133l. 6s. 8d. each.[4] Their income, therefore, which greatly exceeded that

---

[1] Diary of W. Yonge, 48. [2] Rymer, xvii. 347.
[3] Coke, Pref. to 4 Report. [4] Johnson's Life of Coke, i. 348.

amount, must have principally arisen from the fees appertaining to their offices.

Some of the judges when they went the circuit, adopted the ridiculous fashion of carrying a large fan, with a handle at least half a yard long. Sir William Dugdale (who, however, could not have been above ten years old) saw Sir Edward Coke with such a fan ; and the Earl of Manchester (Sir Edward Montagu) also used one.[1]

The plague visited London soon after James's accession, so that Trinity Term was obliged to be adjourned, and Michaelmas Term was held at Winchester. A further visitation in 1606 occasioned Michaelmas Term to be delayed for three weeks: and in 1625, Michaelmas Term was kept at Reading.[2]

After the gunpowder plot, the court and law business were on every 5th of November "intermitted for a little in the morning, whilst the judges in their robes went solemnly to the great church at Westminster, to give God thanks for our great delivery from the powder treason, and hear a sermon touching it ; which done, they return to their benches."[3]

CHIEF JUSTICES OF THE KING'S BENCH.

SIR JOHN POPHAM, the chief justice of the last reign, continued in his place for the remainder of his life.

SIR THOMAS FLEMING, the chief baron of the Exchequer, succeeded him on June 25, 1607, and presided till his death. His place was filled by

SIR EDWARD COKE, the chief justice of the Common Pleas, on October 25, 1613, till his discharge three years afterwards; when

SIR HENRY MONTAGU, recorder of London and king's

---

[1] Legal Observer, ii. 352.; Diary of Walter Yonge, 89.
[2] Rymer, xvi. 555.; Croke Jac.   [3] Spelman, Reliq. p. 93.

serjeant, was raised to the chief justiceship on November 16, 1616; and filled the office till he was appointed lord high treasurer.

SIR JAMES LEY, attorney of the Court of Wards and Liveries, was then advanced to the head of the court on Jannary 29, 1621; and retired from it, like his predecessor, on obtaining the treasurership.

SIR RANULPHE CREW, one of the king's serjeants, was thereupon constituted chief justice on January 26, 1625, only two months before the king's death on March 27.

JUSTICES OF THE KING'S BENCH.

I. 1603. March.	Francis Gawdy,	⎫	the former judges,
	Edward Fenner,	⎬	received new pa-
	Christopher Yelverton,	⎭	tents.
1604. Feb. 4.	David Williams, a fifth judge, was added.		
III. 1606. Jan. 13.	Laurence Tanfield, vice F. Gawdy.		
V. 1607. June 25.	John Croke, vice L. Tanfield.		
X. 1612. Nov. 25.	John Doderidge, vice C. Yelverton.		
XI. 1613. April 21.	Robert Houghton, vice D. Williams.		
XVIII. 1620. Oct. 8.	Thomas Chamberlayne, vice J. Croke.		
XXII. 1624. Oct. 17.	William Jones, vice R. Houghton.		
18.	James Whitelocke, vice T. Chamberlayne.		

The fifth judge of this court had been discontinued at the death of Sir Edward Fenner. At the end of the reign the judges were

Sir Ranulphe Crew, chief justice,

Sir John Doderidge,   Sir William Jones,

Sir James Whitelocke.

CHIEF JUSTICES OF THE COMMON PLEAS.

SIR EDMUND ANDERSON, Queen Elizabeth's venerable chief justice of the Common Pleas, received a new patent, and presided in the court for nearly two years and a half under King James. At his death,

SIR FRANCIS GAWDY, one of the justices of the King's Bench, was raised to the chief seat in the Common Pleas on August 26, 1605; but died within a year, when

SIR EDWARD COKE, the attorney-general, was constituted chief justice on June 30, 1606. On his advancement to the head of the Court of King's Bench,

SIR HENRY HOBART, the attorney-general, succeeded him on November 26, 1613, and presided in this court for the rest of the reign.

JUSTICES OF THE COMMON PLEAS.

I. 1603.	March.	Thomas Walmesley,	resumed their seats
		George Kingsmill,	under new patents.
		Peter Warburton	
	1604. Feb. 3.	William Daniel, a fifth judge, was added.	
III.	1606. Jan.	Thomas Coventry, vice G. Kingsmill.	
V.	1607. Nov. 24.	Thomas Foster, vice T. Coventry.	
IX.	1611. Nov. 7.	Humphrey Winch, vice W. Daniel.	
X.	1612. Nov. 26.	Augustine Nichols, vice T.Walmesley.	
XV.	1617. May 3.	Richard Hutton, vice A. Nichols.	
XIX.	1621.	William Jones, vice P. Warburton.	
XXI.	1624. Feb. 11.	George Croke, vice T. Foster.	
XXII.	Oct. 18.	Francis Harvey, vice W. Jones.	

The four judges of this court, the place of Sir Humphrey Winch not having been filled, at the end of the reign were

Sir Henry Hobart, chief justice,
Sir Richard Hutton,   Sir George Croke,
Sir Francis Harvey.

CHIEF BARONS OF THE EXCHEQUER.

SIR WILLIAM FERYAM, retaining his former place of chief baron, enjoyed it for about eighteen months under James I. Upon his death,

SIR THOMAS FLEMING, then solicitor-general, was appointed on October 27, 1604; but being removed in less than three years to the chief justiceship of the King's Bench, he was succeeded by

SIR LAURENCE TANFIELD, a judge of the King's Bench, on June 25, 1607, who continued to preside in the Exchequer for the remainder of the king's reign.

BARONS OF THE EXCHEQUER.

I. 1603. March.	John Sotherton, Robert Clarke, John Savile	} received new patents for their former places.
II. 1604. Oct. 14.	George Snigg, as a fifth baron.	
IV. 1606. July 8.	* Nowell Sotherton, vice J. Sotherton.	
1607. Feb. 9.	James Altham, vice J. Savile.	
V. Nov. 5.	Edward Heron, vice R. Clarke.	
VII. 1610. Feb. 6.	Edward Bromley, vice E. Heron.	
VIII. May 26.	* Thomas Cæsar.	
Oct. 24.	* John Sotherton.	
XV. 1617. May 2.	John Denham, vice J. Altham.	

* These three seem to have been merely cursitor barons.

The bench of the Exchequer at the end of this reign was filled by

Sir Laurence Tanfield, chief baron.

Sir Edward Bromley   Sir John Denham.

Sir George Snigg's place was not filled up.

TABLE OF THE CHANCELLORS AND KEEPERS OF THE SEAL, AND OF THE MASTERS OF THE ROLLS.

A. R	A. D.	Lord Chancellors and Keepers.	Masters of the Rolls.
1	1603. March 24	Sir Thomas Egerton, *Keeper*	Sir Thomas Egerton
	May 18	—	Edward Bruce, Lord Kinloss.
	July 19	created Lord Ellesmere	—
	24	— *Chancellor*	
8	1611. Jan. 14	—	Sir Edward Phellips
	1614. Sept. 11	—	Sir Julius Cæsar.
12	1616. Nov. 7	created Viscount Brackley	—
14	1617. March 3	resigned	—
	7	Sir Francis Bacon, *Keeper*	—
	1618. Jan. 4	„ „ *Chancellor*	—
15	July 11	created Lord Verulam	—
16	1621. Jan. 27	„ Viscount St. Albans	—
18	May 1	removed	
19	July 10	John Williams, Bishop of Lincoln, *Keeper*	

The king died March 27, 1625.

TABLE OF THE CHIEF JUSTICES AND JUDGES OF THE KING'S BENCH.

A. R.	A. D.	CHIEF JUSTICES.	JUDGES OF THE KING'S BENCH.						
			Francis Gawdy	Edward Fenner	Christopher Yelverton	David Williams			
1	1603, March	John Popham		—	—	—			
	1604, Feb. 4	—		—	—	—			
3	1606, Jan. 13		Laurence Tanfield	—	—	—			
5	1607, June 25	Thomas Fleming	John Croke		John Doderidge	Robert Houghton			
10	1612, Nr. 25	—	—		—	—			
11	1613, April 21	Edward Coke	—		—	—			
	Oct. 25		—		—	—			
14	1616, Nov 16	Henry Montagu	Thomas Chamberlayne		—	—			
18	1620, Oct. 8	—			—	William Jones			
21	1621, Jan. 29	James Ley	James Whitelocke		—	—			
	1624, Oct. 18	—			—	—			
22	1625, Jan. 26	Ranulphe Crew	—		—	—			

TABLE OF THE CHIEF JUSTICES AND JUDGES OF THE COMMON PLEAS.

A. R.	A. D.	CHIEF JUSTICES.	JUDGES OF THE COMMON PLEAS.			
1	1 603, Mch	Edmund Anderson	Thomas Walmesley	George Kingsmill	Peter Warburton	William Daniel
	1 604, Feb. 3	Francis Gawdy	—	—	—	—
3	1 605, Aug. 26	Edward Coke	—	Thomas Coventry	—	—
4	1 606, Jan.	—	—	—	—	—
	1 606, June 30	—	—	—	—	—
5	1 607, Nov. 24	—	—	Thomas Foster	—	Humphrey Winch.
9	1 611, Nov. 7	—	—	—	—	—
10	1 612, Nov. 26	—	—	—	—	—
11	1 613, Oct. 26	—	Augustine Nichols	—	—	—
13	1 617, May 3	Henry Hobart	Richard Hutton	George Croke	William Jones	—
15	1 621	—	—	—	Francis Harvey	—
19	1 624, Feb. 11	—	—	—	—	—
21	1 624, Oct. 18	—	—	—	—	—
22	1 625, Feb. 4	—	—	—	—	died.

TABLE OF THE CHIEF BARONS AND BARONS OF THE EXCHEQUER.

A. R.	A. D.	CHIEF BARONS.	BARONS OF THE EXCHEQUER.			? CURSITOR BARONS.
1	1603, Mch	William Peryam	John Sotherton	Robert Clarke	John Savile	Nowell Sotherton.
2	1604, Oct. 14	Thomas Fleming	George Snigg	—	—	
	" 27	—	—	—	—	
4	1606, July 8	Laurence Tanfield	—	—	James Altham.	
	1607, Feb. 9	—	—	Edward Heron	—	Thomas Cæsar.
5	June 25	—	—	Edward Bromley	—	John Sotherton.
	Nov. 5	—	—	—	—	—
7	1610, Feb. 6	—	—	—	—	
8	May 26	—	—	—	—	
	Oct. 24	—	—	—	—	
15	1617, May 2	—	—	—	John Denham.	

The name of CURSITOR BARON first occurs in this reign, in an order of the Inner Temple, to be presently noticed; and that such an officer, distinct from the rest of the barons, was now for the first time appointed, seems to be fully established by a consideration of the following facts.

It is true that the office of cursitor baron is, according to the general acceptation, as old as the Exchequer itself, whether the introduction of that department of the state is dated at the time of the Conquest, or in the reign of Henry I. And for this there is some semblance of probability; for the same duties which were, till a recent alteration[1], entrusted to the cursitor baron, have been performed by some officer of the Exchequer from the most distant period. It has therefore not unnaturally been presumed that the executor of those duties in ancient times bore the same title as the officer of the present day. But if it were so, how is it that we never meet with the name of cursitor baron for more than five centuries after the introduction of the Exchequer? Is it not rather extraordinary that it never occurs in any ancient record?— that it is not mentioned in the elaborate history of the court by Madox?—and that it is not noticed in any subsequent work from the end of the reign of Edward II., at which Madox terminates his history, till the early part of that of James I.?

This universal silence — especially on the part of that careful historian Madox, who gives the name and describes the duty of every officer of the court, from the chief justiciary who presided, down to the pesour and the fusour of the metal — cannot fail to create in the mind of any intelligent inquirer a strong doubt whether an officer so called then existed; and to induce him to seek for some further evidence,

---

[1] By stat. 3 and 4 William IV. c. 99., some of these duties are now transferred to the Commissioners for Auditing Public Accounts.

in the hope of finding the time when, and the reason for which, he was actually created.

The principal duty devolving upon the cursitor baron, until the recent act of parliament, was the examination and passing of the accounts of the sheriffs of all the counties in England. There can be no doubt that this duty was originally performed by one of the regular barons, and that at one time they used to travel for some of the purposes connected with it. By a statute of Edward I., it is enacted, " that at one time certain every year, one baron and one clerk of our said Exchequer shall be sent through every shire of England, to inroll the names of all such as have paid that year's debts exacted on them by green wax. And the same baron and clerk shall view all such tallies and inroll them. And shall hear and determine complaints made against sheriffs and their clerks and bailiffs, that have done contrary to the premisses."[1] The examination of the sheriffs' accounts was generally performed in London, and when completed, the baron and the clerk assisting him signed their names at the head. It does not distinctly appear in what order the barons acted; but probably they at first took the duty in turn, and, as after the appointment of a chief baron the others were called the second, third, and fourth baron, it then perhaps became the peculiar province of the junior of these three.

It is therefore evident that at some period this duty was transferred from the regular barons to a distinct officer; and in order to discover when and under what circumstances this probably took place, attention must be directed to the changes that have occurred in the ancient constitution of the court.

In the original institution of the Exchequer, all the judges were lords of the land and actual barons; and until the reign of Henry III. they were indiscriminately styled "Jus-

---

[1] Stat. de Finibus Levatis, 27 Edw. I.; Statutes of the Realm, i. 129.

ticiarii et Barones."[1] On the division of the courts in that reign, the real barons having in the meantime gradually seceded from the employment, special persons were assigned to sit in the Exchequer, "tanquam Baro;" thus retaining the name of baron; and in order to distinguish their business from that of the two other courts, from which they were now separated, their duty was expressly limited "pro negotiis nostris quæ ad idem Scaccarium pertinent."[2] One of these persons, Alexander de Swereford, had previously been a clerk in the Exchequer, and thus was fully cognizant of all the details of the court.

All these barons held equal rank until the reign of Edward II., when, for the first time, one of them was distinguished by the title of Chief Baron.[3] He was sometimes selected from the legal profession; but the other barons were generally men who had acquired practical knowledge of the revenue in the minor offices of the court. They manifestly held an inferior rank to the judges of the other courts, and were not reckoned among them in judicial proceedings. In the statute of Nisi Prius, 14 Edward III., it is enacted, "that if it happen that none of the justices of the one bench nor of the other come into the county, then the Nisi Prius shall be granted before the chief baron of the Exchequer, *if he be a man of the law:*"[4] thus excluding the other barons, and even the chief baron, unless he were a regular lawyer. The same distinction occurs in the reign of Henry IV.[5]; and even the rank of the chief baron does not seem to have been higher than that of the puisne judges of the King's Bench and Common Pleas, if so high; since no less than seven of the chief barons, from the reign of Henry IV. to the middle of that of Henry VIII.[6], held, in addition, the

---

[1] Madox's Exchequer, i. 199, 200.   [2] Ibid. i. 54.

[3] Rot. Pat. 5 Edw. II., p. 2. m. 17.   [4] Statutes of the Realm, i. 287.

[5] Rot. Parliamentorum, iii. 498.

[6] John Cockayne, William Babington, John Juyn, Peter Arderne, Humphrey Starkey, John Fitz-James, and Richard Broke.

judgeship of one of those courts, which two of them subsequently retained in preference to the offiee of chief baron.

By the poll tax of 2 Richard II., though the chief baron is placed in the same class with the other judges, the puisne barons are not even named[1]; and in a commission in the fifth year of that reign, to inquire into the abuses of the different courts, the barons and great officers of the Exchequer are named *after* the serjeants at law.[2]

Some of the barons in the reign of Henry VI., as Nicholas Dixon, William Derby, and Thomas Levesham, were in holy orders; others were members of parliament; and two of them — Roger Hunt and Thomas Thorpe — were speakers of the House of Commons; all during the time they were barons. Fortescue also, who wrote in this reign, does not include them among the judges; and in reference to the rings given by the serjeants on taking their degree, says that those for " every justice" must be of the value of "one mark," while " to each baron of the Exchequer, &c." they are to be " of a less value in proportion to their rank and quality."[3]

Under Henry VII. and Henry VIII., the same marked difference still existed, none of them being summoned as attendants on the House of Lords, as the judges of the two other benches were, nor being privileged like them to have chaplains.[4] But they were already advancing in legal education, and entering into the inns of Court. Several instances occur of their being members, and even readers there, after they had become barons. But they still were selected principally from the officers of the Exchequer, and one even was raised from the inferior position of clerk of the Pipe.[5]

No change took place in the reigns of Edward VI. and Mary. One of the barons had been engrosser of the Great

[1] Rot. Parl. iii. 58.
[2] Ibid. iii. 102.
[3] De Laudibus (ed. 1741), 115.
[4] Statutes of the Realm, iii. 457.
[5] Nicholas Lathell. — *Rot. Parl.* vi. 97.

Roll[1]; and at the serjeants' feasts their servants were not allowed liveries, though those of the judges were provided with them. The rings of the judges were of the value of 16s., while those given to the barons were only 14s.[2], which was still further reduced under Elizabeth to 10s.[3]

There is no doubt therefore that, from the reign of Henry III. to that of Elizabeth, the barons of the Exchequer were inferior in degree to the judges of the two other courts, and that, in fact, they were little more than superior officers of the revenue, raised to the bench on account either of their long service, or of their known aptness in the details of that department. But by degrees the business of the Exchequer had materially increased; the causes that were tried there ceased to be confined to cases of revenue; and by means of the writ of *Quo minus* all sorts of civil actions were by a legal fiction introduced. No wonder, then, that the chief baron, who was the only lawyer among them, required some assistance to cope with this accumulation of business, and that it was found necessary to graft a little more legal learning on the bench, in order to give weight to decisions on intricate points that were daily arising.

Accordingly in the month of June, 1579, 21 Elizabeth, two vacancies in the court, occasioned by death or resignation, afforded the opportunity of trying the experiment. One of them was filled up in the accustomed manner by John Sotherton, who had held the office of foreign apposer for twenty years[4]; but the other was supplied by Robert Shute, as second baron, who for the first time was selected from the serjeants at law; and in the patent he received was contained a new and special clause, ordering that " he should be reputed and be of the same order, rank, estimation, dignity, and pre-eminence, to all intents and purposes, as any puisne

---

[1] John Darnall. — *Dugdale's Chron. Ser.* 86.
[2] Dugdale's Orig. 129, 130.   [3] Ibid. 125.   [4] Stowe's London, 332.

judge of either of the two other courts." [1]   He was the first who was thus put on an equality with the other judges, and was consequently privileged to go the circuits, and to hold assizes as they did.   John Birch, the baron who remained in the court at their nomination, is represented by Dugdale to have been also a serjeant; but from various circumstances already detailed, there is little doubt that the author confounded him with another John Birch, who was a serjeant. The vacancy on his death, and all future vacancies in Elizabeth's reign, were supplied by serjeants; so that at the accession of James I. the whole court consisted of men of the law, except the above John Sotherton, the fourth baron, who was the only one left on the bench accustomed to the routine duties of the Exchequer.

Eighteen months after James came to the crown, George Snigg, a serjeant at law, was appointed; so that then the legal phalanx of four barons of the coif was complete.   Ou John Sotherton's death in July, 1606, he was succeeded by Nowell Sotherton, who was not a serjeant; and although of Gray's Inn, he is not mentioned by any of the reporters as an advocate, nor, although the names of all the other barons occur in the books, is he ever mentioned as sitting in court.

In May, 1610, Thomas Cæsar, the brother of Sir Julius Cæsar, master of the Rolls, was, according to Dugdale, appointed a baron; and for the first time the designation of Baron-Cursitor is used with regard to him.   This entry occurs in the books of the Inner Temple on his election :—
" That the said Thomas Cæsar, then being the puisne baron of the Exchequer (commonly called the baron-cursitor), should not be attended to Westminster by any but the officers of the Exchequer; for as much as none but such as are of the coif ought to be attended by the officers of the house." And in the following month another order was made in these

---

[1] Dugdale's Chron. Ser. 94.

terms: — "That Thomas Cæsar, then one of the benchers of this house, notwithstanding an act made 7 June, 5 Jac. —viz. that none who should thenceforth be called to the bench, that had not read, should take place of any reader or have a voice in parliament—having not read, but fined for not reading, and then called to be a puisne baron of the Exchequer, should have place at the bench table, the said order notwithstanding."[1] These entries show, first, that he was not a serjeant; next, that he had not attained the dignity of reader to the society; and thirdly, that his appointment of puisne baron or baron-cursitor, was a new occurrence requiring a special order of the bench; and the omission of his name by the reporters proves that he had no judicial function to perform.

Thomas Cæsar dying before October of the same year, another John Sotherton, of the same inn of Court, was nominated a baron; and here is the entry in the Inner Temple books with reference to him: — "That John Sotherton, one of the barons of the Exchequer, being called to the bench, should have his place at the bench table above all the readers in such sort as Sir Thomas Cæsar, *late* puisne baron of the Exchequer had."[2] Thus it is clear that he was not even a bencher at the time of his appointment; and though the reporters of the period frequently mention all the barons who sat in court, they never introduce his name. From these facts it may be inferred that he held the office of cursitor baron only; and that it was of greatly inferior grade to that of the regular barons is proved by his name being placed in a special commission to inquire into defective titles, issued in 1622, after the attorney-general, though two other barons, Denham and Bromley, are inserted previous to that officer. This order of precedence again occurs in a similar commission in the next year; and in another, relative to nuisances in

[1] Dugdale's Orig. Jurid. 149.　　　　　[2] Ibid.

London in 1624, several knights and the recorder of London intervene between the regular barons and him.[1]

While, therefore, it is apparent that the office of cursitor baron was not, *eo nomine*, an ancient office, the probability afforded by the circumstances above detailed, that it had its origin in the reign of James I., is greatly strengthened by considering the state of the court at that time. John Sotherton (the elder) was the last of the regular barons according to the *ancien régime*, and the only one who was practically acquainted with the mode of accounting and other formal business of the Exchequer. George Snigg, who was appointed fifteen months before Sotherton's death, being bred a lawyer, could not any more than the other barons left on the bench, have the requisite knowledge of the technical matters of account indispensable for the due investigation of the sheriffs' returns, and other minute matters which up to that time had been customarily performed by one of the regular barons. George Snigg, owing probably to John Sotherton's last illness, made an attempt to master this duty; for his name is attached to the current accounts of the year of his appointment.[2] This audit, no doubt, was sufficient to prove that the duty could not be satisfactorily performed by men whose habits and previous education led them in a very different direction. The exercise also of this laborious but necessary employment must have been so onerous an interference with their judicial functions, that it was deemed necessary to appoint some intelligent officer who was conversant with the duties and competent to perform them.

Accordingly, nine months after, Nowell Sotherton, who, no doubt, was bred up in the Exchequer, and was the relative probably of John Sotherton the last baron, was appointed; and as in no list of the barons which the reporters

[1] Rymer, xvii. 388. 512. 540.
[2] 2 & 3 Jac. I. in the Record Office, Carlton Gardens.

give as forming the judicial bench of the Exchequer, do we find his name, the natural inference seems to be, that his appointment was for the sole purpose of auditing the sheriffs' accounts and of transacting all the customary business with regard to them, and the other *matters of course* which were merely ministerial.

It is observable also, that although King James I. in the first year of his reign added a fifth judge to each of the courts of King's Bench and Common Pleas, his order did not extend to the Exchequer, which then had only four, till eight months afterwards; yet when the judges of the two other courts were, after a few years, again reduced to four, the Exchequer, besides the four legal barons, still retained the cursitor baron.

The title, baron-cursitor, was evidently adopted in imitation of the ancient cursitors in Chancery, who, holding the second place under the chief clerks or masters of that court, were called in Latin *Clerici de Cursu*, and prepared all original writs and other writs *of course*. So also the barons cursitor held a secondary rank, and were solely employed, like their prototypes, in doing the formal business, the settled rule of the Exchequer.

Dr. Cowell, in his " Interpreter," published in November, 1607, by stating under the word " Baron," that there were only *four* barons of the Exchequer, manifestly shows that he describes the state of the court at an earlier period than the date of his book; no less than sixteen months having then elapsed since the appointment of Nowell Sotherton as a fifth baron. The author was a civilian, resident at Cambridge, and being professionally ignorant of the practice of the court, was evidently not aware of the change. His account turns out to be a mere abridgment of the narration of the duties of the barons and other officers, written by Sir Thomas Fanshawe, the queen's remembrancer, for the instruction of Lord Buckhurst when he was appointed lord high treasurer in

1599 [1]; and that narration of course applied to the state of the court as it existed at that time, and for the twenty previous years — viz. ever since the introduction of legal barons.

Both say that the lord chief baron " answereth the. barre in matter of lawe ; "—that the second baron, "in the absence of the lord chief baron," doth the like ;—that the third baron, " in the absence of the other two," has the same duty ;—and that the fourth baron "is always a coursetour of the court, and bath bene chosen of some one of the clerks of the Remembrancers' offices, or of the clerke of the Pipe's office. . . . . . . He informeth the rest of the barons of the course of the court in any mater that concerneth the king's prerogative." This was precisely the position of John Sotherton (the elder) when all the others had become legal barons. The words " a coursetour of the court," are evidently used merely as descriptive of the duties of the fourth baron, not as denoting his title, for neither he nor his predecessors are ever designated by any other title than that of fourth baron. When, however, on his death, all the four regular barons became legal barons, and none of them were competent to perform the duties which hitherto had devolved on the fourth baron, then an extra and an inferior officer was added to the court to exercise those formal functions ; and as by the constitution of the court these duties could not be performed but by a baron, he received the designation of cursitor baron; but he was not invested with any judicial power.

In a work on the Exchequer published by Christopher Vernon, in 1642, the proper distinction is made. The author there says—" The chiefe baron and *three* other learned barons, and the puny or cursitor-baron, are all in the king's

---

[1] These instructions seem to have remained in manuscript till 1658, when they were published under the title of " The Practice of the Exchequer Court, with its several Offices and Officers. Written at the request of the Lord Buckhurst, some time Lord Treasurer of England. By Sir T. F." Pp. 23–34.

gift. The said cursitor baron being so called because he is chosen most usually out of some of the best experienced clerkes of the two Remembrancers', or clerke of the Pipe's office, and is to informe the bench and the king's learned counsel from time to time, both in court and out of court, what the course of the Exchequer is." [1] The first instance to be found of the designation, " baron of the coife," being applied to the regular barons is in the patent appointing George Snigg in 1604. [2]

It may then be concluded that Nowell Sotherton was the first person who was added to the four regular barons, as an appendage to the court, with the special denomination of cursitor baron ; that Thomas Cæsar was the second, which will account for the expression in the Inner Temple order, " commouly called;" and that John Sotherton (the younger) was the third. The latter continued in office in the reign of Charles I.; and when Michaelmas Term was adjourned on account of the plague that raged in the sixth year, the Essoigns were kept by Baron Sotherton, that duty being merely a matter *of course.*

One of the most showy functions of this officer was then, as it till very lately continued to be, to convey the public announcement of the crown's approval of the election to the sheriffs of London and Middlesex,— a duty perhaps imposed upon him because the time of their inauguration occurs in the middle of the vacation, when the other barons are absent. A quaint and humorous speech made, or pretended to be made, on one of these occasions by a cursitor baron in the time of the Protectorate[3], proves not only that his rank was

---

[1] Considerations for Regulating the Exchequer. Per C. Vernon, De Scaccario Dom. Regis, 1642, p. 33.

[2] Rot. Pat. 2 Jac. p. 7.

[3] " Baron Tomlinson's learned Speech to the Sheriffs of London and Middlesex, when they came to be sworn at the Chequer." London : printed in the year 1659. The real name was Tomlins.

subordinate, but that his dress was inferior to that of the regular barons. After jocosely alluding to the warmth and the colour of the sheriffs' gowns, he says, " 'Tis true, I have a gown too, but they make me wear *the worst* of any baron of the Exchequer; 'tis plain cloth, as yee see, without any lining; yet my comfort is, I am still a baron, and I hope I shall be so as long as I live; when I am dead, I care not who's baron, or whether there be a baron or no." And again a little further on—" Gentlemen, I am the puisne baron of the Chequer, that is to say, the meanest baron; for though I am not guilty of interpreting many hard words, yet this hath been so continually beaten into my head that I do very well understand it. However, I could brook my means well enough (for some men tell me that I deserve no better), were it not the cause of my life's greatest misery, for here I am constrained, or else I must lose my employment, to make speeches in my old age, and when I have one foot in the grave, to stand here talking in publike." He concludes thus, " Now, Mr. Sheriffs, get yee home, kiss your wives, and by that time the cloth's layed, I'll be with you, and so God by till I see you again." Whether this be the real speech or only a burlesque on his usual style of address, it is equally curious and interesting as a record of the practices of the time.

About a month before King James's death, he erected by letters patent a new court of the Marshal of the Household within the verge, to hold pleas for those not of the household.[1]

ATTORNEYS-GENERAL.

| I. 1603. March. | Edward Coke, who had held the office for the nine previous years, was continued in it till he was made chief justice of the Common Pleas, when |

---

[1] Rushworth, ii. 104.

IV. 1606. July 4.   Sir Henry Hobart was appointed. He vacated it on being raised to the same chiefship; and

XI. 1613. Oct. 27.   Sir Francis Bacon, the solicitor-general, received the appointment, and held it till he was nominated lord keeper.

XIV. 1617. March 12.   Sir Henry Yelverton was then advanced to this place from that of solicitor-general, but on his being sequestered, he was superseded by

XVIII. 1621. Jan. 11.   Sir Thomas Coventry, the solicitor-general, who held it till the end of the reign.

SOLICITORS-GENERAL.

I. 1603. March.   Thomas Fleming, the late queen's solicitor-general, was adopted by King James; who in the next year raised him to the head of the court of Exchequer.

II. 1604. Oct.   Sir John Doderidge succeeded; but being made king's serjeant,

V. 1607. June 25.   Sir Francis Bacon was appointed, and held the place from this time till he became attorney-general, when

XI. 1613. Oct. 29.   Henry Yelverton was advanced to it. On Bacon's receiving the Great Seal, Yelverton succeeded him as attorney-general, and

XIV. 1617. March 14.   Thomas Coventry was constituted solicitor. On his superseding Yelverton as attorney-general,

XVIII. 1621. Jan. 22.   Robert Heath was nominated solicitor-general, and continued so till the king's death.

Sir Francis Bacon told the king that his place of attorney was "honestly worth 6000*l.* a year." [1] Nine months before he was made lord keeper he was sworn in as a privy councillor, retaining his office of attorney-general. This elevation prevented him from pursuing his ordinary practice at the bar: but it appears by his letter to the university of Cambridge, that he still could give counsel, and if anything weighty or urgent occurred, was even allowed to plead.

---

[1] Bacon's Works (Montagu), xii. 31.

SERJEANTS AT LAW.

The added initial marks the inn of Court to which they belonged; and those who became judges have a *.

I. 1603.   * John Croke (I.),   * Augustine Nichols (M.),
       * Thomas Coventry (I.)   * Robert Houghton (L.),
       * Laurence Tanfield (I.),   Thomas Harris (L.),
       * Thomas Foster (I.),   Henry Hobart (L.) [1],
       Robert Barker (I.),   * James Altham (G.).
       * Edward Phellips (M.),

They were summoned by Queen Elizabeth; but her death before the return of the writ rendered a new one necessary. To them were added

       John Shirley (M.),   * John Doderidge (M.) [2],
       * George Snigg (M.),   * James Ley (I.).
       * Richard Hutton (G.),

IV. 1606.   * Edward Coke (I.) [3],   * Humphrey Winch (L.).
       John Davies (I.),

VII. 1609.   * John Denham (L.),   * Edward Bromley (I.).

VIII. 1610.   * Henry Montagu (M.).[4]

IX. 1611.   * William Methwould (L.).

XII. 1614.   * Robert Hicham (G.),   * ThomasChamberlayne(G.),
       * Ranulphe Crew (L.),   Thomas Athowe (G.),
       George Wilde (I.),   Leonard Bawtry (L.),
       William Towse (I.),   John More (L.),
       Francis More (M.),   John Chibon (L.),
       * Francis Harvey (M.),   * Thomas Richardson (L.).
       Henry Finch (G.),

XIV. 1616.   * Edward Henden (G.),   * William Jones (L.).

XV. 1617.   Francis Ashley (M.).

XVIII. 1620.   John Shirley (M.),   * James Whitelocke (M.).

XXI. 1623.   * George Croke (I.),   * Francis Crawley (G.),
       Rice Gwyn (I.),   Richard Diggs (L.),
       John Bridgman (I.),   John Dany (L.),
       Heneage Finch (I.),   John Hoskins (M.),
       Richard Amherst (G.),   Egremont Thyn (M.),
       Thomas Crew (G.),   * John Bramston (M.),
       * Humphrey Davenport(G.), John Lloyd (I.).
       Thomas Headley (G.),

---

[1] Exonerated 3 Jac. I., previous to being made attorney-general.

[2] Exonerated in 2 Jac. I., on being made solicitor-general; but in 5 Jac. I. made king's serjeant without further ceremony.

[3] Sir Edward Coke took for his motto " *Lex est tutissima cassis.*"

[4] Sir Henry Montagu's motto was " *Deo, Regi, et Legi.*"

Croke states that Anthony Heronden (L.) also had a writ to be made a serjeant with these, but that a *supersedeas* was delivered on the same day, and he was denied to join them.

KING'S SERJEANTS.

I. 1603.	John Heale (I.),	* John Croke (I.).
	* Edward Phellips (M.),	
III. 1606.	* Thomas Coventry (I.).	
V. 1607.	* John Doderidge (M.).	
VIII. 1611.	* Henry Montagu (M.).	
X. 1612.	John Davies (I.).	
XII. 1614.	* Ranulphe Crew (L.).	
XIV. 1616.	Henry Finch (G.),	Robert Hicham (G.).
XXI. 1623.	* George Croke (I.).	
XXII. 1624.	* Thomas Richardson(G.),	Thomas Crew (G.).

Lord Ellesmere in a letter to Mr. Lake, then with the king on his coming into England, thus expresses himself: — "Besydes, I thynke yt not amysse to put you in remembrance that the late queene, consideringe that moost of the judges are aged, and the serjeantes at lawe now servinge at the barre not so sufficyent to supplye judiciall places as were to be wyshed (*ne quid dicam durius*), made choyce of certen persons of great learninge and sufficiencye fitte to be called to that degree, and awarded writtes unto theym for that purpose returnable the seconde returne of next terme, which writtes are now by her deceasse abated, and the gent alredye bene at very great charge to prepare themselves."[1] He therefore sends a warrant for the king's signature; and it is a curious circumstance that of the new-made serjeants, who were named in Queen Elizabeth's writ, nine out of the eleven were within a few years raised to the bench; thus justifying the lord keeper's recommendation.

There were three great calls of serjeants in this reign, 1603,

[1] Egerton Papers, 372.

1614, and 1623. The feast of the first is not mentioned; those of the two latter were given in the Middle Temple hall.

When Sir Edward Bromley was called, the treasurer of the Inner Temple presented him with a purse and 10*l*. in money.[1] He and Sir Edward Coke were the only persons in this reign who received the degree of the coif for the purpose of being elevated to the bench.

Scarcely any office was granted in this reign without a fee to King James; not even the serjeants escaped. Sir John Bramston, speaking of the great call of fifteen serjeants in 1623, says that his father " gave 500*l*. for a present to his Majestie (as did all the rest of that call) as I find by an acquittance for the monie."[2]

The prodigality with which the king granted the honour of knighthood occasioned some questions as to the precedency of lawyers who received the title. In 1611 the serjeants petitioned the king to decide the question of precedence between them and such of them as were made knights since they were called to be serjeants, — " and the rather for that the degree of knighthood is bestowed upon diverse utter-barristers and professors of the lawe." The decision is not given[3]; but the society of the Inner Temple had previously cut the Gordian knot, by ordering, May 10, 1605, " that if any then, or thenceforth, of this society should be called to the bench, at that time, or that thereafter should be a knight, that notwithstanding such his dignity of knighthood he should take place at the bench table according to his auncienty in the house and no otherwise." The same rule was afterwards adopted by the other houses[4],—a plain proof that this lavish distribution of honours was beginning to be held cheap.

The serjeants had at this time the precedency of the attorney and solicitor-general in all cases in which the crown

---

[1] Dugdale's Orig. 138.
[2] Autobiography, 6.
[3] Manning's Serviens ad Legem, 263.
[4] Dugdale's Orig. 148. 345.

was not interested. Sir Francis Bacon, when he was attorney-general, disputed the point. A serjeant at law (not
a king's serjeant) having a short motion, offered to move
before Sir Francis, who " was much moved, saying he marvelled he would offer this to him. Upon this, Coke, chief
justice, said, ' No serjeant ought to move before the king's
attorney when he moves for the king; but for other motions,
any serjeant at law is to move before him; and when I was
the king's attorney, I never offered to move before a serjeant,
unless it was for the king.' "[1] Making all allowance for the
jealousy that existed between these two great men, there is
no reason to believe that the chief justice was wrong in his
dictum according to the practice of that time. It would
appear that Bacon even assumed precedence above a king's
serjeant; for in a report made to the king in January, 1613-14,
on the case of Cotton, he signs before Henry Montagu the
king's serjeant, and the solicitor-general after.[2] The offices
of attorney and solicitor-general were considered incompatible
with the degree of serjeant at law ; for many instances occur
in which the one is resigned on the other being taken. William Huse, the attorney-general to Edward IV., was made a
serjeant after he had held that office seven years ; and it is at
least doubtful if he retained it afterwards. Sir John Popham
in 1579, and Sir Thomas Fleming in 1595, were exonerated
from the degree when they were respectively appointed solicitor-general ; and in this reign Sir Henry Hobart as attorney-
general, and Sir John Doderidge as solicitor-general, ceased to
be serjeants on attaining those offices.

The precedence of the serjeants began to be disputed by
other parties besides the attorney-general. Doctors of the
civil law and masters in Chancery claimed to rank before
them ; and they were obliged to stand up in defence of their

[1] Manning's Serv. ad Legem, 55., quoting 3 Bulstrode, 32.
[2] Bacon's Works by Montagu, xii. 471.

order. Among the MSS. in the British Museum, is a paper entitled " Certeine pretended reasons" against both claims. As to doctors, it is alleged that they have only a private degree from the universities, while the serjeants have a public degree from the king; that the former are made after twelve years' study, and in unlimited numbers, while the latter are sparingly appointed and seldom under twenty-five years' study and practice of the law; that their inauguration is very expensive and solemn, graced with the presence of nobility, and even kings; that they are brothers to, and are frequently employed in the stead of, the judges, who can only be made from their order; and that they are privileged to wear their coif in the royal presence. Some of the same reasons are alleged against the claims of the masters in Chancery; in addition to which it is urged that when holding assizes, the serjeants wear their red and purple robes, while the masters are not judges but referentiaries; and also that at coronations and other solemnities, they take by custom the highest place.[1] The masters in Chancery were not slow in their response; on the merits of which it is not necessary to decide. But the contest shows the jealousy of the serjeants of any encroachment on their ancient rights, and their anxiety to arrest the decline of their order, evidenced by the nomination of special counsel for the king, in addition to the ordinary offices of attorney and solicitor-general.

There can be no doubt that in this reign both the Serjeants' Inn in Fleet Street, and that in Chancery Lane, were occupied by the judges. Coke, in the preface to his 3rd Report, published either at the end of Elizabeth's or the beginning of this reign, says, " the judges and serjeants are equally distinguished into two higher and more eminent houses"; but this might mean the judges were in one, and the serjeants in the other. They, however, soon after occupied both indis-

---

[1] Add. MSS. 12497, fo. 170.

criminately, for in p. 121 of his 12th report, he states that a question was resolved in 12 Jac. (1614) by " the chief baron and the justices of Serjeants' Inn in Chancery Lane," and that " of the same opinion was the chief justice and the justices of Serjeants' Inn in Fleet Street."

SERJEANTS' INN, FLEET STREET.—This was evidently the principal house. When any conference of the judges is mentioned by either Coke or Croke as having taken place at Serjeants' Inn, that in Fleet Street is invariably named where the place is designated ; and Coke says also in 8 Jac., " It was agreed *ad mensam* by all the justices and barons in Fleet Street."[1] The judges seem to have frequented the church of St. Dunstan's. In 1614 the churchwardens ordered " a dozen green cushions for the judges' pews in the church, and a seat for Edward Lile the warder." The society in 1614 purchased a tenement in the White Friars abutting on the inn; and the grantees were five judges, viz., Sir Edward Coke, Sir Henry Hobart, Sir Augustine Nichols, Sir George Snigge, and Sir James Altham; and eleven serjeants, viz., Sir Henry Montagu and Sir Randall Crewe, king's serjeants, and Shirley, Barker, Wilde, Towse, Finch, Athowe, F. More, J. More, and Harvey, serjeants at law.

SERJEANTS' INN, CHANCERY LANE.—It would seem that this inn was resumed as the residence of some of the judges at the beginning of this reign. The earliest books of the steward's and treasurer's accounts commence from Michaelmas, 1604. By them it appears that there was a curate or reader for doing duty in the chapel of the inn, and that the business of the society was transacted at what were termed " Boards of green cloth."

Mr. Justice Houghton had chambers in the inn, and died there in 1623.

That Sir Francis Bacon claimed to have been named by

---

[1] Coke, vol. vi. 62., vii. 33., xii. 74. 130.; Cro. Jac., 149. 482.

Queen Elizabeth as her special counsel, and that he certainly received the appointment from King James, has been already shown.[1] Some doubt, however, seems to have existed whether any other person received a similar compliment in this reign, at least till after Bacon was entrusted with the Great Seal. In his speech on taking his seat in the Court of Chancery on May 7, 1617, after noticing that the attorney-general (Yelverton) was son of a judge, that the solicitor-general (Coventry) was likewise the son of a judge, and that he was a chancellor's son, he stated that he had this "fancy," that "besides these great ones" he would hear "any judge's son before a serjeant, and any serjeant's son before a reader; if there be not many of them."[2] From the omission of any mention of king's counsel, an inference might be drawn that such an appointment did not then exist; yet in the patent granted to the two Temples in 1608, Sir Henry Montagu, the recorder, is designated "one of our counsel learned in the law." Sir Henry, however, in 1617, was chief justice; so that there might at that time have been no king's counsel.

COUNSEL.

The initials show the courts to which those who became judges were first appointed.

E. Abdye,	J. Barksdale,	J. Bridgman,
J. Altham, B. E.	E. Barthelet,	J. Briscoe,
R. Amherst,	W. Bastard,	W. Brocke,
E. Andrews,	L. Bawtree,	E. Bromley, B. E.
F. Ashley,	A. Ben,	C. Brooke,
T. Athowe,	H. Binge,	G. Brooke,
W. Ayloffe,	R. Blundell,	T. Brooke,
T. Aynscombe,	W. Bourn,	H. Brownlow,
F. Bacon, Chanc.	J. Boys,	T. Cæsar,
J. Bankes,	F. Brackyn,	R. Callice,
R. Barker,	J. Bramston,	C. Calthorpe,
T. Barker,	E. Brantingham,	E. Cason,

[1] *See* Vol. V. p. 420.   [2] Bacon's Works (Montagu), vii. 256.

J. Cavell,
T. Chamberlayne, K. B.
C. Chibborne,
N. Chomley,
J. Clerke,
E. Coke, Ch. C. P.
N. Collyns,
H. Compton,
T. Coventry, C. P.
T. Coventry, L. K.
R. Cowper,
M. Cratcherood,
F. Crawley,
H. Cressy,
R. Crew, Ch. K. B.
T. Crew,
G. Croke, C. P.
J. Croke, K. B.
P. A. Croke,
E. Curle,
M. Dale,
R. Dale,
W. Daniel, C. P.
C. Danvers,
J. Darcy,
W. Darell,
R. Daston,
H. Davenport,
H. Davies,
J. Davies,
R. De la Bere,
J. Denham, B. E.
H. Denne,
W. Denny,
R. Diggs,
J. Doderidge, K. B.
R. Downes,
N. Ducke,
A. Dyot,
W. Ellis,
E. Estcourt,
F. Eyre,
R. Eyre,
T. Farmer,

J. Farwell,
Hen. Finch,
Hy. Finch,
J. Finche,
W. Fishe,
H. Fleetwoode,
T. Fleming, Ch. B. E.
W. Fletcher,
E. Floyde,
R. Foster, C. P.
T. Foster, C. P.
T. Gardner,
G. Gascoigne,
P. Gerard,
— Germyn,
W. Gibbs,
J. Glanville,
— Godfrey,
A. Gray,
T. Green,
R. Gwyn,
E. Hadde,
M. Hadde,
W. Hakewill,
H. Hall,
H. Hanlo,
J. Harding,
H. Hare,
J. Hare,
J. Harris,
T. Harris,
F. Harvey, C. P.
G. Hastings,
J. Hayward,
R. Heath,
T. Hedley,
E. Hele,
J. Hele,
E. Henden,
E. Herbert,
A. Herenden,
F. Heron, B. E.
J. Hetley,
R. Higgins,

R. Hitcham,
T. Hitchcock,
H. Hobart, Ch. C. P.
R. Hodson,
W. Holt,
J. Hoskins,
R. Houghton, K. B.
W. Hudson,
H. Hughes,
T. Hughes,
R. Hutton, C. P.
L. Hyde,
N. Hyde,
J. Jackson,
J. Jefferys,
D. Jenkyn,
C. Jenny,
J. Jermy,
T. Jones,
W. Jones, C. P.
N. Jordan,
A. Irby,
T. Ireland,
N. Lacon,
T. Levinge,
J. Ley, Ch. K. B.
E. Littleton,
J. Lloyd,
T. Locke,
L. Lovelace,
J. Low,
— Lutwych,
B. Man,
R. Martin,
W. Martin,
R. Mason,
J. Mayne,
W. Methwould,
H. Montagu, Ch. K. B.
F. Moore,
J. Moore,
F. Morgan,
P. Mutton,
F. Myngaie,

A. Nichols, C. P.	R. Shilton,	R. Trefusis,.
W. Noy,	J. Shirley,	T. Trevor,
E. Osburne,	R. Shute,	T. Trist,
N. Overbury,	W. Sidley,	G. Tucker;
R. Owen,	E. Skipwith,	G. Vernon,
T. Paget,	R. Smythe,	J. Wakering,
C. Pepper,	G. Snigge, B. E.	E. Walmesley,
P. Phesant,	T. Southe,	J. Walrond,
E. Phillips, M. R.	T. Southworth,	J. Walter,
A. Powell,	T. Spenser,	R. Waltham,
W. Powell,	E. Stapleton,	R. Wandsford,
E. Prideaux,	T. Stephens,	R. Warde,
R. Pritheroe,,	J. Stone,	D. Waterhouse,
L. Prowse,	J. Strode,	T. Watman, .
W. Pye,	W. Swanton,	H. Weare,
H. Pyne,	R. Swayne,	J. Welsh,
J. Pyne,	L. Tanfield, K. B.	T. Wentworth,
R. Ratcliffe,	R. Tanfield,	J. Weston,
W. Ravenscroft,	F. Tate,	R. Wheler,
R. Reynell,	R. Taylor,	J. Whitelocke, K. B.
T. Richardson, Ch. C. P.	E. Thelwall,	G. Wilde,
H. Robins,	W. Thomas,	D. Williams, K. B.
E. Rolt,	H. Thoresby,	H. Winch, C. P.
T. Rysden,	R. Thorpe,	T. Wode,
W. Ryves,	E. Thynne,	J. Wolveridge;
T. Sanderson,	T. Tildersley,	T. Woodward,
A. Sayer,	J. Tindall,	W. Wotton,
A. Scamler,	H. Topham,	E. Wrightington,
J. Selwyn,	H. Townsend,	G. Wrightington,
— Serjeant,	W. Towse,	H. Yelverton.
H. Sherfield,		

Cecil, Earl of Salisbury, does not give a flattering character of the lawyers of this reign. In 1610 he tells Sir Henry Yelverton, "Most of our lawyers and judges, though learned in their profession, yet, not having other learning, they upon a question demanded, bluntly answer it, and can go no further, having no vehiculum to carry it by discourse or insinuation to the understanding of others." [1]

The government remuneration to counsel was liberal, con-

[1] Archæologia, xv. 52.

sidering the value of money at the period. Serjeant Altham had 20*l.*, and "Master Stevens and Master Walter" 13*l.* 16*s.* 8*d.* each, for their pains and attendance on the lords of the Council and the judges " for defence of the rights and privileges of the Court of Exchequer " in March 1605-6 ; and again Randell Crew and John Walter received 10*l.* apiece for defending the king's title of Alnage before the House of Lords in 1607.[1]

A new set of orders for " the Reformation and better Government of the Inns of Court and Chancery" was issued in 12 James I., 1614, by the benchers of the four societies, and approved by the king and the judges. It acknowledges that some former orders have failed in execution, but declares a settled and constant resolution to cause these to be strictly observed. It directs general searches twice in every Michaelmas Term and once in every vacation for " ill subjects and dangerous persons ; " it orders every person who shall not receive the Communion once in every year to be expelled ; that no foreigners or discontinuers, but only utter barristers, be allowed to lodge there ; that no common attorney or solicitor shall be admitted of any of the four inns of court ; that not above eight shall be called to the bar from each society in any one year ; and that no utter barrister shall begin to practise publicly at any bar at Westminster until he has been three years at the bar, unless he has been a reader at an inn of Chancery. In the regulations about Christmas, it recognises playing at the dice, but prohibits any other persons except gentlemen in commons to play in the hall, and directs the benefits of the boxes to go to the butlers. It also forbids the members to come into their several halls with cloaks, boots, spurs, swords or daggers.[2]

Sir Edward Coke gives the following account of the degrees in the law. " *Moote-men,* which are those that argue

---

[1] Pell Records, Jac. I., p. 32. 64.   [2] Dugdale's Orig. 317.

Readers' cases in Inns of Chancery both in terms and vacations. Of Moote-men after eight years study or thereabouts are chosen *Utter Barristers*. Of these are chosen *Readers in Inns of Chancery*. Of Utter Barristers after they have been of that degree twelve years at least, are chosen *Benchers* or *Antients*. Of which one that is òf the puisne sort reads yearly in summer vacation, and is called *Single Reader;* and one of the antients that had formerly read, reads in Lent vacation, and is called a *Double Reader;* and commonly it is between his first and second reading, about nine. or ten years." [1]

In the first year of his reign, the king commanded through the judges "that none be henceforth admitted into the society of any house of court, that is not a gentleman by descent." [2]

LINCOLN'S INN.—The freehold of this house now belonging to the society, they proceeded liberally with their improvements. They inclosed their garden, built several sets of chambers, and erected the library, to the furnishing of which with books the members contributed rateably. The old chapel being ruinous and not large enough for the members, the first stone of a new one was laid, about the year 1618, by Dr. John Donne, then their lecturer, who also upon Ascension day in 1623, being then dean of St. Paul's, preached the sermon at its consecration by Dr. George Mountain, Bishop of London. The architect was Inigo Jones, the king's surveyor general.

While they thus ornamented their property and prepared accommodation for an increase of their body, they were equally attentive to the health of their members, by taking steps to prevent the free circulation of air from being impeded. Attempts being made to cover Lincoln's Inn Fields with build-

---

[1] Pref. to 3 Coke.   [2] Dugdale's Orig. 316.

ings, the society complained to the king of this infringement of his proclamation, restraining the erection of new buildings in the skirts and confines of the city, and succeeded in obtaining an order from the Privy Council, directing the justices of the peace to restrain the intruders, and to commit those who disobeyed to prison.[1]

The fine on the admission of any person who had not previously been a member of any inn of Chancery was raised to 3l. 10s.[2]

In 12 James I. new tables were set up in the library and hall, touching orders for exercise, showing that due attention was then paid to the instruction of the students, in regulations for the bolts and the moots to be charged and performed both in term and vacation, and forming a favourable contrast with the lax discipline of the present day. The day before and the day after the term were exempt from exercise; in the quaint language of the order there was "Neque Post, neque Præ, neque Bo, neque Mo, neque Le."[3] But relaxation was deemed so essential to the students, that on one occasion in 7 James, when the whole bar had offended by not dancing on Candlemas day according to the ancient order of the society, when the judges were present, the *under barristers*, for example sake, were by decimation put out of commons, and threatened with being fined or disbarred if the offence was repeated.

The society proved its loyalty by expending no less a sum than 1086l. 8s. 11d. upon a masque, which its members and those of the Middle Temple jointly presented before the king on the occasion of his daughter's marriage with the Prince Palatine in 1613, and again in contributing, in 1616[4], every bencher 40s., every barrister of above seven years' standing 30s., every barrister under, 20s., and every gentle-

---

[1] Dugdale's Orig. 234. 268.; Spilsbury's Lincoln's Inn.
[2] Dugdale's Orig. 243.   [3] Ibid. 269.   [4] Ibid. 246.

man 13*s*. 4*d*. for defraying their share of the charge of the performance of the Barriers in honour of the king's son Charles being created Prince of Wales. Forty gentlemen were appointed, ten from each house.

THE TEMPLE.—Since the dissolution of the knights of St. John of Jerusalem, the two Temples had held the premises they occupied as tenants of the crown. But in the sixth year of this reign, August 13, 1608, letters patent were obtained granting the " Hospicia et capitalia messuagia cognita per nomen de le Inner Temple et le Middle Temple ; " (an odd mixture of Latin, French and English) to Sir Julius Cæsar, otherwise Adelmary, knight, then chancellor of the Exchequer; Sir Henry Montagu, then recorder of London ; William Towse, and Richard Daston, Esq., then the two treasurers ; Sir John Boyse, Andrew Grey, Thomas Farmer, Ralph Radcliffe and others, then benchers of the two houses ; to hold to them, their heirs and assigns for ever, for the entertainment and education of the professors and students of the laws residing there, as of the manor of East Greenwich, in free and common socage, by fealty only, and in chief. The annual rent to be paid was 10*l*. by each house ; and the king reserved to himself the nomination of the master of the Church ; to whom the granters covenanted to make a yearly payment of 17*l*. 6*s*. 8*d*., in addition to the sum of 20*l*. to be paid by the king. For this patent, which subsequently caused " disputes and differences " between the societies, they made the king " a most magnificent present of a stately cup of gold — weighing 200½ ounces of pure gold."[1]

INNER TEMPLE. — In the same year in which the grant was obtained from the crown, the society of the Inner Temple began the erection of the buildings on the east of the gardens, called Paper Buildings, together with various other chambers

---

[1] Dugdale's Orig. 145.; Report, Inns of Court, 57. 207. Pell Records, Jac. I., p. 257.

for the accommodation of the members. In 1620 it is stated that "the bridge and stayres" were made. This is no doubt the signification of the expression contained in the mandate of 3 Edward III., where the "bridge" is ordered to be repaired.[1] "Pons" is the word in the record, and Virgil uses it metaphorically much in the same sense in Æn. x. 653.

> " Forte ratis . . . .
> Expositis stabat scalis, et ponte parato."

The order before adverted to, regulating the precedence of the benchers without reference to their knighthood, was made in the third year; and in the fifth year another order appeared, that none who should be called to the bench and had not read should take place of any reader, nor have voice in their parliament. This regulation was suspended in the eighth year in favour of Thomas Cæsar and John Sotherton, who were successively appointed puisne (or as it has been before suggested) cursitor barons of the Exchequer.

In February 1611, the benchers prohibited the performance of plays on the feast of All Saints and on Candlemas day, " for future prevention of disorder and scurrility ; "[2] but this order, probably on account of its unpopularity, was repealed before the end of the year.

This house in conjunction with Gray's Inn, rivalled the other two inns of Court in producing a masque in honour of the princess's marriage with the Count Palatine of the Rhine. They selected Beaumont (who was a member of the Inner Temple) to compose it, who chose for his device, the Marrying of the Thames to the Rhine; and the machinery and contrivances were by Inigo Jones. The show that the two societies made on Shrove Tuesday, February 16, 1613, in their procession by water in illuminated barges from Winchester stairs in Southwark to Westminster, exceeded in brilliancy any previous exhibition. But on their arrival at

---

[1] *See* Vol. IV. 263.   [2] Dugdale's Orig. 148, 149.

the court they were doomed to disappointment; the expense of their river pageant, above 300*l.*, had been incurred in vain, and the performance of the masque was deferred till the following Saturday. Some accounts ascribe this postponement to the hall being so crowded that there was not room for the masquers, or the ladies of rank who graced the galleries to see them land, to enter, while the greater probability is, that the king, who had witnessed the Middle Temple and Lincoln's Inn masque the night before, and who was not so fond as his queen of these spectacles, "was so satiated and overwearied with watching, that he could hold out no longer." On the Saturday, as some amends, the new banqueting house was granted to them to perform in; and on the next day the king entertained the competitors with a solemn supper in the new marriage room, and used them so well and graciously that he sent both parties away well pleased with this great solemnity.[1]

The contribution of the Inner Temple to the Barriers on the creation of the Prince of Wales does not seem so liberal as that of Lincoln's Inn, being only 30*s.* from each bencher, 15*s.* from each barrister of seven years' standing; and 10*s.* from all other gentlemen in commons[2]; but the number perhaps was greater, and consequently a less sum from each was required.

MIDDLE TEMPLE. —After the confirmation of the grant from the crown, several sets of chambers were erected near the Middle Temple gate, and in Vine Court. The only order that requires to be noticed in this reign is one in 1613, directing that none should be called to the bar under seven years' standing.[3]

The society united with Lincoln's Inn in the performance of a splendid masque before the court on Monday, February

---

[1] Dyce's Lives of Beaumont and Fletcher, xxxix , London (1841), p. 9.
[2] Dugdale's Orig. 150.　　　　　　　　　[3] Ibid. 188. 191.

15, 1613, in honour of the marriage of the Princess Elizabeth with the Count Palatine. George Chapman was employed to compose it, and Inigo Jones to invent its machinery. The masquers made their procession on horseback
from the house of the Master of the Rolls in Chancery Lane,
the description of which, together with the masque itself, was
soon after published, printed by G. Eld, for George Norton,
and "sould at his shoppe near Temple Bar."[1] When misfortunes afterwards overtook this royal couple, great interest
was felt on the princess's behalf. A letter of the time gives
the following account of the extent to which it was carried.
"The lieutenant of the Middle Temple played a game this
Christmas time, whereat his Majestic was highly displeased.
He made choice of some thirty of the civillest and best-
fashioned gentlemen of the house to sup with him, and, being
at supper, took a cup of wine in one hand and held his sword
drawn in the other, and so began a health to the distressed
Lady Elizabeth, and, having drunk, kissed his sword, and,
laying his hand upon it, took an oath to live and die in her
service; then delivered the cup and the sword to the next,
and so the health and ceremonie went round." The lieutenant was Sir R. Buller's son, of Cornwall, who was appointed
to that offiee for the revels at Christmas, 1622-3.[2]

GRAY'S INN.—Several orders were made during this reign
as to admission to chambers, and also regulating the bolts
and moots. The readers' table, by an order in 1611, was
to be allowed no wine at the general charge, but an exception was made in 1614 in favour of Mr. Thomas Southworth and Mr. Thomas Athowe, the then readers, in consequence of three members, of whom Mr. Athowe was one,
being included in the new call of serjeants, and each gentleman of the house then contributing 3s. 4d. Two hogsheads

---

[1] Dyce's Lives, &c. xxxviii.
[2] Diary of Walter Yonge, 66.; Letter of Rev. Joseph Meade.

of wine were therefore allowed, which with certain other allowances of the house, viz. 30 bushels of flour, 30 lbs. of pepper, reward for 30 bucks, and 2 stags, were to be equally divided between the two readers; and the *grotes* of the gentlemen in commons and the allowance for eight gentlemen coming to the readers' table, 36s. 8d., was wholly allowed to Mr. Southworth.   In 1623 a reader was fined 20l. for refusing to read.

In 1612, the *commons* were fixed at 6s. in term, and 5s. in vacation; and strict regulations were made enforcing the payment of them; but in consequence " of the smallness of the number that then kept commons, in comparison of times past," the price was raised ten years after to 7s. 6d. in term, and 6s. in vacation.   Suppers and banquets in respect of the moots, " which had grown to an excessive charge," were altogether forbidden; and no beer was to be taken in above 6s. a barrel.

The number of utter barristers that might be called by the readers, which in 1608 was fixed at four, was in the next year limited to two; and they were to be of seven years' standing, and to have performed six grand moots and six moots in the library.

Among other penalties with regard to apparel is one in 1609 of 12d. upon every gentleman of the society who shall fail to wear his cap in the hall, except the master of the Requests and the king's solicitor (Bacon); and in the last year of the reign there was an order that members of parliament should not be exempt from serving their vacations, as other ancients and barristers.

The actors in the masque at the royal marriage in 1613, already mentioned, which was encouraged " by the countenance and loving affection " of Bacon, then solicitor-general, were provided with their masking apparel at the expense of the house; the ancients subscribing 4l., those about to be

called ancients 2*l.* 10*s.,* barristers 2*l.,* and students 1*l.,*—and
after the performance they were ordered to bring it all in.
The charge upon the members of the house for the expense
of the Barriers in 1616 was the same as that collected in
Lincoln's Inn.[1]

Christmas continued to be celebrated with the usual re-
velries.   In 1622, the gentlemen of this society carried their
riotous frolics a little too far.   Having borrowed from the
Tower as many "Chambers" as would fill four carts, they
shot them all off on Twelfth-night with such a tremendous
explosion, that King James, awakened by the noise, started
out of bed, crying "Treason! Treason!"   The court was
raised and almost in arms, the Earl of Arundel ran to the
bed-chamber to rescue the king's person, and the whole city
was in an uproar.[2]

The payment of 6*l.* 13*s.* 4*d.* by the crown to "the treasurer,
students, and fellows" of this house, as their annuity, "for
the yearly salary of one chaplain there," continued in this
reign.[3]

CLIFFORD'S INN.—This Inn had been held by the society
as tenants to the family of Clifford ever since the reign of
Edward III.; but on the 29th of March, 1618, Francis, Earl
of Cumberland, the then representative of the family, together
with Henry Lord Clifford his son, in consideration of 600*l.*
paid to them, made a grant of the property to Nicholas
Sulyard, the principal of the house, and other members of it,
to hold to them for ever at the yearly rent of 4*l.,* so that the
same might for ever retain its title of Clifford's Inn, and be
continued as an inn of Chancery for the good of the gentlemen
of that society and the benefit of the commonwealth.

NEW INN.—The claim of the Middle Temple to the freehold of this inn, which was the subject of the Chancery suit

[1] Dugdale's Orig. 274—286.   [2] Nichols's Progresses, James I. iv. 751.
[3] Pell Records, Jac. I. p. 256.

between the two societies, mentioned in a former volume[1], originated in the sixth year of this reign, and was founded on certain deeds then executed. But the dispute having been settled by the award of Lord Hardwicke, the society remained in possession of the premises, subject only to their former payment of 1*l.* every term.

BARNARD'S INN.—In 1608, the books of this society give the first intimation of the attempt to introduce attorneys into it. An order of November 8 recites that two chambers " are in the hands of the principal, and it is to be feared that they might come into the hands of attorneys and clerks unable to perform what is required by this house; " and it thereupon orders " that these rooms shall be appropriated to students who shall keep the moots and acts of learning required of them." That some members, even of the inns of Court, instead of being called to the bar, had become attorneys, is evident from the repeated orders for their exclusion, commenced so early as the reign of Philip and Mary. Notwithstanding the above order of Barnard's Inn, attorneys quickly acquired a footing in the inns of Chancery, of which they are specifically recognised as members in the next reign; — an order of the judges saying that if " any attorney, clerk, or officer of any court of justice *being of any of the Innes of Chancery*".

Youthful irregularities in this inn were visited by immediate punishment. One of the companions being found in bed with a " lewd woman," " to the great dishonour of God and scandal of the society," he was made an example by being fined 20*s.*, and expelled the society. Another was turned out of commons for contemptuously refusing to take the Sacrament, according to the order to do so on Ascension day.[2]

STAPLE INN.—This society consists of a principal and

---

[1] *See* Vol. IV. p. 405.

[2] Barnard's Inn Books; Dugdale's Orig. 243. 311, 312. 317. 320.

twelve ancients or grand fellows, and an indefinite number of junior fellows. The principal is elected every three years, by a majority of ancients and juniors, three of the ancients being put in nomination. The reader (who had precedence of the principal) was appointed by Gray's Inn; but the society had the choice out of three names submitted to it. Another officer was called the pensioner, elected by the ancients, whose duty was to keep the accounts, and make out the admission to, and receive the rents of the chambers. He formerly gave a pair of white kid gloves to the principal and ancients, for which a treat to the mess has been since substituted. Several other customs used to prevail in this society : the members attended their principal in the hall the first Sunday after his election, and after partaking of tea and coffee, accompanied him in their gowns and with nosegays to St. Andrew's church, the officers walking before them ; the city trumpeters used to play in the garden every Hilary Term; and bonfires were lighted on certain days before the outer gate: but all of them have been long since discontinued.

In 1617 an attempt was made to revive the practice of having salaried reporters. By an ordinance then issued, two persons were to be appointed, to be named by the king, as reporters of the law, who were to " attend the judges of such courts where the judgments shall passe, with their reports to be reviewed by the judges before they be published," each of whom was to receive a fee of 100*l*. a year.[1] As this did not contain a prohibition against other persons, it soon became a dead letter.

[1] Rymer, xvii. 27.

BIOGRAPHICAL NOTICES

OF

THE JUDGES UNDER THE REIGN OF JAMES I.

ALTHAM, JAMES.

B. E. 1607.

JAMES ALTHAM was of civic descent, both paternally and maternally. His grandfather, Edward, was sheriff of London in 1531; his father, James, of Mark's Hall, Latton, Essex, was sheriff of the same city in 1557, and of the county of Essex in 1570; and his mother was Elizabeth, daughter of Thomas Blanke, citizen and haberdasher, and the sister of Sir Thomas Blanke, lord mayor of London in 1582.[1] Being the third son, the law was selected as his profession; and after pursuing his legal studies at Gray's Inn till he was called to the bar, he was chosen reader there in autumn, 1600. He was again appointed to that honourable post in Lent, 1603, on the occasion of his being summoned by Queen Elizabeth to assume the degree of the coif in the following Easter Term.[2] Her decease happening before that period, King James renewed the writ with the same return.

He represented Bramber in the parliament of 1589, and had acquired such a character in his profession (his name

[1] See an interesting paper on the Residence of the Blankes in the Parish of St. Mary-at-Hill, London, formerly the Abbot of Waltham's House, by G. R. Corner, Esq., F.S.A., *Archæologia*, xxxvi. 400–417.

[2] Dugdale's Orig. 295.

occurring in the Reports as early as 1588), that when the
king, soon after his accession, had determined to add a fifth
judge to the courts of King's Bench and Common Pleas,
Chief Justice Popham named Altham as one of the serjeants
from whom the choice might be made.[1] He was not, however, selected on that occasion; but on the death of Sir
John Savile he was appointed a baron of the Exchequer on
February 1, 1607, when he received the honour of knighthood.

Lord Chief Justice Coke seems to have been in the habit
of treating the judges rather superciliously, since Justice
Williams told Archbishop Abbott, who reported it to Lord
Chancellor Ellesmere, "of his utter dislike of all the Lord
Coke his courses; and that himself and Baron Altham did
once very roundly let the Lord Coke know their minde, that
he was not such a maister of the lawes as he did take on him,
to deliver what he list for lawe, and to despise all other."[2]

After filling the judicial seat for ten years, Sir James Altham
died on February 21, 1616–17; and Sir Francis Bacon, in a
speech to his successor, calls him "one of the gravest and
most reverend judges of this kingdom."[3] He was interred
in the chapel of Oxhey House, near Watford in Hertfordshire, which he had founded in 1612, under a monument on
which he is represented in his robes.

He was thrice married. His first wife was Margaret,
daughter and heir of Oliver Skinner, Esq., by whom he had
one son; his second was Mary, daughter of Hugh Stapers,
Esq., who brought him one son and three daughters; and
his third was Helen, daughter of John Saunderson, merchant of London, and widow of John Hyde, citizen and
mercer of London, by whom he had no children. His male
issue soon failed; but all his daughters married into noble
families. One of them was united to Arthur Annesley the
first Earl of Anglesea; and her second son by him, christened

---

[1] Egerton Papers, 388.   [2] Ibid. 448.   [3] Bacon's Works (Montagu), vii. 267.

Altham, was created Baron Altham in Ireland, his descendants eventually succeeding to the earldom. The sixth earl's son failed to make good his claim to the English peerage, which thus became extinct; but he succeeded in regard to the Irish titles, and was created Earl of Mountnorris in Ireland, which title also failed on the death of its second possessor. Another daughter of Sir James Altham married Richard Vaughan, second Earl of Carberry, a title which became extinct in the next generation. The third daughter had three husbands — Sir Francis Astley, of Hill Morton in Warwickshire, knight; Robert, Lord Digby in Ireland; and Sir Robert Bernard, baronet, serjeant at law.[1]

ANDERSON, EDMUND.

Ch. C. P. 1603.

See under the Reign of Elizabeth.

A YOUNGER son of the ancient family of Anderson of Northumberland having migrated into Lincolnshire, the first named as resident in that county is Roger, who had an estate at Wrawbey, and was grandfather of Henry, whose son Edward, of Flixborough in the same county, married Joan Clayton, niece to the Abbot of Thornholme. They had three sons — Thomas, who married Ellinor a daughter of Judge Dalison; Richard, of Roxby; and Edmund, the future chief justice.[2]

Edmund was born about the year 1530, and, being designed for the law, after receiving the principal·part of his education at Lincoln College, Oxford, was removed thence to the Inner Temple in June 1550. In due degree he rose to the office of reader in Lent, 1567; but for some unexplained

---

[1] Morant's Essex, ii. 565.; Wotton's Baronet. iii. 66. 364., iv. 402.

[2] From a pedigree in the family, for which and for several facts in this sketch I am indebted to the kind communication of Sir Charles H. J. Anderson, of Lea Hall near Gainsborough, Bart., where there is a portrait of him.

cause his reading was deferred till autumn. He became duplex reader in Lent, 1574, having in the meantime attained
sufficient practice as a barrister to be noticed in Plowden's
Reports in Easter Term, 1571. He was one of seven who
were called to the degree of the coif in Michaelmas, 1577;
and two years afterwards he was nominated queen's serjeant.[1]
In this character he went as assistant judge on the Western
Circuit in that year[2], and in November, 1581, conducted the
trial of Edmond Campion and others for high treason. His
introductory speech, which is described as having been " very
vehemently pronounced with a grave and austere countenance," is a fair example of the vicious rhetoric of the bar at
that period. It seems to be directed more against the pope
than the prisoner; and whatever may have been Campion's
guilt, he certainly beats the crown lawyers both in eloquence
and argument.[3]

Within six months the death of Sir James Dyer left a
vacancy in the office of chief justice of the Common Pleas;
and it was said that large sums were offered for the place by
Chief Baron Manwood. Serjeant Anderson was, however,
appointed on May 2, 1582, and soon after knighted. The
recorder Fletewood, in a letter to Lord Burleigh, relates
that on the day of his investiture the lord chancellor (Hatton) "made a short discourse what the dewtie and offiee of a
good justice was;" and that after he was sworn, " *Father*
Benloos, because he was auncient, did put a short case, and
then myself put the next." To both, he continues, the new
chief " argued very learnedlie and with great facilitie."
Fletewood then alludes to the rumour of bribes offered " by
one of the Exchequer," and adds that it was well that Lord
Burleigh had prevented him from succeeding. Anderson sat
as president of that court not only during the remainder

---

[1] Dugdale's Orig. 119. 165   [2] Cal. State Papers (Lemon), 639.
[3] State Trials, i. 1051.

of Elizabeth's reign, but for more than two years under James I., a period in the whole exceeding twenty-three years. In the state trials which disgraced the earlier part of his judicial career there is certainly nothing that distinguishes the chief justice from his fellows; all were involved in the disgusting barbarity of the proceedings. He was one of the performers in the farce of Secretary Davison's trial, and was equally puzzled with the rest in drawing that distinction beween the propriety of the act itself and the impropriety of its performance, which was necessary for the purpose of justifying the required condemnation. A strenuous supporter of the discipline of the Church of England, he showed himself too severe a condemner of all sectarians; and Browne, the founder of the Brownists, on his trial, and Udall, the Genevan Minister, on his examination, felt that the chief justice was not an unprejudiced censor.[1] He discouraged, however, the "insolence of office;" and when the mayor of Leicester, who had caused a Maypole to be pulled down, had committed a poor shoemaker for saying that " he hoped to see more morice dancing and Maypoles soon," the chief justice, on coming to the assizes there in 1599, instantly ordered the lover of old customs to be discharged.[2]

As a judge in civil cases he was patient and impartial; his knowledge of law was extensive, and he was ready in its application; and the " Reports " which he collected, and which were afterwards published, prove the industry and devotedness with which he pursued his profession. His firmness in supporting the privileges of his place was shown in his resistance of an attempted encroachment on them in the case of Cavendish, to whom Queen Elizabeth, at the instigation of Lord Leicester, had granted letters patent for making out writs of *supersedeas* upon exigents. The chief justice and his fellows refused to admit him, on the ground

---

[1] State Trials, i. 1229. 1271.   [2] Hist. of Leicester, 305.

that the queen had no power to grant the office, and that the
fees belonged of right to the ancient officers of the court.
Though renewed in various forms, the judges succeeded in
defeating the attempt, and even in satisfying her Majesty of
the justness of their opposition. The boldness evinced in
entering into this contest, and in persevering in it in defiance of courtly interference, speaks highly of judicial independence in those arbitrary times.

Camden says that on the trial of Cuffe as an abettor in the
Earl of Essex's treason, the attorney-general (Coke) arguing
with him in a logical method, and Cuffe answering in the
same style, Chief Justice Anderson, " being unable to keep
his temper, and telling them that they were both but indifferent disputants, pressed him close with the statute of treason." It is curious that in the report in the State Trials the
presence of Anderson is not mentioned, though the proceedings preserved in the " Baga de Secretis " prove that he was
one of the twenty named in the commission. David Lloyd, in
repeating this, calls him a " pure legist . . . always alledging
a decisive case or statute, without any regard to the decency
or respect to be had towards a state or government;" and
asserts that he was " so much the less useful as he was in-
compliant." He thus confounds the character of the judge
and the statesman, evidently considering the want of that
which might be politic in the one to be a blemish in the
other.[1]

Sir Edmund died on August 1, 1605, and was buried in
the church of Eyworth in Bedfordshire, where a handsome
monument was erected over his remains, on which he is
represented in his robes.

His first residence was at Flixborough, then at Arbury in
Warwickshire, where he built a house out of the ruins of the

---

[1] Camden's Elizabeth, in Kennet, ii. 638. ; State Trials, i. 1409. ; App.
4 Report Pub. Rec. 296. ; Lloyd's State Worthies, 803.

monastery. This he exchanged with the Newdigates for Harefield in Middlesex, to be nearer the courts; and there he entertained the queen, who gave him a ring set with diamonds, which was long preserved in the family; till one of them had it reset, and afterwards gave away the jewels. Thus losing their identity, the present representatives will not probably be so fortunate as one of the Northumberland Andersons is said to have been, who, having dropped a ring into the sea, gave it up for lost, when some time after, having bought a cod in the market, on opening the fish the ring was found in his maw.

The judge married Magdalen, daughter of Christopher Smyth, Esq., of Annables in Hertfordshire and Ackthorpe in Lincolnshire, and by her had nine children. His eldest son, Edmund, died without issue. His second son, Sir Francis, was the father of Sir John Anderson of St. Ives, who was created a baronet in 1628, and the grandfather, by another son, of Sir Stephen Anderson of Eyworth, who received a baronetcy in 1664; but both these titles have been long extinct. From this Sir Francis also, through another grandson, descended Charles Anderson of Manley, in the parish of Broughton in Lincolnshire, who, upon inheriting the estates of his maternal great-uncle Charles Pelham of Brocklesby in the same county, assumed that name, and was raised to the peerage in 1794 as Baron Yarborough, a title which was erected into an earldom in 1837; the second possessor of which now represents the chief justice in the House of Lords. The third son of the judge was William, of Lea (a manor in Lincolnshire given to him by his father), whose son, Edmund Anderson of Broughton, was advanced in 1660 to a baronetcy, which is still enjoyed by his lineal representative.[1]

---

[1] Wood's Ath. Oxon. i. 753.; Wotton's Baronet. iii. 191. 427.; Collins's Peerage, viii. 393—398.

BACON, FRANCIS, Lord Verulam, Viscount St. Albans.

Lord Keeper, 1617. Lord Chanc. 1618.

THE greater the reputation which an author acquires by his works, the less probability is there of forming a correct estimate of his personal character.   The admiration which is unreservedly bestowed on the public instructor, extends itself to the private individual; and, dazzled by the glory that surrounds his intellect, biographers are too apt to conclude that his actions must exhibit the same brightness, regardless of the earthly vapours that may dim it.   This is somewhat the case with Bacon.   Every one acknowledges the enlarged powers of his mind; and the productions of his pen are universally appreciated and admired.   The general incidents of his life are also well known; but his biographers, in relating them, have endeavoured to accommodate the practice which he pursued to the principles which he advocated, as if he were perpetually influenced in the world by the inducements which he recommended in the study.   Even those who cannot shut their eyes to his failings endeavour to excuse and extenuate them, finding a sort of justification in the conduct of his contemporaries, whose characters they depreciate, and whose motives they misrepresent.

Such memoirs, however agreeable to the partisan, are not satisfactory to the historian, who, leaving to others to describe the progress made and the results obtained by the philosopher, must judge of a public man by his public acts, interpreting his aims and aspirations, the course which he chooses, and the impulses which direct him, by such light as can be collected from his history.   There is no want of materials for this purpose in Bacon's life; his correspondence gives the biographer every advantage, extending as it does through the whole of his public career from the age of nineteen till his death. No juster interpretation of a man's transactions, no better explanation of his policy, can be found than that which his own letters furnish; and in the following sketch those of Bacon have been carefully used in order to form an impartial and unbiassed judgment of his real character. His letters have been collected, in the edition of his works by Mr. Basil Montagu, from the various publications through which they were dispersed; though their value has been much diminished by the carelessness of the editor, and the total want of chronological arrangement. To that edition, however, the references in the following sketch must of necessity be made.[1]

Francis Bacon was born at York House in the Strand on January 22, 1560-1, when his father, Sir Nicholas, had been lord keeper of the Great Seal for two years. His mother, Sir Nicholas's second wife, to whose early instructions the future philosopher owed much of his celebrity, was Anne, one of the five daughters of Sir Anthony Cooke, tutor of Edward VI., another of whom was Mildred, the second wife of Sir William Cecil, soon after ennobled by the title of Lord Burleigh. Anthony and Francis were the only issue of this union.

As no person has claimed the honour of being Francis Bacon's early instructor, it is to be presumed that he spent the first twelve years of his life at home, where, besides the tuition he received from his accomplished mother, he had all the advantage that could be derived from association with the great and learned men who frequented his father's house. In Queen Elizabeth's occasional visits to Gorhambury, she is said to have been so pleased with his readiness, that she

---

[1] The defect here complained of is about to be removed under the careful superintendence of Mr. Spedding, in the last volumes of an excellent collection of all Bacon's works, edited by that gentleman in conjunction with Messrs. Ellis and Heath, now passing through the press.

called him her young lord keeper; and his answer to her question how old he was, "Two years younger than your Majesty's happy reign," is somewhat too easily accepted as a proof of his early wit.

When little more than twelve years old, he was sent with his brother Anthony to Trinity College, Cambridge, then presided over by Dr. Whitgift, in addressing whom when Archbishop of Canterbury, he always subscribed himself "your dutiful pupil."[1] By the master's books, the account with him began on April 5, 1573, but he was not matriculated till June 10; and according to the same account he paid for sizings up to Christmas 1575.[2] It is stated that he left the university from disgust at the system of education then adopted there, and which remained without much alteration to the days of Milton; but it seems unlikely that his father should have been induced to listen to such an objection from a boy not yet sixteen. His removal was probably caused by other plans being formed for him, which had diplomacy for their object; for in the course of the next year he went to France with Sir Amyas Paulet, our ambassador there. Sir Amyas having occasion to send to England, entrusted Bacon with the mission; and the queen is said to have expressed her approbation of the manner in which the youthful messenger performed the duty. After spending not quite two years and a half in France, during which his journeys into the interior seem to have been only those in which he accompanied Sir Amyas as his "companion," his father's death in February, 1578-9, caused him to be suddenly summoned home from Paris.

At this period he was just turned eighteen; and, as the youngest of a large family, for his father had six children by his first wife, the provision that came to his share was not

---

. [1] Works (Montagu's edit.), xii. 189.   [2] British Mag. xxxiii. 444.

sufficient for his maintenance without some aid from his own exertions. He naturally selected the law for his profession, and entered himself at Gray's Inn, as his father had done before him. The date of his entry is uncertain; but in the questionable MS. of the society, already noticed[1], it is stated to be November, 1576; and, although at that date he was either gone or going to Paris, it is possible that his father might have entered him previous to his departure; but he could not have kept his terms, or began his studies, till his return in March, 1578.

Shortly afterwards he made some suit to his uncle Lord Burleigh, the precise nature of which, from the involved language in which he urged it in two letters addressed to his uncle and aunt[2], it is difficult to unravel. It was evidently connected with the law, and required the queen's approval; but his request being, as he acknowledges, "rare and unaccustomed," and one which might be deemed "indiscreet and unadvised," it will not excite much wonder if a youth not yet twenty should have failed in his application. It has been supposed that a letter without date, which Montagu extracts from the "Cabala[3]," thanking Burleigh for his intercession with the queen on his behalf, was written in the next month after this application.[4] But, adverting to the fact that he was then a minor, and to the contents of his subsequent letters to his uncle, it seems to belong to a much later date, speaking as it does of the queen having "appropriated him to her service," and of "her princely liberality," of which there are no signs at this time, nor were there for a long time after.

During the next five years there is no account of Bacon, except that in the Gray's Inn MS. he is stated to have been

---

[1] See antè, Vol. IV. p. 273. [2] Sept. 16, 1580, Works, xii. 471.
[3] Works, xii. 7.
[4] Strype dates it October 18, 1580; I know not on what authority.

called to the bar in 1582. On February 10, 1586, there is
an order that he "may have place with the readers at the
readers' table, but not to have any voice in pension, nor to
win anciety of any that is his ancient, or shall read before
him."[1] To a copy of this order some notes of Lord Burleigh
are appended, being memoranda of the successive favours
shown by the inn to Bacon. These are — 1. That he had
a "special admittance to be out of commons, sending for
beer, bread, and wine ; " which, if he was entered in 1576,
might be because he was going abroad : 2. "Admitted to
the Grad. Sop., whereby he hath won anciety of 40, being
bar. of 3 years continuance ; " which is perhaps explained
by the next : 3. "Utter barrister upon three years study ; "
by which he would attain seniority over those who were not
to be called till their full term of five or seven years' study
had expired : 4. "Admitted to the high table where none
are but readers." None of these memoranda have any
date; but the last refers to the order of February, 1586,
which proves he was then made a bencher.

For this early call to the bench he was apparently
indebted to Lord Burleigh, who was himself a member of
the Inn. He evidently refers to it in a letter to his Lordship in the following May, when speaking of " a late motion
of mine own," wherein " I sought an ease in coming within
bars."[2] In the same letter he alludes to some reports to his
prejudice, upon which his lordship had admonished him.[3]
At the end of that year, having obtained a seat in parliament,
he was "vehement against the Queen of Scots[4]; but he does

---

[1] Lansdowne MSS. 51. art. 6.

[2] Both Montagu in his Life, and Macaulay in his Critique, suppose that this
application was that he might be called *within the bar*, or, according to the
modern acceptation of the term, to be made a queen's counsel. This is a
mistake. It had merely a reference to his position in the inn. He calls it in
his letter, "not any extraordinary or singular note of favour."

[3] Works, xii. 473.   [4] Parl. Hist. i. 837.

not appear to have taken any other part in the business of the session.

In Lent, 1588, he was elected reader, no doubt in his regular turn; for he did not become double reader till twelve years afterwards, in Lent, 1600, when his reading was on " The Statute of Uses," which was not published till seventeen years after his death.[1] In the meantime, however, he had been actively employed in improving and ornamenting the premises of the society : and various sums were allowed to him for planting the gardens, &c.[2] He took also a prominent part in promoting those dramatic entertainments for which the society was famous, and with the performance of which the queen was so much gratified. In 1587 a comedy was played in their hall before Lord Burleigh ; in 1588, " certaine devices and shows " were presented by them before the queen at Greenwich, Bacon being among the dressers[3] ; and he offered to Lord Burleigh on another occasion, when a joint masque of the four inns of Court failed, to furnish a masque by " a dozen gentlemen of Grey's Inn."[4]

Soon after this his uncle procured for him a grant of the reversion of the registrarship of the Star Chamber, an office worth 1,600*l.* a year, which " mended his prospect, but did not fill his barn," as he truly said ; for he had to wait nearly twenty years for the vacancy.[5] It is evident that during

---

[1] Works, xiii. 313.; Dugdale's Orig. 295.

[2] Dugdale's Orig. 273. There is now in the garden of Gray's Inn a tree with all the marks of age and incipient decay, which is reputed to have been planted by Bacon. But I have the unexceptionable authority of my friend the Rev. John Mitford, to whom it was pointed out by the gardener, that the tree is a catalpa, which was not introduced into this country from America till 1720, a century after Bacon's death. The probability is that the elm which he did plant having died, the catalpa was placed there to commemorate the spot. *See* also Loudon's *Arboretum*, iii. 1391.

[3] Pearce's Inns of Court, 86.   [4] Works, xii. 477.   [5] Ibid. 142.

this time he was not getting on in his profession; for none of the reporters as yet mention his name, and in a letter renewing his applications to Lord Burleigh in 1592, when he was "one and thirty years" old[1], he threatens, "if his Lordship will not carry him on," to sell his inheritance and purchase some office of gain that shall be executed by deputy, and so "become a sorry bookmaker." Though his views were afterwards altered, his petitions do not seem at this time to aim at any active legal place; for he says, "I confess that I have as vast contemplative ends as I have moderate civil ends, for I have taken all knowledge to be my province." His suit not receiving so much encouragement from his uncle as he hoped, he applied to his cousin Sir Robert Cecil, to press it. At last Lord Burleigh, in September, 1593, tells him that he had induced the lord keeper (Puckering), who had been required by the queen to give to her the names of divers lawyers to be preferred, to put him down as a meet man, but not equal to Brograve and Branthwait, two other barristers whom Puckering specially recommended.[2]

In the meantime he had again appeared in parliament. In that which met in February, 1589, he busied himself in promoting the supply, being appointed to confer with the queen's learned counsel thereon.[3] So in the next parliament, in February, 1593, being then member for Middlesex, he supported the motion of his cousin Sir Robert Cecil, to the same purport[4]; but on a subsequent day he lost the credit he had gained, by objecting to the course proposed for its collection. He soon discovered that he had overstepped discretion; and in the remaining debates, which continued for nearly three weeks, he had the prudence to be silent. For this interference he so deeply incurred the queen's dis-

---

[1] Works, xii. 5. [2] Ibid. xiii. 72. [3] Parl. Hist. i. 855. [4] Ibid. 881.

pleasure, that it had not subsided when he received Lord Burleigh's favourable note, nor till some time after.[1]

In April, 1593, Sir Gilbert Gerard, the master of the Rolls, died; and though this place was destined for Sir Thomas Egerton, it was kept vacant till his successor as attorney-general was determined on. The list of lawyers to be preferred, which the lord keeper was required to give, had no doubt reference to this vacancy; for though Sir Edward Coke, as solicitor-general, had the first claim to the succession, it is evident that efforts were making to set aside his just pretensions. Bacon put himself forward as Coke's opponent[2], endeavouring to break through the accustomed routine; but, as he was then only a young man, and had not yet acquired any reputation either as a lawyer or as a writer, it is difficult to understand on what his claims to an office which had been lately increasing in importance were founded. He could not expect that his legal descent would alone avail him, and his parliamentary character had been lately damaged; so that his principal dependence must have been on the influence of his friends at court. There, in addition to Lord Burleigh and his son, he had enlisted the Earl of Essex in his cause.

The earl became his most strenuous advocate. His letters show that both he and the lord treasurer were zealous pleaders for him; for the queen was strongly prejudiced against him, telling them that none but they thought him fit for the place.[3] It is grievous to be obliged to add that Bacon's letters betray an underhand endeavour to impede Coke's success by depreciating his abilities, and nicknaming him the Huddler.[4] History may be searched in vain for an earlier example of such degrading solicitation for legal honours, and for such unworthy attempts to decry a rival; and it is to be lamented that almost all Bacon's future struggles for ad-

[1] Works, xii. 28., xiii. 275. [2] Ibid. xiii. 77. [3] Ibid. 75. [4] Ibid. 74.

vancement were sullied by the same unprincipled accompaniments. Coke, however, could not with decency be passed over. He received the appointment on April 10, 1594; and in filling up the office of solicitor-general, which he vacated, a longer delay intervened, and a similar disappointment awaited Bacon.

This vacancy lasted from April 10, 1594, to November 6, 1595, a period of nineteen months. Bacon exerted every effort to get the place, in letters to Lord Burleigh and his son[1], to Lord Keeper Puckering[2] and to the Earl of Essex, to whom he says in one of them, " The objections to my competitors your Lordship knoweth partly; I pray spare them not, not over the Queen, but to the great ones, to show your confidence and work their distrust."[3] Notwithstanding the intercessions of the earl and some others of his friends, and his own petitions and new year's gifts to the queen[4], both of which she refused to receive[5], she was so disgusted by his pertinacity that she said if he " continued in this manner she would seek all England rather than take him;"[6] and in the end the office was given to Sir Thomas Fleming. Bacon was precluded from complaining of this appointment; for in a letter to the lord keeper, written in the previous July, he had said, " If her Majesty settle her choice upon an able man, such a one as Mr. Serjeant Fleming, I will make no means to alter it."[7]

During this contest the degree of Master of Arts was conferred upon him by the university of Cambridge on July 27, 1594[8]; and at the end of it Essex, attributing to himself Bacon's want of success, gave him, as some compensation for his disappointment, an estate at Twickenham, which was afterwards sold for 1,800l.[9] Lord Burleigh's " constant and

---

[1] Works, xii. 3. 475., xiii. 78. 85.
[2] Ibid. xiii. 51. 56.
[3] Ibid. 77. 79. 82.
[4] Ibid. xii. 109. 166; xiii. 73.
[5] Ibid. xiii. 81.
[6] Ibid. 83.
[7] Ibid. 56.
[8] Ibid. xvi. app. 3. B.
[9] Ibid. vi. 249.

serious endeavours to have him solicitor," he gratefully acknowledges; but in the same letter complains that his lordship does not employ him in his profession in any services of his own.[1]

In May, 1596, Egerton was made lord keeper, but as he still retained the mastership of the Rolls, no vacancy immediately occurred in that office. Neither Bacon nor his friends appear to have applied for it; but Serjeant Heale seems at one time to have been encouraged by Egerton in his hopes for the place.[2] Coke and Fleming, probably, did not aspire to it, as they were common lawyers. They remained in their respective posts during the rest of the reign, so that there was no opportunity for any further intrigue; and Bacon was obliged to content himself with receiving occasioual employment in the service of the queen.

He has been represented as the first who held the office of queen's or king's counsel, distinct from the usual law officers; but that he had any special warrant for that purpose from Queen Elizabeth, there is no evidence whatever from any existing record. Montagu and Macaulay say that he was so appointed in 1590; but the preceding facts sufficiently prove that it could not have been so early; and the precise time at which he began to be engaged in the queen's causes still remains in doubt. From his correspondence it seems probable that he was first employed shortly after Coke became attorney-general in April, 1594, during the vacancy in the office of solicitor. There is a mysterious expression in a letter to the queen, dated July 20, 1594, which may probably refer to the royal promise so to use him: " a gracious vail, it pleased your majesty to give me." [3] The undated letter to Lord Burleigh, already mentioned, apparently written about this time, seems also to allude to it.

[1] Works, xii. 162.   [2] Egerton Papers, 315.   [3] Works, xiii. 81.

Bacon says in it, that it is an exceeding comfort and encouragement to him, " putting himself in the way of her majesty's service," and, " seeing it hath pleased her majesty .... to vouchsafe to appropriate me unto her service. "[1] While engaged in his application for the solicitorship, he writes to Foulk Grevil, " Her Majesty had by set speech more than once assured me of her *intention* to call me to her service; which I could not understand but of the place I had been named to."[2] The queen, however, evidently had no such meaning; and it soon appears that she merely intended him to hold some of her briefs; for Bacon tells his brother Anthony, January 25, 1594-5, that the queen, complaining of his pertinacity, says, " she never deals so with any as with me, *she hath pulled me over the bar*, she hath used me in her greatest causes."[3] Yet any such regular employment does not seem to be consistent with his absenting himself during that term, as he tells Lord Burleigh he did, in a letter dated in the following March, in the latter part of which he adds, " This last request I find it more necessary for me to make, because (though I am glad of her majesty's favour, that I may with more ease practise the law, which, percase, I may use now and then for my countenance); yet, to speak plainly, though perhaps vainly, I do not think that the ordinary practice of the law, not serving the queen in place, will be admitted for a good account of the poor talent that God hath given me."[4] There is also a letter from Lord Burleigh to Sir Robert Cecil, dated February 14, 1594-5, which plainly proves that Bacon was not then recognised as a queen's counsel. His lordship is advising his son as to some rents to be reserved on the nomination of the new bishops of Winchester and Durham, about which he had spoken to the attorney-general (Coke), who,

---

[1] Works, xii. 7.   [2] Ibid. 160.   [3] Ibid. xiii. 83.   [4] Ibid. xii. 475.

he says, complained of the want of other counsellors, " seeing ther is but one sargeant and no sollicitor ; alledging that ther ar many weighty causes of her majesty to be ordered." [1] Thus it is clear that the queen had not then bestowed on him any distinct appointment ; and that the occasional employment he had for the government was not of such importance as to render his absence inconvenient. It may also be inferred, that his business as a barrister was then so trifling, as to allow him to spend the term in the country.

That Bacon was engaged in some crown causes during the vacancy of the solicitorship, there can be no doubt ; but whether as having the independent management of them, or as junior barristers are now employed, in assistance of the attorney-general, it is difficult to say. That he was desirous of producing the former impression, is evident from two letters to Lord Keeper Puckering in 1594 and 1595, during the vacancy, in which he uses it for the purpose of being urged in furtherance of his suit. Both of them, curiously enough, are dated the same day in each year, September 25. In the first, he says, " I was minded according to the place of employment, though *not of office,* wherein I serve, for my better direction, and the advancement of the service, to have acquainted your lordship, now before the term, with such of her majesty's causes as are in my hands ; which cause ... I find ... your lordship of your favour is willing to use for my good, upon that satisfaction you may find in my travels." In the second he says, " I hope your lordship will not be the less sparing in using the argument of my being studied and prepared in the queen's causes." [2] From a letter of his to King James, certainly written between July, 1606, and June, 1607, his own opinion as to the time when he was regularly employed

---

[1] Peck's Desid. Cur. B. v. 6. [2] Works, xiii. 53. 58.

may be collected; for in it he urges his "nine years' service of the crown,"[1] which would not make it earlier than 1597.

Whatever was the date, it is clear he was not a sworn adviser, nor had any patent conferring upon him the office of queen's counsel. That he was not so considered when, at the end of the reign, the names of all the existing officers were sent to King James for re-appointment, is manifest from the omission of his. His activity and the interest of his friends, however, soon got this omission remedied, by procuring the introduction of his name in a warrant on a totally different subject, dated April 21, 1603, thus, " Where[as] we have perceaved, by a lettre from our councell at Whitehall, that Francis Bacon, Esq., was one of the learned counsell to the late Queen, our sister, by speciall commandment, and that in the warrant granted by us to them for the continewance of their places, he is not named, we have thought good to allow him *in such sort as she did.*"[2] He held this equivocal position for the sixteen following months, for it was not till August 25, 1604, that he obtained a patent formally appointing him " consiliarium nostrum ad legem, sive unum de consilio nostro erudito in lege," with such precedence as any other learned counsel, or as he had " ratione *verbi regii* Elizabethæ, vel ratione warranti nostri; " and granting a fee of 40*l.* a year.[3] He himself confirms this view of his position, by stating in one of his letters to King James, " You formed me of the learned council extraordinary, without warrant or fee, a kind of *individuum vagum.* You established me and brought me into ordinary; soon after you placed me solicitor."[4]

This discussion is of more importance than it at first appears, because the judgment to be formed of Bacon's conduct in pleading against the Earl of Essex before the

[1] Works, xii. 107.   [2] Egerton Papers, 367.
[3] Rymer, xvi. 596.   [4] Works, xii. 402.

council, and on his trial in February, 1601, mainly depends on the question, whether the nature of his employment did or did not impose upon him the necessity for such appearance. So general was the disapprobation it caused, that he wrote two letters in defence of himself to Sir Robert Cecil and Lord Henry Howard (nearly copies of each other)[1]; and so long did the stigma attach to him, that he found it necessary, nearly three years afterwards, to address an elaborate apology for his conduct to the Earl of Devonshire, Lord Lieutenant of Ireland.[2] His justification is but a lame one, and can have satisfied few; and in pleading the necessity of his place as one of the queen's counsel, he forgets that, if his duty was absolute and compulsory, his position must have been so notorious, that blame would not have been imputed, nor exculpation needed.

He was on the closest terms of friendship with Essex; the earl had been his most energetic advocate in his aspirations to the offices of attorney and solicitor-general, and had even made his success a personal matter with the queen; and when Bacon had been disappointed of both the places, Essex generously presented him with an estate worth 1800*l.* All this Bacon is forced to acknowledge, but with respect to the latter he asserts, in his apology, that he said to the earl, " My Lord, I see that I must be your homager, and hold land of your gift; but do you know the manner of doing homage in law? Always it is with a saving of his faith to the king and his other lords; and, therefore, my Lord, I can be no more yours than I was, and it must be with the antient savings: and if I grow to be a rich man, you will give me leave to give it back again to some of your unrewarded followers." The reliance that is to be placed on this minute report of a conversation occurring eight years

---

[1] Works, xii. 168. 171.   [2] Ibid. vi. 245.

previously, may be estimated by the fact, mentioned in the same letter, that, notwithstanding this flourish about giving the estate back to some of the earl's unrewarded followers, he had already sold it for 1800*l.* to Mr. Reynold Nicholas. In such intimate relations as existed between the earl and him, both gratitude and common decency ought to have prevented him from taking any active part in the prosecution, unless absolute necessity compelled him. If there was no such necessity, some strong personal object must have prompted him " officiously to intrude himself into the business." To prove a necessity, it would be incumbent on him to show that there was a deficiency of the queen's ordinary legal counsel; but besides the attorney and solicitor-general and Serjeant Yelverton, all of whom assisted at the trial, there were two other queen's serjeants, Daniell and Drew, whose services would have fallen within the regular course of their duties. Even if additional aid was required there was the whole bar to choose from, and the name of " Nicholas Kempe, counsellor at law," is actually recorded as taking some of the examinations.[1] As to Bacon's services being indispensable, he, according to his own showing, held no office, but a new and extraordinary appointment; and it is a curious fact, that in a memorandum for the order of the arraignment, in Coke's handwriting, preserved in the State Paper Office, Bacon's name was not proposed in the list of counsel to be retained. There is, however, a note from the lords of the Council, written the day before the trial, addressed to " Mr. Francis Bacon, one of her Majesty's counsel learned."[2] The non-introduction of his name in Coke's memorandum is a strong proof that his appearance was not a necessary part of his duty. No precedent could be urged against his refusal, if he had been earnest in his resistance;

---

[1] Works, vi. 378. 380. [2] Jardine's Crim. Trials, i. 385.

and if his aid was demanded by the council, with the knowledge of his connection with the earl, he ought to have felt that they sought rather to degrade, than to advance or honour him.   The truth, however, peeps out, even in the apology itself, in his avowal that one of his objects was " to uphold himself in credit and strength with the Queen; " and in another place, that as " she was constant in her favours, and made an end where she began," he was resolved to endure his condition " in expectation of better."   The queen was offended at his friendship for Essex, which, he says, he " saw would overthrow " him ; and consequently he pursued a course by which he incurred the contempt of the world, without producing, as the event proved, any advantage for himself.   Had he acted a more honourable part, he would have obtained the credit, without incurring the danger, of Sir Henry Yelverton, who refused to plead against his patron Somerset, and Sir John Walter, who indignantly rejected a brief against Sir Edward Coke.

This disposition to undertake anything with a view to his own advantage is still more manifest in the " Declaration of the Treasons of the Earl of Essex," published by him soon after the trial.[1]   Though he says that he wrote it at the queen's command, " her majesty taking a liking to my pen," it is impossible to believe that he might not have avoided the task.   In it he vilifies and blackens the earl's character to such an extent, that it is surprising he should so long have associated with him without discovering or suspecting his criminal intentions ; and it is curious to observe that in the " Apology," after the queen was dead, and when the enemies of the earl were in rather doubtful odour, all the criminal imputations against him are softened down to " his misfortune," and the designation of traitor converted into " the unfortunate earl."

[1] Works, vi. 299.

Another remarkable circumstance connected with this conspiracy requires explanation. Catesby, afterwards known as a principal in the Gunpowder Plot, was also implicated in this, but succeeded in obtaining his pardon by the payment of a fine of 4000*l.* to the queen. By a letter from the council to Mr. Attorney-General Coke, the queen's orders were conveyed to him to divide the said fine money among "Mr. Francis Bacon, Sir Arthur Gorges, and Captain Carpenter;" and the share appropriated to Bacon was 1200*l.* The date of this warrant is August 6, 1601, and it is signed by eight privy councillors.[1] Whatever may have been the motive with the royal donor inducing this extraordinary gift, it is difficult, under all the attendant circumstances, to draw an inference favourable to the courtly recipient.

To return. Within ten days after the appointment of Sir Thomas Egerton, Essex wrote to him to have a care of Bacon during his absence in Spain.[2] The new lord keeper had always been friendly to him, and, when he was a candidate for the solicitorship, had supplied him with observations for the exercise of the office.[3] Bacon's crown business no doubt would, with such patronage, be materially increased, and his personal access to the queen become more frequent. Her Majesty even occasionally honoured him with her presence at his house in Twickenham Park.

This advance in favour had the natural effect of making him think more highly of his position than the actual nature of his employment warranted. That he was inclined to encroach beyond his province is apparent from the scene that occurred in the Court of Exchequer about 1601,[4] when, Bacon having moved for the reseizure of certain lands, Coke, probably deeming it an interference with his duties, "kindled at it;" and insulting and scornful words passed between

[1] Council Reg. Eliz. xvii. 336.   [2] Works, xii. 91.
[3] Egerton's Life, 165.   [4] Works, xii. 277.

them. Among the rest, Coke bade him "not meddle with the queen's business," and said he "was unsworn.[1]"

He had in 1578 been an unsuccessful rival of Coke for the favours of lady Hatton; and the Earl of Essex, with his wonted zeal, had been his advocate with both her parents. His disappointment in not obtaining the lady, whose violent temper had not yet been displayed, no doubt increased the feeling of jealousy and dislike which he already indulged against Coke, and which did not diminish as years rolled on.

Whatever reputation Bacon may have acquired among his friends and associates by his private studies, he was not yet known to the public in his literary character; nor was it till the year 1598 that he made his first appearance as an author. In it he published his "Essays," which, as it was the first, so it was, and still remains, the most popular of his works. He dedicated the book to his brother Anthony, in a letter dated January 30; and so highly was it appreciated, that no less than nine editions, the later being greatly enlarged, were issued during his life.

Notwithstanding all the professed advantages he enjoyed from his legal engagements, they did not keep him free from pecuniary pressure. His involvements were so great, and his credit so small, that he was taken in execution and detained in a house in Coleman Street, in September, 1598. This fact appears from a letter to lord keeper Egerton, complaining that it was a breach of privilege, as he was coming from the Tower in "a service of no mean importance" for the queen.[2] The result of his complaint is not stated; but his letters to Mr. Michael Hickes and Lord Cecil show that his difficulties were still existing, at least as late as 1603.[3]

In the last two parliaments of Elizabeth in 1597 and 1601,

---

[1] Works, vii. 338.   [2] Ibid. xii. 275.   [3] Ibid. 278. 478, 479.

he was a frequent speaker in support of the queen's measures.

No sooner was Queen Elizabeth's death announced than Bacon, instead of waiting with a decent and dignified patience for the king's arrival in London, exerted all his influence among persons high and low, to get himself favourably mentioned to the new monarch. To Mr. Davis he writes:— "I commend myself to your love and the well-using my name, as well in repressing and answering for me, if there be any biting and nibbling at it in that place, as by imprinting a good conceit and opinion of me, chiefly in the king, as otherwise in that court."[1] To Mr. Foules he writes two letters, "to further my being known by good note unto the king."[2] Dr. Morison, Sir Thomas Challenor, and Lord Kinloss, were addressed in the same degrading style[3]; and the Earl of Northumberland (to whom he volunteered a proclamation on the king's entry), the Earl of Northampton, and even the Earl of Southampton, were reminded of his services.[4] It must have been a severe mortification to him to find that he had not been even named among the queen's servants to be re-appointed; but the efforts of his friends were, as already stated, successful in obtaining the warrant issued a month afterwards, allowing him as one of the learned counsel "in such sort" as Queen Elizabeth did.

That at first he was not much encouraged, notwithstanding a most fulsome letter to the king,[5] may be judged from a letter in July to Cecil, who was now raised to the peerage, wherein he says, "I desire to meddle as little as I can in the king's causes, his majesty now abounding in council;" "my ambition now I shall only put upon my pen, whereby I shall be able to maintain memory and merit of the times succeeding." He, however, accepted the "prostituted title of

---

[1] Works, xii. 114.   [2] Ibid. 26. 114.   [3] Ibid. 101. 113; xiii. 63.
[4] Ibid. 24. 29. 48. 102. 115   [5] Ibid. 99.

knighthood," as he calls it, with three hundred others, at the coronation on July 23, 1603, and assigns as reasons for doing so, "because of this late disgrace" (probably another arrest); " and because I have three new knights in my mess at Gray's Inn commons ; and because I have found out an alderman's daughter, a handsome maid to my liking."[1]   This maid was Alice, one of the daughters and co-heirs of Benedict Barnham, an alderman of London, whom he soon after married, his means being much increased by her fortune.

Bacon penned another voluntary proclamation touching the king's style, which had the same fate as the former[2] ; and in the session of parliament in that and the following year, being member for Ipswich, he made himself usefully prominent, delivering, however, a speech to the king himself fulsomely flattering[3], and another with reference to him still more so.[4]

The only fact which is recorded of him in the second year of James's reign is his redeeming a jewel on August 21, on the security of which Lord Ellesmere had lent him 50l.[5] Four days afterwards he received the patent already mentioned, appointing him king's counsel with a salary of 40l. per annum ; and on the same day he had a grant in addition of a pension of 60l. for services performed by his deceased brother Anthony and himself.[6]

He was not employed in the trial of Sir Walter Raleigh in November, 1603, though, besides the attorney-general, serjeants Heale and Phillips were ; nor in any of the crown prosecutions before he was made solicitor-general, the queen's serjeant being the only assistant to the attorney-general. From these omissions of his services some judgment may be formed as to the necessity of his appearing against the Earl of Essex ; the remembrance of which was probably the cause

---

[1] Works, xii. 278, 279.   [2] Ibid. vii. 179.   [3] Ibid. vi. 3.
[4] Parl. Hist. i. 1014.   [5] Egerton Papers, 395.   [6] Rymer, xvi. 597.

of his being now so much in the shade. He occupied the interval in the composition of works, some addressed to the king himself, and others evidently intended for the king's eye, which, however excellent in their matter, contained more of flattery than became a great philosopher. Such were his letter to Lord Ellesmere, suggesting a History of England,[1] and his letter to King James, " On the True Greatness of the Kingdom of Britain."[2] To these may be added his tract on the union of the two kingdoms, and his speech on the subject.[3] His leisure was not wholly devoted to politics, for he published his " Advancement of Learning" in 1605.

In spite of his endeavours to force himself forward, Bacon did not obtain the object of his ambition till he had suffered two, or indeed three, more disappointments. He was passed over in October, 1604, when Fleming was appointed chief baron, Sir John Doderidge being made solicitor-general. The death of Sir Edmund Anderson in August, 1605, created another vacancy ; but, instead of Coke, Sir Thomas Gawdy was selected to supply it. On the elevation of Coke to the chief justiceship in June, 1606, Bacon was again set aside, Sir Henry Hobart being called upon to fill Coke's place, and Doderidge remaining solicitor-general. In a letter to Mr. Matthew, at the coming in of the king, he comforts himself that " the canvassing world is gone, and the deserving world is come."[4] But he soon altered his opinion, for on this last occasion he renewed his application to Cecil (now Earl of Salisbury), somewhat depreciating the place, but professing to desire it chiefly to increase his practice.[5] An expedient was suggested by which Doderidge should vacate the solicitorship on being made king's serjeant. This plan he pressed in letters to the king, recapitulating all his

---

[1] Works, xii. 69.   [2] Ibid. v. 311.   [3] Ibid. 16. 47.
[4] Ibid. xii. 230.   [5] Ibid. 14. 63.

deserts, parliamentary and literary[1]; and also to the lord chancellor.[2] Chief Justice Popham died in the following year, and Chief Baron Fleming was put in his place; and instead of either the attorney or solicitor-general succeeding, Judge Tanfield was placed at the head of the Exchequer. The opportunity was, however, taken to effect the plan of making Doderidge king's serjeant; and Bacon, after fourteen years' expectance, obtained at last his desire of entering the king's service by being created solicitor-general on June 25, 1607. His prosperous star was then in the ascendant, for in the next year his reversion in the Star Chamber fell in by the death of Mr. Mylle, and in July, 1608, he was sworn in.[3]

One of the first fruits of his leisure in his new office was, " Certain considerations touching the Plantations in Ireland," which he presented to the king as a new year's offering.[4] He was employed also in preparing his great work, " Instauratio Magna," and sent the draught of various parts of it to different friends and men of learning for their critical censure. The " Cogitata et Visa," he submitted in the beginning of 1608 to Sir Thomas Bodley, the Bishop of Ely (Dr. Hetou), and Mr. Toby Matthew[5]; and in 1609 he published " De Sapientia Veterum,' a collection of Fables of the antients moralised.

In 1611 he was appointed joint-judge of the Knight-Marshals' Court. His cousin, the earl of Salisbury, died on May 24, 1612; and within a week Bacon wrote to the king, disparaging his abilities, saying, " that he was a fit man to keep things from growing worse, but no very fit man to reduce things to be much better; " and, " that he was more *in operatione* than *in opere*." Comparing this with his letters to the earl himself, full of professions of gratitude and admi-

---

[1] Works, xii. 94.   [2] Ibid. 105.   [3] Egerton Papers, 427.
[4] Works, v. 169; xii. 73.   [5] Ibid. xii. 82–92.

ration, either they must be taken as mere flattery, or this must be regarded as false and ungrateful. But neither were without an object. The earl could no longer promote his advancement; while in this and other letters to the king, depreciating the earl's powers, he recommends his own "little skill" in the House of Commons, where he "was never one hour out of credit," and asks "leave to meditate and propound some preparative remembrances touching the future parliament."[1]

Bacon held the office of solicitor-general rather more than six years, during which several puisne judgeships were filled up, for which it does not appear that he applied. He, however, was not idle. He sent one of his petitionary epistles to the king, begging his promise of the "attorney's place whenever it should be void:" and another when the attorney was ill, indecently reminding his Majesty of the promise he had received.[2] The attorney recovered; but upon the death of Fleming, the chief justice of the King's Bench, in August, 1613, Bacon lost no time in urging upon the king, that no one but the attorney and he should be thought of for the place, and that, if the attorney should refuse, he should not be passed over, intimating that the king would then have "a Chief Justice which is sure to your Prerogative."[3] But before the vacancy was supplied, Bacon, perhaps fearing that he should be overlooked, took another course, and in a paper presented to the king, pointed out "Reasons why it should be exceeding much for his Majesty's service, to remove the Lord Coke from the place he now holdeth to be Chief Justice of England, and the Attorney to succeed him, and the Solicitor the Attorney."[4] In it his ill-feeling toward Coke again shows itself. He says, "It will strengthen the King's causes greatly amongst the judges; for my Lord Coke

---

[1] Works, xii. 281. 285.   [2] Ibid. 96. 121.   [3] Ibid. 286.   [4] Ibid. vii. 340.

will think himself near a Privy Counsellor's place, and there-upon become obsequious;" and, "the remove of my Lord Coke to a place of less profit, though it be with his will, yet will be thought abroad a kind of discipline to him for opposing himself to the king's causes; the example whereof will contain others in more awe." After this shameless encouragement to destroy the independency of the Bench, he proceeds in one breath to speak in terms of disparagement of his deceased relative and his present senior, thus : " The attorney-general sorteth not well with his present place, being a man timid and scrupulous, both in parliament and other business, and one that in a word was made fit for the Treasurer (Cecil)'s bent, which was to do little with much formality and protestation." Not forgetting himself, however, he takes care to enhance his peculiar adaptation to the office : adding, " whereas the now Solicitor going more roundly to work, and being of a quicker and more earnest temper, and more effectual in that he dealeth in, is like to recover that strength to the King's prerogative, which it had in times past, and which is due unto it." This cunning plan was adopted. Coke, two months after, was removed to the King's Bench ; Hobart, the attor-ney-general, went to the Common Pleas ; and Bacon obtained, at last, his step of promotion, being made attorney-general on October 27, 1613.

In the two parliaments called by James in the first fourteen years of his reign, the one sitting from 1604 to 1610, and the other from April to June 1614, Bacon was of course an active member. So acceptable had he made himself to the House, and so highly were his qualities as an orator appreci-ated, that in the second Parliament, though it was alleged that no attorney-general had ever been elected a member, he was allowed to sit; but this was not to be a precedent for the future.

One of the first cases in which Bacon exercised his office

of attorney-general, was an information in the Star-Chamber
against Priest for sending, and Wright for delivering, a chal-
lenge, when he exposed the practice of duelling so forcibly,
that the judges, in condemning the defendants to heavy fines,
ordered that their decree should be penned by the attorney-
general, with all his arguments, and read at the assizes for
Surrey, where the offence was committed.[1] With less foundation in reason or justice was his next proceeding against
James Whitelocke (afterwards the judge), for giving a verbal
opinion, or perhaps for arguing as a barrister on the legality
of a commission from the crown.[2] The defendant probably
owed his pardon as much to the bungling efforts of Bacon to
justify the absurd charge, as to the submission which he discreetly made. The attorney's speech in the following year
against Oliver St. John, for writing a letter showing the
unlawfulness of Benevolences (for which he was fined 5000l.),
is loaded with flattery to the king, and futile arguments to
prove that a Benevolence is not a tax. In reference to the sentence on St. John, he adopted the unusual course of corre-
sponding with the king[3], a novel practice which he introduced,
and which he more particularly continued in the cases of
Peacham and Owen.[4]

The charge against Peacham was founded on certain passages contained in a sermon which had never been preached,
but which had been discovered in his study. The king was
most desirous of proving that the mere writing constituted
treason, and Bacon interested himself too much to procure a
conviction. He wrote several letters to the king, with accounts of his examinations of the prisoner, to whom torture
was applied in the course of them ; and he describes his artful
management in obtaining the separate opinions of the judges.
Coke for some time resisted the " auricular taking of opinions

[1] Works, vi. 108–137.   [2] State Trials, ii. 766.
[3] Works, xii. 127.; xiii. 64.   [4] Ibid. xii. 62. 123–136. 289.; xiii. 108.

single and apart;" but eventually was forced to submit to this
most unconstitutional mode of prejudging the case. In
Owen's business the same course was suggested, but not
adopted; probably on account of Coke's opposition with regard to Peacham. In both cases it is difficult to justify Bacon's
conduct.

Then followed the trials connected with Overbury's murder,
in the progress of which the letters of Bacon show his desire
to assist the king in his determination to convict, and afterwards to save, the principal offenders.[1]

When Sir Edward Coke resisted the jurisdiction of the
Court of Chancery, though Bacon made to the king a fair
exposition of the controversy, he could not refrain from aiming
a blow at his rival, suggesting that, " *at this time* " he should
not be disgraced, though " this great and public affront" to
the chancellor, " thought to be dying, which was barbarous,"
and to the High Court of Chancery, may not, he says, " pass
lightly, nor end only in some formal atonement." His total
disregard for the independence of the Bench is further shown
in this letter; for he proceeds to say that " if any of the puisne
judges did stir this business, I think that judge is worthy to
lose his place: I do not think there is anything, a greater
Polycreston ad multa utile to your affairs, than upon a just
and fit occasion to make some example against the presumption of a judge in cases that concern your Majesty ; whereby
the whole body of those magistrates may be contained in
better awe ; " and he then recommends, " that the judges should
answer it on their knees before your Majesty and your council,
and receive a sharp reprimand." [2] In the case of the *commendams*, or " *Rege inconsulto*," he not only took the part of
the king, but was the principal instigator in calling the judges
to account before the privy council [3]; a course which has too

---

[1] Works, vi. 219–241.   [2] Ibid. xii. 36.   [3] Ibid. vii. 307–338.

much the appearance of being influenced by his inveteracy against Coke, especially when connected with a paper he drew up, enlarging on the various " Innovations into the laws," which Coke, as he alleged, had introduced.[1]

The chancellor's illness occurring during the progress of these proceedings, Bacon set himself about his usual practice of begging for the reversion of the place. In a letter to the king, dated Feb. 12, 1615–16, he not only boasts of what he would do if he had the Seal, but depreciates those who might be competitors for it; particularly Coke, of whom he says, " Your Majesty shall put an overruling nature into an over-ruling place, which may breed an extreme: next you shall blunt his industries in matter of finances which seemeth to aim at another place: and, lastly, popular men are no sure mounters for your Majesty's saddle."[2] He had taken care to secure the affections, or at least the interest, of Sir George Villiers, the new favourite, by a long paper of instructions how to govern himself in the station of prime minister[3]; con-taining excellent advice, some points of which it would have been better if he himself had practised. One he evidently for-got : " If any one sue to be a judge, for my own part, I should suspect him ; " for after having sent a paper to Mr. Murray, of the King's Bedchamber, "concerning my honest and faith-ful services to his Majesty," he applied to Villiers, more than a year before the chancellor's resignation, to get it from him and go on " with my first motion, my swearing privy coun-cillor, not so much to make myself more sure of the other, and to put off competition." Six days later he again urges the suit[4], and repeats it on May 30; and when in the following June the king gave him the choice either to be sworn privy councillor, or to have the assurance of succeeding Lord Elles-

[1] Works, vii. 401. [2] Ibid. xii. 31.

[3] Ibid. vi. 400. [4] Ibid. xii. 143. 148., Feb. 1615–16.

mere, he wisely accepted the former[1], and accordingly took his seat at the board on the 9th of that month.

In the nine months that followed, Bacon kept up a constant correspondence with Villiers, not only on public matters, but with reference also to the favourite's private concerns, — the peerage which was conferred on him in August, and the grants which were made to him to support his title, with the contrivances adopted for his benefit. Even in these, apparently for no other object than that of flattering Villiers, he speaks slightingly of " the Cecils, father and son."[2] During this time also the proceedings took place which expelled Coke from his seat in the King's Bench, in which Bacon, so far from attempting to moderate the king's groundless anger, took every means to justify and inflame it. The minute of Council, and the " Remembrances," prepared by him, are evidently composed in this spirit.[3] Nor did he show more generosity towards the chief justice, in reference to the absurd direction as to " expurging of his Reports: "[4] and if the long letter addressed to Coke, as soon as his disgrace had been rendered certain, was, as it has always been considered, the production of Bacon, it exhibits the mean spirit of triumphing over a fallen adversary, by dwelling, under the pretence of friendly admonition, on all his faults and infirmities, and painting them in colours which, however true to the life, reflect on the writer the imputation of their being dictated by cowardly and malicious feelings.[5]

Lord Ellesmere's last days were approaching. During the two previous years he had petitioned to be relieved from his office, but could not prevail on the king till March 3, 1616-17. Four days afterwards Bacon attained the object of his late endeavours, by receiving the Great Seal from the king's hand, with

---

[1] Works, xii. 149.   [2] Ibid. 59, 60. 152. 237.
[3] Ibid. vii. 307–338. 349.   [4] Ibid. xii. 304.   [5] Ibid. vii. 296.

the title of lord keeper.[1]   In another week Lord Ellesmere died; and on May 7 Bacon took his seat in the Court of Chancery, delivering a long speech, stating his resolutions as to the practice.   Even in this speech he could not refrain from giving a sly and contemptuous blow at Sir Edward Coke, by saying, in allusion to complaints against judgments at law, "wherein your Lordships may have heard a great rattle and a noise of præmunire, and I cannot tell what."[2]   He first removed from Gray's Inn to Dorset House in Fleet Street, and soon afterwards to York House in the Strand, where he was born.

On receiving the Seal he immediately wrote to Villiers (now created Earl of Buckingham), in strong terms of gratitude, stating that he "shall count every day lost," wherein he shall not "do your name honour in speech, or perform you service in deed."[3]   The earl made good use of this promise, by writing numerous letters to Bacon in favour of suitors; and the success of his influence may be judged by the frequency of the applications.[4]   Herein both the earl and the lord keeper forgot the advice formerly given by the one to the other : — "By no means be you persuaded to interpose yourself, either by word or letter, in any cause depending in any court of justice."[5]

Within four months, however, his inveteracy against Coke, and his fear lest his old enemy should again triumph, induced him to interfere in a matter which the earl was likely to re-sent.   He wrote letters to the king and the earl (then both in Scotland), advising against the projected marriage between the earl's brother, Sir John Villiers, and Coke's daughter by Lady Hatton, and representing the inconvenience to the State "if there be but an opinion of his (Coke's) coming in."[6]   From

[1] Claus. 16 Jac., p. 15. n. 13.   [2] Works, vii. 243.   [3] Ibid. xii. 241.
[4] Ibid. passim, from 314 to 411.   [5] Ibid. vi. 413.   [6] Ibid. xii. 245.

the former he received a severe letter of rebuke [1]; when he not only made an abject submission, but reversed his policy by furthering the match, and altering his carriage towards Sir Edward Coke.[2] Buckingham was not so easily appeased, but " professed openly against " him, as reported in a letter from Sir Henry Yelverton, who gave him some sound advice how he should act.[3] The earl was, however, soon afterwards apparently reconciled [4]; and not only was the correspondence between them resumed, but Bacon was so entirely restored to the king's favour, that he received the title of lord chancellor on January 4, 1617-18.

The king had indeed much reason to be satisfied with Bacon's industry ; for there was scarcely a single business touching the royal interests to which he did not devote himself. His correspondence with the king was incessant, comprehending all subjects — political, judicial, and, what seems out of his province, economical. It would be more satisfactory if it did not contain too many proofs of his endeavours to conciliate favour by occasional symptoms of his inclination to stretch, and even to overstep, the law for James's benefit[5], and by perpetual flattery and allusions to the superiority of the king's judgment, which are repeated *ad nauseam.* In reward for his " many faithful services," the king, on July 11, 1618, created him Baron Verulam [6]; and Bacon, three months afterwards, applied to Buckingham to obtain for him a grant of the farm of the Alienation, " a little to warm the honour." [7] In the following May he received a more substantial favour in the grant of 1200*l.* a year [8]; and in writing to Buckingham on Dec. 12, 1619, as to the appropriation of the fines imposed on the Dutch merchants for exporting gold and silver coin, he says : " And if the king intend any gifts, let them

---

[1] Works, xii. 327.   [2] Ibid. 250. 324.   [3] Ibid. 331.   [4] Ibid. 342.
[5] Ibid. 264. 374.   [6] Rymer, xvii. 17.   [7] Works, xii. 260.   [8] Ibid. 369.

stay for the second course (for all is not yet done), but nothing out of these, except the king should give me the 20,000*l.* I owe Peter Vanlore out of his fine, which is the chief debt I owe." He adds: " This I speak merrily." Might he not have said " advisedly " too?[1]

His efforts in this case of the Dutch merchants, and in several other proceedings which resulted in fines, were dictated, to all appearance, too much by the desire of relieving the king's pecuniary difficulties, and avoiding the necessity of calling a parliament. To this, however, it became necessary at last to resort; and on November 6, 1620, a proclamation, in the preparation of which, both as to the business to be transacted, and the members to be chosen, Bacon took an active part, was issued for one in Jannary, being six years and a half since that assembly had met. Bacon was advanced in the peerage with the title of Viscount St. Albans.[2] This additional title, though it made his subsequent fall the greater, was no doubt given in gratitude by the king, who, whatever may be thought of Bacon's services, could not fail to see in them a constant desire to please and assist him, and to whom the blow that was being silently prepared was as sudden and unexpected as it was to Bacon himself.

Before the parliament met, Yelverton, the attorney-general, who had incurred Buckingham's enmity, was prosecuted in the Star Chamber for introducing certain clauses in a charter to the city of London not authorised by the king's warrant. Bacon, who had been on friendly and familiar terms with him, seems to have pressed the case too hardly against him; and his letters bear the mark of his having been influenced in doing so by a desire to curry favour with Buckingham.[3]

In the preceding October, he published his great work, " Novum Organum," which he dedicated to the king; to

---

[1] Works, xii. 380.   [2] Rymer, xvii. 279.   [3] Works, vii. 446–9.

whom in a private letter he says, " there be two of your council and one other bishop [Andrews] of this land, that know I have been about some such work near thirty years."[1] The king received it most graciously, promising "to read it thorough with care and attention, though I steal some hours from my sleep, having otherwise as little spare time to read it as you had to write it."[2]

The parliament assembled on January 30; and Bacon, after the king had addressed it, made a short speech in the exaggerated style of flattery he was in the habit of using: "I am struck with admiration in respect of your profound discourses, with reverence to your royal precepts, and contentment in a number of gracious passages, which have fallen from your Majesty in your speech," &c. The Commons were not so well satisfied with the king nor with his system; and though they were liberal in their grants and respectful in their language, they resolved to investigate and repress the evils under which the people suffered, and to punish the oppressors. For this purpose they formed a committee of grievances, which proceeded to inquire into the various monopolies, patents, and grants of concealments, which had caused so much suffering and injustice. One of the first objects of their attack was Sir Giles Mompesson, a member of their house, the charge against whom was taken into the House of Lords; and while Bacon, as chancellor, was assisting in the examination, the committee of the Commons, on March 15, made a report, charging him with corruption in his high office, which was communicated on the 18th to the Lords.

Bacon seems to have been wholly taken by surprise at this accusation, which was at first confined to two cases. He immediately took to his bed, and addressed a letter to Sir James Ley, then acting as speaker in his stead, praying

[1] Works, xii. 392.   [2] Ibid. 154.

that the house would maintain him in their good opinion till his cause was heard, and for time to advise with his counsel, and to make his answer. On March 22nd, four more charges were brought against him; and on the 26th the parliament adjourned till April 17, three committees of the Lords being authorised to examine witnesses during the recess. On the renewal of the session the lord chamberlain announced that Bacon had had an interview with his Majesty, who had referred him to the Lords; and on the 24th Bacon sent them a general confession, stating that, though not communicated formally from the house, he found in the charges "matter sufficient and full" to move him to desert his defence. This submission not being deemed satisfactory, the Lords resolved that he should be charged with the several briberies and corruptions, and that he should make a particular answer by the 30th. The charges had been greatly increased in number. They consisted of his having in no less than twenty-two instances received bribes and presents amounting to above 11,000*l.*, from one or the other, or from both, of the parties in suits before him.

On April 30 he sent in his submission, confessing *seriatim* the receipt of the several sums charged. Some few he acknowledged were given while the suit was depending; but he asserted that others were not presented till after he had pronounced his decree. Some he said were New Year's gifts, and some presents towards the furnishing of his house; and that there were "few or none that are not almost two years old." On the same day the Great Seal was sequestered, and, three days later, Bacon being excused from attending on account of illness, the Lords pronounced sentence against him — of a fine of 40,000*l.*; imprisonment in the Tower during pleasure; incapacity to hold any office, &c., in the State; and prohibition against sitting in parliament, or coming within the verge of the court. They negatived the proposition that he should be suspended from all his titles of nobility during his life.

It has been suggested that Bacon was induced to " desert his defence " at the instigation of the king and Buckingham. What passed at the interview between the former and Bacon cannot of course be known ; but it is not improbable that the king, desirous as he must have been of putting a stop to the investigations of the Commons, lest other persons nearer to him should be implicated, advised him, if he had not a clear defence against all the charges, not to lengthen the proceedings. But it is impossible to read the evidence on which the charges were founded, or even the circumstances alleged by Bacon in extenuation of some of them, without feeling that it must have been more the consciousness of guilt than any tenderness towards other parties that dictated the submission that he offered. Indeed, his own letters, both previous and subsequent to this confession, contradict the idea that he sacrificed himself for the sake of others. In his first letter to the king after the charges were made, though he hopes he may not be found to have " a depraved habit of taking bribes to pervert justice," he adds, " howsoever I may be frail, and partake of the abuses of the times."[1] In another, petitioning his Majesty to save him from the sentence, he ventures to say, " but because he that hath taken bribes is apt to give bribes, I will go further, and present your majesty with a bribe." And in a third letter pleading for pardon, he instances Demosthenes, Titus Livius, and Seneca, as having been restored after being condemned for bribery and corruption.[2] To Sir Thomas May also, in acknowledging and qualifying a present he had received from the Apothecaries, he says, " as it may not be defended, so I would be glad it were not raked up more than needs. I doubt only the chair, because I hear he useth names sharply."[3] The language in

---

[1] Works, xii. 66.   [2] Ibid. xiii. 30. 32.   [3] Ibid. xii. 406.

these and other letters cannot by any interpretation be read as that of an innocent man.

When he signed his submission, his advice to Buckingham must have risen up as a witness against him : " Judges must be chaste as Cæsar's wife, neither to be, nor to be suspected to be, unjust[1];" and one of the features in the picture of a good judge, which he painted in his address to Judge Hutton, could not but be painfully brought to his mind: " That your hands, and the hands of your hands, I mean those about you, be clean and uncorrupt from gifts, from meddling in titles, and from serving of turns, be they of great ones or small ones."[2]

After his sentence, he expresses in his letters no compunction for his offence, nor exhibits any shame at his exposure. How little he felt his disgrace appears in a letter to the Bishop of Winchester, in which he talks of his consolation being in the examples of Demosthenes, Cicero, and Seneca, —" all three ruined, not by war, or by any other disaster, but by justice and sentence as delinquent criminals; all three famous writers, insomuch as the remembrance of their calamity is now as to posterity but as a little picture of night-work, remaining amongst the fair and excellent tables of their acts and works."[3] In a letter also to Buckingham he says, " I confess it is my fault, though it may be some happiness to me withal that I do most times forget my adversity."[4] Neither was it any impediment to his wit, for when Sir Henry Montagu, Earl of Manchester, who had been chief justice, and was lately removed from the office of lord treasurer to the less important one of lord president of the Council, expressed to the fallen chancellor how sorry he was to see him made such an *example*, Bacon replied, " It did not trouble him, since his lordship was made a *precedent*."[5]

---

[1] Works, vi. 413.   [2] Ibid. vii. 271.   [3] Ibid. 113.
[4] Ibid. xii. 424.   [5] Aubrey, 225.

Camden says his imprisonment lasted but two days [1], and his letters prove that one of them was the 31st of May, and that the next day he was at Sir John Vaughan's at Parson's Green.[2] From this retirement he was allowed at the end of the month to remove to Gorhambury.[3] In the following September he pressed his suit for some assistance in his fallen fortunes; and on October 8 he thanked the king for the remission of his fine, and offered his history of Henry VII. for correction.[4] The fine was pardoned, and, at the same time, assigned to trustees to prevent the importunity of his creditors; to the passing of which Lord Keeper Williams at first made some objections, the proposed assignment being, as he said, " full of knavery and a wicked precedent." From a letter addressed to him by John Selden in February 1621-2, he seems to have at one time contemplated overturning the judgment against him, on account of a doubt he raised whether that meeting of parliament was a legal session; but he received no encouragement.[5] He continued his importunities till his friends succeeded in March in obtaining a release from his confinement at Gorhambury, and a permission to go to Highgate.[6] Subsequently he tells the Lord Treasurer Cranfield, who was negotiating with him for the purchase of York house, that he had taken a house at Chiswick[7]; and at the end of 1622 Buckingham obtained for him an interview with the king.[8] He continued, by means of friends and letters, his correspondence with Buckingham till the marquis in February, 1623, accompanied the prince on his romantic pilgrimage to Spain, when, as he says, " the better to hold out,"[9] he retired to his chambers in Gray's Inn. He never returned to York house, which became Buckingham's in 1624.

During the marquis's absence in Spain, Bacon appealed to

---

[1] Camden in Kennett, ii. 657.   [2] Works, xii. 490., xiii. 31.
[3] Ibid. xii. 408.   [4] Ibid. 410.   [5] Ibid. 421.   [6] Ibid. 425.
[7] Ibid. 428.   [8] Ibid. xiii. 37.   [9] Ibid. 439.

the king himself in a long letter, which would have been pathetic but that it is over-laboured, praying his Majesty to pity him so far as that he " that hath borne a bag be not now in his age forced in effect to bear a wallet, nor he that desired to live by study, may not be driven to study to live."[1]   So reduced does he appear to be, by all his letters, that upon a vacancy in May, 1623, he applied to the king, but unsuccessfully, for the provostship of Eton, "a cell to retire unto."[2]

To Buckingham, while abroad (then created duke), his letters were frequent and flattering; and to Mr. Toby Matthew, who was also in Spain, his desires to keep him in the prince's and the duke's remembrance show his anxiety to be again received into favour.   On their return in October he offered the duke counsel for his conduct, advising him to " do some remarkable act to fix " his reputation, and reminding him of an old Spanish proverb, " he that tieth not a knot upon his thread loseth the stitch."[3]   In January, 1624, he tells the duke that he is " almost at last cast for means[4] ;" but it was not till November that he succeeded in getting " three years advance," to relieve him of his necessities.[5] Shortly before this he had received a full pardon of his whole sentence.[6]

King James died on March 27, 1625, and King Charles immediately calling a parliament, Bacon had the firstfruits of his full pardon by receiving a writ of summons.   Ill health, which had begun to make inroads upon him, prevented him from taking his seat, and for the whole of that year his correspondence was much curtailed.   Such letters as remain show a continuance of straightened means.   He writes to Sir Robert Pye " to dispatch that warrant of a

---

[1] Works, xii. 49.   [2] Ibid. 440.   [3] Ibid. 450. 452.
[4] Ibid. 455.   [5] Ibid. xiii. 7.   [6] Ibid. 70.

petty sum, that it may help to hear my charge of coming up to London; "[1] and at the end of the year he tells the Duke of Buckingham that "his wants are great."[2]   Even as late as Jannary, 18, 1626, he shows that his hopes of court favour are not exhausted, by requesting the French ambassador, the Marquis d'Effiat, to procure for him some mark of the queen's good will, and to take occasion to whisper something to his advantage in the Duke of Buckingham's ear.[3]   Indeed a great part of the industry which he displayed during the five years that intervened between his disgrace and his death seems to have been employed in attempts to regain his lost consequence, and to forward his personal advantage.   He sent his History of Henry VII. to the king for correction; he dedicated it to the prince; he requested his majesty "to appoint me some task to write, and that I should take for an oracle,"— and "to give me a theme to dedicate to my lord of Buckingham, whom I have so much reason to honour."[4]   The rest of his time was consecrated to higher and better purposes. No moment seems to have been unoccupied; and his industry is manifested in the number of his original productions during that period, and in the publication of translations of his "Advancement of Learning," with great additions, and of some other of his works, into Latin.

His death was caused by the trial of an experiment whether flesh could not be preserved in snow as well as in salt.   For this purpose, while taking an airing with Dr. Witherspoon, the king's physician, he went to a poor woman's cottage at the bottom of Highgate hill, and bought a hen, the body of which he stuffed with snow.   In doing this the chill seized him so suddenly and violently that he was unable to proceed, and was obliged to be carried to the Earl of Arundel's house in the neighbourhood, where the bed in which he was placed

---

[1] Works, xii. 460.   [2] Ibid. 462.   [3] Ibid. 463.   [4] Ibid. xiii. 37.

being damp, he caught so severe a cold that he died of suf-
focation.[1]　His last letter, addressed to the earl on his death
bed, is preserved in his works[2]; and his last breath was
drawn in the arms of his benevolent relative, Sir Julius
Cæsar.　He expired on Easter Sunday, April 9, 1626,
having exceeded the completion of his sixty-fifth year by
nearly three months.

He was buried at St. Michael's church, at St. Alban's,
where his faithful friend and servant Sir Thomas Meautys
erected a monument, representing him seated in contem-
plation.

His wife, by whom he had no children, survived him till
June 30, 1650, and was buried at Egworth, in Bedfordshire,
having had for her second husband Walter Doble, of Sussex.[3]

Authors differ in their accounts of Bacon's pecuniary
means in the last years of his life.　Howell says he died so
poor that he scarce left money to bury him.　Wilson, the
historian, confirms this account, and adds that Lord Brook
denied him beer to quench his thirst.　Aubrey tells that Sir
Julius Cæsar sent him 100l. in his necessities; and the perpetual appeals to the king and Buckingham for assistance
seem to support the conclusion.　But, on the other hand, it is
related that the prince, on seeing him in a coach followed by a
number of gentlemen on horseback, observed, " Well, do
what you can, this man scorns to go out like a snuff." Indeed,
his income after his pardon was apparently adequate, if prudently managed, to the demands of his station, consisting of
his pension of 1200l. and his grant of 600l. a year from the
Alienation Office, besides the profits of his own estate.　Both
stories may, however, be true, and their discrepancy accounted
for by remembering with what irregularity pensions were
then paid, and the negligence and imprudence in money mat-

---

[1] Aubrey, 227.　　　　　　　[2] Works, xii. 274.
[3] Works, xvi. note H. II. H.; Hasted's Kent, v. 304.

ters generally attributed to him. His reported gift of 50*l.* to the keeper who brought him a buck from the king, politic or ostentatious as it may be interpreted, does not, if true, apply to his fallen state.

As a lawyer Bacon's reputation does not, perhaps, stand so high as it ought. Queen Elizabeth said of him: "Bacon had a great wit and much learning; but in law showeth to the uttermost of his knowledge, and is not deep:" and hers was probably the echo of the general opinion. But this was said when he was a candidate for the office of solicitor-general; and he had not then had the practical advantages which he afterwards enjoyed. With the knowledge of the principles of law which his writings evidence, it is not improbable that the experience he subsequently obtained made him as finished a lawyer as most of his contemporaries. His acquirements in this branch, whatever they were, were overshadowed by his eminence as a philosopher. He composed several legal treatises, but none of them were published during his life. His speeches, which remain, are fair specimens of forensic eloquence in his peculiar style, with sufficient mastery of legal learning, and with ample illustration from history.

In the performance of his judicial duties he boasts of extraordinary activity. He tells Buckingham on June 6, 1617, a month after he took his seat in the court, that there is "not one cause unheard; the lawyers drawn dry of all the motions they were to make; not one petition unanswered. And this, I think, could not be said in our age before."[1] His boasting might be passed over; but it becomes offensive when depreciating his predecessor, as he does in the following December :—"This very evening I have made even with the causes of Chancery, and comparing with the causes heard by my lord, that dead is, of Michaelmas Term was twelve

---

[1] Works, xii. 318.

month, I find them to be double so many and one more; besides that the causes which I dispatch do seldom turn upon me again, as his many times did." He makes an awkward addition to this letter for one who was sworn to administer justice to the people. "That should have been no excuse for me, who shall *ever assign both to the causes of the subjects,* yea, and to my health, *but the leavings of times* after his majesty's business done."[1] Again, in May, 1619, he writes to the same correspondent, "Yesterday was a day of motions in the Chancery. This day was a day of motions in the Star Chamber; and it was my hap to clear the bar that no man was left to move anything, which my lords were pleased to note they never saw before."[2] To this account of his industry should be added his own view of his integrity. When imprisoned in the tower, he says to the duke, "I have been . . . . the justest chancellor that hath been in the five changes since my father's time."[3] When writing also to Buckingham of his poverty, he says, "I never took penny for any benefice or ecclesiastical living; I never took penny for realising anything stopped at the Seal; I never took penny for any commission, or things of that nature."[4] The conviction of Wraynham, prosecuted in the Star Chamber for slandering Bacon, who had pronounced a decree against him in favour of his opponent Sir Edward Fisher, would, on the statement of the case, appear to be just[5], but for the subsequent discovery that the chancellor had shortly afterwards received from Fisher a suit of hangings worth about 160*l.*[6]

The biographers of Bacon have been puzzled how to give to his personal character the praise that he merited for his literary attainments and productions. By the former he must be judged of as the man, by the latter as the philosopher;

[1] Works, xii. 340.   [2] Ibid. xiii. 17.   [3] Ibid. xii. 490.

[4] Ibid. 466.   [5] State Trials, ii. 1059.   [6] Ibid. 1107.

and who but must regret that there is so much of contrast between them? who but must feel that the system of the one was in direct contradiction to the acts of the other? Bacon, as a lawyer, a politician, and a man, seems to be of a totally distinct nature from Bacon as a writer and propounder of everlasting truths. Considering him solely in the former view, taking by themselves the incidents of his life and the evidences of his character, as interpreted by his own letters, would any biographer venture to pronounce a eulogy upon him? Are there grounds for it in his ardent desire for place, betrayed through every phase of his career? in his pertinacious and degrading applications for patronage? in his depreciation of his rivals? in his adulation of his sovereign? in his flattery of the favourite? in his double ingratitude to Essex, in pleading against his life and in blackening his memory? in his envy of Coke, and his underhand proceedings against him? in his attacks on the independence of the judges? in his encouragement of the despotic principles of James? in his acceptance, however extenuated, of the bribes which he acknowledged? in the indifference to shame which he exhibited in his disgrace? or in the unblushing attempts which he made to regain his ascendancy? Would not these, if he had been a common man and undistinguished as a writer, have been visited with the contempt and indignation they merited? And how does his position as an author alter the feeling thus forcibly impressed? Must it not be more deeply imprinted by the conviction that he was acting contrary to his principles, that he had not the moral courage to withstand any temptation, and that in every act of his life he was pursuing a course which his conscience condemned? There is scarcely a fault of which he has been guilty, against which he has not written strongly and truly; and he stigmatises the vices to which he is subject at the very time he is committing them. To himself may be applied the close of his essay " Ou the

Wisdom for a Man's self." " Wisdom for a man's self is, in many branches thereof, a depraved thing. It is the wisdom of rats, that will be sure to leave a house somewhat before it falls. It is the wisdom of the fox, that thrusts out the badger who digged and made room for him. It is the wisdom of crocodiles, that shed tears when they would devour. But that which is specially to be noted is, that those which (as Cicero says of Pompey) are ' sui amantes, sine rivali,' are many times unfortunate; and whereas they have all their times sacrificed to themselves, they become in the end themselves sacrifices to the inconstancy of fortune, whose wings they thought, by their self-wisdom, to have pinioned." [1]

BRACKLEY, VISCOUNT. See Thomas Egerton.

BROMLEY, EDWARD.

B. E. 1610.'

See under the Reign of Charles I.

BRUCE, EDWARD, Lord Kinloss.

M. R. 1603.

THE third son of Robert de Brus, the first chief justice of the Court of King's Bench as newly constituted under Henry III., and one of the competitors for the crown of Scotland in the following reign [2], was John de Brus, to whose grandson, his cousin King David II. granted in 1359 the castle and manor of Clackmannan, with various other manors in the county of that name. In the middle of the sixteenth century, Sir Edward Bruce, the second son of one of the lineal holders of this property, acquired the estate of Blair-hall, and by his marriage with Alison, daughter of William Reid, of

---

[1] Essay xxiii.   [2] See Vol. II. p. 269.

Aikenhead, in the same county, and sister of Robert Reid, Bishop of Orkney, had three sons, the second of whom, Edward, is the subject of the present article.[1]

Edward Bruce was born about the year 1548, and was, according to the most probable accounts, brought up to the law, and practised at the Scottish bar.[2] In 1597 he was preferred to be one of the senators of the College of Justice, and in 1600 he was selected by King James as his ambassador to the English court, for the professed purpose of congratulating the queen on her escape from the earl of Essex's insurrection, but with the secret mission to forward James's views on the succession, and to sound the disposition of the people in regard to it. He effected this object with so much judgment and address, that he obtained the private assurance of most of the leading men of the country that they would support James's pretensions; and he opened a secret correspondence with Sir Robert Cecil (afterwards published by Lord Hailes), which insured the earliest communication of every detail that would aid the conjuncture.[3] Even before his royal master had reaped the fruits of his diplomacy, he received, in reward for his services, a grant of the dissolved abbey of Kinloss, in the shire of Elgin, and was created Lord Bruce of Kinloss by patent dated February 22, 1603.

On Queen Elizabeth's death, Lord Bruce of course accompanied his sovereign to witness that peaceful accession to the English throne which he had been so instrumental in securing. He was not long in being placed in a post which had some slight relation to his early studies. The office of master of the Rolls, which had been previously always a distinct appointment, and the possessor of which had been considered as an assistant to the lord chancellor in his court,

---

[1] Collins's Peerage, v. 120.

[2] Biog. Peerage, iii. 75.; quoting Craufurd and Douglas.

[3] Robertson's Scotland, iii. 136. Burnet's Own Time, i. 8.

had for the last few years been held by Sir Thomas Egerton
in conjunction with the custody of the Great Seal, somewhat
to the inconvenience of the suitors. The restoration of this
office to its original efficiency was therefore by no means
undesirable, and King James was glad of such an opportunity of promoting his faithful servant to a place somewhat
congenial with his former avocations. Accordingly, in less
than three weeks after his arrival in England, Lord Bruce
received the appointment, the date of his patent being May 18,
1603. Sir Thomas Egerton was compensated for his loss
by being created Lord Ellesmere, and changing his official
title from lord keeper to lord chancellor.[1]

Lord Bruce was at the same time admitted into the king's
new council, and in the first parliament obtained an act of
naturalisation for himself and his family.[2] King James
showed his continued favour to him by promoting the marriage of his daughter Christian with William, afterwards
second Earl of Devonshire, giving her away with his own hand,
and making up her fortune to 10,000l. Of Lord Bruce's
performance of the judicial duties devolving upon him nothing
is known, but his remains are deposited close to the court in
which he sat for nearly seven years, namely, in the chapel of
the Rolls, where his effigy in his official dress is represented
on a monument, the inscription on which states that he died
on January 14, 1610–1, and concludes with these two
lines : —

> "Conjuge, prole, nuro, genero, spe, reque beatus;
>   Vivere nos docuit, nunc docet, ecce, mori."[3]

He had not a very high opinion of his royal master, if the
answer he gave to Sir Robert Cecil, who inquired into
James's character, be true as related by Lord Dartmouth : —

---

[1] Dugdale's Chron. Series.   [2] Statutes of the Realm, iv. 1016.
[3] Dugdale's Orig. 335.

" Ken ye a John Ape? en I's have him, he'll bite *you :* en you's have him, he'll bite *me.*"[1]

By his wife, Magdalen, daughter of Alexander Clerk, of Balbirnie in Fife, Esq., he had, besides the daughter already mentioned, two sons who successively possessed the title. Edward, the elder, was killed in a duel with Sir Edward Sackville, afterwards Duke of Dorset. Thomas, the younger, was created Earl of Elgin in Scotland in 1633, and Lord Bruce of Whorlton in England in 1641. To the last title his son received the addition of the earldom of Aylesbury in 1664. The male descendants of this branch of the house failed in 1747, by the death of the third Earl of Aylesbury and fourth Earl of Elgin. The title of Earl of Elgin devolved, according to the Scotch patent, on the heir male, who was the Earl of Kincardine, a descendant from Sir George Bruce of Carnock, younger brother of Edward, the master of the Rolls, and the two titles of Elgin and Kincardine are now enjoyed by the present peer, who has also an English barony of the former name, granted in 1849.

The title of Earl of Aylesbury became extinct; but the last earl having obtained another barony specially limited to his nephew, the youngest son of his sister, the wife of the Earl of Cardigan, the earldom of Aylesbury was added to it in 1776, and his son was in 1821 created Marquess of the same place.[2]

CÆSAR, JULIUS.

M. R. 1614.

See under the Reign of Charles I.

---

[1] Burnet, i. 8. note.

[2] Collins's Peerage, v. 120., i. 325.; Archæologia, xx. 515.; Nicolas's Synopsis.

CÆSAR, THOMAS.

CURSITOR B. E. 1610.

In the city of Treviso near Venice, the noble family of Adelmare had long resided, when a member of it, named Peter Maria Adelmare, who was eminent as a civilian, married a daughter of the house of Cæsarini, and had three sons, the second of whom was christened, after his mother, Cæsar. This Cæsar Adelmare pursued his studies at Padua, and having taken the degree of doctor in medicine, came to England to practise in 1550. Here he obtained such repute that he was employed by Queen Mary, and on one occasion, according to her council book, received the enormous fee of 100l. for his attendance.[1] He obtained letters of naturalisation on August 28, 1558.[2] Queen Elizabeth also placed him at the head of her medical department, and granted to him some beneficial leases under the crown. He fixed his residence in the close of the priory of Great St. Helens, Bishopsgate, where he died in 1569. By his wife, Margaret, daughter of Martin Perin, or Porient, treasurer in Ireland, he left eight children, two of whom obtained judicial appointments — Julius Cæsar, the eldest son, of whom an account will be given in the next reign, and Thomas, the third son, the subject of this article.

Thomas Cæsar was born in 1561, and was educated at Merchant Taylors' School in London, which he left in 1578. In October, 1580, he was entered of the Inner Temple, where he was not called to the bench until he was appointed a baron of the Exchequer, and never held the post of reader to the society. He seems to have used his father's name during the early part of his life, and to have afterwards partially adopted that of Cæsar, at first with an *alias*, and sub-

---

[1] Burgon's Gresham, ii. 464.   [2] Rymer's Fœd. xv. 487.

sequently alone. His first wife, whose mother's name was Chapman, describes herself in her will, " Susan, wife of Thomas Dalmare, alias Cæsar." In this he no doubt followed the example of his brother, Sir Julius, who was then holding a prominent judicial situation, and was aiming at higher posts, for which he perhaps imagined his Italian surname might be deemed a disqualification.

Thomas's name does not appear in any of the Reports, nor did he ever receive the degree of the coif. Indeed, no account is given of his professional career, nor of any office which he held, before his appointment as a baron on May 26, 1610, as the successor of Nowell Sotherton, who died before the 27th of October, 1608; a certificate of that date recommending Thomas Cæsar to the office on account of " his honesty, learning, and sufficiency," having been addressed by the other barons to the lord high treasurer.[1] Thus no less than seventeen months elapsed between the recommendation and the patent. On his receiving it, the Inner Temple ordered that " he should not be attended to Westminster by any but the officers of the Exchequer, forasmuch as none but such as were of the coif ought to be attended by the fellows of the house." He is there described as " the puisne baron of the Exchequer (commonly called the baron cursitor)." Another order was made on June 10, that though he had not read, but fined for not reading, he should have his place at the bench table notwithstanding a previous Act, " That none who should thenceforth be called to the bench that had not read, should take place of any reader, or have a voice in parliament."[2] It is thus manifest that the office of baron which he held was not of the same degree of dignity as the other barons; and that he had no judicial function is apparent from the absence of his name from all the Reports of the period.

[1] Add. MSS. Brit. Mus. 12,504., No. 123.   [2] Dugdale's Orig. 149.

But whatever was his position, he did not long retain it. His patent as baron of the Exchequer is dated May 26, 1610; he was knighted on June 25, at Whitehall; and he died on the 18th of the following month. Lodge, in his memoirs of the Cæsar family, states his death to have occurred on June 9, 1621; but that he was in error is sufficiently proved, first, by a letter from the Rev. D. Crawshawe of Chancery Lane, who attended him in his last illness, which, though undated, is indorsed and indexed by his brother, Sir Julius, to whom it was addressed, with the date of July 18, 1610, and the addition, "Mr. D. Crawshawe's testimony of my brother Sir Thomas Cæsar's godly disposition that morning he died;"[1] and next, by the appointment of a cursitor baron in his place in the October following. He was buried in the church of Great St. Helens, Bishopsgate.

His first wife died in 1590, leaving three children who did not live to grow up. He married, secondly, Anne, the daughter of George Lynn, of Southwilk, Northampton, Esq., and widow of Nicholas Beaston, Esq.; but she dying early without children, he took for his third wife, in January, 1592–3, Susan, daughter and co-heir of Sir William Ryther, knight, an opulent alderman of London. The Mote near Maidstone, now the seat of the Earl of Romney, with various other estates in the county of Kent, fell to her share. After his death, she took for her second husband Thomas, second son of Sir John Philpot, knight, of Compton Wascelin, Hants.

Sir Thomas had by her three sons,— Thomas, Augustus, and Ferdinando,— and five daughters. Some of his descendants were eminent in the profession which first introduced his father to notoriety.[2]

---

[1] Add. MSS. 12,497., No. 406.   [2] Memoirs of the Cæsars, 39–41.

CHAMBERLAYNE, THOMAS.
Just. K. B. 1620.
See under the Reign of Charles I.

CLARKE, ROBERT.
B. E. 1603.
See under the Reign of Elizabeth.

OF the progenitors of Robert Clarke, or Clerke, no account
has been discovered.   That his family lived in the county of
Essex can be only surmised from the fact that he purchased
the Mansion-house of Newarks, or Newlands-fee, in the parish
of Good Estre, and made it his residence; and that he also
possessed the manor of Gibbecrake, in Purley in that county.[1]
He was admitted of Lincoln's Inn on February 15, 1562, was
called to the bar in 1568[2], and is recorded as a reader in
autumn, 1582.[3]   Notwithstanding the irregular entries in
pp. 96 and 97 of Dugdale's Chronica Series, by which he is
constituted a baron of the Exchequer in June, 1588, 30 Eliz.,
it would seem that he was separately called to the degree of
the coif on June 12, 1587, 29 Eliz., for the purpose of being
invested with the judicial ermine on the 22nd of the same
month; inasmuch as in Coke's 3rd Report, p. 16, his name
clearly appears as baron, and one of the judges of Assize at
Hertford in the summer of that year.   In the summer of
1590 he was the judge of Assize at Croydon, before whom
John Udall, the Puritan, was tried for the publication of the
alleged libel called " The Demonstration," — a trial which,
notwithstanding the evident wish of the judge to be lenient
with him if he would have submitted, is a curious instance of
the shameful and absurd manner in which criminal proceedings were then conducted.[4]   On the accession of King James,

[1] Morant's Essex, i. 345., ii. 459.   [2] Black Book, iv. 377., v. 75.
[3] Dugdale's Orig. 253.   [4] State Trials, i. 1277.

his patent was renewed, and on July 23, 1603, he was knighted. He sat on the bench for nearly twenty years; and a few months before his death the information against Bates, raising the great constitutional question whether a duty could be imposed on the subject by the mere act of the king, was heard in the Exchequer. The baron's argument in Michaelmas Term, 1606, in which he gave judgment for the Crown, is fully stated in Lane's Reports, p. 22. He manifestly felt the weakness of the case, for never was there a more feeble production.

He died on January 1, 1606–7, and directed by his will, dated on December 4th preceding, that no more than 20*l.* should be expended on his funeral, but that 40*l.* should be distributed among the poor. He was buried at Good Estre.

Morant says that he had only two wives; but to these one, or perhaps two more, must be added, and all of them were widows. In his will he charges his son Jeremic to pay 17*l.* a year to the Merchant Taylors' Company, in discharge of his bond for Garson Hills for his life, which charge he says he had by his marriage with his mother. He also gives to his son-in-law, Edmond Chapman, his leases in Southwark, which he states he had by marriage with his mother. Now Garson Hills and Edmond Chapman might possibly be the sons of one mother, who might have been twice a widow before she married the baron; but they could not have been the sons of either of the wives whose names are recorded.

The first of these was Margaret, the daughter of John Maynard, M.P. for St. Albans, and grandfather of the first Lord Maynard. Her first husband (to whom she was second wife) was Sir Edward Osborne, Lord Mayor of London in 1582, and ancestor of the first Duke of Leeds. He died in 1591, leaving no issue by her; and she then married Baron Clarke, and died in 1602. The baron records these facts on a monument he erected to her and her first husband in the church of St. Dionys Backchurch, London.[1]

The name of the baron's second recorded wife was Joice (Jocosa), whose monument, still remaining in the church of St. Saviour's, Southwark, describes her as having been twenty-two years the wife of James Austin, and then for four years the wife of Sir Robert Clarke, and to have died in 1626 at the age of sixty-six, after having been twenty years a widow.

The baron must therefore have married Joice Austin very soon after the death of his wife Margaret; but as he could not have married the latter before 1591, four years after he ascended the bench, there is no difficulty in supposing that he was previously united to one or two widows, the mothers of Garson Hills and Edmond Chapman, especially as at the date of his will five of his daughters were already married.

The parish register of Good Estre settles the question, for there it is recorded that " Mary Clarke, the wife of Robert Clarke, Esq., was buryed the 26 daie of February, 1585 ; " and that " Catheran Clarke, the wife of Mr. Baron Clarke, was buryed ye 16th daie of January, 1590." These, there-fore, were the baron's first two wives, and the same register shows that by the second of these he had two of his children, Esther, born in 1587, and Jeremiah, born in 1589. His eldest son, Robert, and his five married daughters, were therefore the issue of his first wife. He had two more daughters by his wife Margaret.

Robert, who was afterwards knighted, succeeded to the manor of Newarks; that of Gibbecrake was bequeathed to Jeremiah.[1]

---

[1] Collins's Peerage, i. 234., vi. 282. In the latter she is called Dorothy.

[2] Morant, ut supra. I have gratefully to acknowledge the kindness of George R. Corner, Esq., F.S.A., in furnishing me with the wills and inscriptions and other particulars of the family.

COKE, EDWARD.

CH. C. P. 1606.   CH. K. B. 1613.

THE ancestors of Sir Edward Coke are traced as far back as the twelfth century; Henry Coke, of Doddington, in Norfolk, bearing arms and being mentioned in a deed dated 8 John.[1] In direct descent came Robert Coke, Sir Edward's father, of Mileham in the same county, who was a lawyer, and, according to the evidence of his son, a bencher of Lincoln's Inn, though Dugdale does not include him in his list of governors. He married Winifred, daughter and coheiress of William Knightley, of Morgrave Knightley in Norfolk, and dying at his chambers in Lincoln's Inn on November 15, 1561[2], he was buried in St. Andrew's Church, Holborn. There Sir Edward erected a monument to his memory, as he did also, in the church of Tittleshall, to that of his mother, who, after marrying Robert Bosanne and having by him a son named John, died in January, 1569.

Edward Coke, who was the only son out of eight children, was born at Mileham on February 1, 1551–2; so that he was ten years old when his father died, and near eighteen at the decease of his mother. He received the rudiments of his education at the grammar school at Norwich, and was thence removed in September, 1567, to Trinity College, Cambridge, where he remained three years and a half. On the 21st of January, 1571, he was admitted a student of Clifford's Inn, and after going through the usual elementary course of law,

---

[1] Hasted's Kent, ii. 479.

[2] This and many of the subsequent dates and facts are taken from notes in Coke's handwriting in an interleaved copy of Littleton's *Tenures*, preserved among the Harleian MSS. in the British Museum, No. 6687., part i. They were used by the able writer of Coke's Life in the *Penny Cyclopædia*, and have been since extracted and arranged chronologically by John Bruce, Esq., in the *Collectanea Topographica et Genealogica*. Coke is said to have called it his *Vade Mecum;* and under that name it is afterwards quoted.

was in the following year, on April 24, entered of the Inner Temple. In the six years that he spent there he distinguished himself by his studious application, and at the end of them, on April 20, 1578, he was called to the bar.[1] In the very next term he held his first brief in the Court of King's Bench, and was successful in defending Mr. Denny, a clergyman of his native county, in an action brought against him by Lord Cromwell for *scandalum magnatum*.[2] His reputation for learning was already so great, that within a year after his call the benchers of his house selected him as reader at Lyon's Inn[3],—an honour usually conferred on an older barrister,—where his lectures fully confirmed the character he had acquired.

On August 13, 1582, he married his first wife, Bridget, the daughter and heir of John Paston, Esq., deceased, of Huntingfield, in Suffolk[4], a descendant of Judge Paston. At this time his name was pronounced Cooke, and is so spelled in the registry of his marriage, as also in a special commission ten years later, when solicitor-general.[5] His acquisition of a fortune of 30,000*l.* with his wife, in addition to his paternal inheritance, did not diminish his industry; for from this date he seems to have been engaged in almost every prominent case noticed by the different reporters. About 1585, he was chosen recorder of Coventry; in the next year the same office was given to him by the citizens of Norwich; and in January, 1591-2, the corporation of London called him to the distinguished post of recorder of the metropolis. The latter office he retained for six months only, resigning it on being selected by Lord Burleigh as solicitor-general in the room of Sir Thomas Egerton, on June 16, 1592. In the previous Easter Term he had been nominated autumn reader of the Inner Temple; and accordingly

---

[1] Vade Mecum, fo. 13.   [2] 4 Reports, 14.   [3] Vade Mecum, fo. 17.
[4] Ibid. fo. 10.   [5] App. & 4 Report Pub. Rec. 284.

composed seven lectures on the Statute of Uses, five of which he delivered to 160 auditors in August, when, on the appearance of the plague, he was compelled to withdraw from London. In his progress to his seat at Huntingfield, he says that "nine of the benchers, forty of the bar, and other fellows of the Inner Temple," accompanied him as far as Romford.[1]

Hitherto he had confined himself to his legal avocations: he was now to enter on his political career. Before the parliament of 1593 was assembled, and even before Coke had been elected a member of it, the queen and council, on January 28, named him as the speaker.[2] On the 5th of February he was returned as representative of his native county, "nullo contradicente;" and he proudly adds that it was a free election, "sine ambitu, seu aliqua requisitione, ex parte mea." On the meeting of the house he was elected speaker, as had been previously arranged. The parliament lasted only seven weeks; and his speeches in it have the same ponderous verbosity for which they were ever remarkable, and too much of sycophantic subserviency, ill according with the boldness of his later years. But he was then a seeker after advancement, and he felt he had a mistress with whose power no one dared to trifle.

Exactly one year after his speakership terminated, on April 10, 1594, he became attorney-general, again succeeding Sir Thomas Egerton, who was appointed on the same day master of the Rolls. This latter office had been vacant for more than a year by the death of Sir Gilbert Gerard, and the interval was occupied by the intrigues of Bacon to obtain it for himself. These intrigues were continued for another year and seven months for the solicitorship, during which Coke had the double labour of performing the duties of both offices.[3] The interest of Essex was exerted on Bacon's behalf on each occasion; and he was also assisted by Egerton, who supplied

---

[1] Vade Mecum, fo. 13.   [2] Ibid.   [3] Ibid. fo. 14.

him with instructions for the exercise of the latter office[1]; but other influences prevailed, and, to Bacon's second disappointment, Sir Thomas Fleming was at last nominated solicitor-general. In 1596 Coke was elected treasurer of the Inner Temple.[2]

Coke had lived happily with his first wife for sixteen years, when he lost her on June 27, 1598. Within five months after this event he entered into another matrimonial speculation, which began inauspiciously, and was fatal to his future peace. His second wife was Elizabeth, relict of Sir William Hatton, and daughter of Thomas Cecil, who had just succeeded his father as Lord Burleigh, and the marriage took place at her house in Holborn on November 6, 1598[3], without either banns or licence. Even his friend, Archbishop Whitgift, could not overlook this irregularity, and it was only by a humble submission, and the extraordinary plea of ignorance of the law, that Coke and all the parties concerned escaped excommunication. Within a fortnight after the marriage the archbishop issued a pastoral letter to the bishops of his province, dated November 19, requiring them to warn all ministers of the consequence of offending against the canons of the church.[4] The powerful connections and the large fortune of the lady had also attracted Bacon, who had previously become a suitor for her hand; and the success of his great rival did not tend to diminish the hostile feelings between the parties.

Coke continued attorney-general during the remainder of Elizabeth's reign, no vacancy having occurred in the chief seats of the Common Law Courts during the nine years that it lasted. The only important State Trial which is reported in the interval, was that of the Earls of Essex and Southampton in February, 1601. Here he gave the first specimen of that

[1] Egerton's Life, 165.   [2] Dugdale's Orig. 170.

[3] Vade Mecum, fo. 12.   [4] Strype's Whitgift, p. 522.

objurgatory and coarse style, which makes his oratory so painfully remembered. He designates the prisoners as "a Catiline,
popish, dissolute, and desperate company; " he calls the Earl
of Essex " treason-bird; " and uses these harsh and indecent
expressions: " But now, in God's Judgment, he of his Earldom shall he Robert the last, that of the Kingdom thought to
be Robert the first; " and, " Well, my Lord, we shall prove
anon what you are, and what your pride of heart and aspiring
mind have brought you unto."[1] That this kind of language
was not the mere result of professional excitement is manifest
from the arrogance and ill-temper he displayed in 1601,
when Bacon, in the Court of Exchequer, made some motion
which Coke thought trenched upon his duties. Kindling at
it, he said, " Mr. Bacon, if you have any tooth against me,
pluck it out, for it will do you more hurt than all the teeth in
your head will do you good." Bacon's sneering answer, "Mr.
Attorney, I respect you; I fear you not; and the less you
speak of your own greatness, the more I will think of it," drew
this reply from Coke: " I think scorn to stand upon terms of
greatness towards you, who are less than little, less than the
least; " with other insulting language. " Herewith stirred,"
Bacon proceeds, "yet I said no more but this: Mr. Attorney,
do not depress me too far ; for I have been your better and may
be again, when it please the queen "— a truth that was subsequently realised. After many more disgraceful words, the
scene ended by Coke's threatening to " clap a *cap. utlegatum* "
on his back.[2]

On the commencement of the new reign, Coke, who had
cordially cooperated in the arrangements for the peaceable
accession of James, was not only confirmed in his office, but
received the honour of knighthood. He soon had ample opportunity of exhibiting his zeal in the prosecution of State

---

[1] Jardine's Crim. Trials, i. 318—329.　　　　[2] Bacon's Works, vii. 338.

offenders. On Sir Walter Raleigh's trial, his heartless and unmanly behaviour forms an appropriate introduction to the shameful mode in which the proceedings were conducted, and the disgraceful verdict given by the jury; and his fulsome adulation of the king's wisdom and innocence has an awkward illustration, in the absurd farce which the monarch caused to be performed at the intended execution of the lords implicated in the same treason, and in the cruel tragedy which, thirteen years after, he perpetrated in Raleigh's death on that condemnation. Of this king he says, " I shall not need speak anything ; " and then, with a well prepared exception, adds, "nor of the bounty and sweetness of his nature ; whose thoughts are innocent, whose words are full of wisdom and learning, and whose works are full of honour ; although it be a true saying, *Nunquam nimis quod nunquam satis.*" To Raleigh, a prisoner on trial for his life, he brutally says, " Thou art a monster ; thou hast an English face, but a Spanish heart ; " — " Thou viper, for I *thou* thee, thou traitor l " — " Thou art thyself a spider of Hell ; " — " Oh damnable atheist ! " &c. Even Chief Justice Popham felt it necessary to apologise; " Sir Walter," said he, " Mr. Attorney speaks out of the zeal of his duty for the service of the king ; and you for your life ; be patient on both sides : " and Secretary Cecil endeavoured to soften him ; " Be not so impatient, good Mr. Attorney, give him leave to speak." On which Coke angrily exclaimed, " I am the King's sworn servant, and must speak ; if I may not be patiently heard, you discourage the King's Counsel, and encourage Traitors ; " — and sat down in a chafe. [1] A more disgusting scene had never been witnessed in court.

The death of Sir Edmund Anderson in August, 1605, seemed to offer a favourable opportunity for Coke's advancement. Whether he preferred his present post as the more

[1] Jardine's Crim. Trials, i. 407. 410. 428. 443. 446.; State Trials, ii. 7., &c.

profitable, or that the Court could not then dispense with his services, or that Sir Francis Gawdy, as was reported, offered a greater temptation, Coke was passed over, and Sir Francis was raised to the chiefship of the Court of Common Pleas.   During the ten months that he survived, the trials of the conspirators in the Gunpowder Plot occurred, in which Coke repeated his gross flattery of the king, and his cruel language to the prisoners.   Their termination was almost immediately followed by his elevation to the bench as chief justice of the Common Pleas.   He succeeded Sir Francis Gawdy on June 30, 1606, having been on the same day made a serjeant, and taken for his motto, " Lex est tutissima cassis." [1]

On ascending the judicial seat, he discarded all appearance of subserviency, and boldly asserted the independence of the judge.   He did not hesitate to oppose James in his attempts to extend his prerogative; and in the very next year after his appointment he told the king, in the case of Prohibitions, that his Majesty had not power to adjudge any case, either criminal or between party and -party ; but that it ought to be determined in some court of justice ; and upon the king's saying that he thought the law was founded on reason, and that he and others had reason as well as the judges, Coke answered that, " true it was that God had endowed his Majesty with excellent science and great endowments of nature, but his Majesty was not learned in the laws of the realm of England ; " with which the king was greatly offended.[2]   In another case, in 1608, when he and the other judges were summoned before the council to account for a judgment they had given, he said to the lords, " We do hope that where[as] the Judges of this realm have been more often called before your Lordships than in former times they have been, which is much observed, and gives much emboldening to the vulgar, that after this day we

---

[1] Vade Mecum. fo. 14.   [2] 12 Reports, 64.

shall not be so often, upon such complaints, your Lordships being truly informed of our proceedings, hereafter called before you."[1]   In 1610 he gave an opinion, in opposition to the council, that the king could not, by his proclamation, create any offence which was not an offence before.[2]   In the next year, he and the other judges of the Common Pleas discharged Sir William Chancey, brought before them by Habeas Corpus, who had been imprisoned by warrant from the High Commission in Causes Ecclesiastical, and afterwards justified their decision before the council.   When a new Commission was issued, in which he was named, he refused to sit upon it.[3]

His old enemy, Bacon, did not fail to take advantage of Coke's resistance.   On the death of Sir Thomas Fleming, he recommended the king to remove Coke from the Common Pleas to the King's Bench ; and, among others, he gave the following reasons for this measure: " It will strengthen the King's causes amongst the Judges, for my Lord Coke will think himself near a Privy Counsellor's place, and thereupon turn obsequious." " The remove of my Lord Coke to a place of less profit... will be thought abroad a kind of discipline to him for opposing himself in the King's causes; the example whereof will contain others in more awe."[4]   His craft succeeded: Coke was *promoted* to the office of chief justice of the King's Bench on October 25, 1613 ; and was sworn of the Privy Council on November 4.   He received a sincerer and more welcome compliment in the following June, by his unanimous and unsought election as steward of the University of Cambridge.   " Sit Deo gratias," he writes at the conclusion of this entry.[5]   At the beginning of the reign he had obtained for the University the privilege of sending two members to parliament.[6]

---

[1] 12 Reports, 51.   [2] Ibid. 74.   [3] Ibid. 82. 84. 88.
[4] Bacon's Works (Montagu), vii. 340.   [5] Vade Mecum, fo. 12. 15.
[6] Seward's Anecdotes, iii. 396.

Coke was not more "obsequious" in his new office than he had been in his old. Some portion of his uncomplying conduct may perhaps be attributable to his being brought. frequently into collision with Bacon, now attorney-general, whom he despised, and whom he could not but consider as a watchful spy on his conduct, and a delighted tale-bearer of his supposed lapses. In Bacon's letters to the king, his offences are carefully reported. The infamous case of Peacham was the first of these. The king having desired to have the private opinion of the judges, whether Peacham could be convicted of treason, Bacon undertook to procure it. Coke, however, told him, "that this auricular taking of opinions, single and apart, was new and dangerous;" but on being pressed that the other judges had given theirs, he consented; and, to Bacon's disappointment, it was in writing, and was apparently against the prosecution.[1] Notwithstanding the infinite pains he took in regard to the murderers of Sir Thomas Overbury, he offended also on those trials by some mysterious and indiscreet expressions he used in the course of them. In their progress he not only repeated his flattery of the king, but resumed the coarse invectives in which he had formerly indulged; degrading the seat of justice by telling Mrs. Turner, before the verdict was given, that " she had the seven deadly sins, viz., a whore, a bawd, a sorcerer, a witch, a papist, a felon, and a murderer." Guilty as the parties undoubtedly were, Coke conducted the trials most unfairly; and the daily letters that passed between James and him on the subject of them are in strong contrast with his former protest against giving auricular opinions.[2]

But the immediate causes that appeared to determine the court to remove him, were his independent refusal to submit to its interference in the case of Commendams, and his more

---

[1] Johnson's Life of Coke, i. 246.   [2] Great Case of Poisoning, 360—420.

doubtful denial of the power of the Court of Chancery. In the first case, the legality of Commendams having been incidentally disputed by a counsel in his argument in a private cause, the king's pleasure was signified to the judges that they should not go on with the case till they had first consulted his Majesty. But the judges thought it their duty, this being only a dispute between party and party, to proceed, notwithstanding the king's mandate; and all the twelve signed a letter to the king, stating their reasons and justifying their conduct. They were immediately summoned before the council, and, being reprimanded by the king, they all fell down on their knees, and acknowledged their error, except Coke, who defended the letter; and upon further interrogation, whether they would stay their proceedings on a future command, Coke said, " When the case should be, he would do that which should be fit for a judge to do."[1]

In the other case, Coke had not only resisted the power of the Court of Chancery to touch any cause which had been decided in the Courts of Common Law, but had encouraged indictments being presented against all who had been concerned in a case where relief in equity had been applied for, including the counsel and solicitor to the parties, and even the master in Chancery to whom it had been referred. The question was taken up by the king, whose decision, confirming the Court of Chancery in all the powers which it claimed, is acted on to this day.

On both of these occasions Bacon's hand is visible. In the case of the Commendams, he enlarges, in his letter to the king, on Coke's contempt; and in the Chancery question, he dwells on the time chosen for pressing the indictments, " that which all men condemn — the supposed last day of my lord chancellor's life:" as if that was in the power of the chief

---

[1] Bacon's Works (Montagu) vii. 307—338.

justice to select.   The result of all this "turbulent carriage,"
as the king called it, was, that on June 30, 1616, he was sequestered from the council table, and ordered to "forbear to
ride the summer circuit." This was soon followed by his removal from office, his discharge from which, on November 15,
he is stated to have "received with dejection and tears."

A private job is said to have hastened his supersedeas.   Buckingham wished to have the lucrative post of chief clerk of the
Court of King's Bench, the profits of which, when it became
vacant, Coke intended to apply to the augmentation of the
salaries of the judges.   As the place was in his gift, the only
means of obtaining it was by removing him, and by pledging
his successor, as the condition of appointment, to transfer it
to the favourite.   No sooner was Sir Henry Montagu sworn
into office than the admission of Buckingham's trustees to the
disputed place showed the success of the negotiation.   On
Coke's receiving a hint that his compliance would prevent his
dismissal, he refused the temptation, saying, " A judge must
not pay a bribe or take a bribe."   Montagu sent him an offer
to purchase the collar of SS; but Coke answered that "he
would not part with it, but leave it to his posterity, that they
might one day know that they had a chief justice to their
ancestor."

Bacon, while this was in agitation, had the meanness to
address a letter to Coke, in which, with an ungenerous and
malicious pen, he describes the character of the chief justice.
He says, "In discourse you delight to speak too much, not
to hear other men.   This, some say, becomes a pleader, not a
judge; for by this sometimes your affections are entangled
with a love of your own arguments, though they be the
weaker, and rejecting of those which, when your affections
were settled, your own judgment would allow for strongest.
Thus while you speak in your own element, the law, no man
ordinarily equals you; but when you wander, as you often

delight to do, you wander indeed, and give never such satisfaction as the curious time requires."—" You cloy your auditory when you would be observed: speech must be either sweet or short."—" You converse with books, not men, and books especially human; and have no excellent choice with men, who are the best books: for a man of action and employment you seldom converse with, and then but with your underlings; not freely, but as a schoolmaster with his scholars, ever to teach, never to learn. . . . As in your pleadings you were wont to insult over misery, and to inveigh bitterly at the persons, which bred you many enemies, whose poison yet swelleth, and the effects now appear, so you are still wont to be a little careless in this point, to praise or disgrace upon slight grounds, and that sometimes untruly, so that your reproofs or commendations are for the most part neglected and contemned: when the censure of a judge, coming slow but sure, should be a brand to the guilty, and a crown to the virtuous. You will jest at any man in public, without respect of the person's dignity or your own: this disgraceth your gravity more than it can advance the opinion of your wit. You make the law to lean too much to your opinion, whereby you show yourself to be a legal tyrant, striking with that weapon where you please, since you are able to turn the edge any way. . . . Having the living of a thousand, you relieve few or none."[1] Whatever truth there is in this delineation, who must not wish it painted by another hand, and at another time?

Ben Jonson's epigram upon him, written between 1613 and 1616, is a better proof of the estimation in which Coke was then held by his contemporaries, as a lawyer and a judge, and affords some evidence that players were not inimical to him, nor he to them.

[1] Bacon's Works (Montagu), vii. 298.

" He that should search all glories of the gown,
    And steps of all rais'd servants of the crown,
    He could not find than thee, of all that store,
    Whom Fortune aided less, or Virtue more.
    Such, Coke, were thy beginnings, when thy good
    In others' evil best was understood :
    When, being the stranger's help, the poor man's aid,
    Thy just defences made th' oppressor afraid.
    Such was thy process, when integrity,
    And skill in thee now grew authority,
    That clients strove in question of the laws,
    More for thy patronage, than for their cause,
    And that thy strong and manly eloquence
    Stood up thy nation's fame, her crown's defence ;
    And now, such is thy stand, while thou dost deal
    Desir'd justice to the public weal,
    Like Solon's self, explat'st the knotty laws
    With endless labours, while the leaning draws
    No less of praise than readers, in all kinds
    Of worthiest knowledge, that can take men's minds.
    Such is thy all, that as I sung before,
    None Fortune aided less, and Virtue more :
    Or if Chance must to each man that doth rise
    Needs lend an aid, to thine she had her eyes."[1]

Milton also thus speaks of him, in a sonnet addressed to his grandson, Cyriac Skinner : —

" Cyriac, whose grandsire on the royal bench
        Of British Themis, with no mean applause,
        Pronounc'd and in his volumes taught our laws,
    Which others at their bar so often wrench." [2]

Coke, at the time of his dismissal, was commanded to expunge and retract " such novelties and errors and offensive conceits as were dispersed in his ' Reports.' " But he showed that there were no more errors in his 500 cases than in a few cases of Plowden ; and delivered in a paper explaining other points. This frivolous inquiry, however, soon ceased ; and though he was not replaced in his judicial seat, he was re-

---

[1] B. Jonson's Works (Gifford), viii. 430.   [2] Milton's Works (1762), ii. 218.

ceived into a certain degree of favour. Bacon also, who had become lord keeper, was sharply rebuked by the king on Coke's account, and was nearly losing the friendship of Buckingham for opposing the marriage of Coke's daughter by Lady Hatton with the earl's brother, Sir John Villiers, afterwards Lord Purbeck. This marriage Coke had evidently negotiated for the purpose of securing the interest of Buckingham, and thus furthering his return to court. In this he was partially successful, being restored to the council table in September, 1617, and appointed, on July 21, 1618, one of the commissioners for executing the office of lord high treasurer.[1] During three years he was employed in various commissions, and his assistance was required in the Star Chamber in all cases of difficulty; but he received no substantial proof of the renewal of the royal confidence; and when the office of lord high treasurer, to which he had aspired, was given or sold to Sir Henry Montagu in December, 1620, and Sir James Ley, in the following month, was appointed lord chief justice of the King's Bench, he saw at once that he must give up all expectation of future preferment.

He had not been in parliament since 1593, the office of attorney-general disqualifying him from sitting in the House of Commons in 1597, 1601, and 1604; and during the short parliament of 1614 he was chief justice. But when James summoned that of 1621, Coke, dismissed from his judicial seat, was again eligible, and was accordingly returned for the borough of Liskeard in Cornwall. His parliamentary career may be truly said to have then commenced, his mouth being no longer stopped by the silence imposed upon him by his former office of speaker. He at once distinguished himself by taking a prominent part against monopolies, patents, and other grievances; and was one of the principal movers against Sir Giles Mompesson. In the impeachment of his

[1] Pell Records, 211.

old enemy, Bacon, he did not, though one of the managers, actively interfere, nor in the other trials which then took place; but on the adjournment in June, he is said to have stood up " with tears in his eyes," and to have " recited the collect for the king and his issue, adding only to it, ' and defend them from their cruel enemies.' " When the house met again in November, it immediately proceeded on the Spanish match and the supply for the palatinate, and Coke was made chairman of a committee to consider these and other subjects. A remonstrance and petition to the king being resolved on, Coke spoke strongly in their support. He made a bold stand also for the privileges of the house; and the protestation, which was then carried, so offended the king, that with his own hand he tore it out of the journals. The parliament was again adjourned on December 18 ; and on January 6, 1621–2, was dissolved by a proclamation enlarging on the " cunning diversions" of " some ill-tempered spirits who sowed tares among the corn." In the interim between the adjournment and the dissolution, several of these " ill-tempered spirits" were visited with the vengeance of the court. Coke had made himself a special mark for the royal indignation. The council debated on the means of excluding him from the general pardon at the end of the year; he was sent to the Tower on December 27 ; his papers were seized; and prosecutions were commenced against him on trumped-up and frivolous charges.[1] His incarceration lasted seven months, at first without intercourse with his family or friends; and even when he obtained his discharge in August, 1622, the king said " he was the fittest instrument for a tyrant that ever was in the realm of England," and ordered him to confine himself to his mansion at Stoke Pogis.

[1] " July, 1622. The great cause concerning the Lord Coke, for 50,000l. followed in the king's behalf in the Court of Wards, is adjudged for my Lord Coke by the three chief judges and Justice Dodderidge."— *Yonge's Diary*, p. 62.

From the new parliament which necessity compelled James to call in February, 1623–4, attempts were made to exclude Coke by sending him into honourable exile. He was joined in commission with Sir William Jones and others to inquire into the church establishment in Ireland, and his passport was actually granted; but the commission not being acted on, he took his seat as member for Coventry. The questions on which he seemed mostly to interest himself were the Spanish match, the means of recovering the palatinate, and the impeachment of the Earl of Middlesex, on each of which he managed the conferences with the House of Lords. The session closed on May 29, and King James died on the 27th of the following March.

In the first parliament of Charles, Coke, who was chosen by his native county, at first dissuaded the house from renewing the committee for grievances, advising a petition for the king's answer to the former application; but afterwards he opposed the grant of a supply without a redress of grievances. This demand, and an evident preparation to bring charges against the Duke of Buckingham, led to a hasty dissolution on August 12, 1625, and to an endeavour to prevent the most unruly members from sitting in the next parliament, which Charles was necessitated to call in the month of February following, by nominating them sheriffs of the counties in which they resided. Coke was made sheriff of Buckinghamshire, but was elected member for Norfolk; and, notwithstanding a message from the king, no new writ was issued, though, in consequence of the parliament being dissolved before his sheriffalty expired, he did not take his seat. Two years elapsed before the third parliament was called; when Coke was returned for two counties, Buckingham and Suffolk, choosing the former because he resided there. It met on March 17, 1628; and in the first session, which ended on June 26, and was the last in which he took any part in public affairs, he advocated the liberty of the subject with an energy that was surprising in a man who had attained the age of seventy-eight. He suggested, and succeeded in carrying, the famous Petition of Right; in the conferences with the Lords being one of the principal managers, and overcoming, by his arguments and perseverance, all the objections and impediments raised against it. In the violent proceedings of the second session of this parliament he took no part: but retiring to his seat at Stoke Pogis, he occupied the five remaining years of his life in publishing that celebrated work on which his fame is permanently established, " The First Institute, or Commentary on Littleton," and in preparing for the press the three other volumes of the Institutes, treating respectively on Magna Charta, on Criminal Law, and on the Jurisdiction of the Courts. These, with his Will and fifty-one other manuscripts, were seized while he was on his death-bed, by an unaccountable order of the privy council, under the pretence of searching for seditious papers; and were not published till seven years afterwards, when, by a vote of parliament, they were delivered up to his son. Four years before his decease, one Nicholas Jeoffes was indicted and fined in the King's Bench for writing a petition wherein he said that Lord Chief Justice Coke was a traitor.[1]

He died on September 3, 1633, being then nearly eighty-two years of age, and was buried in the church of Tittleshall, in Norfolk, in which a marble monument, bearing his effigy at full length, is erected to his memory.

Besides the four books of Institutes, he published eleven volumes of Reports, to which two other volumes were added many years after his death, but not finished or prepared by him for publication. The first part came out in 1600, when he was in the height of his professional fame, and attorney-general to Queen Elizabeth. The others followed in quick

[1] State Trials, iii. 1375.

succession till the eleventh, published in 1615, about a year before he was deprived of his office of chief justice of the King's Bench by James; an example of perseverance and indefatigable industry, which no one occupied as he was with judicial and political duties, and harassed by domestic broils, could have exhibited, had not a cold-blooded temperament made him indifferent to the one, and a habit of early rising enabled him to overcome the other. They are distinguished in Westminster Hall by the name of " The Reports," and his jealous enemy, Bacon, is obliged to say of them, " Had it not been for Sir Edward Coke's reports . . . the law by this time had been almost like a ship without ballast, for that the cases of modern experience are fled from those that are adjudged and ruled in former time." For some law tracts, also, of minor importance, but of great learning, the profession was indebted to him. They were not published till after his death, and are now from the alterations in practice become obsolete.

The early portion of Coke's life was not distinguished from that of any other advocate, except by his deeper studies and a more extensive and successful practice. The reputation he attained for legal knowledge pointed him out without a rival for the office of solicitor-general, which he filled at the age of forty. In less than two years he succeeded as attorney-general, and during the twelve years that he held that office he raised it to an importance it had never before acquired, and which it has ever since preserved. The coarseness and brutality of his language, both at the bar and on the bench, will ever leave a stigma on his memory; but it may be observed, that no such ebullitions occurred till his rivalry with Bacon began, whose underhand endeavours to supplant and annoy him evidently tended to exacerbate his temper, which was not naturally good; and some of his violent and indecent exhibitions — towards Essex, for instance, who was supposed to be Bacon's friend,—may, perhaps, be traced to that influence. His pride and arrogance, however, cannot be doubted, and to them it may be attributed, together with the coldness of his nature and his retired habits, that his biographers record no friendly intimacies, and that fewer sayings of his are repeated than of any person who held so prominent a position in public life. In his station as a judge, which he occupied for ten years, he shone with the brightest lustre; and, making some allowance for his equivocal conduct with regard to Overbury's murderers, he deserves great praise for his resistance of royal interference, and for upholding the independence of the bench; though sometimes, perhaps, he exaggerated his opposition for the purpose of thwarting Bacon, whom he knew to be the encourager, if not the instigator, of the king's arbitrary views. Judge Whitelocke gives testimony of his freedom from the prevailing vice of the time. " Never was man," he says, " so just, so upright, so free from corrupt solicitations of great men and friends, as he was. Never put counsellors that practised before him to annual pensions of money or plate to have his favour. In all causes before him the counsel might assure his client from the danger of bribery."[1] By his subsequent career in parliament, and his energetic advocacy of liberal measures, he would have gained the admiration and applause of the world, was it not for the opinion, by some entertained, that his opposition to the court savoured too much of personal discontent and disappointed ambition. This mixed feeling has prevented him from being a popular character, and has led men to doubt his judgment, and to deny his authority in matters unconnected with his profession; so that many who allow his merit as a great lawyer and an incorrupt judge, refuse to acknowledge his claims as a disinterested patriot, or as an estimable man.

---

[1] Whitelocke's " Liber Famelicus;" a MS. Diary quoted in Bacon's Works by Montagu (vol. xvi. p. cccxvi. note), who omits to state where it is.

Against his private character even his enemies could bring no charge; but the contentions with his second wife, which did not terminate till his death, do not speak well for the temper of either. If his division of the hours of the day, " Quatuor orabis," was the rule of his life, he must be allowed to have been a pious man. Of his friendship to the church he gave many proofs in his settlement of ecclesiastical property, and in his careful selection in the distribution of the patronage attached to his estates. With regard to the first, he threatened a nobleman, who was applying for some lands belonging to the see of Norwich, to put on his cap and gown again and plead in support of its rights; and as to the last he was wont to say, that " he would have church livings pass by livery and seisin, not by bargain and sale." He was liberal in his entertainments, but moderate in his household; and when a great man came to dinner without previously informing him, his common saying was, " Sir, since you have sent me no notice of your coming, you must dine with me; but if I had known it in due time, I would have dined with you." His eagerness for territorial acquisition was so great, that, though inheriting little more than two manors from his father, he possessed at his death upwards of sixty manors in Norfolk and Suffolk alone, besides others in no less than eight different counties. When he was in treaty for the noble domain of Castle-Acre Priory, in Norfolk, King James is said to have told him that he had already as much land as it was proper for a subject to possess. " Then, please your Majesty," replied Coke, " I will only add one *acre* more to the estate." Holkham, the present seat of the family, is said to have been added to the property, by Sir Edward artfully inserting in the marriage settlement of his fourth son, John, with the daughter and heir of Anthony Wheatly, its former possessor, a limitation, in default of heirs male of the marriage, to his own right heirs, to the exclusion of the heirs female; and that it was not discovered till 1671, when John's only surviving son having died childless, the estate, instead of devolving on Johu's seven daughters, fell to Robert, the heir of Henry, Sir Edward's fifth son.

Sir Edward, by his first wife, Bridget Paston, had seven sons and three daughters. The succession to the family estates fell finally on Robert, the grandson of Henry, his fifth son. Robert's grandson, Thomas, was created Baron Lovel in 1728, and Viscount Coke and Earl of Leicester in 1744; but the earl leaving no surviving issue, the titles became extinct in 1759. The estates then devolving on Wenman Roberts, Esq., the son of the earl's sister, Anne, that gentleman assumed the name of Coke, and his son, Thomas William Coke, for many years the representative of Norfolk in parliament, was at last, in 1837, created Viscount Coke and Earl of Leicester; titles which are now borne by his eldest son.

Clement, the sixth son of the chief justice, was the father of Edward Coke of Longford, who obtained a baronetcy in 1641, which became extinct on the death of the third possessor in 1727.

The marriage of Sir Edward Coke's daughter by Lady Hatton proved unfortunate, the lady disgracing herself, and leaving no legitimate issue.

COVENTRY, THOMAS.

JUST. C. P. 1606.

WITH JOHN COVENTRY, lord mayor of London in the reign of Henry VI., and one of the executors of the renowned Richard Whittington, began the prosperity of this family, which derived its surname from the city of Coventry, where it was originally established. One of his descendants, Richard Coventry, was settled at Cassington in Oxfordshire, and by his wife, a daughter of —— Turner, had two sons, the younger of whom was Thomas the future judge. He was born in 1547, and received his education in the university of Oxford, where he took the degree of M.A. on June 2, 1565, and afterwards was elected fellow of Balliol College.[1] He then pursued the study of the law in the Inner Temple, of which society he became reader in autumn, 1593; but, in consequence of the Plague, his reading was deferred to the following Lent, when he gave way to John Heale, newly appointed a serjeant, and at last performed the duty in the autumn of 1594. His name first occurs as an advocate in Coke's Reports in Michaelmas, 1589, and thence frequently till the end of Elizabeth's reign. He was one of those named on Sir Edward Coke's preferment to succeed him in the solicitor's place; and Bacon tells Sir Robert Cecil, though with a profession of disbelief, that it was asserted that Coventry has bought his interest for 2000 angels.[2] Neither of them obtained the promotion; and it was not till two months before the queen's death that Coventry received a writ to take upon him the degree of the coif in the following Easter. Before that time James had ascended the throne, rendering a new writ necessary, which had the same return. On January 13, 1606, he was appointed one of King James's serjeants, that he might with greater honour be elevated to the bench, to which he was immediately called as a judge of the Common Pleas. The register of the Inner Temple enlarges on the error in the order of his procession to Westminster on the occasion, in which he was made to go "formost," instead of "last of all"—an error which, we are solemnly told, was reformed on the next day, when Mr. Justice Tanfield was accompanied with the same ceremony. The dignity of knighthood was conferred on the new judge, who, however, enjoyed his place for less than a year. The last fine levied before

---

[1] Wood's Fasti Oxon. i. 167. [2] Bacon's Works (Montagu), xii. 157.

him was in the following Michaelmas term[1]; and dying on December 12 (1606), he was buried at Croome d'Abitot in Worcestershire. His estate, called Earles Croome, in that parish, he had acquired by his marriage with Margaret, the daughter and heir of —— Jeffreys, of that place, and it still is the chief seat of his family.

The judge left three sons — Thomas, William, and Walter. Thomas was the lord keeper who will be noticed in the next reign. His male descendants failing in 1719, the barony, which had been granted to him in 1628, became extinct; but the Earldom of Coventry, to which one of his successors had been raised in 1697, devolved, according to a special limitation in the patent, on the grandson of the judge's third son, Walter, from whom the present earl is the fifth in descent.[2]

CREWE, RANULPHE.
Ch. K. B. 1625.
See under the Reign of Charles I.

CROKE, GEORGE.
Just. C. P. 1624.
See under the Reign of Charles I.

CROKE, JOHN.
Just. K. B. 1607.

THE original name of the Croke family was Le Blount. Two brothers, Robert and William Le Blount, younger sons of the Count de Guisnes, held high military commands in the army of William of Normandy on his descent upon England. After the Conquest they were rewarded by extensive grants of lands — the former in Suffolk, the latter in Lincolnshire.

---

[1] Dugdale's Orig. 48. 97. 166.; Chron. Ser.
[2] Dugdale's Baronage, ii. 459.; Collins's Peerage, iii. 744.

The elder branch failed by the death of the sixth baron at the battle of Lewes in 1264; and of the younger branch, Sir Robert Blount, who was deeply implicated in the conspiracy to restore Richard II. to the throne after his deposition by Henry IV., was beheaded at Oxford in 1400. Nicholas, his kinsman, being engaged in the same conspiracy, was outlawed, and took service under the Duke of Milan; but four years afterwards he ventured into England, and escaped observation by changing his name to Croke. On the death of Henry IV., he came out of his retirement, and bought lands in Buckinghamshire, where he resided at a place called Easington, in the parish of Chilton. His great-grandson, John Croke, first one of the six clerks, then a master, in Chancery from the reign of Henry VIII. to that of Mary [1], besides purchasing Studley Priory in Oxfordshire, increased his possessions at Chilton, and built a mansion-house there, which became the principal seat of the family. He died in 1554, and by his wife, Prudentia Cave, left a son, who succeeded to his ample inheritance. His name was also John, and he was knighted by Queen Elizabeth when he was sheriff of Buckinghamshire; which county he also represented in Parliament. Marrying Elizabeth, daughter of Sir Alexander Unton, of Chequers, in that county, he had by her a numerous family, the eldest of whom, John, he lived to see on the judicial bench, and the third, George, advancing rapidly towards it. The fifth son, William, is the only one whose male representatives have continued to the present time. One of them, Sir Alexander Croke, judge of the Vice-Admiralty Court in America, has commemorated his family in an elaborate "Genealogical History," of which full advantage has been taken in the present sketch, and also in the memoir of Sir George in the following reign.

---

[1] See his report upon the Ordinances in Chancery, vol. v. p. 341.

John Croke, the eldest son, was born in 1553, and received his legal education at the Inner Temple, where he became a student on April 13, 1570, and having been in due course called to the bar, was admitted a bencher on January 30, 1591. He was appointed Lent reader in 1596, and treasurer in 1598. At a very early period he had acquired so great a reputation for his professional attainments that he was consulted by Sir Christopher Hatton, who gave him as his fee " for his counsell in lawe, a silver gilt hole and cover." It does not appear whether this was before or after Hatton became chancellor in 1587. In 1592 Lord Chief Justice Popham recommended him to be placed in the commission of the peace for Buckinghamshire. Three years after he was elected recorder of London ; and his biographer gives a copy of one of his speeches on presenting the lord mayor to the Court of Exchequer, which, in its elaboration, puts to shame the curtailed addresses of the present day. The same city chose him for their representative in the parliaments of 1597 and 1601 ; he having before, in 1585, been returned for the borough of Windsor.

Of the parliament that met in October, 1601, he was unanimously chosen speaker; and in his speech on presentation, he offered up his solemn prayers to heaven to continue the prosperous estate and peace of the kingdom, which, he said, had been defended by the mighty arm of our dread and sacred queen. Elizabeth, interrupting him, cried out, " No; but by the mighty hand of God, Mr. Speaker." The Court of Aldermen ordered the chamberlain to present him as speaker, with forty marks as their free gift.[1] Early in the session Serjeant Heale, on the question of a subsidy, marvelled much that the house should stand upon granting it, or the time of payment, when all we had, he said, was her majesty's, and she may law-

_____

[1] City List of Recorders.

fully at her pleasure take it; "yea," added he, "she hath as much right to all our lands and goods as to any revenue of the crown." At which all the house laughing and hemming, the speaker was obliged to call them to order, saying that "he that is speaking should be suffered to deliver his mind without interruption." The grievance of monopolies occasioned great debates in this parliament, and the queen having politically anticipated the decision of the Commons, the speaker had the gratification of announcing to the house her resolution to revoke the patents that existed, and not to grant any other. On the division upon the bill for enforcing attendance at church, the ayes being 105, and the noes 106, it was contended that the speaker had a vote which would make the votes even; but Croke said, "He was foreclosed of his voice by taking that place which it had pleased them to impose upon him, and that he was to be indifferent to both parties." At the close of the session on December 19, the lord keeper concluded his speech by saying, "For yourself, Mr. Speaker, her majesty commanded me to say that you have proceeded with such wisdom and discretion that it is much to your commendations; and that none before you have deserved more."[1]

About a year after this Croke received a summons to take upon him the degree of the coif on a day which occurred after the queen's death. The writ in consequence abated; but a new one was issued returnable the same day, the second return of Easter term, 1603 ; previous to which he was knighted by King James, an honour which it was decided by the judges did not give him precedence over his seniors. He was made one of the king's serjeants on May 29, and judge of the counties of Brecknock, Radnor, and Glamorgan; whereupon he resigned the recordership.

On the 25th of June, 1607, he was created a judge of the

---

[1] Parl. Hist. i. 907–956.

King's Bench, and fully sustained the character he had acquired as an advocate. In 1616 he became in some degree implicated in the controversy between Lord Chancellor Egerton and Chief Justice Coke as to the jurisdiction of the Court of Chancery, by introducing into his charge to the grand jury at Westminster the article under the statute of 27 Edw. III. c. 1, " if any man, after a judgment given, had drawn the said judgment to a new examination in any other court." He might, however, very innocently do this, knowing that some indictments under that statute were about to be presented; and, as Bacon says, " it was not solemnly dwelt on," and still more as the bills were ignored, he escaped any public censure, and the prime mover, Coke, only suffered.[1]

After performing his judicial duties for nearly thirteen years he died at his house in Holborn, on Jannary 23, 1620, aged sixty-six. His body was removed to Chilton, and buried there with his ancestors.

His wife was Catherine, daughter of Sir Michael Blount, of Maple Durham in Oxfordshire, lieutenant of the Tower, by whom he had five sons : —

1. John, who was knighted, and was succeeded at Chilton by his son John, said to have been created a baronet, who, rendering himself infamous by conspiring against the life of one Hawkins a clergyman, falsely accusing him of felony, sold the family estate. His son, Sir Dodsworth Croke, died in poverty in 1728, without issue.

2. Sir Henry Croke, clerk of the pipe, whose male descendants failed by the death of all his grandsons before their father.

3. Dr. Charles Croke, professor of rhetoric in Gresham College, and fellow of Eton College, was obliged for his zeal in the cause of Charles I. to retire to Ireland, where he died.

[2] Bacon's Works (Montagu), xii. 38.

4. Unton Croke was a serjeant at law during the Commonwealth; and his sons, Richard, also a serjeant at law, favoured by Cromwell, and Untou Croke, who held a command in the protector's army, outlived the rebellion, but left no traceable descendants.

5. The fifth son, Edward, died young, without issue.[1]

DANIEL, WILLIAM.

JUST. C. P. 1604.

PHILLIPS, in his " Grandeur of the Law " (1684), says that this judge was a younger son of the ancient family of Daniels of Over-Tabley in Cheshire. The name was originally D'Anyers, and is to be found in the list of those who entered England with the Conqueror. Little is known of William Daniel, except that he was entered at Gray's Inn in 1556, and became reader there in autumn, 1579, when his reading was on " Jointures, 2 Henry VII., c. 20." He held the office of treasurer in 1580 and 1587.[2]

In 1584 he was admitted deputy-recorder of London to Serjeant Fleetwoode[3]; and his name appears in Coke's Reports in Hilary, 1591. When about to be advanced to the degree of serjeant at law in 1594, his name was struck out of the list upon an information to his prejudice relative to one Hacket, but was restored at the request of Lord Burleigh, who contradicted the report, and testified to his being " a vearie honest, learned, and discreat man." The same nobleman recommended him as a baron of the Exchequer in 1598[4], but another was chosen. In the beginning of the year 1603–4 he was the first of four serjeants named in Chief Justice Popham's letter to Lord Ellesmere, out of

---

[1] Alex. Croke's Genealogical Hist. of the Croke Family.
[2] Dugdale's Orig. 294. 298.; Pearce's Inns of Court, 67.
[3] City List of Recorders.   [4] Peck's Desid. Cur. B.v. 3. 24.

whom King James was to select the two new judges he had
determined to add to the judicial staff[1]; and he was accordingly constituted a judge of the Common Pleas on
February 3, 1604. There is no record of his argument in
the great case of the Post-nati, but he joined the majority in
the affirmative view of the question.[2]

The last fine levied before him was on the morrow of the
Ascension, 1610, in which year he died.[3]

DENHAM, JOHN.
B. E. 1617.
See under the Reign of Charles I.

DODERIDGE, JOHN.
Just. K. B. 1612.
See under the Reign of Charles I.

EGERTON, THOMAS, BARON ELLESMERE, VISCOUNT BRACKLEY.
M. R. 1603.   LORD KEEPER, 1603.   LORD CHANC. 1603.
See under the Reign of Elizabeth.

THE surname of Egerton was assumed from a manor so
called, as early as the reign of Edward I., by the second son
of David, Baron of Malpas, whose ancestors possessed that
and many other lordships in Cheshire when Doomsday Book
was compiled. In lineal descent came Sir Ralph Egerton,
standard-bearer of England under Henry VIII., whose son,
Sir Richard Egerton of Ridley in the same county, besides
leaving issue by his wife Mary, the daughter of Richard
Grosvenor, Esq., of Eaton, was the father of Thomas Egerton,
the future lord chancellor, by a young woman named Alice
Sparke.

---

[1] Egerton Papers, 388.   [2] State Trials, ii. 576.
[3] Dugdale's Orig. 48. ; Woolrych's List.

He was born in the year 1540, and about 1556 was admitted a commoner at Brazennose College, Oxford, where he remained for three years. At the close of his classical education he commenced the study of the law at Lincoln's Inn on October 31, 1560, by which society he was called to the bar on February 2, 1572. Raised to its bench as a governor in 1580, he was named as Lent reader in 1582, and appointed treasurer in 1587.[1]

His principal practice as a barrister being in the Court of Chancery accounts for the absence of his name from all the Reports during his early career. It was not till 1583 that he is mentioned in Saville's Reports, being two years after he was raised to the office of solicitor-general; his elevation to which took place on June 28, 1581, when Sir John Popham was made attorney-general. As the practitioners in Chancery did not, as now, confine themselves to that court, but occasionally attended the trials at common law,—indeed, so late as the reign of George III. many of them went the circuit, — it is possible that the following story told of Egerton may be true, although it is also related of Attorney-General Noy, and others. Three graziers deposited with a woman in Smithfield a sum of money, which she was not to give up till all the three came together to demand it. One of them afterwards applied to her in an apparent hurry, and pretending to be authorised by his partners induced her to give him the money, with which he immediately absconded. The other two, on hearing this, proceeded against her for the amount; and on the trial of the action her counsel was about to give up the cause, when Egerton, at his request, obtained permission to speak as *amicus curiæ*. He then pointed out to the court that the two plaintiffs had no legal claim against the woman; that she had promised to deliver back the money

---

[1] Black Book, iv. 367.; v. 149.; Dugdale's Orig. 253. 261.

to all three; and that, until they all three came and demanded it of her, she was entitled to retain it. The poor woman was accordingly saved from a verdict, and the young barrister's character for shrewdness was established. It would be scarcely fair to test these traditionary stories by the practice of the present time; but, making allowance for unprofessional embellishment, it is not at all improbable that some such incident occurred. Another anecdote of less likelihood is related, that his appointment as solicitor-general arose from the admiration of Queen Elizabeth on hearing him argue in a cause against the crown, when she is said to have exclaimed, " In my troth, he shall never plead against me again." [1]

During the intervals of his laborious avocations his chief relaxation was in the sports of the field. Lord Paget, in May, 1583, gave him a license to " hunt and kill " in any of his parks in Staffordshire, with a supply of " somer and winter deare " at his pleasure. In August of the same year Henry Earl of Derby appointed him master of the game in the park of Bidstone, in Cheshire, with the fee of a buck of season in summer, and a doe in winter, together with a nominal annuity of five marks. And in December, 1591, Lord Paget's license was renewed by the then possessor, with the allowance of a buck and a doe. No doubt all these parties were clients of the solicitor-general, with whom the Earl of Derby appears to have kept up a correspondence [2], which was continued at his death by his brother Ferdinand, the next earl, who, in 1593, nominated Egerton's son Thomas steward of several of his manors. [3] The two families were

---

[1] Life of Egerton, 8. There is no authority for Lord Campbell's assertion that the Queen, before he became Solicitor-General, " made him one of her counsel ;" nor any appearance in history that such an office then existed " whereby he was entitled to wear a silk gown and have precedence."

[2] Egerton Papers, 95, 96. 131. 157.　　　　　[3] Life, 175.

afterwards more closely united by Ferdinand's widow becoming the chancellor's third wife.

Egerton held the office of solicitor-general for the space of eleven years, till Popham's elevation to the chief justiceship, when he became attorney-general on June 2, 1592, and so remained for nearly two years. During this long period of office he was of course engaged in all the prosecutions for high treason and offences against the state. His name appears in those against Campion and others in 1581; against Abingdon and others in 1586; against Secretary Davison in 1587; against Philip Earl of Arundel, and against Sir Richard Knightly in 1589; and against Sir John Perrot in 1592.[1] If these criminal proceedings were to be judged according to the present enlightened views with regard to the administration of the law, not one of the persons engaged in them would escape condemnation. But this would be palpably unjust. With whatever abhorrence the iniquitous principles on which these trials were conducted may be now regarded, the only fair inquiry which can be raised with respect to the advocates employed in them, is whether they exceeded their duty according to the practice which then prevailed. Looking through the Reports from this point of view, Egerton must receive a full acquittal from all imputation of harshness towards the prisoners. Indeed, if a judgment may be formed from an observation made by John Udall, in the account of his examination about the publication of an alleged libel against the queen, the solicitor-general seems to have had the reputation of being an enemy to persecution. Chief Justice Anderson having called upon him to explain the law, Mr. Udall proceeds thus: " Then Mr. Solicitor (who had sitten all the while very soberly), noting what passed (and if a man's mind may be known by his

---

[1] State Trials, i. 1051. 1145. 1231. 1250. 1269. 1322.

countenance, *seeming to mislike the course holden against me*), upon my Lord Anderson's commandment stood up, and putting off his hat unto me, said," &c.[1]

While he was attorney-general the office of Chamberlain of Chester became vacant, and was conferred upon him between December 22, 1593,—the date of a letter from Lord Burleigh to him on the subject—and February, 1594, when Lord Burleigh inserts in his Diary, "Mr. Egerton, his majesty's attorney, allowed to make his deputy at Chester."[2] It must have been after this date that he was knighted, for in the above letter he is styled "Esquire," and in the entry he is called "Mr." But he received this honour very soon afterwards, as it is attached to his name when he was promoted to the mastership of the Rolls on the 10th of April following. This office had been vacant since February 4, 1593, the date of Sir Gilbert Gerard's death, and no explanation is given for its not having been previously filled up. It is not unlikely to have arisen from Egerton's wish that Sir Francis Bacon should succeed as solicitor-general on the advance of Sir Edward Coke to the post of attorney, and, therefore, that he deferred his own resignation while the negociation held out any promise of success. A letter from Sir Robert Cecil to Egerton, dated March 27, 1594, thanks him for the interest he took in Bacon's promotion by arming him "with your observations for the exercise of the solicitorship."[3] That office was, however, kept open for one year and seven months, and then Bacon's hopes were disappointed by the nomination of Sir Thomas Fleming.

So active and efficient did Egerton prove himself in the office of master of the Rolls, that the queen at once constituted him lord keeper on the death of Sir John Puckering, delivering the Great Seal to him on May 6, 1596.[4] It is univer-

[1] State Trials, i. 1275.
[2] Egerton Papers, 192. 213.
[3] Egerton's Life, 165.
[4] Rot. Claus. 38 Eliz. p. 14.

sally acknowledged that his appointment arose entirely from the high reputation he had attained for his legal knowledge and integrity, and not only without the intervention of any courtly interest, but even, it is said, in opposition to the wishes and endeavours of Lord Burleigh, and his son Sir Robert Cecil. Fuller says, that " all Christendom afforded not a person which carried more gravity in his countenance and behaviour . . . . so much that many have gone to the Chancery on purpose truly to see his venerable garb (happy they who had no other business), and were highly pleased with so acceptable a spectacle ;" adding, that " his outward case was nothing in comparison with his inward abilities, quick wit, solid judgment, ready utterance."[1] He still retained the place of master of the Rolls, and executed during the rest of the reign the whole business of the Court of Chancery in his double capacity. The intrigues of the lawyers, who aspired to the second place, were counteracted by his influence with the queen, and her conviction that he needed no assistance. On Serjeant Heale being recommended to her towards the end of the reign, she applied to the lord keeper for his character; and among the Egerton Papers is the draft of a letter in answer, in which he describes the serjeant as " a grypinge and excessive usurer," " a gredye and insatiable taker of excessive fees," " a notorious and common ambodexter, takyng fee on both sides," and " a great drunkarde ;" to prove which he has preserved minutes of evidence. The serjeant, it seems, had grown enormously rich, and Egerton himself had borrowed 400*l.* from him. This, however, failed to influence the lord keeper's report, and the serjeant called in the debt.[2]

---

[1] Fuller's Worthies (1811), i. 186.

[2] Egerton MSS. before acknowledged, and not included in Mr. Collier's valuable selection published by the Camden Society ; in which are other interesting particulars about this redoubted serjeant. See pp. 315. 391. 399.

In the foolish *émeute* raised by the Earl of Essex in February, 1600, so fatal to himself, the grave lord keeper was placed in a position of some danger. In all the previous imprudences of this generous but headstrong nobleman, Egerton had shown himself a sincere and considerate friend, checking his indignation by salutary counsel when the queen had boxed his ears; procuring his reconciliation at court; acting the part of a polite and liberal host, rather than that of a strict gaoler, when he was committed to the lord keeper's custody at York House for his contempt in returning from Ireland without orders; and eventually mitigating the censure which was pronounced against him for this breach of discipline. Though relieved from the imprisonment to which he was subjected, and in some measure restored to the queen's good graces, his discontent again broke out, and a project was formed by him to seize her person, and revenge himself against those to whose enmity he attributed his various disgraces. To this end he collected at Essex House a band of men of very equivocal character, and was joined there by the Earls of Rutland and Southampton, and by other persons of the better sort. On the queen's being informed of this, she sent the lord keeper, accompanied by the lord chief justice and other lords of the council, to the earl's house, " to understand the cause of this their assembly, and to let them know that if they had any particular cause of grief against any persons whatever, it should be heard, and they should have justice." On being admitted they found the court-yard crowded with armed men, who, after the lord keeper had delivered the queen's message, cried out, " Kill them!"— " Cast the Great Seal out of the window!" &c. The earl, under pretence of conferring privately with them, took the lords into his back chamber, and, telling them that he was going to the lord mayor and sheriffs of London, and would be back in half an hour, left them under lock and key, "guarded by Sir John Davis and others with musket-shot." There they were detained from ten o'clock in the morning till four in the afternoon, when Sir Ferdinando Gorges, who had joined Essex in his progress through the city, and found that he received no encouragement, hastened back and released them. Considering how much the earl was indebted to Egerton, it is to be hoped that his allegation that he locked up the counsellors for their security against his irritated partisans was founded in truth; but the Earl of Rutland in his examination acknowledged that it was purposed to take the lord keeper with them to the court, which they intended to surprise.[1]

During Queen Elizabeth's life Egerton enjoyed her utmost confidence and favour. She employed him in various treaties with the Dutch and the Danes, in the management of which he showed himself a good diplomatist; and she entrusted him with great powers under several special Commissions, which he exercised with mildness and moderation. Within eight months of her death she paid him the honourable but burdensome compliment of a three days' visit to his mansion at Harefield, in Middlesex, recently purchased of Chief Justice Anderson; the enormous expense attending which may well account for her majesty's subjects dreading such visitations.[2]

He was present during the last hours of Elizabeth's life, when she intimated her wishes as to her successor; and no sooner did King James hear of his peaceful accession to the throne, than he issued a mandate from Holyrood House, dated April 5, 1603, appointing Egerton keeper of the Seal during his pleasure. The letter which he wrote seven days afterwards to Sir Thomas Chaloner, and which he knew would

---

[1] See the Lord Keeper's Declaration, State Trials, i. 1340.; and the Examinations of the other parties, 1344–1347

[2] Egerton Papers, 340–347.

be shown to the king, deserves to be recorded as an evidence of his honourable and ingenuous character. He says: —

" Yf I have bene taxed of hautenes, insolencye, or pryde, in my place (as I partely hear relation), I hope it is by theym that have not learned to speake well; and against this poyson I have two precious antidotes:—1. The religious wissdome, royall justice, and princelye vertues of the king my sove-raigne, which wyll soon disperse such foggye mystes. 2. The innocencye and cleernes of myne owne conscience, which is more than *mille testes.* I must confesse that, in the place of justice which I have helde, I was never so servile as to regarde parasites, calumniators, and sycophantes, but always contemned them, and therfore have often fealte the malice of theyr thoughtes and the venym of their touges. I have learned no waye but the kingis hyghe waye; and travelling in that, the better to guyde me I have fastened myne eyes on this marke, *Judicem nec de obtinendo jure orari oportet, nec de injuria exorari.* Yf this have offended any, I will never excuse yt, for I take [it] to be incident to the place by severe examynyng of manie mens actions to offende many, and so to be hateful to many, but those alwayes of the worst sorte, agaynst whom I wyll say no more, but with Ecclesiasticus, *Beatus qui tectus est a lingua nequam.*"[1]

Egerton met King James on his arrival at Broxborne in Hertfordshire, on May 3, when, in the house of Sir Henry Cook, the cofferer, his appointment was confirmed. He was also continued in the office of master of the Rolls till the 19th of the same month, Edward Bruce Lord Kinloss being then named as his successor. Previous to the coronation a new seal was engraven with the king's own image, arms, and titles, which he delivered to the lord keeper on July 19, at the same time creating him Baron of Ellesmere in Shrop-

---

[1] Egerton Papers, 359.

shire; and on the 24th he was constituted lord chancellor.[1] He held this high position for nearly fourteen years under King James, which, in addition to the seven years under Elizabeth, makes his term of service as the head of the law extend to the long period of twenty-one years. Few have filled so prominent a station with so much honour and so few enemies. Looking at the character of the two monarchs whom he served, he must have been endowed with more than ordinary wisdom, prudence, and learning, to suffer no alienation from the caprices of either, and to preserve such continued ascendancy in their councils, without degrading himself by that abject and humiliating flattery to which they were both too much accustomed.

His merits were not only recognised by his sovereigns, but they were acknowledged by the University in which he was educated. On the death of Archbishop Bancroft, he was elected chancellor of Oxford on November 3, 1610, and his presidency lasted till within two months of his death, when he resigned it on Jannary 24, 1617.

The best mode of judging of the character of an individual is to see the reputation which he held among his contemporaries of various grades. That of Egerton will stand the ordeal. Camden records an anagram on his name, " GESTAT HONOREM," which would not have been discovered if it had not been applicable; and he himself repeats the eulogy. Ben Jonson wrote three epigrams in his praise, one of them the last time he sat as chancellor.[2] Bishop Hacket, who might have seen him in his youth, and must have known the estimation with which his memory was regarded, describes him as one " qui nihil in vitâ nisi laudandum, aut fecit, aux dixit, aut sensit." Among the writers of the next generation, Fuller gives the testimony already recorded,

---

[1] Rot. Claus. 1 Jas. p. 12.
[2] Ben Jonson's Works by Gifford, viii. 191. 396.

adding that Camden, had he published a second edition of
his work, would have afforded him a full-faced commendation when this lord had turned his expectation into performance; and Anthony Wood says, " his memory was much
celebrated by epigrams while he was living, and after his
death all of the long robe lamented his loss."

One of the most eminent of these — Sir John Davies, the
poet, statesman, and lawyer, who, after filling the post of
attorney-general in Ireland, was designated, at the hour of
his death in 1626, for the office of Lord Chief Justice of
England — after summing up the characteristics of a good
chancellor in the following sentences, gracefully applies them
to Lord Ellesmere : —

" If, then, the greatest honours do of right belong to the
greatest vertues (for what is honour but *a reflexion and reward of vertue ?*), how vertuous a person must he be,—with
what gifts and graces, with what abilities and ornaments,
both of art and nature, must he be endowed,—who can
worthily supply that great and honourable office?

" Assuredly, besides the naturall faculties and powers of his
mind, which he ought to have in great perfection, and besides
the outward comeliness and dignity of his person (for *Gratior
est pulchro veniens è corpore virtus, et sapientia hominis. lucet
in vulto ejus,* saith *Solomon*), he must be furnished with all
learning that hath any relation to the publick good, divinity,
law, policy, morality, and especial eloquence, to impart and
communicate all the rest. He must withal have a long and
universal experience in all the affairs of the commonwealth;
he must be accomplished and absolute in all points of gravity,
constancy, wisedome, temperance, courage, justice, piety, integrity, and all other vertues fit for magistracy and government ; yet so as the same be seasoned and tempered with
affability, gentleness, humanity, courtesy ; howbeit without
descending or diminishing himself, but still retaining his

dignity, state, and honour. Briefly, he must be a person of such vertue and worthiness, as his life may be a *censure*, and his example a *mirrour*, for all other magistrates. These are the excellences and perfections wherewith that great officer must be qualified and adorned. And this *idea* have I conceived of him, not out of mine own imagination, or weak discourse of reason, but out of an humble observation of your lordship, in whom not only those abilities and vertues before expressed, but many other graces and ornaments, do shine so brightly, as the weakest judgement may collect out of the same a most excellent pattern of a most excellent chancellor."[1]

He is said to have been the first law chancellor since the Reformation who entertained a chaplain in his family. This was Dr. John Williams, whose merits he discovered, and whose interests he advanced, so that the chaplain subsequently filled the same office as his patron, and became also Archbishop of York. Another eminent man, Dr. Donne, afterwards Dean of St. Paul's, spent many years under Lord Ellesmere's roof, as his secretary, and there formed that secret connection with his wife Anne Moore, the niece of the chancellor's second marriage, which had so fatal an influence on his earlier fortunes.

Few of his judicial decisions are reported; but, in the case of the Post-nati, being the question whether persons born in Scotland after the accession of King James to the throne of England were aliens in the latter country, and therefore disabled from holding lands there, he delivered an elaborate judgment that they were entitled to all the rights of natural-born subjects; which by the king's command he published in 1609. Twelve out of the fourteen judges concurring in his opinion, his remarks on the doubts of the other two afford a

---

[1] Preface to Sir John Davies's " Reports of Cases adjudged in the King's Courts in Ireland," published in 1615.

curious specimen of the extraordinary manner in which Scripture allusions were introduced into the oratory of the period. He said, " The Apostle Thomas doubted of the resurrection of the Lord Jesus Christ, when all the rest of the Apostles did firmly beleeve it : but this his doubting confirmed, in the whole Church, the faith of the resurrection. The two worthy and learned judges that have doubted in this case, as they beare his name, so I doubt not but their doubting hath given occasion to cleare the doubt in others ; and so to confirme in both the kingdomes, both for the present and the future, the truth of the judgement in this case." He does not name the two dissentients, and it is uncertain which they were, as three of the judges who pronounced their opinion were named Thomas, viz. Sir Thomas Fleming, Sir Thomas Walmesley, and Sir Thomas Foster, all of the Common Pleas.[1]

In the latter part of this speech, he says in reference to the Ante-nati, " You shall find no such confluence hither ; but some few that have done long and worthy service to his Majesty, have and still do attend him, which I trust no man mislikes : for there can be none so simple or childish (if they have but common sense) as to think that his Majesty should have come hither alone amongst us, and have left behind him in Scotland, and as it were cast off, all his old and worthy servants."[2] At the same time, when he saw the king's profusion to his fellow-countrymen, he cautioned his sovereign not to remunerate them by the alienation of the Crown lands, but to preserve these for his own support, seeing that he and his successors might meet with parliaments unwilling to supply his occasions, but on such conditions as would not be very acceptable.[3]

Besides the publication of this judgment, he printed no

---

[1] State Trials, ii. 669.   Lord Campbell names the two last.
[2] State Trials, i. 695.   [3] Fuller's Worthies, i. 186.

other work during his life; but he left several valuable manuscripts; and some tracts appeared after his death with his name, on the privileges of the Court of Chancery; on the office of lord chancellor; and on Coke's Reports; the genuineness of some of which has been doubted.

He objected strongly to the Statute of Wills, passed in the reign of Henry VIII., saying that it "was not only the ruin of ancient families, but the nurse of forgeries; for by colour of making men's wills, men's lands were conveyed in the extremity of their sickness, when they had no power of disposing of them." He was wont to tell the following merry story as an illustration of its evils: — " A friar coming to visit a great man in his sickness, and finding him past memory, took opportunity, according to the custom of the times, to make provision for the monastery whereof he was; and finding that the sick man could only speak some one syllable, which was for the most part 'yea,' or 'nay,' in an imperfect voice, forthwith took upon him to make his will; and demanding of him, ' Will you give such a piece of land to our house to pray for your soul?' The dying man sounded ' Yea.' Then he asked him ' Will you give such land to the maintenance of lights to our Lady ?' The sound was again ' Yea.' Whereupon he boldly asked him many such questions. The son and heir standing by, and hearing his land going away so fast by his father's word ' yea,' thought fit to ask one question as well as the friar, which was: ' Shall I take a cudgel and beat this friar out of the chamber?' The sick man's answer was again, ' Yea ;' which the son quickly performed, and saved unto himself his father's lands."[1]

In the latter part of his judicial career, he was annoyed by Sir Edward Coke's attempt to restrain the jurisdiction of the Court of Chancery, and by the proceedings which were taken,

[1] Archæologia, xxv. 384. quoted by Mr. Bruce from Harl. MS. No. 1226.

not only against certain suitors there, but against the counsel who were engaged in the causes, and even the masters in Chancery to whom they were referred, to subject them to the penalties of præmunire, to which, under an old statute, all persons were subject who impeached the judgments of any of the king's courts. The inquiry resulted in the complete triumph of Lord Ellesmere, by the confirmation of the powers of his court; and it had no little effect in disgracing Coke, its instigator. In swearing in Sir Henry Montagu, his successor, the chancellor seems to have lost his wonted moderation, indulging in unbecoming sarcasms upon his fallen enemy. Referring to Sir Henry's grandfather, who had been also chief justice, as an example for him, he said, " You shall not find he ever said vauntingly, that he would make latitats latitare. When he did sit chief justice in this place, he contained himself within the word of the writ to be chief justice, as the king called him, *ad placita coram nobis tenenda,* but did not arrogate or aspire to the high title of capitalis justiciarius Angliæ. He desired not any new construction of laws against commissioners and judges of sewers, nor to draw them into the danger of præmunire. . . He never strained the statute 27 Edw. III. c. 1., to reach to the Chancery, and to bring that court and the ministers thereof, and the subjects that sought justice there, to be in danger of præmunire, an absurd and inapt construction of that old statute ; " and so on with other allusions to the faults which were imputed to Sir Edward Coke.[1]

On November 7, 1616, the king rewarded his long services, by advancing him in the peerage to the title of Viscount Brackley, which the wits of Westminster Hall, who objected to his interference with the judgments of the common law courts, converted into Viscount Break-law. He had several times before this, requested the king to allow him to retire

---

[1] Moore's Reports, 826.

from his arduous post, the duties of which he felt were too heavy for his increasing age and infirmities. Sickness at last compelled him to press his resignation, and the Close Roll records, that on March 3, 1617, being ill at his residence, York House, he was visited by the king himself, who then freed him from the custody of the Great Seal, according to his petition; but limited his retirement to two years. Within two weeks from this time, however, his earthly career was closed. He died on March 15; and his body being removed to Doddleston in Cheshire, was there buried.

The king, who appears to have regarded him with great affection, is said to have parted from him with tears of gratitude and respect; and to have signified his intention to raise him to an earldom. Though death prevented the chancellor from receiving this last mark of his sovereign's favour, little more than two months elapsed before his Majesty proved his sincerity by creating the heir Earl of Bridgewater in Somersetshire on May 27, 1617.

The chancellor was thrice married, but had issue by his first wife only. She was Elizabeth, daughter of Thomas Ravenscroft, Esq., of Bretton in Flintshire. His second wife was Elizabeth, sister to Sir George More, knight, of Loseley Farm, Surrey, Lieutenant of the Tower, and widow, first of Richard Polstead, Esq., of Abury, and then of Sir John Wolley, knight, of Pitford, both in the same county. His third wife, whom he married in 1600, was Alice, daughter of Sir John Spencer of Althorpe, knight, and widow of Ferdinando, fifth earl of Derby. She survived him nearly nineteen years, dying on January 26, 1636.

His eldest son by his first wife, Sir Thomas, who distinguished himself in the wars under the Earl of Essex, and whose death in Ireland was celebrated in verses, Latin, English and Greek, having died in his father's lifetime, the succession fell upon John, the second son. The Earldom of

Bridgewater, which he received as before stated, was raised in the person of his great grandson, Scroop, the fourth earl, on June 18, 1720, to a dukedom of the same place. This title was enjoyed by his two sons, John and Francis, in succession; the latter of whom acquired not only a boundless fortune, but a deathless name, as the founder of inland navigation in England. On his death without issue, in 1803, the dukedom became extinct; but the earldom devolved on John William, the grandson of Henry, bishop of Hereford, the younger brother of the first duke. He and his brother, Francis Henry (the author of a Life of his ancestor, the lord chancellor [1]), successively enjoyed it; but on the death of the latter in 1829, the earldom also expired.

The last duke bequeathed the greatest part of his immense possessions to his nephew, Earl Gower (afterwards the first Duke of Sutherland), the son of his sister, Lady Louisa, with remainder to that nobleman's second son, Lord Francis Leveson Gower, who on his father's death assumed the name of Egerton, and was raised to the peerage in 1846 by the titles of Viscount Brackley and Earl of Ellesmere, which have since devolved on his son.

ELLESMERE, LORD.   See THOMAS EGERTON.

FENNER, EDWARD.
JUST. K. B. 1603.
See under the Reign of Elizabeth.

EDWARD FENNER was the son of John Fenner, of Crawley in the county of Surrey, by Ellen his wife, the daughter of Sir William Goring of Burton. Dallaway traces the family for five generations higher, the earliest of which he calls

[1] Life by the last Earl; Collins's Peerage, iii. 170.; Manning and Bray's Surrey, i. 95 ; Wood's Athenæ Oxon. ii. 198.

John atte Fenne.[1]   He took his legal degrees in the Middle
Temple, to which society he became reader in Autumn, 1576.
In Michaelmas in the following year he was made a serjeant
at law, and so remained for thirteen years without further
advance, but enjoying a considerable share of professional
practice.   On May 26, 1590, he was constituted one of the
judges of the Court of King's Bench, in which he sat for one
and twenty years, under Elizabeth and her successor.[2]   In
the January before his appointment he, being a justice of
the peace for Surrey, sat on the bench at the assizes when
John Udall was brought up to receive sentence, and in kind
and considerate language assisted the judges in urging the
prisoner to submit himself to her Majesty.[3]   He does not
appear to have taken any prominent part in the State trials
on which he sat as a commissioner.   As one of the executors
of Lady Dacres, he was defendant in Chancery, Lord Buckhurst being the plaintiff, in the first case in Sir Edward Coke's
first Book of Reports.

He died on January 23, 1611–2, and was buried at Hayes
in Middlesex.   Rayner, in his catalogue of Blackstone's
works (p. 83), notices a curious error in the inscription on
his monument in that church, his name appearing there as
" Jenner " instead of " Fenner."   He had only one son,
Edward, who died three years after him, leaving no issue.

FLEMING, THOMAS.

Ch. B. E. 1604.   Ch. K. B. 1607.

THE family of Fleming may be presumed to have originally
come from Flanders.   It was long settled in Hampshire, and
many of its members, from the early part of the thirteenth
century, held high office in the town of Southampton.   John

---

[1] Parochial Topography of Rape of Chichester, i. 16.
[2] Dugdale's Orig. 218. ; Chron. Ser.   [3] State Trials, i. 1297.

Fleming, established at Newport in the Isle of Wight, was, by his wife Dorothy Harris, the father of Thomas the future judge, who was born there in April 1644. He does not appear to have been educated at either university, but on May 12, 1567, became a member of Lincoln's Inn; and having been called to the bar on June 24, 1574, he arrived at the bench of that society in 1587, and was elected reader in Lent 1590, and double reader in Lent 1594. In the Michaelmas Term before the last date, he had received his summons to take on him the degree of the coif, and the readership was a complimentary duty not unfrequently imposed on a member previous to his leaving· the society. Before the end of the following year he was designated as the successor of Sir Edward Coke in the office of solicitor-general, and even Bacon, who was intriguing for it, acknowledged that he was an able man for the place. In order to hold it, however, it was then deemed necessary to vacate the degree of serjeant, and accordingly he had a writ exonerating him from it on November 5, 1595, and another appointing him solicitor-general on the next day. He was then replaced as a governor of Lincoln's Inn, and so continued till he became lord chief baron.[1]

His name is first mentioned in Croke's Reports in Hilary Term, 1591. He soon had attained sufficient eminence in his profession to be brought forward as a candidate for the recordership of London; a post to which, though he then missed it, he was elected in 1594. He resigned it in 1595 on being made solicitor-general.[2] The only state trial in which he is named as acting, is that of those who participated in the Earl of Essex's plot in 1600. In 1601 and in 1604 he was returned member for Southampton; being the

[1] Dugdale's Orig. 254. 261, 262.; Chron. Series; Bacon's Works (Montagu), xvi. App. LL; Linc. Inn Black Book, v. 64. 183.
[2] Maitland's London, 1206.

last parliament of Queen Elizabeth and the first of King James. The latter sat till July 7, and again met after several adjournments in November, 1605, a period memorable for the grand discovery of the Gunpowder Plot.

During the interval Fleming had received the order of knighthood, and on the death of Sir William Peryam, the king had raised him on October 27, 1604, to the office of chief baron of the Exchequer. Such was the reputation for integrity he had acquired in the House of Commons, that on the meeting after their adjournment it was resolved, that notwithstanding his elevation to the bench, he should still continue a member.[1] When advanced on June 25, 1607, to the chief justiceship of the King's Bench he vacated his seat, and his son was elected for Southampton in his place.

One of the first duties as chief baron was to sit on the trial of the gunpowder conspirators, but he appears to have been quite a silent commissioner. Not so, however, on the great case of Impositions by royal authority, which, so important in its ultimate consequence, was tried in Michaelmas 1606. There, after expressing something like indignation, that a subject should presume to plead that an act of the king was, "indebite, injuste, et contra leges Angliæ imposita," he concluded a long argument which, though certainly most learned and ingenious, was anything but conclusive in favour of the crown. The question of the Post-nati did not arise till after he became chief justice. His argument is not preserved, but his decision was with the majority in support of the claim. The only other important case in which he is recorded to have been engaged, is that in which the refusal of the Countess of Shrewsbury to answer interrogatories relative to the marriage of Sir William Seymour with Lady Arabella Stuart, and her connivance in their subsequent escape, were considered before the Privy Council. It was

---

[1] Duthy's Hants, 383.

a preliminary inquiry as to this being an offence in law, and whether it was cognizable in the Star Chamber, and the chief justice's speech, in favour of the affirmative, is curious as containing a recital of the privileges attached to the nobility, and the consequent duties which they are therefore peculiarly called upon to perform.[1]

After presiding over the court of King's Bench for six years, he died suddenly, in the 69th year of his age, on August 7, 1613. He had retired to bed in perfect health on the previous evening after dispensing his customary hospitalities in "a rearing day" to his tenants at Stoneham Park, which he had purchased of the Earl of Southampton. He was buried in the church of that parish, under a stately monument, on which he is represented in his official costume, with an inscription that he had fifteen children, of whom eight were then living, by his wife, Dorothy, otherwise Mary, daughter of Sir Henry Cromwell of Hitchinbroke, who was the aunt of the Protector.[2]

A prejudiced account of him is given by Lord Campbell, who calls him a "poor creature: "[3] but Sir Edward Coke, who knew him somewhat better, describes him as discharging all his places "with great judgement, integrity and discretion; " adding, that " he well deserved the good will of all that knew him, because he was of a sociable and placable nature and disposition."[4]

The male branch of the family failed in the early part of the last century, when the Hampshire property, including the Stoneham estate, devolved on the descendants of the great antiquary Browne Willis, who had married a daughter of the house. These assumed the name of Fleming, and the present possessor long represented the county in parliament.

---

[1] State Trials, ii. 159. 217. 387. 609. 770. [2] Duthy's Hants, 385.
[3] Lord Campbell's Chief Justices, i. 237. [4] 10 Coke's Reports, 34.

FOSTER, THOMAS.

JUST. C. P. 1607.

THOMAS FOSTER was born about the year 1569. He belonged to the family of Foster in Northumberland, one of whom was gentleman usher to Queen Mary; and another, Sir John Foster, his second cousin, was made a knight-banneret at Musselburg for his valour in defeating the Scots.[1]

The earliest notice of Thomas's name is as a barrister in 1587, when he appears both in Coke's and Croke's Reports. He became reader of the society of the Inner Temple in autumn 1596; and was one of the persons designated by Queen Elizabeth to be serjeants two months before her death. The writ being renewed by King James, he assumed the coif in Easter Term 1603, and was afterwards counsel to Queen Anne and Prince Henry.

On the 24th of November, 1607, he was called to the bench as a judge of the Common Pleas[2]; and sat in that court for four years and a half, performing his duties in such a manner as to acquire the character of "a grave and reverend judge, and of great judgment, constancy, and integrity." He was nominated by Thomas Sutton to be one of the first governors of his hospital—the Charter House.[3]

He died on May 18, 1612, and was buried at Hunsdon in Herefordshire under a massive arched monument of variegated marble, with an effigy of the judge in his robes.[4] His town residence was in St. John Street. Robert, the youngest of his sons became chief justice of the King's Bench in the reign of Charles II.

---

[1] Gent. Mag. lxxxiv. pt. i. 341.

[2] Dugdale's Orig. 161.; Chron. Ser.   [3] 10 Coke's Reports, 235.

[4] I am indebted to the Rev. T. M. Thackeray, the Rector, for an account of it, and a copy of the inscription.

GAWDY, FRANCIS.

JUST. K. B. 1603.   CH. C. P. 1605.

See under the Reign of Elizabeth.

FRANCIS GAWDY was the half brother of his predecessor Sir Thomas Gawdy, being the third son of Serjeant Thomas Gawdy, of Harleston in Norfolk, by his third wife Elizabeth, daughter of Thomas or Oliver Shyres.   He presents an instance as well of the same name being given to two sons, as of a christian name being altered at confirmation.   At his baptism he was called Thomas, which at his confirmation was changed to Francis, and the latter name, " by the advice of all the judges in anno 36 Henry VIII. (1544), he did beare, and after used in all his purchases and grants." [1]

Like his brother he was a member of the Inner Temple, being admitted there in 1549, and six years after him, filled the same office of Lent reader, viz. in 1566.   In Lent 1571, he was appointed duplex reader, and also treasurer to the society.   No further mention is made of him till he was called to take the degree of the coif, which he assumed in Michaelmas Term, 1577.   He was made one of the Queen's serjeants on May 17, 1582 [2]; and in this character he was present at Fotheringay on the trial of Mary, Queen of Scots, but no duty appears to have devolved upon him.   On the arraignment of Secretary Davison in 1587, for forwarding the warrant for that unfortunate lady's execution, he joined in the solemn farce with as serious a face as any of the rest of the actors. [3]

His turn for promotion came in the following year.   On the death of his brother Sir Thomas Gawdy, he was nominated his successor as a judge of the Queen's Bench on November 25, 1588.   In none of the criminal trials on which

[1] Coke Litt. 3a.   [2] Dugdale's Orig. 165. 170.; Chron. Ser.
[3] State Trials, i. 1173. 1233.

he was a commissioner, either in the reign of Queen Elizabeth or of King James (by whom he was continued in his
place and knighted), is he represented as taking any part
except in that of Sir Walter Raleigh, when he is made to
say, "The Statute you speak of concerning two witnesses in
case of Treason, *is found to be inconvenient,* therefore by another law it was taken away."[1]　　He was named as one of
the commissioners to hear causes in Chancery on the death
of Sir Christopher Hatton in 1591.

It seems not improbable that he owed his elevation to the
bench to Elizabeth's favoured chancellor, whose nephew, Sir
William Newport, alias Hatton, about six months after it
took place, married the judge's only daughter Elizabeth.
The ceremony was performed in June, 1589, at Holdenby, the
mansion of Sir Christopher, who is stated to have "danced
the measures at the solemnity, and left the gown in the chair,
saying, 'Lie thou there, chancellor.'"　　The judge perhaps
was also indebted for his next promotion to the marriage of
his granddaughter Frances, the only issue of the above union,
to Robert Rich, second Earl of Warwick.　These nuptials
took place in February, 1605[2]: and on the 26th of the following August, Sir Francis was raised to the post of chief
justice of the Common Pleas, in the room of Sir Thomas
Anderson, deceased.　He enjoyed this high position, for which
he is said to have paid at a dear rate, less than a year.　He
was stricken with apoplexy at his chambers in Serjeants' Inn
about Whitsuntide 1606, and was taken to his mansion at
Eston Hall, Wallington, in Norfolk; but having converted the
parish church into a hay-house or dog-kennel, his body was
obliged to be buried in the neighbouring church of Rungton.

His wife was Elizabeth, the eldest daughter of Christopher Coningsby, the son of William Coningsby the judge.
By her he acquired the estate of Wallington, and having in-

[1] State Trials, ii. 18.　　　　[2] Nicolas' Hatton, 478. 502.

duced her to acknowledge a fine thereof, she is said to have thereupon become distracted, and to have continued so during the rest of her life. He had no other child than Elizabeth, the wife of Sir William Hatton.[1]

HARVEY, FRANCIS.

JUST. C. P. 1624.

See under the Reign of Charles I.

HERON, EDWARD.

B. E. 1607.

THE grandfather of Edward Heron was John Heron, a physician at Barming in Kent, the son of Sir John Heron of Hackney. The judge was the son of Richard Heron, settled at Harsted or Hastings-Hall in Birdbroke, Essex. He pursued his legal studies at Lincoln's Inn, where he was admitted on February 12, 1564; and, having been called to the bar on February 7, 1574, was elected a governor in 1586, and autumn reader in the following year.[2] In 1594, he was called to the degree of serjeant-at-law, which he held for fourteen years before he was advanced to the bench of the Exchequer on November 25, 1607, having been previously knighted. He did not long enjoy his position; his successor, Sir Edward Bromley, being appointed on February 6, 1610.[3]

He was twice married. His first wife was Anne, daughter of David Vincent, Esq., of Bernake in Northamptonshire, the ancestor of the present baronet of that name. By her he had three sons, Edward, John, and William. His second wife was Dorothy, daughter of Anthony Maxey, Esq., of Bradwell near Coggleshall, who brought him a son, named James, settled at Pantfield.[4]

[1] Spelman's Icenia Rel. 140.; Blomefield's Norfolk, vii. 412.
[2] Linc. Inn Black Bk. v. 27. 178.; Dugdale's Orig. 253. 261.
[3] Croke, Jac. 197.   [4] Morant's Essex, ii. 345.

HOBART, HENRY.

Ch. C. P. 1613.

See under the Reign of Charles I.

HOUGHTON, ROBERT.

Just. K. B. 1613.

ROBERT HOUGHTON was born at Gunthorpe in Norfolk on August 3, 1548, and entering himself of Lincoln's Inn on March 1, 1569, was called to the bar on February 10, 1577, became one of the governors in 1587, and was appointed reader in Lent, 1591, and again in Lent, 1600. He was one of several who were nominated by Queen Elizabeth to be serjeants; but in consequence of her death were re-summoued by James, and took the degree in Easter Term, 1603.[1] He represented the city of Norwich in the parliament of 1593, and was chosen its recorder in 1603; an office which he held till he attained a judicial seat in Westminster Hall. This occurred on April 21, 1613, when he was made a judge of the King's Bench and knighted.[2] In Peacham's case, who was tried in 1615 for divers treasonable passages contained in a sermon which was never preached nor intended to be preached, but only set down in writing and found in his study, King James by the advice of Bacon commenced the unconstitutional practice of obtaining the opinion of the judges before trial; and it was arranged that each of the judges of the King's Bench should be applied to separately. Sir Edward Coke for some time resisted "this taking of auricular opinions single and apart," as new and dangerous, and Sir Robert Houghton evidently had the same doubts; for Bacon in his report to the king says, "he is a soft man, and seemeth desirous to confer; alleging that the other three judges had

---

[1] Black Book, v. 97. 224.; Dugdale's Orig. 254. 261.; Chron. Ser.
[2] Blomefield's Norwich, i. 359, 360.

all served the crown before they were judges; but that he had not been much acquainted with business of this nature." Doderidge and G. Croke were the other two judges, and did not hesitate to comply. The trial took place, and though the poor man was found guilty, yet, notwithstanding all Bacon's endeavours, he was not executed; many of the judges being of opinion, as every reasonable man must be, that the offence was not treason.[1]

Sir Robert Houghton died at his chambers in Serjeants' Inn, Chancery Lane, on February 6, 1623–4, and was buried at the church of St. Dunstan's in the West. Croke calls him " a most reverend, prudent, learned, and temperate judge, and inferior to none in his time."

His wife was Mary, the daughter of Robert Rychers, Esq., of Wrotham in Kent; by whom he had three sons and three daughters, one of each of whom died in his life-time.[2] His sister Cecilia married Richard Thurlow of Burnham Ulp in Norfolk, the direct ancestor of Lord Thurlow. The judge held the manors of Threxton, Hemenhales, Curles, Ferthings, and Pensthorpe in Norfolk, which went to his eldest son Francis, and were enjoyed for several generations by his descendants.[3]

HUTTON, RICHARD.

JUST. C. P. 1617.

See under the Reign of Charles I.

JONES, WILLIAM.

JUST. C. P. 1621.   JUST. K. B. 1624.

See under the Reign of Charles I.

KIMBOLTON, LORD.   *See* HENRY MONTAGU.

---

[1] State Trials, ii. 869.   [2] Maitland's London, 1096.
[3] Blomefield's Norfolk, i. 625.

KINGSMILL, GEORGE.

Just. C. P. 1603.

See under the Reign of Elizabeth.

THIS judge was the grandson of John Kingsmill, who held the same office in the reign of Henry VII.; and the second son of Sir John Kingsmill of Sidmanton in Hampshire, by Constance, the daughter of John Goring of Burton in Sussex. He passed through the grades of legal study at Lincoln's Inn, where he was admitted on March 16, 1560, and called to the bar on June 15, 1567.[1] He became reader in autumn, 1578, but the pestilence obliged him to defer his reading till the ensuing Lent. Having been previously appointed one of the governors of the society, he held that position from 1575 till he removed from the inn on being made a serjeant. This degree was conferred upon him in 1594, with the additional honour of queen's serjeant on March 19 in the following year.[2] Lord Burleigh recommended him for advancement as a man " well able to bear the burden of service;"[3] and soon after that minister's death, he was elevated to the bench as a judge of the Common Pleas, on February 8, 1599. After the accession of King James, who knighted him, he retained his post till Hilary, 1606, when he resigned, and in the April following he died.

He married Sarah, daughter of Sir James Harington, of Exton, and widow of Francis Lord Hastings. After the judge's death, she took Edward Lord Zouch, of Harringworth, as her third husband.[4]

KINLOSS, LORD. *See* EDWARD BRUCE.

---

[1] Black Book, iv. 356., v. 61.
[2] Dugdale's Orig. 253. 261.; Chron. Ser.
[3] Peck's Desid. Cur. B. v. 24.   [4] Collins's Peerage, vi. 658.

LEY, JAMES, Baron Ley, and Earl of Marlborough.

Ch. K. B. 1621.

In the parish of Teffont-Evias, in the county of Wilts, the residence of his father Henry Ley, Esq., James, the future chief justice, first saw the light. He was the sixth son of a numerous family, and was born about the year 1552. At the age of seventeen he became a commoner of Brazenose College in the University of Oxford, and having taken a degree in arts, he entered on his legal studies at Lincoln's Inn on February 18, 1577. Being called to the bar on October 11, 1584, he worked his way up to the bench of that society in 1600, and was chosen Lent reader in 1602.[1] On November 22, 1603, he had a separate call to the degree of the coif, probably in preparation for holding the office of lord chief justice of the King's Bench in Ireland, to which he was appointed in the following year, when he was also knighted. While filling that position he was one of the commissioners of the Great Seal of that country from April 6, to November 8, 1605. He presided in the Irish King's Bench about four years, resigning in December, 1608[2]; and Bacon speaks of his "gravity, temper and discretion" in that office.[3] Returning to England he received the profitable place of attorney of the Court of Wards and Liveries, at the same time establishing the right of that office to take precedence in that court of the king's attorney-general; for which he had a Privy Seal dated May 15, 1609. He must then have resigned his rank as serjeant; for in that and the twelve succeeding years he is recorded as one of the governors of Lincoln's Inn.

In 1610 he was named as a commissioner for the better expedition of the plantation in the lands escheated in the pro-

1 Dugdale's Orig. 254. 262.   2 Smyth's Law Off. of Ireland, 26. 28.
3 Bacon's Works (Montagu), vii. 263.

vince of Ulster.[1] On the elevation of Sir Francis Bacon to the Great Seal in 1617, Sir James was a candidate for the attorney-generalship, and the Duke of Buckingham told Sir Henry Yelverton that he offered 10,000*l.* for the office.[2] Not succeeding in this, he was created a baronet as of Westbury in Wiltshire, on July 20, 1619.

On the resignation of Sir Henry Montagu, Sir James Ley was elevated from the attorneyship of the Court of Wards to be lord chief justice of the King's Bench; his patent being dated January 29, 1621. He was then about sixty-nine years of age, and in that year [3] married his third wife Jane, daughter of John Lord Butler, by Elizabeth, the sister of the favourite, George Villiers, Duke of Buckingham, to whose patronage he probably owed his future advance. Within two months after his appointment he was called upon, in consequence of the proceedings against Bacon, to take the place of speaker of the House of Lords; and in that character he had to pronounce their judgment, first, in the cases of Sir Giles Mompesson and Sir Francis Michell, and then against the chancellor himself and Sir Henry Yelverton.[4]

Sir James, after performing the duties of his judicial office for nearly four years, imitated the example of his predecessor by retiring from it, and accepting the profitable place of lord treasurer on December 20, 1624. On the 31st of the same month, he was created Lord Ley of Ley in the county of Devon, the ancient seat of his family. He was more fortunate, however, than Sir Henry Montagu; for he retained the royal purse for the remainder of James's reign, and for more than three years in that of Charles I.; who in the May following his accession created him Earl of Marlborough. He was removed in July, 1628, to make way for Sir Richard

---

[1] Pell Records, Jac. I., 113. 142.
[2] Bacon's Works, xvi. cccix. note; quoting Judge Whitelocke's Diary.
[3] W. Yonge's Diary, 40.   [4] Parl. Hist. i. 1207. 1229. 1250. 1258.

Weston; and retrograded to the almost empty title of president of the Council, which he held for the few remaining months of his life.

He died at Lincoln's Inn on March 14, 1629, and was removed for interment to Westbury, Wilts, in the parish church of which a magnificent monument is erected to his memory.

In the midst of corruption among lawyers and statesmen, and holding the highest offices on the bench and in the council,

" He liv'd in both unstained by gold or fee."

To his character for integrity, was added that of ability, temperance, and erudition; the latter not confined to his legal studies, but extending over subjects of general interest. His professional attainments and industry were exhibited by his " Reports," and by his treatise on the king's right of wardship, &c.; and he contributed various papers to the Society of Antiquaries, of which he was an early member.

He was three times married, a common practice among the lawyers of this period. His first wife was Mary, daughter of John Pettey, of Stoke Talmage in Oxfordshire; his second was Mary, the widow of Sir William Bower, knight; and the third was Jane, daughter of John Lord Butler. By the first he had a large family, but the other two brought him no issue.

His eldest son Henry, and then his grandson James, in turn succeeded to his honours; but the latter being killed in a seafight in 1665, they reverted to the chief justice's third son William, who died without issue in 1679.[1]

LINCOLN, BISHOP OF. *See* J. WILLIAMS.

MANCHESTER, EARL OF, MANDEVIL, VISCOUNT. *See* H. MONTAGU.

MARLBOROUGH, EARL OF. *See* J. LEY.

[1] Dugdale's Baronage, ii. 451.; Wood's Athen. Oxon. ii. 441.

MONTAGU, HENRY, Baron Kimbolton, Viscount Mande-vil, AND Earl of Manchester.

Ch. K. B. 1616.

THE father of Henry Montagu was Edward, the eldest son of Sir Edward Montagu, chief justice of the Courts of King's Bench and Common Pleas in the reigns of Henry VIII. and Edward VI. He was seated at Boughton in Northampton-shire, was sheriff of that county, and its representative in parliament, was knighted by Queen Elizabeth, and died in 1602. By his wife Elizabeth, daughter of Sir James Ha-rington of Exton in the county of Rutland, he had several children, of whom some account has been already given.[1] Henry was his third son, and was born at Boughton about the year 1563. He showed so much intelligence that even at school it was prognosticated " that he would raise himself above the rest of his family." After well employing his time at Christ's College, Cambridge, he became a member of his grandfather's Inn of Court, the Middle Temple, where he attained the rank of reader in autumn, 1606.[2] He had been knighted previous to the coronation of King James, and had already acquired distinction as a lawyer by being elected recorder of London in the year of that king's accession. In this office he was present at the ceremony of opening the New River on Michaelmas day, 1613, and is afterwards named in the patent incorporating the company.[3]

As early as 1601, when he was returned for the borough of Higham Ferrers, he distinguished himself in parliament. In answer to the absurd assertion made by Serjeant Heale, the aspirant for the office of master of the Rolls, " that all we have is her Majesty's, and she may lawfully at her pleasure take it from us," which he " could prove by precedent in the times of Henry III., King John, King Stephen, &c.," he had

---

[1] See Vol. V. p. 313.   [2] Dugdale's Orig. 219.   [3] Stow's London.

the courage to declare, " That there were no such precedents, and if all preambles of subsidies were looked upon, he should find they were of free gift." In the first parliament of King James, which lasted from March 19, 1604, to February 11, 1611, he was elected one of the representatives of the City of London, and took an active part in its important discussions, particularly in that relating to tenures.[1]

The degree of the coif was conferred upon him in February, 1611, and he was immediately constituted king's serjeant.[2] In this character he is only noticed as a commissioner to try the murderers of Sir Thomas Overbury, and as one of the counsel engaged in the prosecution of the great delinquents.[3]

In his private practice he had an action brought against him by one Brook, for words charging the plaintiff with having been convicted of felony. He pleaded that they were spoken by him on a trial in which he was engaged as counsel against the plaintiff, and the court decided that the justification was good ; for a counsel has a privilege to enforce anything pertinent to the issue that is informed him by his client, and not to examine whether it be true or false.[4]

On being selected on November 16, 1616, to succeed Sir Edward Coke as chief justice of the King's Bench, he of course resigned his recordership, when the corporation presented him with 200 double sovereigns as a thankful remembrance for his many careful endeavours for the city.[5] He is described as proceeding three days afterwards in great state to Westminster, arrayed in his robes, and mounted on horseback, with the Earl of Huntingdon on his right hand, and the Lord Willoughby d'Eresby on his left, and above fifty knights and gentlemen of quality accompanying him. The Lord Chancellor Lord Ellesmere, in his speech when Montagu

[1] Parl. Hist. i. 921. 1125.
[3] State Trials, ii. 911. 952.
[5] City List of Recorders.
[2] Dugdale's Chron. Ser.
[4] Croke, Jac. 90.

was sworn in, gives him a significant hint of the tenure by which he holds his place, by reminding him of the "amotion and disposing" of his predecessor "in the peaceable and happy reign of great King James, the great King of Great Britain, wherein you see the prophet David's words true, He putteth down one and setteth up another; a lesson to be learned of all, and to be remembered and feared of all that sit in judicial places." He recommends him to follow the example of his grandfather, Sir Edward Montagu, of whose name he takes advantage to introduce those allusions to the imputed faults of Sir Edward Coke which have been noticed in a previous page.[1] He is said to have procured the place by consenting to give to the Duke of Buckingham's nominee the clerkship of the Court of King's Bench, worth 4000*l.* a year, which Coke, in whose gift it was, refused to part with, although by doing so he might have retained his office.

Sir Henry Montagu's judgments are reported by Croke; and his style of giving them may be seen in that which he delivered in the case of Wraynham for slandering Lord Chancellor Bacon. The method is sufficiently fair and neat, but the language is disfigured by the vice of the age, flattery of the king; of whom he says, "We all know that we have a sovereign of those high and excellent gifts that it is not rhetoric or eloquence that can cast dust in the king's eyes, or cause him anyways to turn aside from justice." It was Sir Henry's fortune to be called on to award execution against Sir Walter Raleigh upon the sentence of death which had been pronounced fifteen years before. His address to the unfortunate prisoner evidently showed his regret in being compelled to the performance of this duty, and its terms do credit to his humanity.[2]

Montagu did not long rest satisfied with the place of chief justice. He aimed still higher, and after sitting in the judi-

[1] Moore's Reports, 826. See ante, p. 150. [2] State Trials, ii. 35. 1080.

cial seat for four years he succeeded in obtaining the more elevated and lucrative post of lord treasurer on December 14, 1620. Nearly two years before he had offered the Duke of Buckingham 10,000*l.* for the place, which, it seems, was not sufficient; for eventually he was obliged to pay 20,000*l.* One of the charges against Buckingham on his impeachment was the receipt of this money; but his answer alleged that it was a voluntary loan to the king, and that he had not a penny of it. The correspondence at the time seems to confirm this [1] : but this view of the fact does not remove the venality of the transaction, nor account for Montagu being deprived of the office on the 13th of the following October, when the unfortunate Lionel Cranfield, Earl of Middlesex, was by the duke's interest named as his successor. While he held it, one of the courtiers ill-naturedly inquired of him whether *wood* was not extremely dear at Newmarket, for there the king had given him the white staff. It was ever considered a place of great charge and profit, and when Montagu was asked what it might be worth per annum, he answered, " Some thousands of pounds to him who after death would go instantly to heaven; twice as much to him who would go to purgatory; and a *nemo scit* to him who would venture to a worse place." [2] While treasurer he was one of the commissioners of the Great Seal from the abdication of the chancellorship by Bacon till July 10, 1621, when Dean Williams received the Seal. [3]

On his appointment to the treasurership he was ennobled with the titles of Baron Montagu of Kimbolton and Viscount Mandevil, and on his removal he was but poorly compensated for his loss by being made lord president of the Council. In this office he remained for the rest of James's reign and

---

[1] Tanner's MSS. in Oxford, quoted in Bacon's Works (Montagu), xvi. ccxxvii.

[2] Lloyd's State Worthies, 1028.   [3] Dugdale's Chron. Series.

for the first three years of Charles's, when he exchanged it for that of lord privy seal, which he enjoyed for the rest of his life. King Charles also in the first year of his reign, on February 5, 1626, advanced him a step in the peerage, creating him Earl of Manchester.

During the sixteen years that he lived in Charles's reign, he was an active minister of the crown and a faithful adherent to the king; maintaining a good reputation and credit with the whole nation. He did not live to witness the fatal termination of Charles's career, but died on November 7, 1642, shortly after the commencement of the hostilities between the royalists and the parliamentary forces. He had nearly attained his eightieth year, and showed as much activity and sagacity in business at that age as at any former period of his life. Fuller says, "When lord privy seal, he brought the Court of Requests into such repute that what formerly was called the alms-basket of the Chancery, had in his time well nigh as much meat in and guests about it (I mean suits and clients) as the Chancery itself." In his last years he published a book entitled "Manchester al Mondo, Contemplatio Mortis et Immortalitatis; or Meditations on Life and Death;"[1] which conveys a most favourable impression of the wisdom and piety of the writer. He was buried at Kimbolton under a noble monument.

Like his grandfather, Sir Edward, he married three wives. The first was Catherine, daughter to Sir William Spencer of Yarnton in Oxfordshire, who, after bringing him four sons and three daughters, died in 1612. By his second wife Anne, daughter and heir of William Wincott of Langham in Suffolk, Esq., and widow of Sir Leonard Haliday, Knt., Lord Mayor of London, he had no issue. His third wife, Margaret, daughter of John Crouch of Cornbury, Herts, Esq., and widow of John Hare of Totteridge, whom he married on April 26,

---

[1] Walpole's R. and N. Authors (Park), ii. 228.

1620, produced him two sons and two daughters. She survived her husband and died in 1653.

His eldest son and successor, Edward Earl of Manchester,
was twice lord commissioner of the Great Seal, and will be
hereafter noticed. The second son, Walter, became a Roman
Catholic, and was made Abbot of St. Martin's Abbey near
Pontoise.

George, the eldest of Lord Manchester's sons by his third
wife, was father of Charles, who in 1694 was made Chancellor
of the Exchequer, in 1700 was created Baron Halifax, and in
1714 was advanced to the Earldom of Halifax. These titles
at his death went by a special limitation to his nephew, but
became extinct in 1772 by the death of the next possessor
without issue.[1]

NICHOLS, AUGUSTINE.

JUST. C. P. 1612.

OF an old and respectable Northamptonshire family, Augustine
Nichols was the second son of Thomas Nichols, Esq., of Hardwick in that county, a lawyer in the beginning of Elizabeth's
reign, and Anne, the daughter of John Pell, Esq., of Eltington.
He was born at Ecton in April, 1559, and being designed
for his father's profession, was entered as a student of the
Middle Temple, in which he became reader in autumn, 1602.
In the following January he received a writ summoning him
to take the degree of the coif, which in consequence of the
death of Queen Elizabeth, was renewed by King James, by
whom he was knighted. He was elected recorder of Leicester
on December 14, 1603 ; and his arguments in Westminster
Hall are reported both by Coke and Croke for the next nine
years, till in November 26, 1612, he was elevated to the
bench as a judge of the Common Pleas. Three years afterwards, on being appointed chancellor to Charles, Prince of

---

[1] Clarendon's Rebellion, i. 96. ; Bridges' Collins's Peerage, ii. 51

Wales, it became necessary for him to have a renewal of his patent, in order that he might " take fee and livery of the prince ; " the usual oath prohibiting a judge from being paid by any but the king himself.[1]   He occupied his judicial seat for little more than four years, dying at Kendal in August, 1616, while on the summer circuit : " judex mortuus est, jura dans," as Fuller describes him.   He was buried there, and has a fair monument in the church.

King James commonly called him " The judge that would give no money ; " and Fuller, with a neighbourly prepossession, being born in the same county, speaks glowingly of his character.   He says, " He was renowned for his special judicial endowments ; patience to hear both parties, a happy memory, a singular sagacity to search into the material circumstances, exemplary integrity, even to the rejection of gratuities after judgment given." [2]

He married Mary, the widow of Edward Bagshaw, Esq., but having no children by her, his estate at Foxton in Northamptonshire, which he had purchased, devolved on his brother's eldest son, Francis, who was created a baronet in 1641.   The title failed on the death of his grandson, the third baronet, in 1717, without issue.

PERYAM, WILLIAM.

Ch. B. E. 1603.

See under the Reign of Elizabeth.

THE father of this judge was John Peryam, an opulent citizen and twice mayor of Exeter ; and his mother was Margaret, one of the daughters and coheirs of Robert Hone, Esq., of Ottery St. Mary.   They had two sons, William and John, the latter of whom was an alderman of Exeter and a knight,

---

[1] Dugdale's Orig. 219. ; Chron. Series ; Croke Jac. Prom.
[2] Fuller's Worthies, ii. 168.

and was a considerable benefactor to Exeter College, Oxford.[1] At this college, William, the elder brother, who was born at Exeter in 1534, is said to have been educated; but Anthony Wood does not mention him; and the Inn of Court at which he pursued his legal studies, is only to be surmised from the fact that his arms are placed in one of the windows of Middle Temple hall. It is curious also that his arguments as counsel are not recorded by any of the contemporary reporters; that the first mention made of him is his receiving the serjeant's coif in Michaelmas Term, 1579, and that the next is his elevation to the bench as a judge of the Common Pleas on February 13, 1581, 23 Eliz.[2]

For the twelve years during which he retained this seat his judgments are reported by Dyer and Coke; and the reputation he enjoyed may be estimated as well by his being named as one of the commissioners to hear causes in Chancery on the death of Sir Christopher Hatton, as by the number of commissions into which his name was introduced for the trial of state offenders. Among these were Mary Queen of Scots, the Earls of Arundel and Essex, Sir John Perrot, and others of less note.[3] The last fine levied before him as a judge of the Common Pleas was on the morrow of the Purification, 1593; and in the course of the same Hilary Term he was promoted to the office of chief baron of the Exchequer, vacant by the death of Sir Roger Manwood. On this occasion he was knighted; and he continued to preside in that court during the ten remaining years of Elizabeth's reign, and for eighteen months under King James I.[4]

After a judicial life of nearly twenty-four years, he died on October 9, 1604, at his mansion at Little Fulford near

---

[1] Chalmers' Oxford, 68.   [2] Dugdale's Orig. 225.; Chron. Ser.
[3] App. 4 Report Pub. Rec. 272—296.; State Trials, i. 1167. 1251. 1315. 1333.
[4] Dugdale's Orig. 48.; Chron. Ser.

Crediton, in the church of which he was buried under a stately monument.

He married three wives. The first was Margery, daughter and heir of John Holcot, of Berkshire, Esq.; the second was Anne, the daughter of John Parker, of North Molton, Devon, Esq.; and the third was Elizabeth, one of Sir Nicholas Bacon the lord keeper's daughters, to whom he was also the third husband, she having been previously married to Sir Robert D'Oyly and Sir Henry Nevill. She survived the chief baron for sixteen years, and founded a fellowship and two scholarships at Balliol College, Oxford.[1]

Leaving no son, his four daughters, whom he had by his second wife, shared his property. They married respectively Sir William Pole, an eminent lawyer, Sir Robert Basset, Sir Robert Pointz, and William Williams, Esq.[2]

PHELLIPS, EDWARD.

M. R. 1611.

EDWARD PHELLIPS, or PHILLIPS, was descended from an ancient Welsh family, which migrated into the county of Somerset, where they long resided at Barrington, a few miles from Montacute. He was the fourth son of Thomas Phellips, Esq., of that place, by Elizabeth, the daughter of —— Smith, Esq., whose second son was father of Sir Thomas Phellips, raised to a baronetcy in 1620, which became extinct in the third generation in 1690.

It is not improbable that Edward studied at Broadgate's Hall (now Pembroke College), Oxford, as Wood notices one of his name taking the degree of B.A. in 1579, and of M.A. in 1582. He kept his legal terms at the Middle Temple, and attained to the rank of reader in autumn, 1596.[3] His

---

[1] Chalmers' Oxford, 50.
[2] Prince's Worthies of Devon; Diary of Walter Yonge, 8.
[3] Dugdale's Orig. 218.

name does not appear in any law reports, except in those of the State Trials after he became a serjeant, to which degree he was called at the end of the reign of Queen Elizabeth, but did not assume it, on account of her death intervening, till the beginning of King James's. He was appointed king's serjeant on the 18th of May following, and was knighted at Whitehall on July 23, 1603. In November he assisted in the trial of Sir Walter Raleigh, but took no part in the brutal manner with which Sir Edward Coke conducted the prosecution.

In January, 1606, he opened the indictment against Guy Fawkes and the other conspirators in the Gunpowder Plot, and his speech on the occasion is a curious specimen of oratory. He commences: "The matter that is now to be offered to you, my lords the commissioners, and to the trial of you the knights and gentlemen of the jury, is matter of treason; but of such horror and monstrous nature that before now the tongue of man never delivered, the ear of man never heard, the heart of man never conceited, nor the malice of hellish and earthly devil ever practised: for if it be abominable to murder at least; if to touch God's anointed be to oppose themselves to God; if (by blood) to subvert princes, states, and kingdoms, be hateful to God and man, as all true Christians must acknowledge: then, how much more than too monstrous shall all Christian hearts judge the horror of this treason; to murder and subvert such a king; such a queen; such a prince; such a progeny; such a state; such a government, so complete and absolute, that God approves, the world admires, all true English hearts honour and reverence; the pope and his disciples only envies and maligns."[1] It would almost seem that he intended to turn into ridicule this most atrocious conspiracy. But the good man was perfectly sincere, and no doubt thought himself very eloquent,

[1] State Trials, ii. 164.

as there are some other similar specimens of his taste as a rhetorician.

In the first parliament of King James, which met on March 19, 1604, Sir Edward Phellips, being returned for his native county, was elected speaker. His address to the king is in the same ponderous style; and he apparently vied with his majesty which should most fatigue the audience by the length of their orations. The reporter, however, was out of patience and leaves his harangue unfinished. On the close of the session in July, his speech is full of the most fulsome absurdities; beginning with solemn pomposity, " History, most high and mighty sovereign, is truly approved to be the Treasure of Times past, the Light of Truth, the Memory of Life, the Guide and Image of Man's present Estate, Pattern of Things to come, and the true Work-Mistress of Experience, the Mother of Knowledge," &c.[1] This parliament continued till February, 1611, during which period there were four more sessions, in all of which Sir Edward acted as speaker; having in the interim been rewarded for his flattery by the reversion of the office of master of the Rolls, granted to him on December 2, 1608.[2] As the death of Lord Bruce of Kinloss, the possessor, did not occur till January 14, 1611, and the parliament, which was prorogued till the 9th of February, was dissolved on that day by commission, Sir Edward's only act in his double character was hearing that commission read. He was also made chancellor to Henry, Prince of Wales.

Of Sir Edward's proceedings in Chancery little more is known than appears incidentally in the report of Wraynham's case, against whom proceedings were instituted for slandering Lord Bacon. A cause in which Wraynham was concerned had been referred to the master of the Rolls, who had made a report adverse to his interests, on which Lord Chancellor

[1] Parl. Hist. i. 989. 1045.   [2] Rot. Pat. 6 Jac., p. 27. n. 4.

Bacon had afterwards founded his decree ; and Wraynham had thereupon conveyed the slander in a petition to the king. Without entering into the merits of the case, which do not touch Sir Edward Phellips, it will be enough to state the character given to him by the attorney-general Yelverton, by Sir Edward Coke, who, though out of office, was one of the commissioners to try it, and by Chief Justice Montagu. Yelverton says that he " was a man of great understanding, great pains, great experience, great dexterity, and great integrity." Coke says, " As for this master of the Rolls never man in England was more excellent in Chancery than that man; and for ought I heard (that had reason to hear something of him) I never heard him taxed with corruption, being a man of excellent dexterity, diligent, early in the morning, ready to do justice." Chief Justice Montagu in speaking of him, however, lets us into a little bit of his real character as a judge; for after declaring that " whoever knew that man, knows him to be a true reporter and a judicious collector of proofs, as ever was," he adds, " I will not dissemble what others thought a fault in him, to be over swift in judging : but this was the error of his greater experience and riper judgment than others had." [1]

He had left the scene long before this trial took place ; having died on September 11, 1614. He built the large and noble mansion still standing at Montacute, which is thus noticed by Thomas Coryat: " For besides many other English Palaces that do surpasse that of the Archbishop of Colen, there is one in mine owne country of Somersetshire, even the magnificent house of my most worthy and right worshipful neighbour and Mecænas, Sir Edward Philippes, now master of the Rolles (whom I name *honoris causâ*) in the town of Montacute, so stately adorned with the statues of the Nine Worthies that they bee at the least equally ranked with this of Bonna, if not something preferred before it." [2]

---

[1] State Trials, ii. 1062. 1073. 1079.   [2] Coryat's Crudities, ii. 483.

He married, first, Margaret, the daughter of —— New-digate, Esq., and, secondly, Elizabeth, the daughter of Thomas Pigott, Esq. of Bucks. By the former he left a family, and the representatives of his eldest son still enjoy the paternal estate.[1]

POPHAM, JOHN.
Ch. K. B. 1603.
See under the Reign of Elizabeth.

POPHAM is a hamlet in Hampshire, where the family from which the chief justice descended were settled early in the twelfth century. One of its most eminent members, also named Sir John Popham, after holding several high employments, was elected speaker of the House of Commons in 28 Henry VI., but was excused on account of his age and infirmities.[2] The estate of Huntworth in Somersetshire was acquired in marriage by a younger son in the reign of Edward I., and remained in that branch of the family till the time of Charles I. There John, the future chief justice, was born about the year 1531, being the second son of Alexander (or as some say, Edward) Popham of that place, by his wife Jane, the daughter of Sir Edward Stradling of St. Donat's Castle, Glamorganshire.

He received his education at Balliol College, Oxford, whence he removed to the Middle Temple to pursue the study of the law. Instead of doing this, tradition charges him with entering into wild courses, and even with being wont to take a purse with his profligate companions. However this may be, he must have soon reformed, and, as Fuller says, "applied himself to a more profitable fencing";[3] for he does not seem to have been delayed in obtaining the usual honours of his

---

[1] Collinson's Somerset, iii. 314.; Burke.
[2] Stow's London (Thoms's Ed.), 143.; Parl. Hist. i. 306.
[3] Aubrey, ii. 492.; Fuller's Worthies, ii. 284.

society. His nomination as reader took place in autumn, 1568, when he was thirty-seven years old: and he became treasurer twelve years afterwards.[1] In the interval between these two dates, he had obtained, as member for Bristol, a seat in parliament, where in 1571, when the subsidy was under discussion, he joined with Mr. Bell (the future chief baron) in calling for the correction of some abuses, and pointed out the evil of allowing the treasurers of the crown to retain in their hands "great masses of money," of which, becoming bankrupt, they only repaid an instalment. In the next year he was one of the committee appointed to confer with the lords on the subject of the Queen of Scots.[2]

Though he is not named by any reporter till Michaelmas, 1576, he must have acquired considerable legal celebrity, as he and Mr. Francis Rodes were specially called to the degree of the coif on Jannary 28, 1578. The entry in the Middle Temple books, that they "non dederunt aurum," arose probably from their being added as a rider to the great call of serjeants which took place in the preceding Michaelmas Term, and their not therefore being required to give a separate feast. In the following year he was offered the place of solicitor-general. This office being inferior in rank to that of a serjeant at law, it became necessary for him to choose between them; and as he considered that the former more certainly led to judicial honours, he obtained a patent exonerating him from the latter degree, and was thereupon appointed solicitor-general on June 26, 1579.[3] While holding that office he was elected speaker of the House of Commons in Jannary 1581, in the place of Sir Robert Bell, who had died during the prorogation. Some idea may be formed not only of the speaker's wit, but also of the lightness of the parliamentary labours during that session, by his reply to Queen

[1] Dugdale's Orig. 217. 221.   [2] Parl. Hist. i. 735. 779.
[3] Dugdale's Orig. 127.; Chron. Ser.

Elizabeth, when, on his attending her on some occasion, she said, " Well, Mr. Speaker, what hath passed in the Lower House?" he answered, " If it please your Majesty, seven weeks."[1] His last and, indeed, principal duty in this capacity, was the making the customary speech to the queen on presenting the subsidy voted at the end of the session. This was on March 18, after which that parliament never again met.[2]

On the elevation of the attorney-general, Sir Gilbert Gerard, to the mastership of the Rolls, Popham succeeded to the former office on June 1, 1581. He held it for eleven years, during which he took part in all those criminal trials, the perusal of which, even where the guilt of the prisoners is most apparent, cannot but excite feelings of indignation at the gross injustice of the proceedings. His conduct in them, however, is not chargeable with any unnecessary harshness; and, even in the opening of the unwarrantable charge against Secretary Davison, he performed the difficult duty without any words of aggravation.[3]

When Sir Christopher Wray's death left a vacancy in the King's Bench, little time was lost in supplying it. In about three weeks, Mr. Popham received his patent as lord chief justice, dated June 2, 1592, and was immediately knighted. He presided in that court for the fifteen remaining years of his life, eleven under Queen Elizabeth, and four under King James.

He accompanied Lord Keeper Egerton in February 1600, to the Earl of Essex's house, as before related[4]; and when Sir Ferdinando Gorges offered to deliver him from his forced detention there, he refused to depart without his companions in confinement, saying that " as they came together, so would they go together, or die together." This fact is not men-

[1] Bacon's Apophthegms (1626) 79.   [2] Parl. Hist. i. 311. 828.
[3] State Trials, i. 1051—1321.   [4] See ante, p. 142.

tioned at the earl's trial either in the chief justice's evidence,
or in Gorges' examination; but it is related by himself on
the subsequent trial of Sir Christopher Blunt and others
implicated in this insurrection, at which was exhibited the
unbecoming spectacle of prisoners tried, and sentence pronounced, by a judge who had himself been a sufferer.[1]

One of his earliest duties after the accession of James was
to preside at the trial of Sir Walter Raleigh,—stained not
only by a conviction founded on weak and unsatisfactory evidence, but also by that disgusting conduct towards the prisoner of Sir Edward Coke, which will ever disgrace his name,
and for which the chief justice felt himself called upon to
apologise; saying to Sir Walter, "Mr. Attorney speaketh
out of the zeal of his duty for the service of the king, and
you for your life; be valiant on both sides."[2] He would have
done better to have silenced the brutal tongue.

The last state trials which he presided over were those
against the conspirators in the Gunpowder Plot; finishing with
that of Garnet the Jesuit, on March 28, 1606.[3] He was then
seventy-five years old; but he sat on the bench for another
year, pronouncing a judgment in the Court of Wards, as late
as Easter Term, 1607.   On June 10, in the following Term,
he died; and was buried under a magnificent tomb in the
church of Wellington in Somersetshire, where he had long
resided in a stately house he had erected, and to which he left
a testimony of his charity and goodwill by the foundation of
a hospital for the maintenance of twelve poor and aged
people.   His mansion there was ruined in the civil war, being
turned into a garrison for the parliament by one Bovet of
Taunton, who got possession of it by stratagem, and defended
it some time against Sir Richard Grenville.[4]

Sir John died in possession of several valuable estates, one

---

[1] State Trials, i. 1340. 1344. 1428.   [2] Ibid, ii. 10.
[3] State Trials, ii. 159. 217.   [4] Gough's Camden, i. 98.

of which was that of Littlecott in Wiltshire. In connection
with this a dark and improbable story is related of its having
come into the chief justice's hands as the price of his cor-
ruptly allowing one Darell, the former proprietor, to escape
on his trial for an atrocious murder. There is no doubt of
the existence of such a tradition; it is told by Aubrey, who
was certainly no admirer of the judge, and it is related by
Sir Walter Scott in illustration of a ballad in Rokeby. Sir
Walter does not give the judge's name, but that appears in full
in other accounts both in prose and verse detailing the horrid
particulars. It would be curious to trace the circumstances to
which such a tradition owes its origin, especially in a case
where every other incident in the career of the party implicated seems to render its occurrence impossible, and where
contemporaries so eminent as Lord Ellesmere, Sir Edward
Coke, and Sir George Croke give voluntary testimony to the
purity of his character.

Lord Ellesmere, in the year after Popham's death, says of
him, " And here I may not omit the worthy memory of the
late grave and reverend judge, Sir John Popham, chief justice of the King's Bench, deceased, a man of great wisdom,
and of singular learning and judgment in the law."[1]   Coke,
not long afterwards, in reporting Sir Drew Drury's case, says,
"And this was the last case that Sir John Popham, the
venerable and honourable chief justice of England, &c. resolved, who was a most reverend judge, of a ready apprehension, profound judgment, most excellent understanding, and
admirable experience and knowledge of all business which
concerned the commonwealth; accompanied with a rare memory, with perpetual industry and labour for the maintenance
of the tranquillity and public good of the realm, and in all
things with great constancy, integrity and patience"[2]; and
Croke, in noticing his death, calls him " a person of great

[1] State Trials, ii. 669.   [2] Coke's 6 Report, 75.

learning and integrity." These are qualities which oppose
the idea of the possessor of them being possibly guilty of such
a dereliction of principle and duty as that with which the
tradition charges him. At the same time it is extraordinary
that no refutation should have been attempted; for if any
had existed it is to be presumed that such a writer as Sir
Walter Scott while detailing the charge would have noticed
the answer. Some light could be surely thrown on the truth
of the allegation by the records of the time, which would
show whether a Darell was ever in fact arraigned for such a
murder, and who was the judge that presided at his trial.
The dates also of the last Darell's death, and of the chief
justice's acquisition of the estate, would afford the means
of either disproving the fact entirely or of increasing the
probability of its occurrence. If the petition which Sir
Francis Bacon, in his argument against Hollis and others for
traducing public justice, states was presented to Queen Elizabeth against chief justice Popham, and which after investigation by four privy councillors was dismissed as slanderous[1],
could be found, it might possibly turn out that this story was
the slander; and the chief justice's subsequent enjoyment of
his high office would be a sufficient proof of its utter false-
hood.

He is reputed to have been a severe judge; and according
to Fuller, to have recommended King James to be more
sparing in his pardons to the malefactors who then infested the
highways. This author adds, "In a word, the deserved death
of some scores preserved the lives and livelyhoods of more
thousands; travellers owing their safety to this judge's severity many years after his death."[2] David Lloyd gives him
credit for having "first set up the discovery of New England
to maintain and employ those that could not live honestly in
the Old; being of opinion that banishment thither would be

---

[1] State Trials, ii. 1029.　　　　　　[2] Fuller's Worthies, ii. 284.

as well a more lawful as a more effectual remedy against these extravagancies."[1] And Aubrey says that "he stockt and planted Virginia out of all the gaoles of England."[2] Neither of these accounts is quite correct, the truth being that having associated himself with Sir Ferdinando Gorges (the knight who released him from the Earl of Essex's house) in a speculation for the establishment of a colony in North America, and a patent having been granted to them and several others, their expedition sailed on December 19, 1606[3], about six months before the chief justice's death; so that whatever might have been his intentions as to transportation, he did not live to see them carried into effect.

After his death some Reports collected by him were published with his name; but the book is considered as of no authority.

The chief justice married Amy, daughter and heir of Robert Gaines of Glamorgan, Esq.,[4] and by her, besides several daughters, left a son, Sir Francis, whose descendants are still in possession of the Littlecott estate.

ST. ALBANS, Viscount. *See* F. Bacon.

SALISBURY, Dean of. *See* J. Williams.

SAVILE, JOHN.

B. E. 1603.

See under the Reign of Elizabeth.

THE ancient family of Savile, long settled in Yorkshire, was represented in the reign of Edward I. by two brothers, John and Henry. John was the ancestor of a branch which received a baronetcy (that of Thornhill) in 1611, the fourth possessor of which was ennobled by the successive creations of Lord Savile of Eland, and Viscount, Earl, and Marquess of

---

[1] State Worthies, 760.   [2] Aubrey, ii. 495.
[3] Bancroft's America, i. 123.   [4] Berry's Hants Visitations.

Halifax; titles which became extinct on the death of the second marquess in 1700. The baronetcy survived till 1784, when on the decease of Sir George Savile unmarried that also expired.[1] Henry, the second of the brothers, was father of several sons. His eldest, John, was the ancestor of the Sir John Savile of Copley, who was created a baronet in 1662, but who died in 1689 without a son to inherit the title. From the youngest son Nicholas descended Henry Savile of Bradley Hall in Stainland, in the parish of Halifax, who by his wife Elizabeth, daughter of Robert Ramsden, was the father of three sons, John, Henry and Thomas, the two elder of whom became eminent in their respective vocations; John as a baron of the Exchequer, and Henry for his profound learning and his valuable publications, — the memory of the latter being perpetuated in the university of Oxford by his endowment of two professorships in geometry and astronomy, which are distinguished by his name.

John Savile was born at Over Bradley in 1545, and became a commoner at Brazenose College in Oxford about 1561, but took no degree at the university. Entering then at the Middle Temple he advanced to the office of reader there in autumn 1586.[2] His pleadings as an advocate are not mentioned in any of the published reports, but that he was a regular attendant in the Common Pleas and Exchequer (in the latter of which he probably practised) is apparent from his Reports of cases decided in those courts, which commence in Easter Term 1580. He was about this time steward of the Lordship of Wakefield, and was called on November 29, 1592, to take the degree of serjeant at law. In less than five years afterwards, on July 1, 1598, he was raised to the bench as a baron of

---

[1] From an illegitimate son of this branch sprang Lord Savile of Pontefract, to which title was afterwards added the Earldom of Sussex. But these titles failed on the death of the second earl in 1671.

[2] Dugdale's Orig. 218.

the Exchequer, being recommended by Lord Burleigh, though described by him as a man of small living.[1] He sat in that court for the remainder of his life, King James renewing his patent in 1603, with the additional honour of knighthood. In 1599 he had been named as a commissioner " de Schismate supprimendo [2]; " and in Michaelmas Term 1606, he joined with his colleagues in giving judgment for the crown in the great case of impositions.[3] This was one of the last legal duties he performed, his death occurring on February 2, 1607. His body was buried at St. Dunstan's in the West, in Fleet Street, London, but his heart was deposited in the church of Methley in Yorkshire, where his ancestors were interred; and over it a magnificent monument was afterwards erected, on which he is represented judicially robed, with an inscription, in which his character is thus described: —

"Vir fuit pietatis zelo, ingenii perspicacia, morum suavitate, rerum Principis et Patriæ agendarum dexteritate, variis et exquisitis animi dotibus, undique conspicuus."

He was fond of historical studies, and was one of the first members of the Society of Antiquaries. An intimacy existed between him and Camden, his letter to whom pointing out a variety of mistakes in the Britannia is extant. His benevolence was equal to his learning, and there was scarcely a manor of his in Yorkshire in which he did not leave some charities behind him.

He married four wives. 1. Jane, daughter of Richard Garth of Morden in Surrey, Esq. 2. Elizabeth, daughter of Thomas Wentworth of Elmshall in Yorkshire, Esq. and relict of Richard Tempest of Bowling, Esq. 3. Dorothy, daughter of Lord Wentworth of the South, and relict of Sir William Widmerpool and Sir Martin Forbisher. And, 4. Margery,

---

[1] Peck's Desid. Cur. b. v. 24. [2] Rymer, xvi. 386.
[3] State Trials, ii. 382.

daughter of Ambrose Peate of London, and relict of Sir Jerom Weston.   He had issue by the first two of these only.

Henry, his son by his first wife, was created a baronet (of Methley) in 1611, but the title died with him in 1632. From John, his son by his second wife, who then succeeded to the estates, descended Sir John Savile, who was installed a knight of the Bath in 1749, and created Baron Pollington in 1753, and Earl of Mexborough in 1765, both in the Irish peerage, the third possessor of which titles still enjoys the family estates of Methley.[1]

SNIGGE, GEORGE.
B. E. 1604.

AMONG the citizens of Bristol the family of Snigge held a distinguished place, and several of that name filled the offices of sheriff and mayor of the city.   George Snigge, the father of the baron, was sheriff in 1556 and mayor in 1574-5, in which year his wife Margery, daughter of —— Taylor, died of the plague.   His son George was born about the year 1545, and was admitted a member of the Middle Temple on August 9, 1567.   He was called to the bar on June 17, 1575, nominated reader in autumn, 1560, and again in Lent, 1598, and in May, 1602, elected treasurer of the society.[2]   He became recorder of his native city ; was raised in Easter Term, 1604, to the degree of the coif ; and on October 14 of that year, was placed in the court of Exchequer as an additional or fifth baron.[3]   In Bates's case, on the duty imposed on currants by the king's authority, he joined with his brethren in the decision in favour of the crown, and was one of the majority in affirming the rights of the *post nati* ; but in neither case is his argument preserved.[4]   After sitting on

---

[1] Wood's Athen. Oxon. i 773.; Biog. Peerage, iv. 81.; Wotton's Baronet. i. 153.; Rayner's Cat. of Blackstone's Works, 72.

[2] Middle Temple Books; Dugdale's Orig. 218. 221.

[3] Rot. Pat. 2 Jac. p. 7.   [4] State Trials, ii. 382. 576.

the bench for nearly thirteen years, he died on November 11, 1617 ; and having lain in state for six weeks in Merchant Taylors' Hall in Broad Street, Bristol, he was buried in St. Stephen's Church in that city under a monument erected by his daughter Anne, surmounted with his effigy, in the habit of a judge, leaning on his right side.

By his wife Alice, daughter of William Young of Ogborne, Wiltshire, he had nine children, of whom the daughters were his only survivors.[1]

SOTHERTON, JOHN.

B E. 1603.

See under the Reign of Elizabeth.

THE name of Sotherton was probably derived from a village so called in Suffolk. The family was for a long time settled at Norwich, to which city it had provided several sheriffs and representatives in parliament. John Sotherton was born there about the year 1525, and being placed in the Exchequer was in 1558 admitted to the office of Foreign Apposer.[2] After performing the duties belonging to it for above twenty years he was raised to the bench of that court as a puisne baron on June 16, 1579. During the long remainder of Elizabeth's reign he continued to occupy the seat ; and receiving the new patent on the accession of James I.,[3] he held it till his death on October 26, 1605. His remains were deposited in the church of St. Botolph, Little Britain, Aldersgate Street, in the same tomb with his two wives, Frances, daughter and heir of John Smith of Cromer in Norfolk, and Maria, daughter of Edward Woton, M.D. By the former he had a son, Christopher ; and by the latter a son, John, and a daughter, Maria.[4]

---

[1] Barrett's Bristol, 514.; MSS. Coll. Arms, G. 77.
[2] Ex inf. of Mr. Adlington, an officer in the Exchequer.
[3] Dugdale's Chron. Series.　　　[4] Stow's London, 332.

Queen Elizabeth granted him the manor of Wadenhall in Waltham, Kent [1]; and he possessed property in Norwich, on which the city Bridewell now stands.[2]

SOTHERTON, JOHN.

CURSITOR BARON, 1610.

See under the Reign of Charles I.

SOTHERTON, NOWELL.

B. E. [? CURSITOR] 1606.

THE connection of Nowell Sotherton with the city of Nor-wich, makes it probable that he was of the same family as John Sotherton the baron who died in October, 1605, and by whom he was in all likelihood introduced into the Exche-quer. He is called of Gray's Inn, but never was a reader there; nor does his name occur in any of the Reports either as an ad-vocate or a judge. Nearly nine months after John Sotherton's death he was made a baron of the Exchequer, his patent being dated July 8, 1606; but as there were at that time already four barons on that bench, who were all serjeants-at-law and entirely unaccustomed to the fiscal duties attached to the office, the probability is, for the reasons stated fully in the survey of this reign [3], that he was the first extra baron ap-pointed for that special service, under the title of cursitor baron : with minor privileges and holding a lower rank than the other barons, and in no way joining with them in their judicial functions.

He died before October 27, 1601, as a certificate of the rest of the barons to the Lord High Treasurer, in favour of Thomas Cæsar, who some time after became his successor, bears that date.[4]   He gave 100*l.* to the corporation of Norwich, with which they purchased a rent charge out of the

---

[1] Hasted's Kent, ix. 322.   [2] Blomefield's Norwich, i. 277., ii. 318.
[3] Ante, p. 16—26.   [4] Add. MSS. Brit. Mus. 12504. fo. 123.

manor of Hawkyns in Burnham Broome, to be paid yearly to the churchwardens of St. Andrew the Apostle, part for a sermon and the remainder to be divided among the poor.[1]

TANFIELD, LAURENCE.
JUST. K. B. 1606. CH. B. E. 1607.

See under the Reign of Charles I.

VERULAM, LORD. See F. BACON.

WALMESLEY, THOMAS.
JUST. C. P. 1603.

See under the Reign of Elizabeth.

OF an honourable family settled at Sholley in Lancashire, where its descendants still flourish, Thomas Walmesley, by his wife, Margaret daughter of —— Livesay, left ten children, of whom the eldest son, Thomas, was the future judge. He was born about 1537, and commenced his legal studies either at Barnard's Inn or Staple Inn, for each claims him as having been a student, before he was entered at Lincoln's Inn in May, 1559. He was called to the bar by the latter society on June 15, 1567; and being elected one of the governors in 1575, he became reader in Lent, 1578, and again in autumn, 1580. On the last occasion he had just received his summons to take the degree of the coif, which he accordingly assumed on October 18.[2] Chief Justice Dyer having named the barristers whom he had selected to receive that honour, Mr. Justice Francis Wyndham wrote to Lord Burleigh, suggesting that two in the list might be spared "in respect of suspicion of their religion." These were Mr. Maryot, of the Inner Temple, and Walmesley[3]; and the judge's representations, though failing in regard to the latter, seem to have been successful against the former.

---

[1] Blomefield's Norwich, ii. 317.

[2] Black Bk. iv. 344., v. 61.; Dugdale's Orig. 253. 261.; Holinshed, iv. 432.

[3] Manning's Serv. ad legem, quoting Lansdowne MSS. xxix. No. 12.

In little more than nine years he was raised to the bench, receiving his patent as a judge of the Common Pleas on May 10, 1589. He was reappointed on King James's accession, and knighted, and was one of the " Thomases " alluded to by Lord Ellesmere as differing both in the House of Lords and the Exchequer Chamber from the majority of the judges on the question of the *post-nati.*[1]

His account of presents received and expenses incurred on some of his circuits, a very curious record, has been preserved among the Petre papers. By this document it appears that he went the western circuit with Mr. Justice Fenner for five consecutive years, from autumn, 1596, to spring, 1601. At each place of holding the assize it was the custom for the mayor and the sheriff to present some article of consumption, varying according to their means or liberality. The eatables consisted of "half a bucke," "one mutten," "one veale," lambs, capons, quayles, conyes, turkies, herneshawes, chickings, ducks, gulles, samons, lobsters, gurnetts, soales, haddocks, and among numerous pies and pasties, "one redd deare pie." Of drinkables there were wine (without naming the sort) and several "hoggesheades of beare." The noblemen and gentry of the county also sent similar contributions of bucks, muttons, &c.; besides which these additional articles are recorded: "One kidd," pigeons, a pecock, pewetts, "two peeces of turbett," "one isle of sturgeon," "artychocks and peases," and "xii suites" (sweets?) The sheriff of Devon seems to have been a most munificent caterer, for besides presenting half a buck and two hogsheads of beer, he provided the judges with an excellent supper during the whole time they were at Exeter, the particulars of which, as showing the substantial fare then consumed at that repast, it may be interesting to copy: —

"Imprimis. Of Mr. Sheriff of Devon one lambes ptinances, a q^r of

---

[1] State Trials, ii. 576. 669.

mutton, veal ij joynts, a q^r of lambe, a capon, a pastie of Veneson, iij chickings, iii quailes, iiij Rabetts, one duck, a gamon pie, a neats tongue pie, for Sundaie supper.

"It. more of him. A q^r of mutton, a brest of veale, a capon, a q^r of lambe, iij chickings, iij rabetts, one ganny, iij quailes, one gull, for Mundaie supper.

"It. more of Mr. Sheriff. A lambe's ptin. a q^r of mutton, veale one joynt, a capon, ij chickings, ij ducks, ij rabetts, a q^r of lambe, one tarte, one gull, for Tuesdaie supper.

"It. more of him. A lambe's ptin. a q^r of mutton, a q^r of lambe, a loyne of veale, ij chickings and ij rabbetts, for Wednesdaie supper.

"It. of Mr. Sheriff. A lambe's ptin. a q^r of mutton, a q^r of lambe, a brest of veale, ij chickings, ij rabbetts, for Thursdaie supper.

"It. of Mr. Sheriff. A lambe's ptin. a q^r of mutton, a brest of veale, a q^r of lambe, ij chickings, ij braynes, one plaice, iiij gurnards, and iiij whitings, for Fridaie supper."

The "Rewardes" paid by the judges for these presents, varying from 5s. down to 6d., amounted to 6l. 15s. Besides what they thus received, they had themselves to furnish a plentiful supply of food, so that their joint expenses of one circuit amounted to 47l. 18s. 10d. To Judge Walmesley's half of this, 23l. 19s. 5d., are added his private charges, for horse-meat, &c., servants, and 20d. at each place " to the poore," amounting to 23l. 2s. 5d., making the whole circuit cost him 47l. 1s. 10d.[1]

He retained his seat above twenty-three years, and died on November 26, 1612, aged seventy-five. He was buried at Blackburn in Lancashire, where his magnificent monument, the exact counterpart of that of Anne, Duchess of Somerset, in Westminster Abbey, was demolished by the parliamentary soldiers in 1642. On it were inscribed the following quaint lines : —

> " Tombs have their period, monuments decay,
> And rust and age wear Epitaphs away.
> But neither rust nor age nor time shall wear
> Judge Walmesley's name that lies entombed here,

[1] I have been favoured with an extract from this account, for the Autumn Circuit of 1596, by my friend W. Durrant Cooper, Esq., F.S.A.

Who never did for favour nor for awe
Of great men's frowns quit or forsake the lawe.
His inside was his outside, he never sought
To make fair showes of what he never thought:
For well appear'd by his bold opinion
In that great case styl'd of the Union,
Deliver'd openly in Parliament,
How free his heart and tongue together went,
When against all the judges he alone
Stood singular in his opinion.
And well King James his bounty likewise there
His Justice, Greatness, Goodness did appeare;
For though that his opinion seem'd to bring
Some crosse to th' Union wish't for by the King,
Yet as he thought he freely spoke his minde,
Neither with favour nor with feare inclin'd,
He did withdraw no grace he show'd before,
But rather of his bounty added more;
For when as old age creeping on apace
Made him unable to supply his place,
Yet he continued by the King's permission
A Judge until his death still in commission;
And still received by his special grace
His fee as full as when he serv'd the place."[1]

He had the repute of having amassed considerable wealth
by great rapacity in his practice of the law; but no evidence
is given of the charge. He became possessed of the estate of
Dunkenhalgh in the parish of Whalley, a few miles from
Blackburn, on which he built a fine mansion. By his wife
Anne, the rich heiress of Robert Shuttleworth, Esq. of Hack-
inge in the same county, he left an only son, whose male descendants failed at the beginning of the last century, and the
large property passed into the families of Lord Petre and
Lord Stourton, who were the first and second husbands of
the last possessor's sister and heir.[2]

---

[1] Lansdowne MSS. No. 973. fo. 88.
[2] Shuttleworth Accounts, Chetham Soc. 1856, part 2. App. 265.

WARBURTON, PETER.

JUST. C. P. 1603.

See under the Reign of Elizabeth.

PETER WARBURTON was descended, indirectly, from the ancient Cheshire family of Warburton and Arley; his father, Thomas Warburton, being an illegitimate son of John Warburton of Northwich in that county, one of the sons of Sir Peter Warburton, knight, an elder of the family. His mother was Anne, the daughter of Richard Maisterson of Winnington.[1]

He was born at Northwich, and, adopting the law as his profession, he began his legal studies at Staple Inn (where his arms are in the south window of the hall), and finished them at Lincoln's Inn. He was admitted a member of the latter on May 2, 1561, was called to the bar February 2, 1572, became one of the governors of the house in 1581, and was elected Lent reader in 1584.[2] He was then, and for some time after, resident in a mansion called the Black Hall, Watergate Street, Chester, formerly the house of the Grey Friars; and in this year he was recommended by Henry, Earl of Derby, to the mayor of Chester, to be an alderman of that city.[3] Though it is evident from the large purchases he made in the county that he had a considerable practice as a barrister, it was, probably, chiefly in the provinces; for his name does not occur in the Reports of Westminster till 1589, four years before he took the degree of the coif, for which he was summoned on November 29, 1593.[4] In September, 1593, soon after the death of the Earl of Derby, who was Chamber-

---

[1] From a Cheshire Pedigree compiled by the late Mr. Hadfield, with which the present representative of the family has kindly furnished me. Wotton's Baronetage, iii. 87., gives an incorrect account, making Sir Peter the Judge, eldest son of Sir John Warburton of Arley, Kent, by Mary, daughter of Sir William Brereton.

[2] Linc. Inn Black Bk. iv. 377., v. 149.; Dugdale's Orig. 253. 261.

[3] Harleian MSS. 2173.　　　　　　　　[4] Dugdale's Chron. Ser.

lain of Chester, Warburton had been appointed to exercise the office of vice-chamberlain, in which he was confirmed in the following March, when Sir Thomas Egerton became chamberlain.[1]   In November, 1599, he appears as one of the commissioners " de schismate supprimendo." [2]

His elevation to the bench at Westminster soon followed, his patent as a judge of the Common Pleas being dated November 24, 1600.   King James renewed it on his accession [3], and soon after knighted him.   In none of the State trials at which he was present does he seem to have taken a prominent part, and no record remains of his argument in the great case of the Post-nati.[4]   The last fine levied before him is dated three weeks of Trinity, 19 James I., 1621 [5], only a few weeks before his death on September 7, in that year.   This event occurred at Grafton Hall in Cheshire, a stately building exhibiting a fine specimen of the domestic architecture of the seventeenth century, erected by Sir Peter on a manor purchased by him after he became a judge.   He was buried in the church of Tilston, the parish in which the manor is situate.[6]

He was thrice married.   His first wife was Margaret, daughter and sole heir of George Barlow of Dronfield-Woodhouse in Derbyshire ; his second was Elizabeth, daughter and coheir of Sir Thomas Butler of Bewsey in Lancashire ; and his third was Alice, daughter and coheir of Sir Peter Warburton of Arley Hall.   By the first only he had issue. His son John died in infancy, and his only surviving daughter, Elizabeth, inherited all his rich possessions.   She married Sir Thomas Stanley of Wever and Alderley, knight, who had a son by her created a baronet in 1660, and whose lineal descendant now graces the peerage by the title of Lord Stanley of Alderley, to which he was raised in May, 1839.[7]

[1] Peck's Desid. Cur. bk. v. 1.; Egerton Papers, 192, 193.
[2] Rymer, xvi. 386.   [3] Dugdale's Chron. Ser.
[4] State Trials, i. 1334., ii. 1. 62. 159. 604.   [5] Dugdale's Orig. 48.
[6] Ormerod's Cheshire, ii. 386.   [7] MSS. Pedigree, ut supra.

Sir Thomas Butler, the grandfather of Sir Peter's second wife, had founded the Grammar School of Warrington, and settled ample endowments on it, of which it was nearly deprived by the husband of another granddaughter obtaining a grant of them as concealed lands. But by the judge's strenuous exertions they were compelled to be restored; and the school exists to this day a flourishing foundation.[1]

WESTMINSTER, Dean of.   *See* J. Williams.

WHITELOCKE, JAMES.
Just. K. B. 1624.
See under the Reign of Charles I.

WILLIAMS, DAVID.
Just. K. B. 1604.

It was not till the reign of Henry VIII. that the Welsh began to abandon the practice of changing their names at each generation. The son had previously assumed the Christian name of his father, uniting it to his own Christian name by the word "ap" (signifying "son of"); in the same manner that the word "Fitz" was used by the English in earlier times before surnames were generally introduced among them.[2] Thus the judge of whom an account is now to be given was originally called David ap William, his father's name being William ap Ychan; and it was not till he removed into England that he adopted the simpler appellation of David Williams.

The father, descended, it is said, from Bleddin ap Maenyrch, Lord of Brecknock in 1091, was a substantial yeoman, whose property was situate in the parish of Ystradvelte in that county. By his wife Margaret, daughter of Rhys Griffith

---

[1] Ex inf. W. Beamont, Esq., Warrington.   [2] See Vol. I. p. 114.

Bevan, Melin, he had three sons, the youngest of whom, this David, born about 1550, went to seek his fortune in England; stimulated, possibly, by the success of his relative, Sir John Price, who by his own merit had raised himself to the presidency of the Council of the Marches. Entering himself at the Middle Temple, he was called to the bar in 1576, and arrived at the post of reader in Lent, 1590. This honour was repeated in Lent, 1594, as a customary compliment on his taking the degree of the coif, according to his writ of summons dated in the previous November.[1] It may be presumed, from his name not occurring in any of the Reports till after he became a serjeant, that his practice was principally in the provinces. That it was considerable, may be inferred from his being appointed recorder of Brecon in 1587; and also from his acquisition of the manors of Shifford and Golofers, as well as of certain lands at Hams Court, all in the parish of Bampton, Oxfordshire; to his possession of which a spot called " Welshman's Bush " in a terrier of the year 1577, and another to this day called " Welshman's Gap," are supposed to owe their designations. He next purchased the neighbouring property of Cockthorpe; and to these he afterwards added the great estate of Guernevet, near the Hay, in his native county; and also Kingston House, Kingston-Bagpuze, in Berkshire, where he principally resided, and to the church of which the parish register records his gift of a new bell-tower.

The Reports of Coke and Croke show that he was extensively employed in the courts after his assumption of the coif; and the estimation in which his professional abilities were held appears from his being mentioned by Lord Burleigh as a proper person to fill a vacancy on the Exchequer bench. His lordship, in writing to his son Sir Robert Cecil, after suggesting the name of Serjeant Heale, adds,

[1] Dugdale's Orig. 218.; Chron. Ser.

"But if there be cause of mislike for such choice, I think Savyl or Williams may supply the place of baron, though they be men of small living;"[1] meaning, probably, men of unostentatious habits. This letter was obviously written about 1598, for Savile, the one selected out of the three named, was appointed in July of that year. Williams, however, was not forgotten, for when King James, soon after his accession, determined to add a fifth judge to each of the two superior courts, Lord Chief Justice Popham, in a letter to Lord Ellesmere, dated January 28, 1603–4, recommended four serjeants, Danyell, Williams, Tanfyld, and Altham, for the king to make choice of two. He calls them " all men lerned and of good estates," and adds, " Yf amongst the rest my brother Williams shold be allowed of by hys Matie for one, that then yt wold pleas your L. to admytt hym into the Court off hys Ma$^{ty's}$ Bench."[2] Within a week the first two were selected, and the chief justice's wish was complied with, by Williams receiving his patent as a judge of the King's Bench on February 4.[3] He was thereupon knighted. In 1608 he coincided with the majority of the judges in the decision pronounced in the case of the Post-nati[4]; but his argument is not reported. Among the Egerton Papers is a letter from Archbishop Abbott to Lord Ellesmere, dated Jannary 22, 1611–2, in which, speaking of the condemnation of Legat and Wightman for imputed heresy, he says:—
" Mr. Justice Williams was with mee the other day, who maketh no doubt but that the lawe is cleare to burne them. Hee told me also of his utter dislike of all the Lord Coke his courses;" who seems to have been of a contrary opinion.[5]

He died exactly a year after the date of this letter. In his will, which was executed a week before his death, is con-

---

[1] Jones's Brecknock, ii. 381., quoting Peck's Desid. Curiosa, p. 182.
[2] Egerton Papers, 388. [3] Dugdale. [4] State Trials, ii. 576.
[5] Egerton Papers, 447, 448.

tained the following curious legacy, which shows the friendly terms on which he lived with his brethren on the bench. "And whereas it hath been heretofore agreed between my good and kind brother Warburton and myself that the survivor of us twayne should have the other's best scarlet robes, now I do will that my said good brother Warburton shall have the choice of either of my scarlet robes, and he to take that shall best like him, praying him that as he hath been a good and kind brother unto me, so he will be a good and kind friend to my children." He likewise gives to the lord chancellor (Ellesmere) a great gilt standing cup with a cover, in token of his love and affection, and begs him to be overseer of his will.[1] A tablet in old Kingston church records that his bowels were interred there; but his body was removed for burial to the church of St. John the Evangelist at Brecon, where there is a sumptuous monument to his memory, presenting his effigy in judicial habiliments. The inscription, by himself, states that out of nine sons and two daughters only four sons and two daughters remained, and concludes with these lines:—

> "Nuper eram judex, nunc judicis ante tribunal
> Subsistens paveo; judicor ipse modo."

These children were all by his first wife, Margaret, a daughter of John Games of Aberbran in the county of Brecon, Esq., by a daughter of Sir William Vaughan of Porthaml. His second wife was Dorothy, daughter and coheiress of Oliver Wellsborn of East Hanney, Berks, Esq., and widow of John Latton of Kingston in that county, Esq., by whom he had no children. Henry, the eldest of Sir David's surviving sons, received in 1644 the dignity of baronet. He was described of Guernevet, where he entertained King Charles when he was a fugitive after the battle

---

[1] Jones's Brecknock, ii. 381.

of Naseby. This title, after being enjoyed for more than 150 years, expired in 1798, on the death of the eighth baronet.[1]

WILLIAMS, JOHN, Dean of Salisbury and Westminster, Bishop of Lincoln, Archbishop of York.

Lord Keeper, 1621.

See under the Reign of Charles I.

WINCH, HUMFREY.

Just. C. P. 1611.

Humfrey Winch was seated at Everton in the county of Bedford. He was born about 1545, and having received his legal education at Lincoln's Inn, of which he was admitted a member on July 19, 1573, and was called to the bar on November 26, 1581, became a bencher there in 1596, and Autumn reader in 1598.[2] Though he is not mentioned in the Reports till the following Michaelmas, nor frequently after that, he had apparently acquired some character as a lawyer; for he sat in the last three of Elizabeth's parliaments for the town of Bedford[3], and was invested with the degree of the coif in Trinity Term, 1606, for the purpose of taking upon him the office of chief baron of the Exchequer in Ireland, to which he was appointed on November 8. He was then knighted; and two years afterwards he succeeded Sir James Ley as lord chief justice of the King's Bench in that country, with a salary of 300l. a year. He only retained that appointment from December 8, 1608, till November 7, 1611[4], during which his character for "quickness,

---

[1] Ashmole's Berks. iii. 341.; Wotton's Baronet. ii. 404. To Benjamin Williams, Esq., F.S.A., of Cote in Oxfordshire, I am greatly indebted for his kindness in supplying many particulars in this sketch.

[2] Black Book, Linc. Inn, v. 170. 335.; Dugdale's Orig. 254. 262.

[3] O'Byrne's Represent. Hist. i. 74. [4] Smyth's Law Off. of Ireland, 88. 140.

industry, and dispatch" is recommended for imitation by Bacon, in his speech to Sir William Jones, on taking the same place.[1]   Sir Humfrey was immediately translated into England, and constituted a judge of the Common Pleas, where he sat for the next fifteen years.   In August, 1613, he was sent into Ireland with three other commissioners to examine into the complaints of the people.[2]   Three years after, he fell deservedly into some disgrace, in consequence of condemning and executing, at the Summer assizes at Leicester, no less than nine women as witches, on the evidence of a boy, who pretended that he had been bewitched and tormented by them.   The king, on a visit to the town a month after the trial, personally examining the boy, discovered and exposed the imposture ; but too late to save the unfortunate victims of this absurd superstition.[3]

He died on February 4, 1625, and was buried in the cloisters of Pembroke Hall, Cambridge.   His reports of "Choice Cases" in his own court, during two of the latter years of his life, were published in 1657 ; and Croke, his colleague on the bench, calls him a "learned and religious judge."[4]

By his wife Cecily, daughter of Richard Onslow, Esq., Recorder of London and Speaker of the House of Commons in 8 Eliz., he left, besides other issue, a son named Onslow Winch, who was sheriff of Bedfordshire in 1633 ; but his male representatives terminated with Humfrey Winch of Hawnes, in that county, who was created a baronet in 1660, and died without male issue in 1703.[5]

---

[1] Bacon's Works (Montagu), vii. 264.   [2] Pell Records, Jac; I. 169.
[3] Borough MSS. Leicester, for extracts from which I am indebted to the kindness of William Kelly, Esq.
[4] Croke, Jac. 700.   [5] Collins's Peerage, v. 466.; Wotton's Baronet. iv. 475.

YELVERTON, CHRISTOPHER.

Just. K. B. 1603.

See under the Reign of Elizabeth.

In direct descent from Sir William Yelverton, the judge of the King's Bench in the reigns of Henry VI. and Edward IV., came, with four generations between them, William Yelverton, who still enjoyed the same property in Norfolk, and pursued the same profession.   He held the office of reader in Gray's Inn in Lent, 1535, and Lent, 1542 [1]; and it was probably he whose name appears in the debates in the parliaments of 1571 and 1572.[2]   He died in 1585, leaving, by his marriage with Anne, daughter and heir of Sir Henry Fermor of East Barsham in Norfolk, a large family.   Henry, his eldest son, succeeded to the estates, and was father to Sir William, who obtained a baronetcy (of Rougham) in 1620, which expired on the death of his son in 1649.   The third son, Christopher, arrived at the same judicial distinction as his ancestor, and is the subject of the present sketch.[3]

Entering himself in 1552 at Gray's Inn, the inn of Court to which his progenitors had been attached, he relieved his legal studies there by an occasional offering to the Muses. When "Jocasta," a tragedy translated from Euripides by George Gascoigne and Francis Kynwelmersh, was performed at Gray's Inn in 1566, the Epilogue was supplied by Yelverton[4]; and he assisted in other devices and shows of the society. He became reader in Lent, 1574, and again in Lent, 1583, but in consequence of the pestilence then raging, his duties were deferred till the following year, at the end of which he was re-elected treasurer, having before held that office in 1573. In Trinity Term, 1589, he was called to the degree of the coif; and Dugdale gives two dates for his appointment as

---

[1] Dugdale's Orig. 293.
[3] Collins's Peerage, vi. 693.

[2] Parl. Hist. i. 747. 762. 779.
[4] Wood's Athen. Oxon. i. 436.

queen's serjeant, May 10, 1589, and May 11, 1598 [1], the latter being obviously the correct one; as he was first recommended for the place by Lord Burleigh in February, 1594–5.[2]

In the parliament of October, 1597, he was elected speaker on the nomination of the court. His disabling speech on that occasion gives so minute a description of his person and position, that part of it is worth extracting :—

" Whence your unexpected choice of me to be your mouth or speaker should proceed, I am utterly ignorant. If from my merits, strange it were that so few deserts should purchase, suddenly, so great an honour. Nor from my ability doth this your choice proceed; for well known it is to a great number in this place now assembled, that my estate is nothing correspondent for the maintenance of this dignity : for my father, dying, left me a younger brother, and nothing to me but my bare annuity. Then growing to man's estate and some small practice of the law, I took a wife, by whom I had many children, the keeping of us all being a great impoverishment to my estate, and the daily living of us all nothing but my daily industry. Neither from my person nor nature doth this choice arise; for he that supplieth this place ought to be a man big and comely, stately and well spoken, his voice great, his courage majestical, his nature haughty, and his purse plentiful and heavy: but contrarily, the stature of my body is small, myself not so well spoken, my voice low, my carriage lawyer-like and of the common fashion, my nature soft and bashful, my purse thin, light, and never yet plentiful. . . . . But if this cannot move your sudden choice, yet let this one thing persuade you, that myself not being gracious in the eye of her Majesty, neither ever yet in account with any great personages, shall deceive your expectation." The prayer which, according to the custom of those times, he composed and read

---

[1] Dugdale's Orig. 295. 298. Chron. Ser.   [2] Peck's Desid. Cur. b. v. 6.

to the house every morning, has much devotional beauty. In this parliament, which was dissolved in the following February, it is observable that the queen " refused or quashed forty-eight several bills which had passed both houses."[1] The allusion to his "not being gracious in the eye of her Majesty," probably refers to an old complaint mentioned in a letter from Sir Walter Mildmay to Sir Christopher Hatton in 1582, wherein he says that Yelverton " doth assure me that he is utterly guiltless of any of those matters whereof her Majesty hath been informed against him, and doubteth not fully to satisfy you when it shall like you to hear him, which my request to you is that you will vouchsafe to do; for it will be grievous unto him that her Highness should retain any such opinion of him, whereof he hath given no just cause."[2] However this may be, his conduct in the house seems to have removed the evil eye, his promotion to be queen's serjeant having taken place three months after the dissolution. In this character he opened the indictments against the Earl of Essex and the other conspirators in 1600, but the principal duty of urging the evidence fell on Coke and Fleming, the attorney and solicitor-general.[3]

Lord Burleigh thought very highly of him, and soon after his appointment as queen's serjeant, named him as most eligible for " learning and auncienty " to fill a vacancy in the Common Pleas; yet considered that he would do the queen more service by continuing queen's serjeant, than by being made a justice.[4] He was not then selected; but four years later, on February 2, 1602, he was nominated a judge of the King's Bench. On the accession of James I. in the following year, his patent was renewed, and he received the honour of knighthood. It fell to his lot to pronounce sentence of death upon Robert Creighton, Lord Sanquire, for procuring the murder

[1] Parl. Hist. i. 897. 905.   [2] Nicolas's Hatton, 248.
[3] State Trials, i. 1336. 1419.   [4] Peck's Desid. Cur. b. v. 24.

of Robert Turner, a fencing màster, who had by mischance struck out his eye while playing with the foils.[1]

Sir Christopher died in November, 1612, at Easton Mauduit, an estate he had purchased in Northamptonshire, which has remained the seat of his family up to the present time. About two years before his decease, Robert Cecil, Earl of Salisbury, gave this character of him to his son Henry: " He is a gentleman, a learned man, and a lawyer; one that will deliver his mind with perspicuous reason and great comeliness."[2]

His wife Margaret, daughter of Thomas Catesby of Ecton and Whiston in Northamptonshire, Esq., brought him two sons and four daughters.   Of his two sons, Henry and Christopher, the former became a judge of the Common Pleas, and will be the subject of an article in the next reign.

YORK, ARCHBISHOP OF.   *See* J. WILLIAMS.

[1] State Trials, ii. 752.   [2] Archæologia, xv. 52.

CHARLES I.

Reigned 23 years, 10 months, and 3 days; from March 27, 1625, to January 30, 1649.

SURVEY OF THE REIGN.

Such was the nominal length of Charles's reign: but he had substantially lost all regal power from August 22, 1642, when he set up his standard at Nottingham in opposition to the parliament; although in the various acts of government and the appointments of officers his name continued to be used. The parliamentary grant of the Marquis of Worcester's lands to Cromwell on April 24, 1648, purports to be from King Charles.[1]

One of the primary causes of the great rebellion, that overthrew the government and that cost the king his head, was the degradation of the bench of justice. The arbitrary principles prevalent in the last reign had by degrees been exercised over the judges, who, some from fear, some from subserviency, and some from honest though mistaken conviction, had gradually become more anxious to support the royal prerogative than to preserve the people's rights. When the encroachments of the crown increased and became oppressive; when the people were subjected to impositions without parliamentary authority, and their representatives were imprisoned for expressing their grievances; above all, when the courts of justice refused their customary aid, and timorously denied them relief; when they found, in addition,

[1] Archæologia, xxix. 383.

that the venerable men who ventured to speak for them were displaced from their seats, and their most time-serving oppressors appointed to fill them; when, in short, they had lost all confidence in that solemn judicature which they had been taught to depend on and venerate, the people might well despair; and no one can wonder at any attempt they might make to extricate themselves from their bondage, though all must regret the lengths to which they were carried in their efforts to procure their liberation.

The disgraceful trading in ministerial and judicial offices which prevailed in the last reign was continued in this. In the Chancery they were notorious objects of traffic. Archbishop Laud, when consulted by Sir Charles Cæsar about the vacancy in the mastership of the Rolls, plainly told him "that as things then stood, the place was not like to go without more money than he thought any wise man would give for it."[1] Sir Charles, notwithstanding this caution, appears to have given 15,000l., with a supplemental loan of 2000l. to the king. On Sir Charles's death, Dr. Buck offered a good sum for the office, and actually paid 3000l. in advance; but the king returned the money, having resolved to keep a promise he had made to Sir John Colepeper.[2] Nor were the common law judges exempt from the same imputation. Chief Justice Richardson was said to have given 17,000l. for his place[3]; and, according to Sir James Whitelocke's diary, Justice Vernon "dedit aurum" for his promotion.[4] The shameful practice was no doubt general, though many instances remain unrecorded, the details being as discreditable to the giver as to the receiver, to the tempted as to the tempter. One inevitable consequence of this was, that men were afraid of losing the places they had paid for; and another, that the public, to whom the corruption of some was known, attri-

---

[1] State Trials, iv. 417.
[2] Life of Clarendon, i. 170.
[3] Walter Yonge's Diary, 97.
[4] Bacon's Works (Montagu), xvi. ccciv.

buted it to all, and distrusted the motives of an adverse judgment, though that judgment might be rightly pronounced.

So strong was the general feeling that bribery exercised an influence in the courts, that it even found vent from the pulpit, and the judges were sometimes compelled to listen to charges against their order. At Thetford assizes, in March, 1630, Mr. Ramsey, the preacher, touched pithily on the corruption of judges " favouring of causes," and of counsellors " taking fees to be silent;" and at Bury assizes, in the summer of 1631, " one Mr. Scott made a sore sermon in discovery of corruption in judges and others." At Norwich, also, " Mr. Greene was more plaine, insomuch that Judge Harvy, in his charge, broke out thus: ' It seems by the sermon that we are corrupt, but know that we can use conscience in our places, as well as the best clergie man of all.' " [1]

Sometimes, however, the judges would resist interference, and refuse obedience to unconstitutional commands. A clergyman, named Huntley, in 1630 had brought an action in the King's Bench against some of the members of the High Commission Court for false imprisonment. Archbishop Laud endeavoured to stop the proceedings, and induced the king to interpose his authority. The judges " stoutly answered that they could not, without breach of their oaths, perform that command," insisting " that it was against law to exempt any man from answering the action of another that would sue him:" and their honest argument prevailed.[2] Hyde, Jones, Whitelocke, and Croke then formed the court.

This High Commission Court, which had exercised unlimited authority in all ecclesiastical matters, was suppressed by act of parliament in July, 1641; and at the same time the people were relieved from the oppression of the Star Chamber.[3] Another grievance which occasioned much com-

---

[1] Diary of John Rous, 50. 62.   [2] Whitelocke, 15.   [3] Whitelocke, 46.

plaint, the Court of Wards and Liveries, was abolished in 1646; and that petty cause of annoyance, the Court of Requests, a minor Court of Chancery, was generally supposed to be put an end to by statute 16 Car. I., c. 10 (1640); but there is a volume of its decrees extending to the eighteenth year, 1642.[1] To these legislative benefits of this reign may be added the Petition of Right, a new Magna Charta, in 1628; and the judicial declaration of all the judges that the punishment by torture is illegal.[2] It has been generally supposed that up to the end of 1640 the judges were always appointed "durante bene placito;" but several instances occur previously of their patents being "quamdiu se bene gesserit." It is sufficient to mention the late one of Chief Baron Walter, whose elevation to the bench in 1625 was in that form, and who refused to be dismissed in 1630 without a scire facias "whether he did bene se gerere or not."[3] From January, 1641, however, that improvement has been universally adopted.

Another inconvenience, arising from the commencement of Michaelmas Term so soon after the feast of St. Michael, was remedied by a statute passed in 1640, 16 Car. I., c. 6, whereby its first two returns were cut off; the effect of which was, that the first day of full Term was put forward from October 9 to October 23.

The title of lord chancellor was not used during this reign. The Great Seal was held with that of lord keeper only; of whom the king appointed five; one being an ecclesiastic—the last that ever filled the office—and the other four lawyers.

---

[1] 12 Report Pub. Rec. 8. 9.   [2] Rushworth, i. 638.
[3] Whitelocke, 11. 16.

LORD KEEPERS.

JOHN WILLIAMS, BISHOP OF LINCOLN, retained his place as lord keeper for exactly seven months after Charles's accession. He was then removed, and the Seal was given to

SIR THOMAS COVENTRY, the attorney-general, on November 1, 1625. He retained it till the day of his death; having been created Lord Coventry on April 10, 1628.

SIR JOHN FINCH, chief justice of the Common Pleas, succeeded him as lord keeper, on January 17, 1640; and on April 7, was created Lord Finch of Fordwich. He held the Seal only eleven months and a few days, flying the country on December 21, to avoid the impeachment of the Commons. '

SIR EDWARD LYTTELTON, chief justice of the Common Pleas, received the Great Seal on January 23rd, 1641; and on February 18, was raised to the peerage by the title of Lord Lyttelton of Mounslow. He joined the king at York, on the breaking out of the civil war, and though a new Great Seal was ordered, and Commissioners for its custody were appointed, by the parliament, he retained the title of lord keeper till his death; when

SIR RICHARD LANE, lord chief baron of the Exchequer, on August 30, 1645, succeeded him with the same title, which he held at the king's decapitation on January 30, 1648–9.

When Lord Lyttelton took the Great Seal to the king at York in May, 1642, the parliament were much puzzled how to act. They had so much respect for that emblem of authority that they for some time took no decided step to provide a substitute: but in about a year the House of Commons, by only a slender majority, passed a resolution "That a Great Seal of England shall be forthwith made to attend the parliament for dispatch of the affairs of the parliament and kingdom." The Lords not agreeing with this resolution, the Commons on July 5, 1643, voted " That a Great Seal be presently made," and that Mr. Simonds have 100*l.* for his pains in making it. After four months' delay, an ordinance was agreed to by both houses on November 16, 1643, invalidating all acts done under the Great Seal since May 22, 1642, and all acts that should thereafter be done; and ordaining that the Great Seal of England already provided by the Lords and Commons should be forthwith put in use; and that it should be placed in the custody of the following commissioners, members of the two houses: —

HENRY GREY, EARL OF KENT[1], and OLIVER ST. JOHN, EARL OF BOLINBROKE, Peers; OLIVER ST. JOHN, solicitor-general; JOHN WILDE, serjeant-at-law; SAMUEL BROWNE, esq.; and EDMUND PRIDEAUX, esq., Commoners; or any two of them, one being a member of one house, and one of the other. These commissioners were accordingly sworn, and among other oaths, took, somewhat curiously, those of allegiance and supremacy.

WILLIAM CECIL, EARL OF SALISBURY, was on July 3, 1646, made a commissioner in the place of the Earl of Bolinbroke, deceased.

In the following October, in consequence of a vote of the House of Lords that there should be three commissioners who were not members of either house of parliament, the above-mentioned commissioners received thanks, and (except the Earl of Salisbury) 1000*l.* each, for their faithful services; and it was ordered that as a mark of honour, those commissioners who were members of the House of Commons should practice within the bar, and have precedence next after the solicitor-general.

But the lords and commons could not agree as to the number, names, or duties of the future commissioners; till at

---

[1] The Earl of Kent was substituted for the Earl of Rutland, who was first appointed, but who desired to be excused.

last, on October 30, 1646, they concurred in appointing the speakers of both houses, viz. : —

EDWARD MONTAGU, EARL OF MANCHESTER, and WILLIAM LENTHALL, Esq., Master of the Rolls; limiting their power to twenty days after the end of Michaelmas term. This period was from time to time extended till March 15, 1648, when

HENRY GREY, EARL OF KENT; WILLIAM GREY, LORD GREY DE WERKE; SIR THOMAS WIDDRINGTON, M. P.; and BULSTRODE WHITELOCKE, Esq , M.P. were nominated commissioners, with a salary of 1000*l.* a year each.[1] They remained in office till the king's death.

On the day of Lord Coventry's appointment a commission was issued to all the puisne judges, and to all the masters in chancery, to assist him in hearing causes: so that he could call in the aid of any of them in case of necessity.[2] His lordship's allowances were the same in amount as those mentioned in the last reign.[3]

The allowance to Sir Richard Lane, when he was appointed at Oxford, was 23*s.* per diem for his diet ; 26*l.* 13*s.* 4*d.* per annum for a winter livery, and 13*l.* 6*s.* 4*d.* for a summer livery; and 300*l.* per annum pension out of the Hanaper; together with all other fines, fees, and allowances belonging to the office.[4] The fee to each commissioner under the parliament was 1000*l.* a year.

On the surrender of the city of Oxford in ·June, 1646, the king's Great Seal and the seals of the several courts were delivered up to the parliament. They were immediately ordered to be defaced and broken, and the pieces

---

[1] Journals of Lords and Commons. Votes were passed in one or other of the Houses for the following gentlemen to be commissioners, but not agreed upon : Mr. Serjeant Bramston, Sir Nathaniel Brent, Mr. Serjeant Greene, Mr. Serjeant Turner, Sir Rowland Wandesford, Sir Thomas Bedingfield, Mr. John Bradshaw, Challenor Chute, esq.

[2] Rymer, xviii. 219.   [3] Ibid. 220.   *See* ant*è*, p. 5.

[4] Docquets, &c. at Oxford.

given to the speakers of the two houses.[1]　The parliament's new Seal, which had been ordered to be made in July, 1643, and had been used by them since November in that year, and which nothing differed from the king's, now continued in undivided operation till January, 1649.

MASTERS OF THE ROLLS.

SIR JULIUS CÆSAR, who had been master of the Rolls for nearly eleven years under King James, retained the office for eleven more under King Charles.　In April, 1629, the reversion of it was granted to Sir Humphrey May; but he died without coming into possession in June in the next year. Sir Julius survived him till April 18, 1636, when

SIR DUDLEY DIGGES, to whom, on the death of Sir Humphrey May, it had also been granted in reversion, entered on the offiee, and held it for about three years.　At his death

SIR CHARLES CÆSAR, one of the masters in Chancery, was placed in the office on March 30, 1639, but enjoyed it but for a short time, dying of the small-pox on December 6, 1642; when the king appointed

SIR JOHN COLEPEPER, the chancellor of the Exchequer, on January 30, 1643.　He was created Lord Colepeper on October 14, 1644, and nominally held the office at the death of the king on January 29, 1649.

On the death of Sir Charles Cæsar, the Commons ordered the rents and profits of the office to be sequestered for the service of the parliament; and one of the first instruments to which the parliamentary Great Seal was attached was a patent dated November 22, 1643, granting the offiee to

WILLIAM LENTHALL, Esq., speaker of the House of Commons; so that for the rest of the reign there were two masters of the Rolls—one appointed by the king, and one by the parliament.

---

[1] Whitelocke, 210. 219.

Masters in Chancery.

Sir Julius Cæsar, M. R. - - -	- 1 to 12	Car. I.
Francis James, LL.D. - - - -	- 1	—
Sir Charles Cæsar, LL.D., afterwards M. R. -	- 1 to 18	—
Richard More - - - -	- 1 to 11	—
Sir John Hayward, LL.D. - -	- 1 to 3	—
Ewball Thelwall - - - -	- 1 to 6	—
Robert Rich - - - -	- 1 to 22	—
John Michell - - - -	- 1 to 20	—
Sir Edward Salter - - -	- 1 to 18	—
Edward Leech - - - -	- 1 to 24	—
Sir Peter Mutton - - -	- 1 to 13	—
Edward Clarke - - - -	- 1 to 14	—
Thomas Eden, LL.D. - - -	- 1 to 16	—
John Page - - - -	- 3 to 24	—
Sir Dudley Digges, afterwards M. R. - -	- 6 to 13	—
Sir Thomas Bennett, LL.D. - -	- 11 to 24	—
William Griffith, LL.D. - -	- 12 to 17	—
Robert Aylett, LL.D. - -	- 13 to 24	—
William Child - - -	- 14 to 24	—
James Littelton - - -	- 15 to 20	—
Thomas Heath, LL.D. - -	- 16 to 21	—
Sir Justinian Lewen, LL.D. - -	- 17 to 24	—
Sir Thomas Colepeper, afterwards Lord Colepeper, M.R.	18 to 24	—
William Lenthall, M. R. - -	- 19 to 24	—
Sir Thomas Mainwaring - -	- 19 to 23	—
John Sadler - - -	- 20 to 24	—
Arthur Duck, LL.D. - -	- 21 to 24	—
Edward Rich - - -	- 21 to 24	—
William Hakewell - -	- 22 to 24	—
Edward Eltonhead - -	- 23 to 24	—

The judges suffered with the rest of the kingdom from the violence resulting from the extreme opinions of the opposing parties. Their removal from the bench was frequent; — by the king during the first ten years of the reign, and by the parliament afterwards. Lord Keeper Williams was an early sacrifice to the cabals of the Duke of Buckingham and his friends, joined to the dislike of the king to receive unwelcome advice. Lord Chief Justice Crewe was dismissed in 1626 for not acknowledging the lawfulness of forced loans. In 1630 Chief Baron Walter was suspended for doubting the legality of proceeding against members of parliament for acts done in the house. The removal of Sir Robert Heath in 1634 was caused either by his discouragement of ship-money, or by his resistance to Archbishop Laud. All these examples arose from supposed·non-compliance with the king's will; others suffered for supporting what he claimed as his prerogative. Lord Keeper Finch, Chief Justice Bramston, Chief Baron Davenport, Justices Berkeley and Crawley, and Barons Weston and Trevor, were impeached by the parliament in 1640 for their opinions in favour of ship-money; Justices Jones and Vernon only escaping the same ordeal by dying before the parliament acted. Chief Justice Banks and Justices Foster and Malet also got into disgrace for their steady adherence to their royal master, and were likewise impeached. The former died, and the two latter were declared to be disabled as if they were dead. The king had hitherto preserved his prerogative of appointing the judges, and had exercised it for the last time on January 31, 1644; but his authority being then entirely set aside, and the twelve judges having by the above impeachments and other casualties been reduced to four, the parliament from thenceforth took upon themselves to supply the vacancies; the Oxford parliament of course declaring that those who acted on these nominations, and all lawyers pleading before them, were guilty of high treason.

These various changes often led to great inconvenience, and obliged the parliament itself to resort to extraordinary measures to preserve the regular administration of justice. In October, 1642, all the judges of the King's Bench being either with the king at Oxford or imprisoned in the Tower, except Judge Berkeley, who had been impeached in the previous year, and arrested while sitting on the bench, an ordinance was passed notwithstanding, resolving that "having carried himself with modesty and humility, and inoffensively to both houses," he should keep the essoigns of Michaelmas term. Another of the impeached judges, Baron Trevor, was allowed on payment of a fine to make his peace, and to resume his judicial functions till the king's death. He was for some time the only baron in the Exchequer; and on September 29, 1645, being too ill to attend the court, and the Cursitor Baron Leeke having joined the king, the parliament was obliged to name another, in order that the form should be preserved of presenting the sheriffs of London, &c., on the next day, which " for the space of three or four hundred years had never been · omitted ;" and Richard Tomlins was accordingly appointed cursitor baron.[1] From Michaelmas, 1645, to the end of the reign two judges only sat in each court.

The suitors also had great reason to complain on account of the frequent adjournment of the terms and the irregular sittings of the courts. In the early part of the reign several adjournments took place on account of the plague which visited the kingdom. In 1625, both Trinity and Michaelmas terms were adjourned, and the latter was ordered to be held at Reading. Michaelmas, 1630, and Trinity and Michaelmas, 1636, were obliged for the same cause to be partially delayed.[2] These could not be avoided; but during the parliamentary conflict other adjournments were attempted under different circumstances. In 1642, the king adjourned Easter and Michaelmas terms from London to York, which the parliament voted to be illegal. In 1643, though the two houses had adjourned Trinity term, they commanded the judges not to adjourn Michaelmas term by colour of any writs from Oxford; and in Hilary, 1644, they ordered that any person delivering such writs " should be proceeded against as spies, according to Marshal law." The same order was re-

---

[1] Lords' and Commons' Journals ; Clarendon, iv. 287.

[2] Rymer, xviii. 116. 184. 206., xix. 192., xx. 20. 23. 71.

peated in the following terms ; and that this was not an idle
threat was sufficiently proved by their actually executing one
of the unfortunate messengers who delivered the writs to
Justice Reeve and Baron Trevor.   Hilary term, 1649, was
adjourned till after the king's trial.[1]

In August, 1643, Whitelocke states that " the courts were
not yet open, no practice for lawyers ;" and on December 12
of the same year, when the new commissioners had been
sworn in, they sealed above 500 writs, " so desirous were
people to have the course of Justice to proceed."   Again,
while the two houses were disputing in October, 1646, into
whose hands the Great Seal should be entrusted, there were
no less than 8000 writs ready to be sealed.[2]

The parliament, on account of " the present distractions,"
forbade the judges to go the usual circuits in Lent, 1643 ;
but afterwards, the assizes were held with tolerable regularity,
according to the position of the respective armies.   The people,
however, were sometimes unwilling or afraid to appear.
Whitelocke relates that at Hereford, in August, 1647, " the
People came not in, so that there was little to do either for
Judges or Lawyers ;" and in August, 1648, the judges were
desired to " avoid going to any place where they shall appre-
hend to be any danger ;" and the judges were to go the
northern circuit " if they please."[3]

The salary of the parliamentary judges was fixed at 1000l.
a year in lieu of all former fees and profits, to be paid out of
the receipts of the Customs ; but it was frequently allowed
to get in arrear, so that there was a peremptory order of the
parliament on December 19, 1648, for the immediate discharge of all that was due, and the punctual payment in
future.[4]

---

[1] Whitelocke, 59. 62. 78. 80. 87. 370. : Journals ; Clarendon, iv. 342.
[2] Whitelocke, 71. 79.   [3] Ibid. 265. 329. 332. ; Clarendon, iii. 536.
[4] Whitelocke, 174. ; Journals.

Chief Justices of the King's Bench.

Sir Ranulphe Crewe, who had held the office only two months in James's reign, was re-appointed in this; but not pleasing the governing powers, was removed on November 9, 1626, and was succeeded by

Sir Nicholas Hyde, a practising barrister, on February 5, 1627. On his death,

Sir Thomas Richardson, Chief Justice of the Common Pleas, was 'on October 24, 1631, removed into this court; over which he presided till his death on February 4, 1635.

Sir John Bramston, king's serjeant, was called to supply his place on April 14, 1635; but had a patent of revocation on October 10, 1642; when

Sir Robert Heath, formerly chief justice of the Common Pleas, but since a judge of the King's Bench, was appointed by the king. The parliament, by an ordinance on November 25, 1645, voted him disabled " as though he were dead;" and he fled to France to avoid their impeachment.

The place was not filled up till little more than three months before the decapitation of the king, when the parliament appointed

Henry Rolle, already a parliamentary judge of the King's Bench, chief justice of that court, on October 12, 1648.

Justices of the King's Bench.

I.	1625.	March.	John Doderidge, ⎫ The judges at the end
			William Jones, ⎬ of James's reign were
			James Whitelocke,⎭ continued by Charles.
IV.	1628.	Oct. 28.	George Croke, vice Doderidge.
VIII.	1632.	Oct. 11.	Robert Berkeley, vice Whitelocke.
XVI.	1641.	Jan. 23.	Robert Heath, vice W. Jones.
XVII.		July 1.	Thomas Malet, vice G. Croke.

XVIII. 1642. Oct. 14.   Francis Bacon, vice R. Heath.
  XIX. 1644. Jan. 31.   Robert Brerewood, vice R. Berkeley.
                          Chief Justice Heath and Justice Malet being
                          disabled by a vote of parliament, the only judges of
                          this court remaining were Sir Francis Bacon, who
                          acted till the end of the reign, and Sir Robert Brere-
                          wood, who was appointed at Oxford, and never
                          appeared in Westminster Hall.
  XXI. 1645. Sept. 30.   Henry Rolle,   ⎫ Appointed by the Parlia-
XXIV. 1648. Oct. 12.   Samuel Browne,   ⎬   ment.
                          Philip Jermyn,   ⎭
              The judges of this court at the king's death were,
                          Henry Rolle, chief justice,
              Francis Bacon,   Samuel Browne,
                          Philip Jermyn.

CHIEF JUSTICES OF THE COMMON PLEAS.

SIR HENRY HOBART, who had been chief justice nearly twelve years, had his patent renewed, and kept his seat till his death on December 26, 1625. The vacancy was not filled up for eleven months, when

SIR THOMAS RICHARDSON, king's serjeant, received the appointment on November 28, 1626; and, being removed to the King's Bench on October 24, 1631, was, two days after, succeeded by

SIR ROBERT HEATH, the attorney-general, who in about three years was suddenly removed from his place, which was given to

SIR JOHN FINCH, the queen's attorney-general, on October 14, 1634. He became lord keeper in January 17, 1640, and

SIR EDWARD LYTTELTON, the king's solicitor-general, received his patent for the place on January 27, 1640. On his promotion at the beginning of the next year to be lord keeper,

SIR JOHN BANKS, the attorney-general, was made chief

justice on January 26, 1641. He died on December 28, 1644; after which the king did not fill up the place, which remained vacant nearly four years. The parliament then appointed

OLIVER ST. JOHN, the parliamentary solicitor-general, chief justice of the Common Pleas, on October 12, 1648.

JUSTICES OF THE COMMON PLEAS.

I.	1625.	March.	Richard Hutton, George Croke, Francis Harvey, } Kept their seats on the Bench.
			Thomas Chamberlayne, (?) for a temporary object.
		May 10.	Henry Yelverton, as a fifth judge; which was not continued after Judge Croke's removal to the King's Bench in 1628.
VI.	1630.	Feb. 2.	Humphrey Davenport, vice H. Yelverton.
VII.	1631.	May 8.	George Vernon, vice H. Davenport.
VIII.	1632.	Oct. 11.	Francis Crawley, vice F. Harvey.
XIV.	1639.	March 24.	Edmund Reeve, vice R. Hutton.
XV.	1640.	Jan. 27.	Robert Foster, vice G. Vernon.
			A vote of parliament having disabled Justices Crawley and Foster, and Chief Justice Banks being dead, the only judge of the court was Mr. Justice Reeve.
XXI.	1645.	Sept. 30.	Peter Pheasant,
XXIII.	1647.	April 30.	John Godbolt, } Appointed by the parliament.
XXIV.	1648.	Oct. 12.	Thomas Bedingfield, Richard Cresheld,

At the death of the king the judges of this court were
Oliver St. John, chief justice,
Peter Pheasant,   Thomas Bedingfield,
Richard Cresheld.

CHIEF BARONS OF THE EXCHEQUER.

SIR LAURENCE TANFIELD, having served for eighteen years under James, was re-appointed at the beginning of this reign; but died in little more than a month.

SIR JOHN WALTER, one of the king's serjeants, was then made chief baron, May 10, 1625. Though suspended from sitting in court, he retained his place till his death on November 18, 1630; soon after which,

SIR HUMPHREY DAVENPORT, from being a judge of the Common Pleas, was raised to the office of chief baron on January 10, 1631. At his death,

SIR RICHARD LANE, attorney-general to the Prince of Wales, was appointed on January 25, 1644; and, though he became lord keeper on August 30, in the following year, his place of chief baron was not filled by King Charles during the unfortunate remainder of his reign. After being vacant for nearly five years,

JOHN WILDE, serjeant-at-law, and late one of the commissioners of the Great Seal, was appointed by the parliament lord chief baron on October 12, 1648.

BARONS OF THE EXCHEQUER.

I.	1625.	March.	Edward Bromley, ⎱ Had their Patents renewed.
			John Denham, ⎰
			John Sotherton, ? cursitor.
		May 10.	Thomas Trevor, vice G. Snigge, who died in the last reign.
III.	1627.	July 4.	George Vernon, vice E. Bromley.
VII.	1631.	May 16.	James Weston, vice G. Vernon.
		Oct. 24.	James Paget, ? cursitor, vice J. Sotherton.
X.	1634.	April 30.	Richard Weston, vice J. Weston.
XIV.	1638.	Oct. 29.	John or William Page, ? cursitor, vice J. Paget.
XV.	1639.	Jan. 22.	Edward Henden, vice J. Denham.
XVIII.	1642.	Nov. 25.	Thomas Leeke, cursitor, vice J. or W. Page.

Chief Baron Sir Richard Lane having been promoted to the office of lord keeper, Sir Richard Weston being disabled by an order of parliament, and Sir Edward Henden being dead, Sir Thomas Trevor was now the only baron remaining in the court, besides Cursitor Baron Leeke.

XXI. 1645. Sept. 29. Richard Tomlins, cursitor, ⎫
　　　　　　Sept. 30. Edward Atkyns, 　　　　　　⎬ Appointed by
XXIV. 1648. Oct. 12. Thomas Gates, 　　　　　　⎭ the parliament.

The following were barons on Charles's death : —
John Wilde, chief Baron,

Thomas Trevor,　　　　Thomas Gates,
Edward Atkyns,　　　　Richard Tomlins, cursitor.

TABLE OF THE LORD KEEPERS, &C., OF THE SEAL, AND
MASTERS OF THE ROLLS.

A. R.	A. D.	LORD KEEPERS.	MASTERS OF THE ROLLS.
1	1625, Mar. 27	John Williams, Bishop of Lincoln	Sir Julius Cæsar.
	Nov. 1	Sir Thomas Coventry	—
4	1628, April 10	*Cr.* Lord Coventry	
12	1636, April 18	—	Sir Dudley Digges.
15	1639, Mar. 30	—	Sir Charles Cæsar.
16	1640, Jan. 17	Sir John Finch	—
	April 17	*Cr.* Lord Finch	—
17	1641, Jan. 23	Sir Edward Lyttelton	—
	Feb. 18	*Cr.* Lord Lyttelton	—
19	1643, Jan. 30	—	Sir John Colepeper.
20	1644, Oct. 14	—	*Cr.* Lord Colepeper.
21	1645, Aug. 30	Sir Richard Lane	—
19	1643, Nov. 10	Henry Grey, Earl of Kent ⎫ Oliver St. John, Earl of Bolinbroke ⎪ Oliver St. John ⎬ *Parl. Commrs.* John Wilde ⎪ Samuel Browne ⎪ Edmund Prideaux ⎭	William Lenthall, Parl. M. R.
22	1646, July 3	William Cecil, Earl of Salisbury, vice Earl of Bolinbroke	
	Oct. 30	Edward Montagu, Earl of Manchester ⎫ *Parl.* William Lenthall, ⎬ *Commrs.* M. R. ⎭	—
24	1648, Mar. 15	Henry Grey, Earl of Kent ⎫ William Grey, Lord Grey de Werke ⎬ *Parl.* Sir Thomas Widdrington ⎪ *Commrs.* Bulstrode Whitelocke ⎭	

TABLE OF THE CHIEF JUSTICES AND JUDGES OF THE KING'S BENCH.

A.R.	A.D.	CHIEF JUSTICES.	JUDGES OF THE KING'S BENCH.		
1	1 65, Mar. 27	Ranulphe Crewe	John Doderidge	William Jones	James Whitelocke.
2	1626, Nov. 9	removed	—	—	—
3	1627, Feb. 5	Nicholas Hyde		—	—
4	1628, 28	—	George Croke	—	—
7	1631, Oct. 24	Thomas Richardson	—	—	Robert Berkeley.
8	1632, Oct. 11	—	—	Robert Heath	—
11	1634, April 14	John Bramston	—		—
16	1641, Jan. 23	—	Thomas Malet	made Ch. K. B.	—
17	July 1	—	—	Francis Bacon	—
18	1642,	Robert Heath	—	—	Robert Brerewood.
	14	—	—	—	—
19	1644, Jan. 31	—	—		
21	1645, Nov. 24	disabled	disabled		
24	Sept. 30	Henry Rolle	Henry Rolle	—	Philip Jermyn.
	1648, Oct. 12	Henry Rolle	Samuel Browne		

TABLE OF THE CHIEF JUSTICES AND JUDGES OF THE COMMON PLEAS.

A. R.	A. D.	CHIEF JUSTICES.	JUDGES OF THE COMMON PLEAS.			
1	1625, March 27	Henry Hobart	Richard Hutton	George Croke	Francis Harvey	? Thomas Chamberlayne.
	May 10	—	—	—	—	Henry Yelverton.
	Dec. 26	died	—	—	—	—
2	1626, Nov. 28	Thomas Richardson	—	made K. B.	—	—
4	1628, Oct. 28	—	—		—	Humphrey Davenport.
5	1630, Feb. 2	—	—		—	George Vernon.
7	1631, May 8	—	—		—	—
	Oct. 26	Robert Heath	—		Francis Crawley	—
8	1632, O. 11	—	—		—	—
10	1634, O. 14	—	—		—	Robert Foster.
14	1639, Mch 24	John Finch	Edmund Reeve		—	—
15	1640, Jan. 27	Lrd Lyttelton	—		—	—
16	1641, Jan. 29	John Banks	—		disabled	disabled.
20	1644, Dec. 28	died	—			
21	1645, Nov. 24.		—			
	Sept. 30		died			
23	1647, March 27		John Godbolt		Peter Pheasant	
	April 30		died		—	
24	1648, about June	Oliver St. John	Thomas Bedingfield		—	Richard Cresheld.
	Oct. 12				—	

TABLE OF THE CHIEF BARONS AND BARONS OF THE EXCHEQUER.

A. R.	A. D.	CHIEF BARONS.	BARONS OF THE EXCHEQUER.			? CURSITOR BARONS.
1	1621, March 27	Laurence Tanfield	Edward Bromley	John Denham	Thomas Trevor	John Sotherton.
	May 10	John Walter	—	—		—
3	1627, July 4	died	George Vernon	—	—	—
6	1630, Nov. 18		—	—	—	—
7	1631, Jan. 10	Humphrey Davenport	—	—	—	—
	May 16		James Weston	—	—	James Paget.
	Oct. 24		—	—	—	—
10	1634, April 30	—	Richard Weston	—	—	John or William Page.
14	1638, Oct. 29	—	—	Edward Henden	—	—
	1639, Jan. 22	—	—	—	—	Thomas Leeke.
18	1642, Nov. 25	Richard Lane	—	—	—	—
19	1644, Jan. 25	made Lord Keeper	—	—	—	—
21	1645, Aug. 30		disabled		—	
	Nov. 24					
	Sept. 29		Edward Atkyns	Thomas Gates		Richard Tomlins.
	30					
24	1648, Oct. 12	John Wilde	—			—

In consequence of various changes which had been introduced from time to time by the judges, partly in the fashion of their robes, but principally in the times of wearing them, a solemn order was made on June 4, 1635, by the whole bench, regulating this important subject, so that there might be certainty and uniformity for the future.   From this order it appears that the judges' various dresses then consisted of black, violet, and scarlet gowns, with hoods and mantles of the same colour; the hood put over their heads, and the mantles above all, with the end of the hood hanging over behind.   The summer facing of the gowns, mantles, and hoods, was changeable taffeta, except the chiefs', which was velvet or satin; the winter facing was white furs of miniver. The summer was reckoned from Ascension Day to the Feast of St. Simon and St. Jude, October 28 ; and the winter comprehended the rest of the year.   They had for the covering of their heads velvet caps, coifs of lawn, and cornered caps.

In Term they were to sit in their black or violet gowns as they chose ; except on holy days, when they were to sit in scarlet.   So also when the Lord Mayor of London came to be sworn ; and upon the 5th of November (being Gunpowder day); also when the judges went to Westminster Abbey to hear a sermon, and after sit in court ; and when they went to St. Paul's, or any other public church in Term.   On these, and all other grand days, the chiefs were to wear their collars of SS above their mantles.

At *Nisi Prius*, in Westminster or London, they were to go in violet gowns, with scarlet casting hoods and tippets; but on holy days in scarlet.

On the circuit they were to go to church, and open the commission in scarlet, with their velvet caps or cornered caps upon their heads.   He who gave the charge and delivered the gaol was to continue the same dress during the assizes;

and he who sat at Nisi Prius commonly used the same coloured robe.

Similar directions are given for the dress at the council-table and the House of Lords, when they attended the king's majesty, or dined at a public feast. In one place the scarlet casting hood is directed to be pinned "near the left shoulder;" but in another, and seemingly in contradiction of this, the order says:—"The scarlet casting hood is to be put above the tippet on the right side, for Justice Walmesley and Justice Warburton, and all the Judges before, did wear them in that manner, and did declare, that by wearing the hood on the right side, and above the tippet, was signified more temporal dignity, and by the tippet on the left side only the Judges did resemble Priests."[1]

Ruffs continued to be worn in the beginning of Charles's reign, but soon after gave way to the falling band. The judges and the bishops were the last who laid them aside.[2] Lord Keeper Lyttelton's portrait by Van Dyck is one of the earliest of the judges represented with the falling collar, which in the Commonwealth was universally worn.

The grant to the Marshal of the Household to hold pleas for those not of the Household, by letters patent in the last days of King James's reign, was renewed "with more per-fection, as was conceived," in November, 1630; but a ques-tion arising whether the proceedings under it were good in law, the king desired the opinion of the judges, which they apparently evaded to give.[3]

ATTORNEY-GENERALS.

I. 1625. March.   Sir Thomas Coventry was continued in this
                   place by Charles I., but was raised to that
                   of lord keeper in seven months, when

---

[1] Dugdale's Orig. 101; Gent. Mag. xxxviii. 457.
[2] Granger, ii. 412.   [3] Rushworth, ii. 104.

		Oct. 31.	Sir Robert Heath, the solicitor-general, succeeded. On his appointment as lord chief justice of the King's Bench, six years after,
VII.	1631.	Oct. 27.	William Noy was made attorney-general, but dying after holding it about three years,
X.	1634.	Sept. 27.	Sir John Banks, the prince's attorney, received the office, and held it till his elevation to the Bench as chief justice of the Common Pleas, when
XVI.	1641.	Jan. 29.	Sir Edward Herbert, the solicitor-general, was appointed. He was discharged by the king, by whom
XXI.	1645.	Nov. 3.	Sir Thomas Gardner was then nominated.

For the trial of the king the parliament appointed

| XXV. | 1649. | Jan. 10. | William Steele to be attorney-general. |

SOLICITOR-GENERALS.

I.	1625.	March.	Sir Robert Heath, the solicitor-general at the death of James I., retained the office till he was advanced to that of attorney-general.
		Nov. 1.	Sir Richard Shilton or Sheldon succeeded him; and after nine years resigned, to make way for
X.	1634.	Oct. 17.	Sir Edward Littelton, who in five years was advanced to the chief justiceship of the Common Pleas.
XV.	1640.	Jan. 25.	Sir Edward Herbert, the queen's attorney, was then made solicitor, and the next year succeeded as attorney-general, when
XVI.	1641.	Jan. 29.	Oliver St. John was put into the office. The king found it necessary to remove him, and gave it to
XIX.	1643.	Oct. 30.	Sir Thomas Gardner, on whose appointment as attorney-general,
XXI.	1645.	Nov. 3.	Jeffery Palmer succeeded him.

The parliament not recognising either of the last two appointments, Oliver St. John still retained the title and performed the duties annexed to the office, till raised to that of chief justice of the Common Pleas, when the parliament made

XXIV.   1648.   Oct. 12.   Edmond Prideaux, solicitor-general; but afterwards,

       1649.   Jan. 10.   John Cook was substituted for the trial of the king.

SERJEANTS AT LAW.

The added initial marks the inn of Court to which they belonged; and those who became judges are distinguished by a *.

I.	1625-6.	* John Walter (I.),	Henry Yelverton (G.).[1]
		* Thomas Trevor (I.),	
II.	1626-7.	* Nicholas Hyde (M.).	
III.	1627-8.	Rowley Ward (M.),	Robert Callice (G.),
		* Robert Berkeley (M.),	* George Vernon (I.).[2]
		William Ayloff (L.),	
VII.	1631-2.	* James Weston (I.),	* Robert Heath (L.).[3]
IX.	1633-4.	* Richard Weston (I.).[4]	
X.	1634-5.	* John Finch (G.)[5],	Ralph Whitfield (G.).[6]
XI.	1635-6.	* Thomas Malet (M.)[7].	
XII.	1636-7.	Timothy Leving (I.),	* Edmund Reeve (G.),
		* John Wilde (I.),	* John Godbolt (G.),
		* Robert Foster (I.),	Arthur Turner (M.)
		Henry Clarke (M.),	Nathaniel Finch (G.),
		Thomas Milward (L.),	Gilbert Boone,
		* Richard Cresheld (L.),	* Philip Jermyn (M.).[8]
XIII.	1637-8.	John Glanville (L.).[9]	
XV.	1639-40.	* Edward Lyttelton (I.).	

[1] Walter and Trevor's motto was "*Regi, Legi, servire Libertas;*" Yelverton's was "*Stat lege Corona.*"

[2] Ward and Berkeley's, "*Lege Deus et Rex;*" Ayloff and Callice's, "*Regis Oracula Leges;*" and Vernon's, "*Lex Regis Regnique Patronus.*"

[3] J. Weston's, "*Servus Regi, serviens Legi;*" Heath's, "*Lex regis vis legis.*"

[4] R. Weston's, "*Rex legem, lex regem, protigit.*"

[5] J. Finch's, "*Rosæ lilia dant purpuram.*"

[6] Whitfield's, "*Religio finem Legi ponit.*"

[7] Malet's, "*Deo, Regi, Reginæ, Legi.*"

[8] The motto of these was "*Rex animat legem.*"

[9] Glanville's was "*Sol regis stirps legis virescit.*"

XVI.	1640-1.	John Stone (I.),	Richard Taylor (L.),
		John Whitwich (I.),	* Edward Atkyns (L.),
		*Henry Rolle (I.),	John Green (L.),
		William Lyttelton (M.),	*Peter Pheasant (G.),
		* Robert Brerewood (M.),	*Francis Bacon (G.),
		Robert Hyde (M.),	Sampson Evre (G.),
			* John Banks (G.).
XIX.	1643-4.	* Richard Lane (M.).	
XXIV.	1648.	* Thomas Widdrington (G.),	* John Puleston (M.),
		* Thomas Bedingfield (G.),	Thomas Chapman, (I.),
		* Richard Keeble (G.),	* Thomas Gates (I.),
		* Francis Thorpe (G.),	William Littelton (I.),
		* John Bradshaw (G.),	William Powell (L.),
		* Oliver St. John (L.),	John Clerke (L.),
		* Samuel Browne (L.),	John Eltonhead (M.),
		* John Glynne (L.),	* Robert Nicholas (I.)
		Erasmus Earle (L.),	* John Parker (G.),
		* Bulstrode Whitelocke (M.),	Robert Bernard,
		William Coniers (M.),	Robert Hutton (M.).

This call being by authority of parliament only, was subsequently declared to be invalid. The survivors were recalled at the Restoration.

KING'S SERJEANTS.

I.	1625.	* John Walter (I.),	Francis Ashley (M.),
		* Thomas Trevor (I.),	* Humphrey Davenport (G.),
		* Henry Yelverton (G.),	
II.	1627.	*Nicholas Hyde,	
III.	1627.	* Robert Berkeley (M.),	
X.	1634.	* John Bramston (M.),	
XI.	1635.	Ralph Whitfield,	
XIII.	1637.	* Robert Heath,	
XVI.	1640-1.	Nathaniel Finch,	John Glanville (L.),
		Sampson Evre (G.),	* Robert Brerewood (M.),
XIV.	1648.	Thomas Widdrington (G.),	Bulstrode Whitelocke (M.).

By an order of Privy Council of March 19, 1636, any serjeant who comes before it to move in any matter, and shall not wear his proper gown, is liable to a fine of 20s., and any counsellor at law, 10s.[1]

King Charles had only two general calls of serjeants — one in 1636, and the other in 1640. The feast of the first was in the Middle Temple hall, that of the last is not named. The other calls were principally for the purpose of qualification to the bench; and the feasts of these occasions (for that ceremony was never omitted, though the customary speeches were frequently dispensed with) were held at the hall of one of the Serjeants' Inns, either in Chancery Lane or Fleet Street.

The same order by which the twelve judges regulated the wearing of their robes contained also directions for the serjeants' dresses, describing how the lord chief justice of the King's Bench was to put on their coif and tie it under the chin, and arrange their hood on the right shoulder; and how they were always to wear their party-coloured robes during the first year, and afterwards to put on violet at Westminster when the judges sat in scarlet; and on all grand days, to wear scarlet gowns and scarlet hoods; " but no serjeants may pin their hoods, nor have used to line their gowns."

Both "Judges and Serjeants when they ride circuits are to wear a serjeant's coat of good broad cloath, with sleeves, and faced with velvet; they have used of late to face the sleeves thick with lace. And they are to have a sumpture, and ought to ride with six men at the least."[2]

At King James's funeral, the king's serjeants had precedence of the masters in Chancery.[3]

Both the Inns in Fleet Street and Chancery Lane were used

---

[1] Dugdale's Orig. 321.   [2] Ibid. 101. 139.; Gent. Mag. xxxviii. 457.
[3] Jones's Rep. 157.

by the judges; and at one time there seems to have been a little jealousy between the residents of the two houses; for on the inauguration of George Vernon in 1627, in the hall in Fleet Street, the judges of the other inn were not present.[1] The meetings of the judges were held sometimes at one and sometimes at the other; but the house in Fleet Street was most frequently selected.

SERJEANTS' INN, FLEET STREET. — A new lease of this inn was granted by the Dean and Chapter of York, in 1627, for forty years, and the lessees included no less than nine of the judges and fifteen serjeants.

When the parliament abolished the title and dignity of bishops in 1646, they passed an ordinance securing to the judges and serjeants the use of the inn during the continuance of their lease; but that at the end of it, the inn should be " in the disposing of both houses of parliament." [2]

SERJEANTS' INN, CHANCERY LANE. — There was evidently some sort of chapel in this inn; for the treasurer's books contain entries of arrangements for administering the Sacrament in every term in 1635 and 1646.

This inn was also secured to the judges and serjeants by a similar ordinance of parliament to that above mentioned.

The appointment of special counsel for the king, separate from the attorney and solicitor-general and the king's serjeants, became more common in this reign. The four following are recorded in Rymer's " Fœdera ": —

1626. March 17. John Finch, afterwards lord keeper.
1632. Nov. 15. George Ratcliffe.
1634. Oct. 7. Richard Shilton, on his resigning the office of solicitor-general, with a salary of 70l. a year, and precedency before the solicitor-general. (Croke, Car. 376.)
1641. July 31. Thomas Levingston.[3]

---

[1] Croke, Car. 85.　　　　　　　　　　　[2] Journals.
[3] Rymer's Fœdera, xviii. 633., xix. 432. 607., xx. 517.

1646. Oct. 1.   The parliament also, though they did not give the title of king's counsel, conferred the same privilege of precedence and of pleading within the bar upon

John Wilde, serjeant at law,
Samuel Browne, and
Edmund Prideaux,

when they were removed from the office of Commissioners of the Great Seal.[1]

COUNSEL.

The initials show the courts to which those who became judges were first appointed.

— Adam,	W. Boothe,	F. Crawley, C. P.,
— Alestre,	— Boreman,	R. Cresheld,
J. Aleyn,	J. Bradshaw, C. G. I.,	H. Cressy,
E. Andrews,	J. Bramston, Ch. K. B.,	T. Crew,
— Archibald,	R. Brerewood, K. B.,	U. Crooke,
F. Ashley,	T. Brickendine,	— Danby,
R. Ashley,	— Bridgeman,	J. Darey,
R. Aske,	J. Briscoe,	H. Davenport, C. P.,
T. Athoe,	C. Brooke,	J. Davies,
E. Atkyns,	— Broome,	H. Denne,
W. Ayloffe,	G. Brown,	T. Denne,
J. Baber,	S. Brown, C. G. I.,	W. Denny,
W. Babington,	J. Bryan,	R. Downes,
F. Bacon, K. B.,	E. Bulstrode,	N. Ducke,
N. Bacon,	R. Callice,	E. Earle,
E. Bagshaw,	H. Calthorpe,	J. Eltonhead,
P. Ball,	T. Chapman,	E. Estcourt,
J. Banks, Ch. C. P.,	— Choke,	S. Evre,
J. Barkesdale,	N. Cholmley,	W. Eyre,
— Barton,	C. Chute,	W. Farrer,
G. Beare,	E. Clerke,	E. Fettiplace,
T. Bedingfield,	H. Clerke,	H. Finch,
R. Berkeley, K. B.,	J. Clerke,	J. Finch, Ch. C. P.,
R. Bernard,	W. Clopton,	N. Finch,
— Bing,	W. Conyers,	T. Fletcher,
E. Bishe,	— Cook,	T. Forde,
T. Bletcher,	G. Copley,	R. Foster, C. P.,
G. Boone,	T. Coventry, L. K.,	J. Franklyn,

[1] Whitelocke, 223.

N. Franklyn,
C. Fulwood,
T. Gardner,
T. Gates, B. E.,
J. Glanville,
J. Glynne, Ch. U. B.,
R. Godard,
J. Godbolt, C. P.,
— Goldsmith,
J. Greene,
T. Greene,
— Griggs,
— Grimston,
P. Gwyn,
W. Hackwill,
E. Hadde,
— Hales,
J. Harrington,
J. Harrison,
R. Hatton,
R. Heath, Ch. C. P.,
— Hedley,
E. Hele,
E. Henden, B. E.,
E. Herbert,
A. Herenden,
J. Herne,
— Hersey,
— Hill,
R. Hitcham,
— Hoddesden,
R. Holbourn,
— Holhead,
C. Holloway,
J. Hoskins,
W. Hudson,
T. Hughes,
W. Hussey,
J. Hutchins,
— Hutchinson,
— Hutton,
L. Hyde,
N. Hyde, Ch. K. B.,
R. Hyde,

D. Jenkins,
P. Jermyn, K. B.,
E. Johnson,
C. Jones,
R. Keble,
— Keeling,
R. King,
R. Lacee,
R. Lane, Ch. B. E.,
T. Lane,
— Latch,
R. Lathom,
W. Lenthall, M. R.,
T. Levingston,
— Lightfoot,
B. Llanden,
J. Lloyd,
J. Lovelace,
G. Ludlow,
E. Lyttelton, Ch. C. P.,
W. Lyttelton,
T. Malet, K. B.
J. Martin,
R. Mason,
— Maynard,
J. Merefield,
T. Milward,
R. Minshall,
— Montague,
J. More,
— Moreton,
P. Mutton,
J. Newton,
R. Nicholas,
W. Norbonne,
W. Noy,
R. Osbaldeston,
E. Palmer,
J. Palmer,
— Panell,
J. Parker, B. E.,
R. Parker,
— Peard,
R. Pepys,

T. Pepys,
P. Phesant,
— Philips,
J. Plat,
— Popes,
— Porter,
W. Powell,
— Prescott,
— Prestwood,
R. Proctor,
— Prynne,
J. Puleston, C. P.,
W. Pye,
H. Pyne,
G. Ratcliffe,
W. Ravenscroft,
E. Reeve, C. P.,
T. Richardson, Ch. C. P.,
T. Riddell,
H. Rigby,
H. Rolle,
W. Rumsey,
O. St. John, C. G. S.,
T. Sanderson,
R. Seaborne,
R. Sheldon or Shilton,
H. Sherfield,
C. Sherland,
W. Shuttleworth,
T. Southe,
T. Spenser,
J. Stone,
R. Tanfield,
R. Taylor,
T. Tempest,
R. Thornes,
F. Thorpe,
R. Thorpe, B. E.,
E. Thynn,
A. Turnour,
R. Townsend,
W. Towse,
— Trevor,
E. Trotman,

J. Tryst,

A. Turner,

T. Turner,

— Twisden,

G. Vernon, B. E.,

J. Wakering,

— Walker,

R. Wandesford,

R. Ward,

W. Warde,

J. Wentworth,

J. Weston, B. E.,

R. Weston, B. E.,

J. Whistler,

W. Whitaker,

J. White,

R. Whitfield,

B. Whitelocke, C. G. S.,

J. Whitwick,

T. Widdrington, C. G. S.,

J. Wightwick,

J. Wilde, C. G. S.,

T. Wilde,

T. Williamson,

— Windham,

R. Wolriche,

E. Woodroofe,

— Worlick,

E. Wright,

J. Wright,

P. Wyat,

— Yard.

The fee paid to four serjeants in a cause in the Court of Wards and Liveries in 1625, " for the day of hearing," was 4*l*. each, and to two other counsel 4*l*. and 3*l*.; but these are stated to be larger than usually allowed.

In 1633 Lord Bayning paid " to Mr. Challenor Chute, the counsellor, for one quarter of a year's allowance, for his council and help in our law business, according to an agreement with him, the sum of 12*l*. 10*s*.; " and in the same year the same gentleman had from his lordship, " for a gratification, for his great pains and care extraordinary on my lord's business, &c., 20*l*."[1]   Challenor Chute was afterwards speaker in Richard Cromwell's parliament.

Before the commencement of the rebellion, the same attention was paid to the education of the students of law as in the preceding reigns.   The readers in all the houses of Court were subjected to new regulations by an order of the judges in Hilary Term, 1627–8.   A double reader was to continue his reading for a week at least; a single reader for a fortnight at least.   They were not to have above ten men in attendance on them; they were to repair on the Sunday before reading to the sermon at Paul's Cross, and wear their caps while there; and were not to practise at Westminster but with their reader's gown, with the velvet welt on the back. All the fellows were directed to repair to the hall at dinner, supper, and exercises, and to the " church, chapel, and place

[1] Gent. Mag. Nov. 1853, p. 478.

of prayer" in their caps, and not in hats.[1]   Another order
was issued by the lord keeper and the judges on April 15,
1630, for the government not only of the inns of Court
but also those of Chancery, principally in repetition of the
order of 1614, which evidently had not been very strictly
obeyed.   It directs that the inns of Chancery shall be subordinate to the inns of Court, by whom the former shall be
surveyed annually, that there may be a competent number
of chambers for the students.   A search is required to be
made in both inns of Court and Chancery three times a
year for ill subjects and dangerous persons; every member is
to receive the Communion once at least in every year upon
pain of immediate expulsion; and no person except members
of the societies are to be "admitted or allowed to lodge in
any of the houses."   Utter-barristers are prohibited from practising publicly at any bar at Westminster until they have
been three years at the bar, unless they have been readers in
some inn of Chancery; and none are to be called to the bar
by readers, but by the bench of the inn, nor unless they have
kept their exercises in an inn of Court and Chancery for at
least eight years.   It forbids hats, cloaks, boots, spurs, swords,
or daggers to be worn in the hall or chapel, and also long
hair.   No attorney or solicitor is to be admitted into any of
the four inns of Court; but attorneys are mentioned as members of the inns of Chancery.[2]

Whitelocke gives an account of a splendid masque performed by the members of the four inns of Court before the
king and queen at the end of Christmas, 1633.   This masque
had a political application, and was suggested by the courtiers
as a means of counteracting the effect of Prynne's *Histrio-
mastix*, and of confuting his opinions against interludes.   The
lawyers, who were at that time eminently loyal, took up the
idea so zealously that they appointed two of the most eminent

---

[1] Dugdale's Orig. 319.   [2] Ibid. 320.

men of the time in each inn to be a committee, to arrange
and conduct the performance. Among those selected were
Sir John Finch, Sir Edward Herbert, Mr. Edward Hyde,
and Mr. Whitelocke, who all afterwards held the Great Seal;
and no less famous were two of the remaining four, viz., Mr.
Selden and Mr. Attorney-General Noy. Distributing the
various duties among them, they seem to have spared no expense or labour to produce the desired effect. Whitelocke
had the management of the music; which, he says, "was
so performed that it excelled any musick that ever before
that time had been heard in England." He engaged Mr.
Simon Ivy and Mr. Laws to compose the airs and songs;
and selected four "most excellent musicians of the Queen's
Chapel," with many others, English, French, Italians, and
Germans, "with forty lutes at one time, besides other instruments and voices in consort." One dispute among "the
Houses," as to precedence, having been settled by throw of
the dice, and another, as to the arrangement of the masquers
in the chariots, having been accommodated by making the
chariots oval, "after the fashion of the Roman Triumphant
Cars," so that each man should sit in front, the procession
started in the evening of Candlemas-day from Ely House,
Holborn, and proceeded down Chancery Lane to Whitehall.
Some extracts from Whitelocke's account of it will not be
unwelcome.

"The first that marched were twenty Footmen, in Scarlet
Liveries with Silver-lace, each one having his Sword by his
side, a Baton in one Hand, and a Torch lighted in the other
Hand; these were the Marshal's Men, who cleared the
streets, made way, and were all about the Marshal, waiting
his Commands. After them, and sometimes in the midst of
them, came the Marshal, then Mr. Darrel, afterwards knighted
by the King: He was of Lincoln's Inn, an extraordinary
handsome proper Gentleman; he was mounted upon one of

the King's best Horses, and richest Saddles, and his own habit was exceedingly rich and glorious; his Horsemanship very gallant; and besides his Marshal's Men, he had two Lacquies, who carried Torches by him, and a Page in Livery that went by him, carrying his Cloak.

"After him followed one hundred Gentlemen of the Inns of Court, five and twenty chosen out of each House; of the most proper and handsome young Gentlemen of the Societies, every one of them was gallantly mounted on the best Horses, and with the best Furniture that the King's Stable, and the Stables of all the Noblemen of the Town would afford, and they were forward on this occasion to lend them to the Inns of Court.

"Every one of these hundred Gentlemen were in very rich Clothes, scarce anything but Gold and Silver-lace to be seen of them; and each Gentleman had a Page and two Lacquies by his Horse-side: The Lacquies carried Torches, and the Page his Master's Cloak. The richness of their Apparel and Furniture glittering by the light of a multitude of torches attending on them, with the motion and stirring of their mettled Horses, and the many and various gay Liveries of their Servants; but especially the personal Beauty and Gallantry of the handsome young Gentlemen, made the most glorious and splendid shew that ever was beheld in England.

"After the Horsemen came the Antimasquers, and as the Horsemen had their Musick, about a dozen of the best Trumpeters proper for them, and in their Livery, sounding before them; so the first Antimasquers, being of Cripples and Beggars on Horseback, had their Musick of Keys and Tongs and the like, snapping and yet playing in a consort before them.

"These Beggars were also mounted, but on the poorest leanest Jades that could be gotten out of the Dirt-carts or elsewhere: and the variety and change from such noble

Musick and gallant Horses as went before them, unto their proper Musick and pitiful Horses, made both of them the more pleasing.

" The Habits and Properties of these Cripples and Beggars were most ingeniously fitted (as of all the rest) by the Committee's direction, wherein (as in the whole business) Mr. Attorney Noy, Sir John Finch, Sir Edward Herbert, Mr. Selden, those eminent Persons, as all the rest of the Committee, had often meetings, and took extraordinary care and pains in the ordering of this Business, and it seemed a pleasure to them."

Then follows an antimasque of birds; after which a satirical antimasque of projectors from the " Scotch and Northern Quarters " is thus described :—

" First in this Antimasque, rode a Fellow upon a little Horse, with a great Bit in his mouth, and upon the man's Head was a Bit, with Head-stall and Rains fastned, and signified a Projector, who begged a patent, that none in the Kingdom might ride their Horses, but with such Bits as they should buy of him.

" Then came another Fellow, with a Bunch of Carrots upon his Head and a Capon upon his Fist, describing a projector, who begg'd a Patent of Monopoly, as the first Inventor of the Art to feed Capons fat with Carrots, and that none but himself might make use of that Invention, and have the Privelege for fourteen years, according to the Statute.

" Several other Projectors were in like manner personated in this Antimasque; and it pleased the Spectators the more, because by it an information was covertly given to the king, of the unfitness and ridiculousness of these Projects against the Law ; and the Attorney Noy, who had most knowledge of them, had a great hand in the Antimasque of the Projectors."

After this and other antimasques, two superb chariots are duly delineated, with their attendant bands of music.

" Then came the first Chariot of the Grand Masquers, which was not so large as those that went before, but most curiously framed, carved, and painted with exquisite Art, and purposely for this service and occasion. The form of it was after that of the Roman Triumphant Chariots, as near as could be gathered by some old Prints and Pictures extant of them. The seats in it were made of an oval form in the back end of the Chariot, so that there was no precedence in them, and the faces of all that sat in it might be seen together.

" The colours of the first Chariot were Silver and Crimson, given by the Lot to Gray's Inn, as I remember ; the Chariot was all over painted richly with these colours, even the Wheels of it most artificially laid on, and the carved Work of it was as curious for that Art, and it made a stately Show. It was drawn with four Horses, all on breast, and they were covered to their Heels all over with Cloth of Tissue, of the colours of Crimson and Silver, huge Plumes of red and white Feathers on their Heads and Buttocks ; the Coachman's Cap and Feather, his long Coat, and his very Whip and Cushion of the same Stuff and Colour.

" In this Chariot sat the four Grand Masquers of Gray's-Inn, their Habits, Doublets, Trunk-hose, and Caps, of most rich cloth of Tissue, and wrought as thick with Silver Spangles as could be placed, large white silk Stockings up to their Trunk-hose, and rich Sprigs in their Caps ; themselves proper and beautiful young Gentlemen."

Then followed similar Chariots of the three other Inns, only differing in their colours. The Middle Temple, with blue and silver ; the Inner Temple, and Lincoln's Inn, whose colours are not mentioned. Their march was slow, " interrupted by the Multitude of the Spectators in the

Streets, besides the Windows, and they seemed loth to part with so glorious a Spectacle."

" In the meantime the Banquetting-house at Whitehall was so crouded with fair Ladies, glittering with their rich Cloths and richer Jewels, and with Lords and Gentlemen of great Quality, that there was scarce room for the King and Queen to enter in.   The King and Queen stood at a Window, looking straight-forward into the Street, to see the Masque come by; and being delighted with the noble Bravery of it, they sent to the Marshal to desire that the whole Show might fetch a turn about the Tilt-yard, that their Majesties might have a double view of them.

" The King and Queen, and all their noble Train being come in, the Masque began, and was incomparably performed in the Dances, Figures, Properties, the Voices, Instruments, Songs, Composures, the Words and Actions were all of them exact, and none failed in their parts of them, and the Scenes were most curious and costly.

" The Queen did the honour to some of the Masquers to dance with them herself, and to judge them as good Dancers as ever she saw; and the great Ladies were very free and civil in dancing with all the Masquers, as they were taken out by them."

Whitelocke estimates the expense of this masque to have been above 21,000*l.*; and he concludes his account of it with this ominous reflection:—" Thus these Dreams past, and these Pomps vanished!"[1]   How little did any of the spectators of this gaudy pageant dream of the melancholy contrast that was to be exhibited a few years after on the same spot, and how many lived to witness it!

The king, to show his gracious acceptance of this masque, invited one hundred and twenty gentlemen of the four Inns

---

[1] Whitelocke's Memorials, 19—22.

of Court to a masque at Whitehall on the Shrove Tuesday following.[1]

The readings at all the Inns of Court were frequently interrupted on account of the plague that visited the city. In the 1st, 6th, 12th, and 13th years of the reign there were no readings "*causâ pestilentiæ.*" During the latter years of the reign, when the civil war — a worse pestilence — raged, the readings entirely ceased.

These were not the only evils suffered by the lawyers in consequence of the rebellion. Though some from the first sided with the parliament, the great majority in the outset were loyal to the king. In 1642 the four Inns of Court presented an address to the parliament, reminding them of their duty to the throne[2]; and even while the king was at Oxford, the members of the profession were numerous enough to form a regiment of foot under the command of Lord Keeper Lyttelton. Few, indeed, were allowed to remain neutral in the contest. The dominant party took the most effectual method of frightening the backward, by stigmatizing their opponents with the title of malignants, and sequestering and selling their property. In 1644 a committee of lawyers was appointed by the parliament for sequestering and selling the chambers belonging to what they called " malignant lawyers;" and in 1646 the benchers of the Inns of Court and the principals of the Inns of Chancery were forbidden to permit any lawyers that had borne arms for the king to be in any of their societies. No surprise can therefore be felt at the following entry in Whitelocke's Memorials: — " The Commissioners of the Seal gave the Covenant to the Lawyers and Officers ; and so many came to take it, that they were fain to appoint another day for it." Some of the barristers took arms in the parliamentary army[3]; and others sold their

---

[1] Dugdale's Orig. 246.   [2] Pearce's Inns of Court, 284.
[3] Whitelocke, 81. 91. 101. 226.

chambers and deserted their profession till order was restored.[1]

When the *Directory* was established instead of the Book
of Common Prayer, and the Presbyterian government substituted for the Prelacy, the parliament, by an ordinance of
March 14, 1645-6, directed that the Chapel of the Rolls, the
two Serjeants' Inns, and the four Inns of Court, should be a
province of themselves, and should be divided into classes;
one consisting of Lincoln's Inn, Gray's Inn, Serjeants' Inn
in Chancery Lane, and the Rolls; and the other of the two
Temples and Serjeants' Inn in Fleet Street.[2]

LINCOLN'S INN. Notwithstanding the prohibition against
attorneys and common solicitors by former orders, it was
found that some persons of that class had contrived to be
admitted into the society. To remedy this " which they
esteemed to be no small disparagement thereunto," the bench
at a council held on June 4, 1635, not only ordered that none
should from thenceforth be admitted, but also that if any
gentleman, after his admission, should become an attorney or
common solicitor, his admittance should be *ipso facto* void.

This society takes the credit of having originated the
masque that was presented before the king in 1634. Besides
the dresses of the individual members, some of which are
stated to have cost 1000*l.* a piece, the expense to this society
was 2400*l.*, which was raised by a tax of 6*l.* on the benchers,
3*l.* and 2*l.* on the utter barristers, and 1*l.* on the students[3];
and the contributions by the members of the other societies
to the cost was much in the same proportion.

Rushworth tells a story of four young men of this inn
being called before the council, on the information of the
drawer at a tavern, for drinking a health " to the confusion
of the Archbishop of Canterbury." They first applied to the

---

[1] Bramston's Autobiog. 103. 　　　　 [2] Rushworth, vii. 226.
[3] Dugdale's Orig. 243. 246.

Earl of Dorset, when his lordship on understanding that the drawer was going out at the door, suggested that he had only heard the first words of the health, and not the last, and that they must have drunk "to the confusion of the Archbishop of Canterbury's *foes*." The young gentlemen gladly took the hint, and using the earl's interpretation before the council, were dismissed with a slight admonition.[1]

INNER TEMPLE. In the early part of the reign this society showed considerable activity in providing accommodation for their members. Among the erections were the great brick buildings over against the garden, those in Fig-tree Court, and those between that place and the Hall. They repaired likewise the east end of the church.

In 1631 more stringent rules for keeping Christmas were enacted by both the Temples. The Christmas Commons was ordered to continue for three weeks only ; the " innovation of treasurers" was abolished, and three stewards restored; drinking of healths was prohibited, and the sale in the house of wine or tobacco; and no play was allowed on Saturday night or Christmas eve after twelve o'clock.

MIDDLE TEMPLE. The society expended no less a sum than 4668*l*. 10*s*. 11*d*. in 1639, in erecting a large brick building between Elm Court, Pump Court, Vine Court, and Middle Temple Lane, where, according to Chauncy's description, the old Hall, which was then pulled down, stood. The "gentlemen that were builders" contributed 2300*l*., each depositing 80*l*. for a whole chamber, and 40*l*. for a half chamber. The remainder was paid out of the treasury, "which did put the house much in debt."

In 1635, the benchers of this house made an order enforcing in all its particulars that issued by the judges in April, 1630. That they denied the authority of the judges to interfere in their internal regulation is evident, as well from their delay

---

[1] Rushworth, ii. 1180.

in issuing this order as from these expressions in its pre-
amble :— " The Masters of the Bench conforming themselves
to the grave advice of the said Judges, and in obedience to
his Majestie's command : and finding all the said particulars
agreeable to the ancient Orders and Constitution of this
House, have agreed," &c.

In 1642, Mr. Robert Ashley, an ancient barrister of this
house, having bequeathed some books to the society, they
were ordered to be kept under lock and key till a library was
built.[1]

A curious contest arose in consequence of the death, during
the Christmas revels of 1628, of Mr. Basing, " an Officer of
Quality in that solemnity." The society ordered him to be
buried according to the dignity of his office, and the expense
to be disbursed out of the public stock of the society. His
father, being applied to, refused to pay the amount; whereupon the society preferred a bill in the Court of Requests,
drawn by the principal lawyers of the day,—Mr. Palmer,
Mr. Maynard, Mr. Noy, and others,—setting forth, " ingeniously and handsomely," the customs of the Inns of Court
for the solemnities of Christmas, and the choice of Christmas
officers, with the other facts ; and praying the repayment of
the money with damages. The father, however, thought
proper to stop here, and to pay the money ; which the society
distributed among the poor prisoners, not taking " one peny
for the publick stock."[2]

A letter from Garrard to the Earl of Strafford of Jannary
8, 1635, will give some idea of the grandeur assumed by
the officers elected for the Christmas revels :—

" The Middle Temple House have set up a prince who carries himself
in great state, one Mr. Vivian, a Cornish gentleman. He hath all his
great officers attending him, lord keeper, lord treasurer, eight white
staves at the least, captain of his pensioners, captain of his guard, two

---

[1] Dugdale's Orig. 189—191, 193.　　　[2] Whitelocke, 11.

chaplains who on Sunday last preached before him, and in the pulpit made three low legs to his excellency before they began, which is much laughed at. My lord chamberlain lent him two fair cloths of state, one hung up in the hall, under which he dines, the other in his privy chamber; he is served on the knee, and all that come to see him kiss his hand on their knee. My lord of Salisbury hath sent him pole-axes for his pensioners. He sent to my Lord of Holland, his justice in eyre, for venison, which he willingly sends him; to the lord mayor and sheriffs of London for wine; all obey. Twelfth day was a great day; going to the chapel many petitions were delivered to him, which he gave to his masters of the requests. He hath a favourite whom, with some others of great quality, he knighted on his return from church, and dined in great state. . . . It costs this prince 2000*l.* out of his own purse; I hear of no other design, but all this is done to make him fit to give the prince elector a royal entertainment, with masks, dancings, and some other exercises of wit in orations or arraignments that day that they invite him." [1]

Mr. Bagshaw, the Lent reader in 1639–40, having chosen for his reading some questions about the bishops and clergy, which trenched too much on the politics of the time, was commanded by the king not to proceed. He of course desisted; but shortly after, went out of town accompanied with a retinue of forty or fifty horse, and in good credit with the gentlemen of the society. This Mr. Bagshaw, though Whitelocke describes him as " much inclined to the Nonconformist's way," being elected member for Southwark in the Long Parliament, joined the king at Oxford, and was afterwards taken, imprisoned, and expelled the house. [2]

GRAY'S INN. — At the commencement of this reign all the orders for the regulation of the society were extracted from registers by three of the readers, — Mr. Osbaldiston, Mr. Clopton, and Mr. Whistler, — and reduced into a form, which was inscribed on a tablet, and hung up in the hall. [3] No subsequent orders of any importance were passed.

BARNARD'S INN. — The gradual admission of attorneys into Inns of Chancery, and the attempts to exclude them, appear

---

[1] Pearce's Inns of Court, 127.   [2] Whitelocke, 33. 92. 116.
[3] Dugdale's Orig. 287—291.

from the following order of this house.   In May, 1630, Mr.
Harvey, late a student, now practising as an attorney contrary to his admission, the principal was ordered to "admit a
Student into the chamber of Mr. Harvey;" and in 1638, the
principal was borne harmless by the society in a suit brought
against him by Thomas Marsh, a companion, for breaking
into his chamber.   Thomas Marsh was discomfited, and besides being committed to the Marshalsea until he could find
bail for his good behaviour, was ordered to be struck off the
roll of attorneys.

In 1639, an order was made that every principal, on being
chosen, should give plate of the value of 5l. at the least for
the use of the house.[1]

[1] Barnard's Inn Books.

BIOGRAPHICAL NOTICES

OF

THE JUDGES UNDER THE REIGN OF CHARLES I.

ATKYNS, EDWARD.
PARL. B. E. 1645.

See under the Interregnum, and the Reign of Charles II.

BACON, FRANCIS.
JUST. K. B. 1642.

IN addition to the four judges of this name who have appeared in these pages, a fifth remains to be noticed, who owed his origin to the same root from which they sprang, being of that branch of the family which settled at Hesset in Suffolk. This was Francis Bacon, whose great grand-parents are stated to be Thomas Bacon of that place and Anne Rowse, and whose father is described in Francis's admission to Gray's Inn, as John Bacon of King's Lynn in Norfolk, gentleman.

He was born about the year 1587, and commencing his legal studies at Barnard's Inn, he pursued them at Gray's Inn, the same school at which his two illustrious predecessors were nurtured. Admitted a member in February, 1607, he was called to the bar in the same month in 1615, and became reader there in autumn 1634.[1] His name does not appear in any of the contemporary reports; his practice probably being in Chancery or the provinces.

In 1624 and 1626, Blomcfield records his reparation of the

---

[1] Gray's Inn Books; Dugdale's Orig. Jurid. 297.

font and east window of St. Gregory's church, in Norwich.[1]
In 1636, he had a grant in reversion of the office of drawing
licences and pardons of alienations to the Great Seal.[2] Four
years afterwards in May 1640, he was included in the batch
of serjeants then called; and on October 14, 1642, he received the then dangerous promotion to a seat in the King's
Bench, his patent being dated at Bridgenorth[3], on the king's
march towards London; when he was knighted. That the
new judge was not obnoxious to the parliament may be inferred from their request in the propositions made to the king,
in February, 1643, that he might be continued in his place.
He does not appear to have joined the king at Oxford, but he
attended his duty in his court at Westminster Hall; where,
in Michaelmas Term, 1643, he was the only judge sitting[4];
and on the trial of Lord Macguire for high treason as the
fomenter of the great rebellion and horrible massacre in Ireland in 1641, before that court in Hilary Term, 1645, he
alone appears to have been present.[5] He is next mentioned
in September, 1647, as having, with Serjeant Creswell or Cresheld, committed James Symbal and others for speaking words
against the king, with whom negotiations were proceeding.
He continued to act till the king was beheaded; when he had
the courage to refuse the new commission offered him by the
Commons.[6]

He lived more than eight years after his retirement, spending the remainder of his days in privacy, and died on August,
22, 1657. His eldest son, Francis (who was a reader in
Gray's Inn in autumn 1662), raised a handsome monument
over his grave in St. Gregory's church, Norwich; the inscription on which states that after his appointment, "nec serviens ad legem, neque Judex apud Westmonasterium, per ip-

---

[1] Blomefield's Norwich, ii. 274.　　　[2] Rymer, xx. 123.
[3] Rymer, xx. 541.　　　[4] Clarendon, iii. 407., iv. 342.
[5] State Trials, iv. 666.　　　[6] Whitelocke, 269. 378.

sum Regem, ordinatus nec constitutis fuit."[1] This, though perhaps strictly correct as to the letter, leads to a wrong inference, and would seem to exclude Chief Justice Heath, Chief Baron Lane, and Judge Brerewood, who all received patents from the king at a subsequent period, though they were sworn in at Oxford.

Sir Francis married Elizabeth daughter of William Robinson, and had several children: but his branch of the family has been long extinct.[2]

BANKS, JOHN.
CH. C. P. 1641.

THE family of this chief justice resided at Keswick in Cumberland, where his father of the same name was a merchant, and his mother was Elizabeth, daughter of ——— Hassell. He was born in 1589, and having received the rudiments of his education at a grammar school in his own county, was sent in 1604 to finish his studies at Queen's College, in the University of Oxford. Without taking any degree there, he entered himself a student at Gray's Inn in May, 1607, and after being called to the bar on November 30, 1614, and to the bench of the society in 1629, he was elected reader in Lent, 1631, and treasurer in the following year.[3] He had previous to arriving at these posts acquired a high reputation in his profession.

Returned to the Parliament of 1628, he confined himself to legal questions[4]; and had been selected in July 1630, to be attorney-general to the newly-born Prince Charles, Duke of Cornwall[5], afterwards Charles II.; whereupon he had been knighted. On the death of William Noy, he was appointed attorney-general to the king on September 27, 1634, and it is some proof of the estimation in which he was held, that a contemporary letter writer says, with somewhat of exaggeration,

---

[1] Blomefield's Norwich, ii. 275.   [2] Wotton's Baronet, i. 2.
[3] Dugdale's Orig. 297. 299.   [4] Parl. Hist. ii. 480.   [5] Rymer, xix. 254.

that he was commended to his Majesty as exceeding Bacon in eloquence, Ellesmere in judgment, and Noy in law.[1] Soon after his advance he purchased the manor of Corfe Castle in Dorsetshire of Sir Edward Coke's widow, Lady Hatton.

Under his official direction the questionable proceedings in the Star Chamber were taken against Bastwick, Burton and Prynne, against Bishop Williams, and against John Lilburn; and though he did not originate the plan for the imposition of ship money, it fell to his lot to support it as the prosecutor. against John Hampden.[2] These duties he performed so satisfactorily to the court, that upon the elevation of Sir Edward Lyttelton to the post of lord keeper, he received that of chief justice of the Common Pleas on January 29, 1641.[3]

Very soon after his appointment a commission was granted to him to sit as speaker in the House of Lords, in consequence of the illness of the lord keeper; and in that character he had the melancholy duty of presiding, when the Earl of Strafford, who had been his client, and with whom he was in habits of friendly intimacy, was brought to the bar on his impeachment by the Commons.[4] Early in the next year, on the king retiring to York, Banks was among the first to join him; when he was admitted into the Privy Council, and subscribed the profession made by the lords of their belief that the king had no intention to make war upon the parliament, but that his anxious desire was to preserve the peace of the kingdom.[5] When Charles took up his winter quarters at Oxford, Sir John Banks received from the university the complimentary degree of Doctor of Laws.[6]

Notwithstanding the part which Sir John had formerly taken in the prosecution and in the case of ship money, and his present assistance to the royal counsels, he does not seem to have been an object of enmity to the parliament; for in the

---

[1] Bankes's Corfe Castle, 54.   [2] State Trials, iii. 711. 771. 1014. 1374.
[3] Rymer, xx. 447.   [4] Bankes's Corfe Castle, 83.
[5] Clarendon's Reb. iii. 72.   [6] Wood's Fasti, ii. 44.

propositions they made to the king for peace in February, 1643, they desired that he should keep his place in the Common Pleas.[1]   This recommendation he owed to his having friends in both houses, with whom he continued to correspond; the Earls of Northumberland and Essex, the Lord Wharton, Daniell Holles, and Green.   These had been desirous of an accommodation, and some of them were aware that Banks by his moderate counsels had hazarded the king's indignation.[2] Soon after the failure of this negotiation, Sir John's real devotion to the royal cause was proved by his liberal subscription to the king's necessities, and by his wife's noble defence of Corfe Castle.

This lady was Mary, the daughter of Ralph Hawtrey, Esq., of an ancient family resident at Ruislip in Middlesex.   At the beginning of the troubles she had retired with her children to the castle, and for some time remained there in peace.   But at length, after several fruitless endeavours by the parliamentary army to surprise her and get possession, she made hasty preparations for its defence, though totally unprovided with cannon.   Laying in a store of provisions and powder, she obtained the assistance of a few soldiers under the command of Captain Lawrence from Prince Maurice's army.   Sir Walter Erle set himself down before the castle on June 23, 1643, with artillery, and a large body of men; and made several furious attempts to take it by assault.   The steadiness of the soldiers in the castle, and the bravery of the lady and her servants, as often succeeded in repulsing the assailants; who after a six weeks' siege, and the loss of an hundred men, alarmed by the report of the advance of the king's forces, fled from the field on August 4, leaving their guns and ammunition to the victors.[3]

The former good feeling of the Parliament towards the chief

---

[1] Parl. Hist. iii. 70.   [2] Corfe Castle, 122—24.
[3] Hutchins's Dorset, i. 180.

justice had been totally changed by his steady adherence to his royal master; and their present inveteracy against him had been excited by his charge to the grand jury at Salisbury in the summer assizes of this year, denouncing the Earls of Northumberland, Pembroke, and Salisbury, and several members of the House of Commons as guilty of high treason in taking up arms against the king. Though the bills were not found, he was ordered to be impeached for his charge; an order which was repeated in the following year on the occasion of his condemning Captain Turpin to be hanged at Exeter.[1] Though by his absence he escaped the consequences of these votes, he paid the price of his loyalty, under another ordinance, by the forfeiture of all his property. Even his books were seized and given by the parliament to Mr. Maynard.[2]

Sir John did not live to see the destruction of his castle, which, at the close of 1645, was again invested, and after a resolute defence of forty-eight days, in which Lady Banks showed the same courage that formerly distinguished her, it fell into the hands of the enemy by the treachery of an officer in the garrison, and was immediately dismantled. Its ruins at the present day tell of its former strength and splendour.

The chief justice, after a short illness, died at Oxford on December 28, 1644, and was buried in Christ Church cathedral. Lord Clarendon describes him as "a man of great abilities and unblemished integrity," but at the same time intimates that he wanted courage to meet the exigencies of the time. All agree that he was thoroughly versed in the learning of his profession, and his whole conduct shows that though cautious and moderate, he was steady in his attachment to the crown. He made a settlement of 30l. a year, and other emoluments, on the poor of Keswick, and chiefly to set up a manufacture there of coarse cottons.[3]

Lady Banks, by compounding, got rid of the sequestration

---

[1] Whitelocke, 78. 96. [2] Ibid. 177. [3] Fuller's Worthies, i. 237.

issued by the parliament.[1]   She had a numerous family by
the chief justice, whose descendants represented Corfe Castle
as long as that borough returned members to parliament; and
his late representative, the Right Honourable George Bankes,
the cursitor baron, remained till his death one of the members
for the county of Dorset.

BEDINGFIELD, THOMAS.
PARL. JUST. C. P. 1648.

SPRUNG from a younger branch of an ancient and knightly
family, which took the name of Bedingfield from a manor so
called in Suffolk, the judge was the second son of Thomas
Bedingfield, Esq., of Darsham Hall in that county; to which
his eldest son Philip succeeded, and sold it to Thomas his
younger brother.   Thomas was admitted a student at Gray's
Inn in 1608, and being called to the bar on February 17,
1615, arrived at the post of reader there in Lent 1636.[2]
He acquired such eminence in his profession that he was
made attorney-general of the Duchy of Lancaster; and was
thereupon knighted.

He was assigned by the House of Lords in 1642 to conduct the defence of Sir Edward Herbert the attorney-general,
against the impeachment of the Commons; but declining to
plead in consequence of the latter threatening any counsel,
who presumed to appear against them, with their displeasure,
he was committed to the Tower by the peers for his contempt
of their commands.   He did not, however, long suffer under
this choice of predicaments, being released from his incarceration in three days.[3]   The Commons showed their estimation
of him in 1646 and 1647, by several times inserting his name
as one of the persons they proposed as commissioners of the
Great Seal: but the appointment never was completed, in
consequence of the disagreement of the Lords.   But both

[1] Whitelocke, 270.   [2] Gray's Inn Books.   [3] State Trials, ii. 1125. 1129.

houses concurred in October 1648, in a vote appointing him one of the judges of the Common Pleas; and, having been first decorated with the coif, he was in the following month sworn in. Not long, however, did he retain his new dignity, for on the decapitation of the king in January 1649, Sir Thomas refused to act under the commission offered by the executioners.[1] Retiring into private life, he outlived the interregnum, and on the return of Charles II. in 1660, he received immediately and in a legitimate manner the degree of the coif.[2]

At his death, the date of which is uncertain, he left a son of the same name, whose descendants for some time retained possession of Darsham Hall, and the judge's other possessions.[3]

BERKELEY, ROBERT.

JUST. K. B. 1632.

THE descent of this unfortunate judge from the noble family of Berkeley, and consequently from the two itinerant justices, Maurice and Robert de Berkeley, already noticed under the reigns of Richard I. and John[4], is thus traced. James, sixth Lord Berkeley, by his second wife Isabel, daughter of Thomas Mowbray, first Duke of Norfolk, had four sons, the youngest of whom was Thomas, whose third son Richard's fourth son William, was Mayor of Hereford in 1545. William's eighth son was Rowland Berkeley, who, the youngest born of a succession of younger sons, had little to begin the world with; but by his industry became a very eminent and wealthy clothier at Worcester, and purchased, among others, a considerable estate in the neighbouring parish of Spetchley. By his wife, Catherine, daughter of Thomas Hayward, Esq., he had a family of seven sons and nine daughters.[5]

[1] Whitelocke, 224. 234. 240. 342. 348. 356. 378.; Journals.
[2] Dugdale's Chron. Series.   [3] Wotton's Baronet. iii. 161. 322.
[4] See Vol. I. 341.; Vol. II. 39.   [5] Chambers's Biog. Illust. Worcester, 85.

Robert Berkeley, the second son, was born at Worcester in 1584. It does not appear that he had the advantage of a university education, and nothing is recorded of him, except that he pursued his legal studies at the Middle Temple, where he was admitted on February 5, 1600, was called to the bar May 6, 1608, and remained till the death of his father in 1611; when he became possessor of the Spetchley estate. In 1613, he was sheriff of his native county, and thirteen years afterwards, in 1626, he became autumn reader of his inn of court. At the commencement of the next year, he was called to the degree of the coif, and on April 12 was nominated one of the king's serjeants. From this time his name appears in the Reports; and it fell to his lot in 1629, to argue for the king that the return made to the Habeas Corpus, obtained by William Stroud and the other members imprisoned for their conduct in the last parliament, was good and sufficient in law; his argument showing great ability.[1]

On October 11, 1632, having been previously knighted, he succeeded Sir James Whitelocke as a judge of the King's Bench; a position perhaps coveted by him as an honourable promotion in his profession, but not to be envied when kings push their prerogative beyond its limits, and parliaments would restrain it within too narrow bounds. Judge Berkeley had a deep feeling in favour of the king's prerogative; and though he agreed that the king could not on all occasions impose charges on his subjects without consent of parliament, saying "The people of this kingdom are subjects not slaves, freemen not villains, to be taxed de alto et basso," yet he contended that his majesty might do so when the good and safety of the kingdom in general is concerned, and that he is the sole judge of the danger. He therefore in the great case of ship money, after a most elaborate and learned argument, which however wrong it may be thought in its founda-

---

[1] State Trials, iii. 844.

tion, at least showed his conscientious conviction of its truth, pronounced his opinion against Mr. Hampden.[1]

For this he was called to severe account by the Long Parliament. He was one of the six judges whom the Lords, on December 22, 1640, bound in 10,000*l.* a piece to answer the charges which the Commons were preparing against them. On February 13, he was singled out for the first example, and, being impeached for high treason, was arrested in open court while sitting on the bench, to "the great terrour of the rest of his brethren, and of all his profession."[2]   The articles of impeachment charged him with endeavouring to introduce arbitrary and tyrannical government against law, and, principally denouncing his opinion on ship-money, added some other judgments given during his judicial career tending to the same consequence; with two other articles, showing that the judge's leaning against the Puritanical party had, in a great measure, influenced the promoters of the prosecution.[3]   He was kept in custody of the Sheriff of London till October 20, 1641, when he appeared at the bar of the House of Lords and pleading not guilty, obtained permission to go with a keeper to Serjeants' Inn to look out papers and advise with his counsel.   The trial, which was fixed for November 2, was put off at the instance of the Commons for want of witnesses.[4]   In Michaelmas Term, 1642, of the three judges of the King's Bench that were then left, Heath being with the king, Malet in the Tower, and Berkeley under impeachment, the two houses at a conference resolved, "That Judge Berkeley having carried himself with modesty and humility, and inoffensively to both houses, be pitched upon for keeping the Essoigns."[5]

The Lords in the following September, — that is, the ten that remained, — sentenced the judge to pay a fine of 20,000*l.*

---

[1] State Trials, iii. 1087—1125.   [2] Whitelocke, 40.
[3] Rushworth, ii. 606—614.   [4] Parl. Hist. ii. 917.
[5] Parry's Parliament, &c.

and to be for ever disabled from holding any office in the commonwealth. But the parliament being then pressed for money to pay an instalment of their subsidy to the Scots, he was let off on payment of half to their own officers.[1] In the conflict that afterwards took place, Sir Robert Berkeley suffered much from the plundering and exactions of both the parties. Cromwell took up his quarters at his mansion of Spetchley; which was afterwards burned down by the Presbyterians, his old enemies, though in the service of the king. He wisely refrained from restoring it, but contented himself with converting his stables into a dwelling-house, and quietly waiting for better times. Even Whitelocke represents him as " moderate in his ways," and acknowledges him to be " a very learned man in our laws, and a good orator and judge."

He outlived his sovereign above seven years, dying on August 5, 1656, at the age of 72. He was buried under a handsome monument, with an excellent marble figure of the judge upon it, in a chancel he had built to the church of Spetchley.

He married Elizabeth, daughter and coheir of Thomas Conyers, Esq., of East Barnet, Herts, by whom he had one son, Thomas, who became a Roman Catholic, and whose descendants still enjoy the family estate.

BOLINBROKE, EARL OF. *See* OLIVER ST. JOHN.

BRAMSTON, JOHN.
CH. K. B. 1635.

IN a pedigree appended to the interesting autobiography of the eldest son of the chief justice, edited for the Camden Society by Lord Braybroke, its president, the first person of this name is William Bramston, who was sheriff of London in 18 Richard II., 1394–95. A descendant of his, John, about two centuries later, was a mercer in the same city, whose son Roger Bramston, of Whitechapel, was the first

---

[1] Clarendon, iv. 286.

who established himself in Essex; having married Priscilla, daughter of Francis Clovile, of West Haningfield Hall, and widow of Thomas Rushee, of Boreham, both in that county. Of that union the chief justice was the eldest son.

John Bramston was born on May 18, 1577, at Maldon, and after receiving his early instruction in the free-school there, finished his education at Jesus College, Cambridge. He entered on the study of the law at the Middle Temple, and having been duly called to the bar, he was chosen in 1607 by his university as one of their counsel. In the preceding year he had married Bridget, daughter of Dr. Thomas Moundeford, an eminent physician of Milk Street, London; and lived then, or soon after, in a large and handsome house in Whitechapel, his inheritance, where his eldest son was born. In regular succession he was admitted to the bench of his inn, and was selected as Lent reader in 1623[1], when his reading was on the statute 32 Henry VIII., c. 2., concerning limitations; and again in the following autumn, when he took the statute 13 Eliz., c. 5., as his subject, treating on fraudulent conveyances. In the Michaelmas Term after his last reading, he was one of the fifteen who took the degree of the coif[2]; not, however, without contributing, as all the others did, 500l. to King James's purse. He obtained great practice as well in the courts of law, as in Chancery, the court of Wards, and the Star Chamber. In 1626 he was selected by the Earl of Bristol to defend him[3]; in 1627 he pleaded for Sir John Heveningham, who was imprisoned for not contributing to the loan[4]; in 1628 he was retained by the city of London as their counsel, with a fee *pro consilio impenso et impendendo;* and in 1630 he was constituted chief justice of Ely, on the nomination of the then bishop of that see, which was confirmed by his successor. He was made the queen's serjeant

---

[1] Dugdale's Orig. 219.   [2] Croke, Jac. 671.
[3] State Trials, ii. 1380.   [4] Ibid. iii. 6.

on March 26, 1632, and King Charles advanced him on July 8, 1634, to be one of his serjeants, and knighted him in November following.

After the birth of a numerous family his wife died at the age of thirty-six, and some few years after, in 1631, he married for his second wife, Elizabeth, the daughter of Lord Brabazon, and the relict already of two husbands, the first being George Montgomerie, bishop of Clogher, and the second Sir John Brereton, the king's serjeant in Ireland. He had no children by her and she died in 1647, leaving him a second time a widower. Soon after his second marriage he purchased the estate of Skreenes in Roxwell, Essex, for 8000*l.* from Thomas Weston, afterwards Earl of Portland.

On the death of Sir Thomas Richardson he was called upon to fill the then not very enviable place of chief justice of the King's Bench, and received his patent on April 14, 1635.[1] The people were discontented and seditiously inclined; King Charles was raising money by various means without the aid of parliament, which had not met for six years; the writs for ship money had just been issued and created general excitement. Bramston, who evidently was conscientious in considering that it was legally imposed, as chief justice headed the opinion in its favour, that was given by all the judges, in answer to the case which the king had laid before them. In the prosecution of Hampden he supported that opinion upon the general principle that the defence of the realm must be at the subjects' charge; but, notwithstanding, gave his vote against the crown upon a technical point, that by the record it did not appear to whom the money assessed was due.[2]

One of the earliest proceedings of the Long Parliament, which met in November, 1640, was to impeach Chief Justice Bramston and five other of the judges who had given this

[1] Rymer, xix. 764.   [2] State Trials, iii. 1243.

answer to the king; and he was obliged to give security in
10,000*l.* to abide his trial.[1]   The principal charge against him
was for signing the opinion, and did not touch his judgment
in the case of Hampden.   His answer, which his son thinks,
though prepared and signed by counsel, was never called for,
was that he, like Croke and Hutton, subscribed only for conformity, for he was overruled by the rest of the judges in his
wish to insert that the charge could not be made except in
case of necessity, and only during the time and continuance of
that necessity.   When the king went to York in July, 1642,
he commanded the attendance of the chief justice, and though
Bramston sent his sons to excuse him on account of the
danger which those who had become bound for his appearance
before the parliament would incur, the injunctions for his presence were reiterated.   Bramston had already applied to the
parliament for leave, and been refused; and, therefore, seeing
the ruin in which both he and his bail would be involved if
he complied, he determined to stay away.

The consequence was, that on October 16, 1642, the king
revoked his appointment [2]; but, as if to show that it was not
from royal displeasure, sent him a patent as king's serjeant on
the 10th of the following February.   It is curious that this
patent was granted a few days after the king had received the
propositions of the Lords and Commons for an accommodation;
one of which was a prayer that he would make Sir John
Bramston chief justice of the King's Bench.[3]   By this it is
evident that the parliament were not very inveterate against
Sir John; and it seems probable that the king appointed him
his serjeant as an earnest of his intention, if the negotiation
had succeeded, to replace him in his office in compliance with
the parliament's request.   As a further proof that that body
held him absolved, and esteemed him to be, as Lord Clarendon
calls him, "a man of great learning and integrity," they made
several attempts to induce him to resume his judicial duties,

---

[1] Parl. Hist. ii. 700.   [2] Rymer, xx. 536.   [3] Parl. Hist. iii. 70.

and, when he refused, as another had superseded him, they ordered him to be advised with on some legal business before them. In January, 1646-7, the Commons named him as one of the Lords Commissioners of the Great Seal; but by his interest with the peers, he induced them to pass him over. In the following March the same attempt was made with the like result. In the interim the Lords had voted that he should sit in their house as an assistant; but without refusing the appointment, he managed to avoid the attendance. And in April a vote was passed that he should be one of the judges of the Common Pleas [1], which he also declined. His son says that Cromwell, after he became Protector, urged Sir John to take the office of chief justice again; but that he excused himself, pleading his old age; which, as this must have been in 1654, when he was verging on seventy-seven, he might well do. On September 22, of that year, he died at Skreenes after a very short illness; and was buried in Roxwell church.

Fuller gives him the character of being " accomplished with all qualities requisite for a person of his place and profession, . . . deep learning, solid judgment, integrity of life, and gravity of behaviour: " adding, that " he deserved to live in better times." [2]

Out of a large family, six children only survived him, three sons and three daughters. The descendants of his eldest son, John, who was made a knight of the Bath by Charles II., have given members to the county of Essex in very many parliaments; and one of them is its present representative, and now resides at Skreenes. This property, Morant says [3], " has been all along in families that have raised themselves by their merit and eminence in the law." The mansion took its name from Serjeant William Skrene, who was called to the degree of the coif by Henry IV. from the society of Clifford's Inn [4]; and

---

[1] Whitelocke, 108. 234. 237. 240. 245.　　[2] Fuller's Worthies, i. 349.
[3] Morant's Essex, ii. 73.　　[4] See Vol. IV. p. 141.

it was afterwards possessed by Richard Weston, judge of the
Common Pleas in the reign of Elizabeth, whose grandson
became Earl of Portland.   From one of that family it was
purchased by Chief Justice Bramston, by whom the charter
was still kept up; for Moundeford, his second son, was a
master in chancery and knighted; and Francis, his third son,
became a baron of the Exchequer, and will be noticed in the
reign of Charles II.[1]

BREREWOOD, ROBERT.
Just. K. B. 1644.

THE family of Brerewood were flourishing citizens of Chester,
many of them enjoying the municipal honours of that ancient
city.   The judge's grandfather is called a wet-glover there,
and was thrice mayor.   His uncle, Edward, was a famous
scholar, and became the first Gresham professor of astronomy.
His father, John, who was the mayor's eldest son, was sheriff
of Chester; and the judge himself was born there about 1588.
He was admitted into Brazenose College, Oxford, in 1605;
and two years afterwards became a member of the Middle
Temple; where, after somewhat more than the usual seven
years' probation, he was called to the bar on November 13,
1615.   After a lengthened practice of two-and-twenty years,
during which he published several of his uncle's works, he
was appointed a judge of North Wales in 1637; was chosen
reader to his inn in the Lent following, and at Easter, 1639,
was elected recorder of his native city.   The degree of the
coif was conferred upon him in 1640, and in Hilary Term,
1641, he was made king's serjeant.   Receiving the honour of
knighthood in December, 1643, he was advanced to the bench
on the 31st of the next month, and was sworn into offiee at
Oxford on February 6.[2]   The exercise of Sir Robert's judicial

---

[1] The incidents in this memoir, for which no other authority is cited, are derived from Bramston's Autobiography.

[2] Middle Temple Books; Dugdale's Orig. 220.; Chron. Ser.

functions were, however, of short continuance, and were never exercised in Westminster Hall.

Witnessing the extinction of regal authority and lamenting his royal master's untimely death, he passed the remainder of his days in the retirement of his home; and dying there on September 8, 1654, he was buried in St. Mary's church, at Chester.

He married, first, Anna, daughter of Sir Randle Mainwaringe, of Over Pever, in Cheshire, and, secondly, Katherine, daughter of Sir Richard Lea, of Lea and Dernhall, of the same county; and left several children by each of them.[1]

BROMLEY, EDWARD.

B. E. 1625.

See under the Reign of James I.

THIS is the third member of the same family who has been adorned with the judicial ermine; Sir Thomas Bromley, the chief justice in the reign of Queen Mary, being the son, and Sir Thomas Bromley, the lord chancellor in the reign of Queen Elizabeth, being the grandson, of Roger Bromley, of Mitley, Esq.; and Edward, the subject of the present notice, being the son of Sir George Bromley, justice of Chester, the elder brother of the chancellor.

Of his antecedents before he was constituted a baron of the Exchequer, there is no account, except that he kept his terms at the Inner Temple, and was a reader there in Lent, 1606. He was made a serjeant for the purpose of his being raised to the bench; his call taking place on February 5, and his patent as baron being dated February 6, 1610. During the remaining sixteen years of James's reign, and for above two years in that of Charles I., he performed the functions of his office; and, according to Croke, he died in the

---

[1] Wood, Ath. Oxon. ii. 140; Gent. Mag. lxi. 714.

summer vacation of 1627.[1]　It does not appear that he left any issue.

BROWNE, SAMUEL.

PARL. COM. G. S. 1643.　JUST. K. B. 1648.

See under the Reign of Charles II.

CÆSAR, JULIUS.

M. R. 1625.

See under the Reign of James I.

THE parentage of the Cæsar family has already been given in noticing Sir Thomas Cæsar, the cursitor baron of the Exchequer in the last reign.　He was the third, while Sir Julius Cæsar was the eldest, son of Cæsar Adelmare, physician to Queens Mary and Elizabeth, by his wife Margaret Perin or Perient.　Julius was born at Tottenham in Middlesex in 1557, and enjoyed royal patronage from his infancy; Queen Mary, by her proxy Lady Montacute, being his sponsor, together with William Paulett, Marquis of Winchester, lord high treasurer, and Henry Fitzalan, Earl of Arundel.　He received the names of Julins Cæsar; the latter of which he seems very early to have substituted for that of his ancestors; though even so late as 1608 he was designated by both names with an *alias* in formal documents.　Thus in King James's patent to the Inner and Middle Temple, he is described " Sir Julius Cæsar, otherwise Adelmare, knight."

Having lost his father when he was twelve years old, and his mother having married again, he was sent to Oxford, where he became a student at Magdalen Hall, and took the degree of B.A. in 1575, and that of M.A. in 1578.　In October, 1580, he was admitted a member of the Inner Temple, and proceeding to Paris, he took the degree there of doctor in both laws in 1581; after which he returned to Ox-

---

[1] Dugdale's Orig. 138. 167.; Chron. Ser.; Croke, Car. 85.

ford, and proceeded to the same degree in that university in 1583.[1]

In the meantime he had received in October, 1581, two public appointments, one being "Justice of the peace in all cases of piracy," and the other, chancellor to the master of St. Catherine's near the Tower. In the following February he married Dorcas, daughter of Sir Richard Martin, an alderman of London, afterwards master of the Mint, and widow of Richard Lusher. In 1583, he became counsellor to the city of London, and commissary of Essex, Herts, and Middlesex; and on April 30, 1584, he was made judge of the Admiralty Court. Although possessed of so important a post at the early age of 27, he was not contented. In March, 1587, he petitioned the queen to grant him a lease of such of her manors for forty years as should amount to 100 marks yearly; or to give him one of various specified preferments; viz., a deanery, or a hospital, or the provostship of Eton College, or the place of one of the masters of requests. His influence must have been great to have warranted these applications; in which he was only so far at that time successful, that in October, 1588, he was admitted one of the masters in Chancery, an office which was then frequently filled by doctors of the Civil Law. He still continued his importunities, alleging that he had spent 4000*l.* above his gains in the execution of his office of judge of the Admiralty, and in relieving the poor suitors of his court. This statement it would be scarcely possible to credit, if his unlimited charity were not evidenced by the following confirmatory anecdote. "A gentleman," says David Lloyd, "once borrowing his coach, which was as well known to the poor as any hospital in the kingdom, was so followed and encompassed with the London beggars, that it cost him all the money in his purse to satisfy their importunities, so that he might have hired twenty hackney coaches

[1] Wood's Fasti, i. 224.

on the same terms."[1] Isaac Walton says of him that, when grown old, " he was kept alive beyond nature's course, by the prayers of those many poor he daily relieved."

At last his perseverance procured for him, in addition, the appointment of a master extraordinary of the Court of Requests on January 10, 1591; but it was not till August 17, 1595, that he was admitted one of the ordinary masters of that court, which gave him immediate access to the queen. During this time it is amusing to see how he paid his court to the influential ministers and favourites; and how ingeniously he contrived to remind them of his claims in his letters conveying New Years' Gifts, some curious specimens of which are preserved among the Lansdowne MSS. In 1593, without having passed through the grade of reader, he was elected treasurer of the Inner Temple, and on December 8 in the same year he was appointed governor of the mine and battery works throughout England and Wales. Having already procured (by a bribe of 500*l* to Archibald Douglas, the Scottish ambassador, to use his influence with the queen) the reversion of the Mastership of St. Catherine's, he succeeded to it on June 17, 1596.

His wife dying in June, 1595, he entered in the following year into a second matrimonial connection with Alice, daughter of Christopher Green, and widow of John Dent, a rich merchant of London. This lady had two daughters by Mr. Dent, for the wardship of whom she paid the queen 1000*l*. Sir Julius was desirous of securing them in marriage for his two sons, Julius and Charles, but the ladies were not compliant, and two documents are extant, dated in 1606 and 1608, recording their respective refusals.[3] Two years after this marriage, in September, 1598, her majesty inflicted on him the honour of a visit to his house at Mitcham, the

---

[1] State Worthies, 937.　　　　　　[2] Life of Wotton, 178.
[3] Add. MSS. Brit. Mus. 12497. fo. 357. 359.

expense of which, with the customary offering, amounted to 700*l.* sterling. No other incident occurred to him in Elizabeth's reign, except that he obtained a verdict of 200*l.* against a man for asserting that he had pronounced a corrupt sentence against him in the admiralty.[1]

King James knighted him on May 20, 1603; and in the same year reappointed him master of the Court of Requests, and master of St. Catherine's. He was further favoured with grants of the manor of Linwood in Lincolnshire, and of the Forest of High Peak in Derbyshire, for life.[2] On April 11, 1606, the important office of chancellor and under treasurer of the Exchequer was conferred upon him, and in the next year he was sworn of the privy council. During the eight years in which he performed the onerous duties of his place, his main difficulty seems to have been the supplying means to meet the idle profuseness of his master. He had prepared his way for relieving himself from its responsibilities, by obtaining from the king, so early as January 16, 1611, a reversionary grant of the mastership of the Rolls; but he did not come into possession for nearly four years. He was sworn in on September 13, 1614; but as the former grant was questionable, he deemed it advisable, before he took his seat, to have a new patent, dated October 1.

Four months before he entered on his new office, he lost his second wife; but seven months afterwards he entered into espousals with Anne, the daughter of Henry Wodehouse, of Waxham in Norfolk, by Anne, daughter of Sir Nicholas Bacon, lord keeper, and widow of William Hungate, of East Brudenham in the same county.

In the previous year he took a most prominent part in the proceedings for a divorce by the Countess of Essex against her husband for impotency, almost making himself a party in the cause. Abbot, Archbishop of Canterbury, who was at

---

[1] Croke, Eliz. 805.   [2] Rot. Pat. 1 Jac. p. 21.; 2 Jac. p. 13.; 7 Jac.

the head of the commission, could not be prevailed on to give judgment for the nullity of the marriage; and so anxious was the king for it, that he issued a new commission, adding two bishops, so that a majority was obtained over those who dissented.[1]   The lady, two months afterwards, married the Earl of Somerset.

Sir Julius continued master of the Rolls till his death, a period of more than twenty-one years; and during the interval between the disgrace of Lord Chancellor Bacon, and the delivery of the Seal to lord keeper Williams, viz., between May 21 and July 10, 1621, he had a commission to hear causes in Chancery.   To Bacon, with whom he was connected by marriage, he continued a kind friend; assisting him by his bounty, affording him an asylum in his misfortunes, and receiving his last breath in his arms.

He had not any great reputation as a judge, and it is said that counsel would occasionally pass " a slye jeste" upon him. A hubbub occurring in court, one of them cried out, " Silence there, my masters, you keep such a bawling, the master of the Rolls cannot *understand* a word that is spoken."[2]   Clarendon relates, that towards the close of his career, having outlived most of his friends at court, Weston, Earl of Portland, the lord treasurer, taking advantage of this and his old age, procured the appointment of one Mr. Fern, who had bribed him with 6000*l.*, to be one of the six clerks.   This place was in the gift of the master of the Rolls, and he had designed it for his son, Robert Cæsar, " a lawyer of good name, and exceedingly beloved;" but he was easily frightened into admitting the treasurer's nominee.   The transaction made a great noise, and the king hearing of it, promised that " if the old man chanced to die before any other of the six clerks, that offiee, when it should fall, should be conferred on his son, whosoever should succeed him as master of the Rolls;"

---

[1] State Trials, ii. 785., &c.   [2] Anecdotes and Traditions (Camden Soc.), 23.

and the treasurer promised to procure a declaration of this under the sign manual. One day the Earl of Tullibardine, who was nearly allied to Mr. Cæsar, asked the treasurer " whether he had done that business?" To whom he answered, " that he had forgotten it, for which he was heartily sorry; and if he would give him a little note in writing, for a memorial, he would put it among those which he would despatch that evening." The earl presently writ upon a little paper, *Remember Cæsar,* and gave it to him, and he put it in his pocket. Many days passed, but Cæsar never was thought of. At length, when he changed his clothes, his servant brought him all the notes and papers in those he had left off. When he found this little billet, *Remember Cæsar,* which he had never read before, he was exceedingly confounded, and knew not what to think of it. After a serious and melancholic deliberation with his friends, it was agreed that it was the advertisement, by some friend who durst not own the discovery, of a conspiracy against the treasurer's life by his many and mighty enemies. They all knew Cæsar's fate by contemning such a notice, and therefore concluded that he should pretend to be indisposed, that he might not stir abroad all that day. The porter was ordered to open the gates to nobody, nor to go to bed till the morning; and some servants were ordered to watch with him, lest violence should be used at the gate; and they themselves, and some other gentlemen, would sit up all night, and attend the event. It was late next morning before any one was admitted. At last the Earl of Tullibardine came, and asking whether he had remembered Cæsar, the truth flashed upon the treasurer, who could not forbear telling the jest to his friends.[1]

[1] Clarendon, i. 94. The name of Mr. Fern does not appear in Mr. Duffus Hardy's List of the Six Clerks. Mr. Robert Cæsar was appointed three months before his father's death.

Sir Julius died on April 18, 1636, at the age of seventy-nine, and was buried at Great St. Helen's, Bishopsgate, where his father lay. Over his remains was placed a monument with an inscription written by himself, in the form of a deed with a pendant seal, the connecting silk of which is broken.

He had no issue by his last wife; but his other two brought him eight children. Of the five by his first wife only one survived him, viz., Charles, who, three years after the death of his father, became master of the Rolls. His second wife produced to him three sons: John, who was knighted at the age of ten; Thomas, who became a doctor in divinity; and Robert, who obtained the place of one of the six clerks in Chancery; no descendants of any of whom remain.[1]

CÆSAR, CHARLES.

M. R. 1639.

CHARLES CÆSAR, the eldest surviving son of Sir Julius, the master of the Rolls, was born on January 27, 1589. Destined to pursue the profession by which his father had risen, he was sent to All Souls' College in the university of Oxford, and was admitted to the degree of doctor of laws on December 7, 1612.[2] Commencing practice in the Ecclesiastical Courts, he received the order of knighthood on October 6 in the following year, and was gradually promoted, first to the office of the master of the faculties, and then to that of judge of the audience.[3] According to a common practice in those times, of selecting the masters in Chancery from among the doctors of laws, Sir Charles Cæsar attained that appointment on May 19, 1615[4], no doubt by the interest of his father, who had been sworn in as a judge of that court in the preceding year. In his customary attendance on the House

[1] Lodge's Memoirs of the Cæsars.
[2] Wood's Fasti, i. 348.
[3] State Trials, ii. 1452.
[4] Hardy's Catalogue, 89.

of Lords, it fell to his duty to carry down to the Commons the Duke of Buckingham's answer to the articles of impeachment against him.[1] This is the only incident related of Sir Charles till the death of Sir Dudley Digges, in 1639, who had succeeded his father three years before as master of the Rolls.

Sir Charles was desirous to obtain this place, and went to Archbishop Laud to consult him about it, when that prelate " told him plainly that as things then stood the place was not like to go without more money than he thought any wise man would give for it."[2] Sir Charles was not disheartened, and bid so highly that it appears by a memorandum made by his son that he paid for that " high and profitable place " no less than 15,000l., " broad pieces of gold," with a loan of 2000l. more when the king went to meet his rebellious Scottish army. He received his patent for the office on March 30, 1639. It is difficult to regret that he did not live long enough to profit by this iniquitous traffic of the judicial seat, as disgraceful to one party as the other. In November, 1642, the small-pox seized the family, and proved fatal to one of his daughters on the 2nd of that month, to himself on the 6th of December, and to his eldest son five days after. They were buried at Bennington in Herts, where his estate was situate ; and his monument there bears an inscription commemorative of his personal worth and his judicial integrity. It records besides, that he had two wives — the first, Anne, daughter of Sir Peter Vanlore, knight, an eminent London merchant ; and the second, Jane, daughter of Sir Edward Barkham, knight, lord mayor of London ; and that he had six children by the first wife, and nine by the second. Of these fifteen only five survived him, two daughters and three sons — Julius, who lived but five days after his father ; Henry, who and

---

[1] Parl. Hist. ii. 191.　　　　[2] State Trials, iv. 417.

whose son and grandson were successively members of parliament for the county of Herts; and Charles, of Great Grandsden in Huntingdonshire, whose son was treasurer of the navy in the reign of Queen Anne. The patrimonial possessions were eventually dissipated, and no male descendant now preserves the name of the family.[1]

CECIL, WILLIAM, Earl of Salisbury.

Parl. Com. Great Seal, 1646.

THE appearance of William Cecil, second Earl of Salisbury, in these pages arises from his filling the place of one of the parliamentary commissioners of the Great Seal for less than four months. His grandfather was the renowned Lord Burleigh, and his father was Robert Cecil, the wise minister of Queen Elizabeth and James I., who, after serving both sovereigns, and after passing through the two lower grades of the peerage, was created Earl of Salisbury in 1605. On his death, in 1612, this William succeeded, but did not do much credit to his lineage. At first the obsequious servant of his sovereign, he concurred in every act proposed by the court, and attended King Charles when he retired in his troubles to York, joining the peers in signing the declaration that the king had no intention to take warlike measures. Soon after, without any apparent reason, he fled from court, deserting the king's party for that of the parliament, and forming one of the small knot of lords who legislated at Westminster. He had the effrontery to appear before the king at Oxford as a commissioner to treat for peace, and was named in the same capacity in the proposed treaty at Uxbridge. Though totally without credit with either party, he was appointed a commissioner of the Great Seal on July 3, 1646, in place of the Earl of Bolinbroke deceased, but was not sworn in till Au-

---

[1] Lodge's Lives of the Cæsars.

gust 11. The parliament, however, withdrew their confidence from him and the other commissioners on October 30, and placed the Seal in the custody of the speakers of the two houses.

On the decapitation of the king he allowed himself to be nominated one of the Council of State, and, as if this was not a sufficient degradation, he got himself, on the abolition of the House of Lords, returned as a member of the House of Commons for Lynn in Norfolk, in September, 1649. After being expelled with the rest by Cromwell in 1653, he joined the Rump a its meeting in 1659, to be again expelled, and again restored. In none of these variations is any act of his recorded, save the bare mention that they actually took place. His insignificance probably saved him on the restoration of Charles II., who no doubt thought that the contempt which all men felt for the degraded earl was a sufficient punishment.

He died on December 3, 1668. His descendants have wiped out his disgrace, and, at the end of nearly two centuries, flourish with the additional title of marquess, granted in 1789.[1]

CHAMBERLAYNE, THOMAS.

JUST. C. P. 1625.

See under the Reign of James I.

THIS family claims a noble origin, being descended from William, Count Tankerville, who was one of the Norman followers of William the Conqueror, and whose son John became lord chamberlain to Henry I. ; the same office being held by several of his descendants, its name thus became attached to them. They spread through various counties, and were eminent in different departments of the State. One of the branches of the family, William Chamberlayne, brother of

---

[1] Dugdale's Baron. ii. 407. ; Clarendon's Hist. i. 279., iii. 559. ; Whitelocke, 376. 409. 425. ; Parl. Hist. iii. 1547. ; Journals.

Sir Thomas Chamberlayne who was employed in diplomacy by Henry VIII. and his three successors, settled in Ireland, and was the father of the subject of the present article.

Thomas Chamberlayne began his career as a student in Gray's Inn. Admitted there in 1577, he was called to the bar on January 25, 1585, and became autumn reader in 1607.[1] From several letters among the Egerton MSS., he appears at this time to have been in the confidence of Lord Chancellor Ellesmere[2], to whose patronage he probably owed his further advancement. He was called to the degree of the coif in Michaelmas Term, 1614, and was soon after advanced to the office of chief justice of Chester, and knighted. From this position he was selected to be one of the judges of the King's Bench on October 8, 1620.[3] In that court he remained only four years; for, whether from feeling the duties too onerous, or from some other cause, he retired from it on October 18, 1624, and resumed his judicial seat at Chester[4], which he retained till his death on September 17, 1625.

But before that event occurred he seems, on the accession of Charles I., to have been recalled to Westminster Hall. In a commission dated May 12, 1625, he is described not only as chief justice of Chester, but also as one of the judges of the Common Pleas. He is likewise mentioned by Sir William Jones, under Easter Term, 1 Car., as one of the Judges before whom the case of Lord Sheffield v. Ratcliffe was argued in the Exchequer Chamber, in which it appears that after various hearings, extending over two years, the judges were equally divided. The probability is that the case, being a very important one, and the former arguments having been made before him, it was deemed expedient that he should take part in the last hearing, and that he was accordingly appointed *pro hac vice*. Mr. Justice Godbolt, in reporting the

[1] Gray's Inn Books.
[2] Egerton Papers, 453.
[3] Dugdale's Chron. Series.
[4] Croke, Jac. 690.

same case, says, that in consequence of the equality of voices, Sir Henry Yelverton was raised to the bench, so as to give a preponderance according to his view of the case.[1]

Sir Thomas married Elizabeth, daughter of Sir George Fermor, knight, of Easton Nestor in Northamptonshire, and widow of Sir William Stafford, knight, of Blatherwick in the same county. His eldest son, Thomas, of Wickham in Oxfordshire, was a loyal adherent to King Charles in his misfortunes, and was by him created a baronet in 1642, a title which lasted 134 years, and expired, on the death of his grandson Henry without issue, in 1776.[2]

COLEPEPER, JOHN, Lord Colepeper.
M. R. 1643.
See under the Reign of Charles II.

COVENTRY, THOMAS, Lord Coventry.
Lord Keeper, 1625.

THE civic descent of this family has been given in the memoir of Sir Thomas Coventry, one of the judges of the Common Pleas in the last reign. The lord keeper, who bore the same name, was the eldest son of the judge, by Margaret, daughter and heir of . . . . Jeffreys, of Earles-Croome, *alias* Croome D'Abitot, in Worcestershire. He was born there in the year 1578, and, having passed the first fourteen years of his life under the tuition of his parents, he was placed as a gentleman-commoner at Balliol College, Oxford, of which his father had been a fellow, at Michaelmas, 1592. At the end of three years he was admitted a member of the Inner Temple, where his father had studied before him; and having, after passing through the regular legal

---

[1] Rymer, xviii. 67 ; W. Jones's Reports, 70. ; Godbolt's Reports, 300.
[2] Wotton's Baronet. ii. 374.

course, been called to the bar, he entered on his professional career. He is mentioned in Coke's Reports as an advocate so early as 1611, and soon becoming a bencher of his Inn of Court, he was elected reader in autumn, 1616, and treasurer in the next year.[1]

By the respect he showed to Sir Edward Coke, he entailed upon himself the enmity of Bacon, who sought to impede his professional advance by prejudicing the king against him. When Coventry was a candidate for the recordership of London, on Sir Henry Montagu being raised to the office of chief justice of the King's Bench, Bacon suggested to the king, that "it is very material, as these times are, that your Majesty have some care that the Recorder succeeding be a temperate and discreet man . . . . The man upon whom the choice is like to fall, which is Coventry, I hold doubtful for your service; not but that he is well learned, and an honest man, but he hath been, as it were, bred by Lord Coke, and seasoned in his ways."[2] The shaft fell harmless: the testimony to his learning and integrity prevailed more than the insinuation against his courtly pliancy; and Coventry was not only elected recorder on November 16, 1616, but on March 14, 1617, was taken into the king's own service as solicitor-general, and knighted. Four years after, also, when Sir Henry Yelverton, the attorney-general, was sequestered from his place, pending the proceedings against him in the Star Chamber, Sir Thomas Coventry received a patent on June 28, 1620, directing him provisionally to perform its duties in the interim; and on Sir Henry's condemnation, he received the appointment absolutely on January 11, 1621.[3] One of the first duties he had to perform in his new offiee was to take a message from the Lords to Bacon, requiring him to send specific answers to the charges against

---

[1] Dugdale's Orig. Jur. 167. 171.   [2] Bacon's Works (Montagu), xii. 310.
[3] Dugdale's Chron. Series; Rymer, xvii. 231.

him.   Soon after he had to prosecute Edward Floyde for his presumption in calling the king's daughter and her husband " Goodman Palsgrave and Goodwife Palsgrave ;" but he was not answerable for the brutal sentence which the Lords pronounced upon the silly speaker.[1]

On King James's death he was retained in his office by King Charles, and before the end of the year was called upon to supply the place of Bishop Williams, whom Buckingham had succeeded in dismissing; receiving the Great Seal as lord keeper on November 1, 1625.   His letter to Buckingham forms a strong contrast with Bacon's on a similar occasion. It is a manly and modest doubt of his own capacity for the place, a dutiful submission, after full consideration, to the royal will, and a courtly acknowledgment of the duke's favour.[2]   But there is nothing in it that shows any previous application, nor any undue reliance on the interference of the favourite.   A week before his appointment Bacon, though he had thrown impediments to his early advance, wrote to him about the reversion of his titles, which it seems he was then seeking, and with bad taste begging a place under the new lord keeper for one of his servants.   Coventry answered him kindly as to his own affair; but with respect to his servant, gave him no hopes; reminding him that he had servants and relations of his own, and many applications from the court.[3]   The name or circumstances of the servant are not mentioned; but it would be difficult to explain, even if Bacon had not been inimical to Coventry, what claim he had, nearly five years after his dismissal, to foist one of his servants by anticipation upon Coventry; or still more, why his refusal should be called " unfeeling and discreditable."[4]

He had to open the second parliament of the reign, and soon after to deliver the king's reprimand to the Commons

[1] Parl. Hist. i. 1239. 1260.   [2] Harl. MSS. quoted by Lodge.
[3] Bacon's Works (Montagu), xii. 461.   [4] Lord Campbell, ii. 507.

for their negligence in completing the supply, and their encouragement of seditious speeches. This he did in terms so absolute, that the Duke of Buckingham was obliged afterwards to qualify and explain them. He had little to do in reference to the imprisonment of the Earl of Arundel and the demand of the peers for his release, except as the messenger of the king and the organ of the house.[1] The angry dissolution of this parliament, notwithstanding his earnest endeavours to prevent such a termination, soon after taking place, the king endeavoured to supply his necessities by forced loans; but, not succeeding to his wish, he called a third parliament in March, 1628. Sir Thomas Coventry opened this in an eloquent speech, which would have been more effective had it not contained an intimation that, if there were not a readiness in voting supplies, the king might resort to other means by the use of his prerogatives. But before the end of the session he had to pray of the king a more explicit answer to the Petition of Right; which was accordingly given on June 7, 1628, in the well-known formula, " Soit droit fait comme il est désiré."[2]

On April 10, more than three months before the prorogation of the parliament, the lord keeper was created a baron, by the title of Lord Coventry of Aylesborough, in the county of Worcester. When Buckingham applied for the dormant offiee and almost unlimited powers of lord high constable, Lord Coventry showed a patriotic spirit in opposing the grant, and thus incurring the hatred of the favourite. Peremptorily accosting him, the duke said:—"Who made you lord keeper?" " The king," said Coventry, boldly.—" It's false," said Buckingham; "'twas I did make you, and you shall find that I who made you, can and will unmake you." Coventry retorted, "Did I conceive I held my place by your favour, I would presently unmake myself, by rendering the Seal to

---

[1] Parl. Hist. ii. 39. 56. 60. 125.   [2] Ibid. 218. 409.

his Majesty." Buckingham would have put his threat into execution, and probably have obtained the Seal for Sir Henry Yelverton, had he not been assassinated in the following August.[1] This parliament, after another session, was hastily dissolved like the former; the close of it being distinguished by the forcible detention of the speaker (Sir John Finch) in the chair, while the Protestation of the Commons against Tonnage and Poundage was passed.

No other parliament met for the eleven remaining years of Coventry's life, — a circumstance which, however impolitic, could not be distasteful to his personal disposition. He was more of a lawyer than a politician, and would no doubt be glad to be relieved from defending measures which he could not honestly justify. The holder of the Great Seal was no longer, as in Wolsey's time, the director of the State; other and more active spirits acquired the ascendancy, and their opinions prevailed. No one can read the history of the time without seeing that Coventry had but little influence in the councils of his sovereign, which were in a great measure directed personally by the king, under the guidance, first of a favourite, and then of unscrupulous and intemperate advisers. In times when all men's actions were open to censure, and none escaped who could be charged with too violent a support of the royal prerogative, or with too manifest a tendency to infringe on the liberty of the subject, the very absence of the name of one who held so high an official position, tells strongly in his favour, as showing that his personal demeanour and his imputed principles were not to any great extent obnoxious to those who were assuming the rule and punishing their opponents. In Lilburn's case, though Coventry presided on the condemnation, his estate was not in the first instance attempted to be charged with the compensation awarded; and it was not till the estates upon which the reparation was voted, were dis-

---

[1] Hacket's Bp. Williams, ii. 19.

posed of in another manner, nor till eight years after the lord keeper's death, that the pertinacious sufferer conceived the idea of coming on Lord Coventry's heir.[1] The attempt was frustrated, even in the strong excitement of that period, by a large majority; and the vote, though perhaps influenced by some personal motives, was no doubt dictated principally by the conviction, that the cruelty and illegality of the sentence against Lilburn could not be justly imputed to the lord keeper. At the same time it is difficult altogether to excuse his Lordship from participation in the iniquitous punishments which were too often awarded in the Star Chamber, except on the presumption that, though presiding, he had but a single voice, and that, by the course of the court, he gave his opinion last, and was compelled to pronounce the censure of the majority. That his inclinations were on the side of mercy, the judgment in Chambers's case[2] proves. In Henry Sherfield's case, for breaking a painted glass window[3], he was, after giving a lenient sentence, actually out-voted; and in the case of Dr. Leighton, for publishing " A Plea against Prelacy [4]," and in other similar accusations, it requires not much discrimination to decide to whom the severity of the punishment is to be attributed.

At the introduction of the imposition of ship-money, originally proposed by Attorney-General Noy, Lord Coventry, in the speech which, according to the practice of the times, he addressed to the judges previously to the commencement of the circuits in June, 1635, enlarged upon the necessity of providing for the defence of the realm; announced the intended issue of writs, not only to the maritime towns, but to the whole kingdom besides; and enjoined the judges, in their charges to the grand jury, to urge the people to pay their contributions with alacrity and cheerfulness. And in his speech to them before the next Lent Assizes, he reiterated

---

[1] State Trials, iii. 1315.   [2] Ibid. 374.   [3] Ibid. 519.   [4] Ibid. 383.

these injunctions, and read publicly the king's letter to the
judges on the subject, and their joint answer confirming the
king's claim to the impost.[1]   From his position as lord keeper,
he was precluded from giving any legal opinion on the case
of Hampden, who resisted the Levy, the judgment being pronounced by the twelve judges alone ; and he was not a party
to, nor a witness of, the consequences that resulted from these
proceedings, his death taking place before the next parliament
met.   That event occurred at Durham House in the Strand
(where the Adelphi now stands), on January 14, 1640; and
his remains were removed for interment in the family vault at
Croome D'Abitot.   His last message to the king was a request, " That his Majesty would take all distastes from the
Parliament summoned against April with patience, and suffer
it to sit without an unkind dissolution." [2]

He had held the Seal for above fourteen years ; and every
writer of any authority has refrained from making any specific
charge against him.   Even Whitelocke, who had evidently
no good will towards him, can say no more than that he was
" of no transcendant parts or fame."   His other contemporaries differ from this judgment, and unite in praising him.
Croke calls him " a pious, prudent, and learned man, and strict
in his practice, . . . he died in great honour, and much lamented
by all the people."   The Sloane MS.[3] describes him as " of
very quick apprehension, and of an exceeding judicious and
expeditious dispatch in all affairs, either of state or of the
tribunal; . . . an helper or coadjutor of counsel at the bar, and
understood better what they would have said in a case than
what they sometimes did say for their clients."   After giving
a most favourable account of his temper and dispositions, this
writer, who, as a sufferer by one of his decisions, had no reason
for partiality, adds, " For his erudition and acquisition of art,

---

[1] Rushworth, ii. 294. 352.   [2] Hacket's Bp. Williams, ii. 137.
[3] Quoted in Lodge's Portraits, vol. v.

though all knew he was learned in the sciences, and most profound in his profession, yet such was the happiness of his constellation, that he rather leaned to his native strength than depended on any artificial reliance." Clarendon says he discharged all his earlier offices " with great ability and singular reputation for integrity," and that in his place of lord keeper " he enjoyed it with an universal reputation (and sure justice was never better administered)." Of his " parts " the same author says, " He was a man of wonderful gravity and wisdom, and understood not only the whole science and mystery of the law, at least equally with any man who had ever sate in that place ; but had a clear conception of the whole policy of the government, both of Church and State, which by the unskilfulness of some well meaning men, justled each the other too much. He knew the temper, disposition, and genius of the kingdom most exactly ; saw their spirits grow every day more sturdy, inquisitive, and impatient ; and therefore naturally abhorred all innovations." In answer to those who " thought he was not active and stout enough in opposing those innovations," the writer explains, " that he was seldom known to speak in matters of State, which, he well knew, were for the most part concluded before they were brought to that public agitation." " To conclude, his security consisted very much in his having but little credit with the king ; and he died in a season most opportune, in which a wise man would have prayed to have finished his course, and which, in truth, crowned his other signal prosperity in the world."

Anthony Wood, Fuller, and David Lloyd are equally encomiastic. The comeliness and gravity of his aspect, the dignity of his carriage, the grace of his elocution, and the kindness and affability of his manners, were so universally acknowledged, that it is not surprising that he had, as Lord Clarendon says in recording his death, " the rare felicity in being looked upon generally throughout the kingdom with great affection, and a singular esteem, when very few men in any high trust were so." [1] A charge of bribery was got up against him by a disappointed suitor, but was so palpably unfounded and malignant, that the Star Chamber visited the contriver and all his assistants with severe penalties of purse and person. [2]

Lord Coventry was twice married. His first wife was Sarah, daughter of Edward Sebright, of Besford in Worcestershire; and his second was Elizabeth, daughter of John Aldersey, of Spurston in Cheshire [3], and widow of William Pitchford, Esq. By both of them he left issue. His grandson, Thomas, was advanced in 1697 to the titles of Viscount Deerhurst and Earl of Coventry, with a special limitation, under which they are now held by the descendants of Walter, the lord keeper's brother; the original barony having become extinct in 1719, by the death of the fourth earl without male issue. [4]

CRAWLEY, FRANCIS.

Just. C. P. 1632.

FRANCIS CRAWLEY was of a Bedfordshire family, residing at Someris, near Luton, in that county. [5] He received his legal education at Staple Inn and Gray's Inn; to the latter of which he was admitted on May 26, 1598, and, having been called to the bar in the usual time, was elected autumn reader in 1623, on the occasion of his being summoned to take the degree of the coif. [6] In 1626 he was one of the counsel whom the Earl of Bristol desired to be assigned to him on his impeachment [7]; and, on Sir Francis Harvey's death, he

---

[1] Clarendon, i. 80. 231.   [2] Rushworth, ii. App. 30.

[3] Bramston, in his Autobiography, p. 251., says that the name of this lady's father was Hoskins

[4] Wood's Ath. Oxon. ii. 650.; Fuller's Worthies, ii. 470.

[5] Grandeur of the Law (1684).   [6] Gray's Inn Books.   [7] Parl. Hist. ii. 98.

was appointed a judge of the Common Pleas on October 11, 1632, and knighted. In the great case of Ship-money, he not only joined the rest of the judges in their answer to the king's letter affirming its legality, but in an elaborate argument in the Exchequer Chamber, in February, 1638, he gave a decided opinion in favour of the king against Hampden, which he repeated at the assizes, asserting in his charge to the grand jury, " That ship-money was so inherent a right in the crown, that it would not be in the power of a parliament to take it away." For these opinions, and particularly the last, he was impeached by the Long Parliament, the charge against him being introduced in July, 1641, in a powerful speech by Mr. Waller, who warmly urged the enormity of the doctrine.[1] In August the house resolved that the impeached judges should have no commissions to go the circuits; but it appears that they still continued to sit in Westminster Hall. Justice Crawley joined the king at Oxford in 1642, and on the following Jannary was made doctor of civil law in that university.[2] The state of the kingdom probably prevented his trial from taking place, notwithstanding his extreme unpopularity; but on November 24, 1645, the Commons passed an ordinance disabling him and four others " from being judges, as though they were dead." [3]

He died on February 13, 1649, having survived his sovereign only a fortnight, and was buried at Luton. His wife was Elizabeth, daughter of Sir John Rotherham, knight, of that place, by whom he left two sons. The eldest, John, dying without children, the patrimonial property devolved on his brother, Francis, who is described, in 1660, in the list of those qualified to be knights of the contemplated order of the Royal Oak, as possessed of an estate in Bedfordshire worth

[1] State Trials, iii. 1078. 1301.   [2] Wood's Fasti, ii. 44.
[3] Whitelocke's Mem. 181.

1000*l.* a year[1], and who became cursitor baron of the Exchequer in the reign of Charles II.[2]

CRESHELD, RICHARD.
PARL. JUST. C. P. 1648.

IN the propositions made by the parliament to the king in February, 1643, they name " Mr. Serjeant Creswell " as one of those whom they desire to be appointed justices of the Common Pleas.[3]   In September, 1647, " Mr. Serjeant Creswell " is mentioned by Whitelocke as accompanying Mr. Justice Bacon on the circuit, and there committing a person for words spoken against the king.   On October 12, 1648, the same writer states that " Mr. Serjeant Creswell " was made a judge of the Common Pleas by the parliament; and again states that " Creswell " was one of the judges who refused to act after the death of the king.[4]

Notwithstanding these authorities, there was no serjeant of the name.   The person intended is Richard Cresheld, who was summoned to take the coif in 1636[5], and who is recorded under that name in Dugdale's List of Serjeants.   By an abbreviated mispronunciation of the name it became corrupted to Creswell, for even in Sir W. Jones's Reports of the period he is called, when appointed, " Creswell."[6]

He was admitted into the society of Lincoln's Inn on June 18, 1608, under the description of " Richard Cresheld, son of Edward Cresheld, of Mattishall-Burgh in the county of Norfolk; " and having studied for seven years he was called to the bar on October 17, 1615, and became bencher in

---

[1] Wotton's Baronet. v. 353.

[2] I am indebted to Henry H. Gibbs, Esq., a relative of Chief Justice Sir Vicary Gibbs, for information of the family of Judge Crawley, with which he is maternally connected.

[3] Clarendon, iii. 407.

[4] Whitelocke, 269. 342. 378.

[5] Rymer, xx. 22.

[6] W. Jones's Reports, 390.

1633.[1] He sat for the borough of Evesham in Worcestershire in King James's last parliament, and was returned member for the same place (of which he was recorder) in all the parliaments in King Charles's reign.[2]   In 1628 he led the van in the Committee of Grievances, presided over by Mr. (afterwards lord keeper) Lyttelton, in a speech sufficiently complimentary to the king, but arguing strongly against the legality of imprisonment without declaration of the cause.[3] He does not appear to have often taken part in the debates; and in the Long Parliament his return was contested, or rather that of his colleague, Mr. Sandys, who was displaced by Mr. Coventry; but the same confusion of the name appears.[4]   On his receiving his writ of summons to take the coif, the usual compliment was paid him by his inn of appointing him Lent reader[5] before he retired from the society; and, when his inauguration took place, he was presented with a purse of ten guineas, as the customary viaticum.[6]

That he accommodated himself to the views of the popular party is apparent by **his** receiving the thanks of the Commons on November 2, 1642, for " the good service done by Serjeant Cresweld in the country upon the matter of contributions, and other services[7]," by their proposing him to be a judge in 1643, and by their appointing him one in 1648; but that he disapproved of their violent proceedings is equally apparent from his refusal to act under their usurped authority on the death of the king.   It is to be regretted that no further information remains of a judge who had the courage to vacate his seat in such perilous times.

One of his daughters married William Noel of Kirkby Mallory.[8]

---

[1] Lincoln's Inn Books.   [2] Notes and Queries, 2nd S. i. 460.
[3] Parl. Hist ii. 240., where, quoting Sir J. Napier's MSS., he is called Creskeld.   Rushworth i. 506., giving the same speech, calls him Creswell.
[4] Rushworth, iv. 9.   [5] Dugdale's Orig. 255. 266.
[6] Lincoln's Inn Books.   [7] Commons' Journal, ii. 831.
[8] Wotton's Baronet. iii. 93.

CREWE, RANULPHE.

Ch. K. B. 1625.

See under the Reign of James I.

CREW or Crue is a manor in Cheshire, which gave the name
to a family in the reign of Edward I.[1], from a younger branch
of which the chief justice traces his descent.   His father,
John Crewe, was settled at Nantwich, and is said to have
been a tannèr in that town.   By his wife Alice Mainwaring,
he left two sons, both of whom were the ancestors of noble
families.   Ranulphe (as he himself spelled it), the elder, whose
career is now to be narrated; and Thomas, the younger,
a serjeant at law, and speaker of the House of Commons in
the last parliament of James I. and in the first of Charles I.,
whose son, John Crewe, in 1661, was created Baron Crewe,
of Stene in Northamptonshire.   This barony became extinct
in 1721, on the death of Nathaniel, Bishop of Durham, the
third baron, without issue.[2]

Ranulphe Crewe was born about the year 1558.   Of his
early life there are no particulars, till he was admitted a member
of Lincoln's Inn, on November 13, 1577, and was called to
the bar, after the customary seven years' study, on November
8, 1584.[3]   Though he had acquired sufficient eminence to be
elected member for Brackley in the parliament of 1597[4], his
name is not mentioned as an advocate in any of the Reports
till Michaelmas, 1598.   In that year he married Juliana, the
daughter and heir of John Clipsby, of Clipsby in Norfolk,
with whom he had a fair inheritance.[5]   He was admitted to
the bench of Lincoln's Inn on November 3, 1600, and filled
the office of reader to the society in autumn, 1602.[6]   Judging

[1] Cal. Inq. p. m. i. 119.
[2] Collins's Peerage, ix. 326.
[3] Linc. Inn, Black Bk. v. 230. 364.
[4] Hinchcliffe's Barthomley, 222.
[5] Fuller's Worthies, i. 188.
[6] Dugdale's Orig. 254. 262.

from the published Reports, he does not seem to have been much employed in the courts, yet it is evident that his reputation as a lawyer must have been considerable, as he was selected to defend the king's title to alnage in the House of Lords in 1606, for his "travail and pains" in which he received 10*l.*[1]; and as his professional income was so considerable, that he was enabled, two years afterwards, to gratify the great object of his ambition by the acquisition of the aucestral property from which he derived his name. He purchased the manor of Crewe from Sir Edward Coke and his wife Lady Elizabeth Hatton; and thus becoming repossessed of the estate which for nearly three hundred years had had no Crewe for its owner, he built the magnificent seat there, which has ever since been the seat of the family.

Of that parliament which met on April 5, 1614, and was so hastily dissolved on the 7th of the following June, to which he was returned as representative of his native county, he had the honour to be selected as speaker[2]; but he did not participate in the king's displeasure towards the other members, since he was knighted the day after the dissolution, and, being called to the degree of the coif on July 1, was (though not so recorded by Dugdale) a few days afterwards made king's serjeant. In this character he sat, in 1615, as a commissioner on the trial of Weston for the murder of Sir Thomas Overbury; and was one of the counsel for the crown against the Earl and Countess of Somerset.[3] He was also concerned in the shameful trial of Edward Peacham for treason at Taunton.[4]

He was not in the next parliament of 1620; but conducted the proceedings in the House of Lords against Sir Francis Michell, the monopolist, Sir Henry Yelverton, late attorney-general, and Sir John Bennet, judge of the Prerogative

---

[1] Pell Records, Jac. 64.
[2] State Trials, ii. 911. 952. 989.
[2] Parl. Hist. i. 1153.
[4] Walter Yonge's Diary, 28.

Court.[1] In the parliament of 1624, he opened some of the charges against Cranfield, Earl of Middlesex[2]; and when Sir James Ley succeeded that nobleman as lord treasurer, Sir Ranulphe was selected to fill his place as chief justice of the King's Bench, to which he was promoted on January 26, 1625.

King James died in the following March. His successor having angrily dissolved two parliaments in less than fifteen months, was compelled to resort to unconstitutional means to replenish his exhausted exchequer. One of these was by forced loans from his subjects according to the amount they would have paid towards a subsidy. The judges, who among the rest were applied to, paid the money demanded; but refusing to subscribe a paper recognising the legality of the collection, Chief Justice Crewe was selected as an example, and was discharged from his office on November 9, 1626, having held it not quite two years. In 1628, he wrote a manly and modest letter to the Duke of Buckingham, pleading for his restoration to the king's favour, in which he took credit to himself that he had declined to be in the parliament just prorogued, "distrusting that I might be called upon to have discovered the passages concerning my removal."[3] Whatever intentions the duke might have had of repairing the injury he had done to the chief justice, they were frustrated by his assassination by Felton, in the August of that year. After another application to the king himself, which produced no result, Sir Ranulphe retired from public life. He survived his dismissal more than nineteen years, witnessing the calamitous effects of those illegal measures to which he had refused his judicial sanction, and suffering much from the consequences of the civil war, his revenues being seized and his mansion ransacked by the soldiers of that parliament which

---

[1] State Trials, ii. 1136. 1143. 1146.   [2] Parl. Hist. i. 1447.
[3] Yonge's Diary, 98.; Rymer xviii. 791 ;. Erdeswicke's Staffordsh. 71.

had made those measures the ostensible motive of the rebellion.[1]

He died at his house in Westminster on January 13, 1646 ;
and his remains, deposited in a stone coffin, on the lid of which
his effigy is carved, were interred so late as the 5th of the
following June, in a chapel he had erected in the church of
Barthomley, the parish in which Crewe Hall is situate.

As a lawyer he was learned and painstaking ; as a judge
he was assiduous and patient; of his honesty, independence,
and integrity (so justly lauded by Mr. Hollis in parliament[2]),
he gave the best proof that man can offer; and of his eloquence he has left a most favourable specimen, in his speech
to the Lords on the titles of De Vere.   After describing the
500 years of unbroken lineage in the family, he exclaimed :
" I have laboured to make a covenant with myself that affection may not press upon judgment ; for I suppose there is no
man that hath any apprehension of gentry or nobleness, but
his affection stands to the continuance of so noble a name and
house, and would take hold of a twig or a twinethread to
uphold it.   And yet Time has his revolutions ; — there must
be a period and an end of all temporal things —*finis rerum,*
—an end of names and dignities, and whatsoever is terrene;
and why not of De Vere?   For where is Bohun ?   Where is
Mowbray ?   Where is Mortimer ?   Nay, which is more and
most of all, where is Plantagenet?   They are entombed in
the urns and sepulchres of mortality.   And yet let the name
and dignity of De Vere stand so long as it pleaseth God!"[3]

By his first wife, who died in 1623, he left a son, Clipsby
Crewe, whose grandson dying without issue, his sister (married to John Offley, Esq., of Madeley in Staffordshire) succeeded to the inheritance.   Their son took the name of Crewe,
and both he and his son and grandson represented their native

---

[1] Barthomley, 238.   [2] Rushworth, ii. App. 266.
[3] Sir W. Jones's Reports, 101.

county until 1806, when the latter was elevated to the peerage by the title of Lord Crewe, of Crewe in Cheshire. His grandson now enjoys the title and estate.

Sir Ranulphe married, secondly, another Juliana, daughter of Edward Fnsey, of London, and relict of Sir Thomas Hesketh, Knt., by whom he had no children.[1]

CROKE, GEORGE.
Just. C. P. 1625.   Just. K. B. 1628.
See under the Reign of James I.

SIR GEORGE CROKE was the third son of Sir John Croke of Chilton in Buckinghamshire and Elizabeth Unton; and was seven years junior to his brother Sir John Croke the judge in the last reign, being born about 1560. He received the rudiments of his education at the school at Thame founded by Lord Williams, and completed it at Christ Church College, Oxford, where he was admitted in 1575. In the same year on February 7th, he was entered of the Inner Temple, where, having been called to the bar in Hilary Term, 1584, he became a bencher on November 5, 1597, was appointed autumn reader in 1599, and again in Lent, 1618, having in the interim, in 1609, filled the office of treasurer.[2] He commenced his parliamentary career in 1597 as member for Berealston.

Though not mentioned in his own Reports as an advocate till Michaelmas 1588, he had commenced his collections for them seven years before; showing an early devotion to the practical part of his profession. He did not attain legal honours, however, till four years after his brother's death, when he was made serjeant at law and king's serjeant nearly at the same time; his writ being dated in June 1623, and his inauguration taking place in the following Michaelmas. King James knighted him on the occasion. Long before this period

---

[1] Barthomley, 239.   [2] Dugdale's Orig. 167. 171.

his professional profits were so considerable as to enable him in 1615 to purchase the estate of Waterstock in Oxfordshire of Sir William Cave; and Studley Priory in 1621 of his nephew. Judge Whitelocke, in his diary, says that he did not receive the coif sooner, because he refused to give money; and offence was taken at his saying he thought "it was not for the King:"—so common it was in those days to pay for honours, and so large a part of these unholy payments were known to be appropriated by those about the court.

He had not been eighteen months a serjeant ere he was raised to the bench on February 11, 1625, as a justice of the Common Pleas, in the place of Sir Humphry Winch.[1] In six weeks the death of James I. occurred, when his patent was renewed by King Charles; who, on October 9, 1628, removed him to the court of King's Bench on the death of Sir John Doderidge. He had no successor in the Common Pleas; the opportunity being taken to reduce the judges from five, to which they had been increased by James I., to the original number of four.[2]

The twelve years that he sat there were those that immediately preceded the great Rebellion; which the courts of justice were greatly instrumental in hastening. They were used as tools to enforce the unconstitutional behests of the crown, which by the subservient decisions of the judges were declared to have the force of law. This servile spirit did not extend over the whole bench, and Sir George Croke was one of the minority, whom neither the threats of power nor the hopes of favour could induce to swerve from the dictates of conscience. He was the only judge of the King's Bench excepted in the vote of the House of Commons from responsibility for delaying justice towards Selden, Hollis, and the other members of parliament who were committed to the Tower for their speeches there; and in the great case of

---

[1] Croke, Jac. 700.　　　　　[2] Ibid. Car. 127.

ship-money, though he had been induced in the first instance to join the rest of the judges, for the sake of conformity, in signing an abstract opinion declaring its legality, yet when it came judicially before him in Hampden's case, he, in opposition to the majority, gave judgment against the crown; and in this courageous conduct he was imitated by Sir Richard Hutton, Sir Humphrey Davenport, and Sir John Denham. The decision against Hampden was pronounced on June 12, 1638; and all the concurring judges were impeached for high treason by the Long Parliament in December, 1640. About this time Sir George, being then eighty years old, had petitioned to be relieved from his duties, and had received from the king a dispensation from his attendance in court or on the circuit; his judicial title, salary, and allowances being continued to him. The ostentatious disavowal in the instrument that this dispensation was not granted " out of any our least displeasure conceived against him," looks somewhat as if the request which occasioned it was dictated by the court on conditions with which the judge was not unwilling to comply. It has been supposed that Fuller attributed to Sir George's conduct in regard to ship-money the saying " by hook or by crook;" but it is evident that the humorous author only jocularly applies a well-known expression of the time; which is of far greater antiquity, and is derived from an old custom that prevailed in the forests, of taking such wood as could be obtained *by hook or by crook*. Early in Charles's reign one Nicholas Jeoffes was indicted and fined in the King's Bench, for writing a petition wherein he said that the judge was a traitor.[1]

Sir George retired to his estate at Waterstock, where he spent the remainder of his life. He died on February 16, 1641–2, in the 82nd year of his age, and was buried at Waterstock, under a monument on which he is represented

[1] Rushworth, ii. App. 271.

in his judicial robes, with an inscription commemorative of his private virtues and public patriotism, which, unlike the usual language of epitaphs, was acknowledged both by contemporaries and posterity to be a faithful picture of his character. His learning as a lawyer and his bearing as a judge are well described by his son-in-law, Sir Harbottle Grimston, in the preface to his Reports, which were not published till after his death. They were originally written by Sir George in the Norman-French language, but were translated by Sir Harbottle into English; and they consist of three volumes, one being appropriated to each of the reigns of Elizabeth, James, and Charles. The cases commence with the 24th year of the former reign, and end with Michaelmas Term in the 16th of the latter, being the date of his retirement from the court; thus comprehending a period of sixty years, and affording an example of persevering industry not to be equalled. In the abbreviated language of the courts they are referred to, as Cro. Eliz., Cro. Jac., and Cro. Car., and are always quoted with respect for their learning and accuracy.

At Studley he erected a chapel in his mansion house, and settled a stipend of 20l. a year for a clergyman to preach there; and he founded an almshouse for four poor men and four poor women, with excellent regulations, which are still maintained. He gave also 100l. to the library of Sion College.

He married Mary, the daughter of Sir Thomas Bennet, who was lord mayor of London in 1 James I., and whose brother Richard was ancestor to the noble houses of Arlington and Tankerville. This lady is said to have encouraged and confirmed her husband in his resolution not to be influenced by the persuasions of the king's friends to give a judgment in the case of ship-money contrary to conscience. She survived him fifteen years, and died December 1, 1657. By her he had one son and three daughters. The son, Thomas, died either before or immediately after the father, without issue. The eldest daughter, Mary, married Sir Harbottle Grimston, bart., who will be mentioned as master of the Rolls in the reign of Charles II. The second, Elizabeth, became the wife, first of Thomas Lee, Esq., of Hartwell, Bucks, ancestor of Sir William Lee, chief justice of the King's Bench in the reign of George II.; and, secondly, of Sir Richard Ingoldsby, a distinguished officer in Cromwell's army, but afterwards made knight of the Bath for his services in securing the restoration of Charles II. The third daughter, Frances, married Richard Jervois, Esq.

The estate of Waterstock was left by the judge to his nephew, Dr. Henry Croke, the son of his brother Henry; whose son, Sir George, one of the earliest members of the Royal Society, dying without male issue, it was sold to Sir Henry Ashurst.

Studley was devised to his brother William, whose descendants still enjoy it.[1]

DAVENPORT, HUMPHREY.

Just. C. P. 1630.   Ch. B. E. 1631.

CHESTER is the county that claims the birth of Sir Humphrey Davenport. He was the second son of William Davenport, of an ancient and genteel family settled at Bromhall in Cheshire, by Margaret, daughter of Sir Richard Ashton, of Middleton in Lancashire. Born about 1566, he entered Balliol College in 1581, and, without taking a degree, then went to Gray's Inn to study the law; where, passing through the regular course, he was called to the bar on November 21, 1590, and in Lent, 1613, became reader to this society.[2] Ten years afterwards, having gained a con-

---

[1] Sir Alex. Croke's Genealogical Hist. of the Croke Family.
[2] Dugdale's Orig. 296. ; Gray's Inn Books.

siderable practice as a barrister, he took the degree of the coif in the great call of serjeants in June, 1623; and, having been knighted by King James, he was created king's serjeant, shortly after King Charles's accession, on May 9, 1625. In this character he had to argue on the part of the crown in support of the detention of the members imprisoned for forcing the speaker to put a question at the close of the last parliament; and it is not to be wondered at that he did not make much of his argument.[1] The prisoners refused to give sureties for their good behaviour in Michaelmas, 1629, and Davenport was relieved from all further anxiety in the case by being raised to the bench on February 2, 1630, as a judge of the Common Pleas. He had not sat there a year before he was called upon to fill the office of lord chief baron, to which he was nominated on Jannary 10, 1631, as the successor of Sir John Walter, his patent being "durante bene placito," instead of "quamdiu se bene gesserit," as Sir John Walter's was.[2]

In the case of ship money, he gave his opinion assuming the king's power to impose it, but acquitting Hampden on a technical point, that the writ was not good in law.[3] The majority of the judges having decided against Hampden, it became the duty of the lord chief baron, to whose court the cause properly belonged, to deliver the judgment, which afterwards, in the Long Parliament, was declared to be void. His equivocal opinion in favour of Hampden did not avail to prevent that parliament from condemning the support he had given to the king's illegal impositions. Articles of impeachment against him were accordingly carried up to the House of Lords on July 6, 1641[4]; and, in the conference between the two houses, Mr. Hyde (afterwards Lord Clarendon) opened those against him and Barons Trevor and

---

[1] State Trials, iii. 250.　　[2] W. Jones's Rep. 230.; Rymer, xix. 133. 254.
[3] State Trials, iii. 1202.　　[4] Parl. Hist. 869.

Weston.[1] He was ordered to give 10,000*l.* bail for his appearance. It is probable that he then withdrew himself altogether from the duties of his office, for on Jannary 25, 1644, the king appointed Sir Richard Lane his successor. It is curious, however, that Sir Humphrey's patent of revocation is not dated till Jannary 11 in the following year.[2]

The date of his death is not given. Fuller says he "had the reputation of a studied lawyer and upright person[3];" and A. Wood states that "he was accounted one of the oracles of the law."[4] One of his sons, of the same name, was admitted at Gray's Inn in 1619.

DENHAM, JOHN.

B. E. 1625.

See under the Reign of James I.

THE biographers of Sir John Denham, the poet, have been content with recording that he was the son of Sir John Denham, the judge, without tracing his lineage higher. Neither the father's admission at Lincoln's Inn, nor the inscription on his monument at Egham, supply the deficiency, except so far as a marginal note to the former intimates that his domicile was London. In the memoirs of the poet, the judge is described as of Little Horsely in Essex; but whether that was a patrimonial, a purchased, or a rented property, is left in obscurity. He appears to have been a member first of Furnival's Inn, and then of Lincoln's Inn, to which he was admitted on August 19, 1577; and, having been called to the bar on June 29, 1587[5], to have been chosen reader of that society twenty years afterwards, in Lent, 1607.[6]

---

[1] Wood's Ath. Oxon. iii. 1022.
[2] Docquets, &c. Oxford.
[3] Fuller's Worthies, i. 188.
[4] Ath. Oxon. iii. 182.
[5] Black Book, Linc. Inn. v. 271. 407.
[6] Dugdale's Orig. 254.

Eton College employed him as their counsel, and made him their steward; and in 1609 he `was called serjeant, for the purpose of taking the post of lord chief baron of the Irish Exchequer, to which he was appointed on June 5, and was then knighted. From this office he was advanced within three years to that of lord chief justice of the King's Bench, in the same country. This he held for five years, and then exchanged it for a seat in the English Court of Exchequer, in the place of Baron Altham, receiving his patent on May 2, 1617.[1] How well he performed his duties in Ireland may be judged from the address of Lord Chancellor Bacon to bis successor, Sir William Jones, who is recommended to imitate " the care and affection to the commonwealth of Ireland, and the prudent and politic administration of Sir John Denham."[2] He was so good an " administrator of the revenue " there, as Bacon calls him, that he set up the customs, which, bringing first only 500l., were let before his death for 54,000l. per annum.[3]

In the proceedings against his eminent eulogist, three years afterwards, he had the unpleasant duty of delivering the message of the lords to the fallen chancellor, requiring a special answer to the charges against him.[4] In the case of ship money, he joined the other judges for the sake of conformity in the opinion they gave to the king in favour of its legality; but on the hearing of the case against Hampden, he was absent during four days of the argument, and being sick and weak gave a short written judgment on May 28, 1638, in opposition to the king's claim.[5] He lived only seven months after the unfortunate decision of the majority, and died on January 6, 1639, having sat on the judicial bench for thirty years, eight of them in Ireland, and twenty-two in England.

[1] Law Off. of Ireland, 88. 141.   [2] Bacon's Works (Montagu), vii. 264.
[3] Ibid. 316. n.; quoting Borlace's Reduction of Ireland, p. 200.
[4] Parl. Hist. i. 1239.   [5] State Trials, iii. 1201.

He was buried at Egham in Surrey, where there is a monument to him and his two wives. The second of these was Eleanor, the daughter of Sir Garrett Moore, first Viscount Drogheda, whom he married while chief justice of Ireland.

The judge built the mansion called "The Place" at Egham; but his estate was wasted in gambling by his only son, John Denham, equally celebrated as the author of "Cooper's Hill," and other poems, and as a loyal adherent of King Charles through all his adversities. He was rewarded on the Restoration with the post of surveyor-general and the knighthood of the Bath, and died in 1668.[1]

DIGGES, DUDLEY.

M. R. 1636.

ON the monument of Sir Dudley Digges, in the church of Chilham in Kent, there is a pedigree prepared by himself, which commences in the reign of Henry III. The first person named in it is " Joannes filius Rogeri de Mildenhall dictus Digge," who purchased property in Kent, and whose descendants are traced in regular succession down to Leonard, "insignem mathematicum," whose son Thomas, "mathematicum insignissimum," (buried in the church of St. Mary, Aldermanbury), was by Anne, the daughter of Sir Warham de Sentleger, father of Sir Dudley Digges. Both of these progenitors, so eminent for their mathematical studies, the result of which they gave to the world in many well-esteemed treatises, were resident at Digges Court, Barham in Kent, where Sir Dudley was born in 1583. At the age of fifteen he was entered a gentleman commoner of University College in Oxford, where he had for his tutor Archbishop Abbot, with whom he preserved a close intimacy during the remainder of his life, always calling him father; and, says the archbishop,

[1] Aubrey, ii. 320.; Collins's Peerage, ix. 17.; Brit. Biog. v. 453.

" I term his wife my daughter, his eldest son is my godson, and their children are, in love, accounted my grandchildren." [1] He took the degree of B. A. in 1601, and, in the multitudinous distribution of honours by King James, he was knighted soon after the accession.

He was returned member for Tewkesbury to James's first parliament [2], which met in March, 1604, and lasted till February, 1611; but he does not appear to have taken any part in its discussions. During this time he travelled abroad; and was subsequently employed on a mission to the Hague, to obtain from Holland the restitution of some goods which had been intercepted in their voyage from the East Indies. Whether he then held any office at court is uncertain; but he probably did so in October, 1615, when he deposed on the trial of Weston for the murder of Sir Thomas Overbury, that he was sent to Sir Thomas " by a privy counsellor, a great man " (the Earl of Somerset), and that the knight had imparted to him his readiness to be employed in an embassy to Russia, to which the king had appointed him. [3] There is no doubt, however, that he was a gentleman of the king's Privy Chamber in 1618, for he is so described in a commission of that date appointing him " ambassador to the Great Duke and Lord of all Russia, to treat concerning the renewing of the privileges of the king's subjects enjoyed in that dominion, and concerning the loan from the king to the duke." [4] Of this voyage, which was not improbably connected with the mission which Sir Thomas Overbury was imprisoned for refusing, and in which John Tradescant accompanied him as a naturalist, there is a MS. account preserved in the Ashmolean Museum. [5]

In the parliament that met in January, 1621, which was so fatal to Lord Chancellor Bacon, Sir Dudley sat again for

[1] State Trials, ii. 1472.   [2] Parl. Hist. i. 974.
[3] State Trials, ii. 916. 919.   [4] Rymer, xvii. 257.
[5] Notes and Queries, 1st Ser. iii. 392.

Tewkesbury, and was one of the committee that brought forward the charges against the noble delinquent.   His speeches
in the first session had reference, principally, to subjects of
trade and the customs.   In one of them he accounts for the
decay of the former by asserting that the merchants "give
over their trade and turn usurers, as most of the aldermen of
the city do."   In the second and last session he was a more
frequent speaker, but, except his declaration that, if Sir Edwin
Sandys suffered for parliamentary business, " he must, if he
died, say that of right we ought not to be punished for what
we speak here other than by the house," he seems to have
taken a moderate and conciliatory part.   The king, however,
thought otherwise, for though not included among the " ill-
tempered spirits " mentioned in his Proclamation on the Dissolution, whom he committed to the Tower, Sir Dudley and
a few others were punished by being sent into Ireland on a
frivolous commission.   They were dismissed from their penal
employment on February 26, 1623, receiving each thirty-
shillings a day for 124 days, from October 26, when they entered on their commission.[1]

Archbishop Abbot, in his narrative, says of Sir Dudley,
that he had been " a great servant " of the Duke of Buckingham, who, he presumes, lost his friendship for some unworthy
carriage offered to him.   The archbishop also alludes to Sir
Dudley being committed to the Fleet and kept there for seven
or eight weeks, without any known reason for his imprisonment.[2]   It is apparent that these two persons bore great
ill-will towards each other, for Sir Dudley, in the second parliament of Charles I. (1626), was one of the most active managers of the impeachment against the duke.   In the conference
with the Lords he made an eloquent introduction, "comparing
England to the World ; the Commons to the Earth and Sea ;

---

[1] Parl. Hist. i. 1171. 1290. 1302. 1371.; Pell Records, 266.
[2] Rushworth, i. 450.

the King to the Sun; the Lords to the Planets; the Clergy to the Fire; the Judges and Magistrates to the Air; the Duke of Bucks to a blazing Star." In it, having made some allusion to the plaister administered to the late king, Buckingham endeavoured to fasten upon him expressions which were little less than treason to the present king; and thereupon obtained his committal to the Tower. There was evidently a wilful misrepresentation of the words used, and on the murmured resentment of the Commons, Sir Dudley was released after three days' detention.[1]

In Charles's third parliament (1628) Sir Dudley was returned for the county of Kent, and took a prominent part in forwarding the Petition of Right, being appointed to open the conference with the Peers on the subject. The lord president in reporting to the House describes him as " a man of volubility and elegance of speech," and there is nothing in his address that takes it out of that category. At a late period, when the speaker (Sir John Finch) interrupted Sir John Elliot in his reflections on the duke, Digges exclaimed " unless we may speak of these things in parliament, let us arise and be gone, or sit still and do nothing." But in the intervening debates he showed a disposition to pursue temperate measures and to place confidence in the king.[2]

This parliament was angrily dissolved in March, 1629, and the next (which it was not Sir Dudley's fate to see) was not called until eleven years afterwards. In the interim, Sir Julius Cæsar being a very old man, the reversion of his office of master of the Rolls had been granted to Sir Humphrey May, an old officer and constant supporter of the court, but he dying in fourteen months, and no vacancy occurring, the reversion had again become at the king's disposal. On the 29th of the following November (1630) it was given to Sir Dudley Digges, who, though a strenuous advocate for the

[1] Whitelocke, 5.   [2] Parl. History, ii. 254. 260. 277. 331. 402.

liberty of the subject, yet had, since the death of his enemy
the duke, shown no disposition to oppose government measures, and had probably resumed his connection with the
court. On obtaining this grant, he entered himself as a
member of the Society of Gray's Inn, and, *honoris causâ*,
was immediately made a bencher. He had to wait for nearly
five years and a half before Sir Julius Cæsar died; but in
the meantime he was admitted one of the masters in Chancery on January 22, 1631.[1] He thus had a slight opportunity of acquiring some professional knowledge; for neither
he nor Sir Humphrey May, having never studied any branch
of law, could from their legal experience found any claim to
the judicial seat. On Sir Julius's death on April 18, 1636,
Sir Dudley immediately acceded to the office[2]; but of his
proceedings in it, during the three years of his possession,
there is no account.

He died on March 18, 1639, and was buried at Chilham,
the manor and castle of which he acquired by his marriage
with Mary, one of the daughters and co-heirs of Sir Thomas
Kempe of Ollantigh in the next parish. A. Wood says that
the wisest men reckoned his death a public calamity, and
gives him so splendid a character that, were it not taken
verbatim from the epitaph on his tomb, he might rank high
among the worthies of his age. It must, therefore, be received with some little qualification; but there is no doubt
he was intelligent, eloquent, and ready as a public man, and
pious, amiable, and generous in his private life. He bequeathed 20*l.* a year for a running match at Old Wives Lees
in Chilham, to be contested every 19th of May, by a young
man and maiden of Faversham, and a young man and maiden
of Chilham, the male and female winners of the race to receive 10*l.* each. He charged forty acres of his lands in the
parishes of Sheldwick and Preston, since called " the running

---

[1] Hardy's Catalogue, 90.   [2] Dugdale's Chron. Series.

lands," with the payment. The day was kept as a holiday, and a great concourse of the gentry attended, during the whole of the last century, but the diversion has been discontinned under the unsociable fastidiousness of very recent times. He published "A Defence of Trade" during his life; and was the author of "The Compleat Ambassador," printed after his death. The family was famous for literature. Besides his grandfather, his father and himself, his brother Leonard was an accomplished poet, and is connected with the memory of Shakespeare by his commendatory verses, which have been often reprinted. Sir Dudley's third son Dudley was also a good poet and linguist; and in later times the elegiac poet, James Hammond, might claim a descent from his daughter Anne, who married William Hammond of St. Alban's Court, near Canterbury.

Sir Dudley's grandson, Sir Maurice Digges, was created a baronet soon after the Restoration, but by his death without issue within the year (1666) the title became extinct.[1]

DODERIDGE, JOHN,

JUST. K. B. 1625.

See under the Reign of James I.

DEVONSHIRE was undoubtedly the native county of Sir John Doderidge; but there is some uncertainty as to the place in it where he was born, and the parentage from which he sprang. The more received opinion is that he was the son of Richard Doderidge, an eminent merchant at Barnstaple, and Joan Badcock of South Moulton, and that he was born at Barnstaple in 1555. He was entered of Exeter College, Oxford, in 1572, and took the degree of B. A. four years after; and then he became a member of the Middle Temple. At both, his studies were so successful, that Fuller says "it was hard

---

[1] Wood's Athen. Oxon. ii. 634. ; Fasti, i. 290. ; Hasted's Kent, vii. 265.

to say whether he was better artist, divine, civil or common lawyer." Among his other pursuits history was a favourite one, and he joined the learned men who formed the nucleus of the Society of Antiquaries, then meeting at the Heralds' College in Derby House.[1] In 1593 and 1602 he was selected by his inn to deliver lectures at New Inn. The subject of the last course was "advowsons and church livings," published after his death under the title of "A Compleat Parson." In the following year he was appointed Lent reader to his own society; and on January 20, 1604, he was called to the degree of the coif, being at the same time nominated serjeant to Henry Prince of Wales. He had held this degree scarcely nine months when he was discharged from it on October 29, for the purpose of taking the office of solicitor-general. At this time he was the representative in parliament for Horsham in Sussex; and was on the different committees relative to the disputed election for Buckinghamshire.[2]

After filling the office of solicitor-general nearly three years, during which he argued the famous case of the Post-nati[3], he was induced on June 25, 1607, to resign it, and become principal serjeant to the king, in order that Bacon might be put into his place. For this accommodation he was knighted on July 5, with a promise of the first seat that should become vacant in the Court of King's Bench. This did not occur for the next five years; but at length on November 25, 1612, he received his patent as the successor of Sir Christopher Yelverton.[4] In that court he continued during the remainder of his life, being nearly thirteen years in James's reign, and above three in that of Charles.

Three months after he had ascended the bench the vice-chancellor, the two proctors, and five academicians of Oxford, paid him the extraordinary honour of attending in Serjeants'

---

[1] Reliq. Spelman, 69.
[2] State Trials, ii. 96. 110.
[3] State Trials, ii. 566.
[4] Croke, Jac.

Inn hall and creating him master of arts. This degree was
conferred upon him in so distinguished a manner, to show the
gratitude of the university for his great exertions on their
behalf in the legal questions lately agitated between them and
the city.

When the practice of privately interrogating the judges
was adopted, Coke's resistance to which in Peacham's case
was one cause of his dismissal, Bacon, in a letter to the king,
says, " Mr. Solicitor came to me this evening and related to
me that he had found Judge Doderidge very ready to give
opinion in secret:"[1] a course in which it is lamentable to
think that most of his colleagues concurred. When King
James was negotiating for his son's marriage with the Spanish
princess, and was desirous of showing some leniency to the
Catholics, Walter Yonge reports that " Judge Doderidge
saith he thought they [the Judges] should find out a way by
law to dispense with the Statute against recusancy."[2] This
spirit of accommodating their opinions to the royal wishes was
further shown, when the Judges refused to admit Hampden
and others to bail for refusing to subscribe to the late loan.
On their being called before the House of Lords in April,
1628, to assign the reasons for their judgment, Judge Doderidge, though he attempted to justify the decision, seemed to
acknowledge they had committed a mistake, by thus apologe-
tically concluding: " omnia habere in memoria, et in nullo errare,
divinum potins est quam humanum."[3] This speech exhibits
somewhat of the drivelling of an old and failing man ; but in
it he says, " God knoweth I have endeavoured always to keep
a good conscience ; "—an assertion which is borne out by
the general tenor of his life. In conversing on the belief then
existing that some parties had given large sums to purchase
places of judicature, he said, " That, as old and infirm as he

[1] Bacon's Works (Montagu), xii. 125.   [2] Yonge's Diary, 69.
[3] Parl. Hist. ii. 291.

was, he would go to Tyburn on foot to see such a man hanged,
that should proffer money for a place of that nature." He
had the habit of shutting his eyes while sitting on the bench,
for the purpose of concentrating his attention on the argument, without being distracted by surrounding objects; and
was thence jocularly called the Sleeping Judge.

He survived his appearance in the House of Lords only
five months, dying on September 13, 1628, at Forsters, near
Egham in Surrey, and was buried in the Lady chapel in
Exeter cathedral, where there is a stately monument erected
to his and his wife's memory.

Croke, in recording his death, describes him as " a man of
great knowledge, as well in common law, as in other humane
sciences, and divinity : "[1] and Fuller, another of his contemporaries, says of him, "his soul consisted of two essentials,
ability and integrity, holding the scale of Justice with so steady
a hand, that neither love nor lucre, fear or flattery, could
bow him on either side."[2] But it must be acknowledged that
in several instances he betrayed that subservience to the
ruling powers, for which the judicial bench was then remarkable. Anthony Wood, who lived shortly after him, shows
that he had a high reputation for learning. He composed a
variety of works, legal and antiquarian, none of which were
published in his lifetime, and some of which still remain in
manuscript.

He was married three times. His first wife was a daughter of —— Germin ; his second was a daughter of —— Cul-
lum, of Canon's Leigh in Devonshire ; and the third was
Dorothy, daughter of Sir Amias Bampfield, of North Molton,
and widow of Edward Hancock, of Combe Martin, Esq. By
the two former he had no issue, and by the latter only one
son, who died before him. He was succeeded in his property
by his brother, Pentecost Doderidge, of Barnstaple, whose

---

[1] Croke, Car. 127. [2] Fuller's Worthies, i. 282.

son became recorder of that town, and edited one of his uncle's tracts concerning Parliament."[1]

FINCH, JOHN, LORD FINCH OF FORDWICH.
CH. C. P. 1634. LORD KEEPER 1640.

THIS family originally bore the name of Herbert. It is said to have descended from Henry Fitz-Herbert, chamberlain to Henry I., and to have adopted the name of Finch in the reign of Edward I., being that of a manor in Kent, which came into their possession by a marriage with the daughter and heir of its lord. After a long train of succession, Sir Thomas Finch, in the reign of Queen Mary, married one of the coheirs of Sir Thomas Moyle, of Eastwell in Kent, and on his death by shipwreck in 6 Elizabeth, he left three sons. Through two of them his connection with the law is worthy of remark, for he had one son, two grandsons, one great-grandson, and one great-great-grandson, all eminent in Westminster Hall, besides two female descendants connected by marriage with lawyers equally illustrious. Sir Thomas's eldest son was Sir Moyle Finch, whose fourth son, Sir Heneage, a serjeant at law, recorder of London, and speaker in the first parliament of Charles I., was father of Heneage, who became lord chancellor to Charles II., and was created Earl of Nottingham. The earl's second son, Heneage, was solicitor-general to Charles II., and was ennobled by Queen Anne with the title of the Earl of Aylesford; and his eldest daughter married the son and heir of Sir Harbottle Grimston, Bart., master of the Rolls. The addition of Hatton to the family name arose from the marriage of Daniel, the second Earl of Nottingham, with a descendant of Queen Elizabeth's lord chancellor, Sir Christopher Hatton; and one of this earl's daughters became the wife of the first Earl of Mansfield,

---

[1] Wood's Ath. Oxon. ii. 425.; Prince's Worthies of Devon.

whóse name as chief justice of England will not soon be forgotten. Sir Thomas's son, Sir Henry Finch, was an eminent advocate, and one of King James's serjeants, and by his wife Ursula, daughter and heir of John Thwaites, was the father of John, the subject of this article, who brought no credit to the name he bore.

John Finch was born on September 17, 1584, and was admitted of the society of Gray's Inn in February, 1600. In his reply to Lord Keeper Coventry's speech on his installation as lord chief justice, he gives this account of himself: " For the first six years bestowed by me in the books of law by some unhappy means I was diverted, and my resolution fitted in another way for foreign employment, to which after nine or ten years I was designed." Nearly twelve years elapsed before he was called to the bar, on November 8, 1611; but in six years more, assisted by the patronage of Lord Bacon, he became a bencher, and was chosen autumn reader in 1618.[1] In the meantime he had been elected member for Canterbury in the second of James's parliaments, 1614; but neither in that nor in the succeeding parliaments of the reign is he mentioned as addressing the house. He was chosen recorder for the same city in 1617, and held that office till 1621; again representing it in the first three of Charles's parliaments, of the last of which, meeting in March, 1628, he was chosen speaker. Clarendon says that he had " led a free life in a restrained fortune, and having set up upon the stock of a good wit and natural parts, without the superstructure of much knowledge in the profession by which he had to grow; he was willing to use those weapons in which he had most skill."[2] The first effect of his endeavours was his knighthood; the next his appointment as king's counsel, on March

[1] Rushworth, ii. 256.; Gray's Inn Books; Dugdale's Orig. 296.
[2] Clarendon, i. 130.

17, 1626; and then followed his being made attorney-general to the queen on the 13th December in that year.[1]

In his address to the king on his being elected speaker, he showed some of the wit for which Clarendon gave him credit, and too much of the customary adulation. The liberty of the subject, which had been invaded by the imprisonment of those who refused to contribute to the loan, the many grievances under which the people suffered, the Petition of Right, and the remonstrance against Tonnage and Poundage, were among the subjects which agitated this parliament. To avoid doing anything which might deprive him of the confidence of the Commons, or hazard the destruction of his hopes from the king, was, to a man of Finch's disposition, a difficult and delicate task. Through the first session he managed in his speeches to the throne to steer with tolerable safety; and though, towards the end of it, he ran some risk by interrupting, "with tears in his eyes," a speaker who was about, as he supposed, to fall upon the Duke of Buckingham, and requesting to withdraw, he redeemed himself by bringing back a conciliatory message from the king, which elicited the declaration by another member, "Mr. Speaker, you have not only at all times discharged the duty of a good speaker, but of a good man."[2] At the termination, however, of the second session he lost all credit with the house, and incurred their censure by his conduct. After delivering a message from the king, ordering an adjournment, he refused to read a remonstrance against Tonnage and Poundage, proposed by Sir John Elliott, and left the chair. Upon being forced to resume it, he had again recourse to tears, saying, "I am the servant of the house, but let not the reward of my service be my ruin . . . . I will not say I will not, but I dare not." Sir Peter Hayman, a kinsman and a neighbour, called him "the disgrace of his country, and a blot to a noble family."

[1] Rymer, xviii. 633. 866. [2] Parl. Hist. ii. 222. 281. 346. 402. 406.

The door of the house was locked, the usher of the black rod denied admittance, and the speaker was compelled to keep his seat while the resolutions were passed. Eight days after, March 10, 1629, the king angrily prorogued the parliament[1], which was not destined to meet again for eleven years, when Sir John Finch presided over the Lords instead of the Commons.

As a sort of confutation to Mr. Prynn's " Histriomastix," the four inns of Court resolved to unite in presenting a masque for the entertainment of the king and queen, the preparations for which were conducted by a committee formed by members of each society. Its magnificence may be estimated by the cost, which was said to exceed 20,000*l.* ; and the performance, on Candlemas Day, 1634, was so successful, that when Sir John Finch, who managed on the part of Gray's Inn, returned thanks to their majesties for their acceptance of it, they not only praised it highly, but, at the queen's request, the masque was repeated in her presence at Merchant Taylors' Hall, by the invitation of the lord mayor.[2]

But soon Sir John was to act a more prominent part. Noy, the attorney-general, who had invented or revived the tax called ship-money, died in the following August, before the writ for the imposition was issued; the removal of Sir Robert Heath from the chief justiceship of the Common Pleas, without any alleged cause, took place in September, and on the 14th of October (1634) Finch, to the surprise of all, received the latter appointment, having taken the coif a few days before.[3] The writ for ship-money being issued six days after, naturally induced the public to associate the removal, the substitution, and the writ, as in some way connected together. Lord Clarendon says that Finch " took up

---

[1] Parl. Hist. ii. 487—492.   [2] Whitelocke's Mem. 19—22.
[3] Croke, Car. 375. Dugdale, by mistake, makes him a puisne judge at this date.

ship-money where Noy left it, and, being a judge, carried it up to that pinnacle from whence he almost broke his own neck; having in his journey thither had too much influence on his brethren to induce them to concur in a judgment they had all cause to repent." Though he denied having known of the writ at the time of his appointment, he 'acknowledged having collected his brethren's opinions on the subject; and when the case of Hampden came under discussion, he gave so absolute an opinion in its favour, and contended so strenuously against the argument of his brother judges, Hutton and Croke, that he confirmed the general feeling that he was elevated to the bench for the purpose of carrying through the obnoxious impost; and, as Lord Clarendon says, by the judgment he delivered he made it " much more abhorred and formidable" than before.[1]

On his appointment in the place of Heath, and Sir John Banks succeeding Noy as attorney-general, the following specimen of bar wit was circulated : —

> *Noy's* flood is gone,
>   The *Banks* appear ;
> *Heath* is shorn down
>   And *Finch* sings here.[2]

The prejudice against him was in no degree diminished by his heartless remark, when Mr. Prynn was brought up for sentence upon his second libel, " I had thought Mr. Prynn had no ears, but methinks he hath ears." Thus noticed, the hair was turned back, and the clipped members exposed; "upon the sight whereof the lords were displeased they had been formerly no more cut off." And the consequence was, that the unfortunate gentleman was condemned to lose the remainder, which was done so cruelly and closely, that a piece of his cheek was cut off with it.[3]

---

[1] State Trials, iii. 1216.; Clarendon, i. 127. 130.
[2] Wood's Athen. ii. 584.   [3] State Trials, iii. 717. 749.

His conduct in the circuit in Eyre, when he is charged with extending the boundaries of the forest in Essex, and annihilating the ancient perambulations, excited the hatred and suspicion of the people [1]; and the feeling was confirmed by his subsequent declaration that an order of the Lords of the Council "should be always ground enough for him to make a decree in Chancery."[2]

Finch's unpopularity in the kingdom tended to advance his favour with the king, and accordingly within three days after Lord Coventry's death, he was appointed lord keeper [3], and on Jannary 23, 1640, was sworn in court. He opened the parliament that met on April 13 (having been previously ennobled, on the 7th of that month, with the title of Baron Finch, of Fordwich in Kent) with a fulsome speech, in which, alluding to the royal condescension in calling them together, he says, that the king " is now pleased to lay by the shining beams of Majesty, as Phœbus did to Phaëton, that the distance between sovereignty and subjection should not barr you of that filial freedom of access to his person and counsels." His Majesty, however, felt it necessary to resume his beams in less than three weeks, and hastily dismissed the assembly on May 5. In the meantime the Commons had visited the lord keeper with a vote, declaring that his conduct as speaker at the close of the last parliament was a breach of privilege [4]; and the offence was not forgotten when the king was compelled to summon a new parliament in the following November. Lord Finch, finding by the resolution then passed by the Commons against ship-money and those who advised it, that preparations were making for proceeding against him personally, applied to the house, desiring to be heard in his own defence before it came to a vote; and his request being granted, he delivered, on December 21, an artful and inge-

[1] Parl. Hist. ii. 695.
[2] Clarendon, i. 131.
[3] Rymer, xx. 364.
[4] Parl. Hist. iii. 528. 552. 571.

nious speech in his own vindication. But notwithstanding his grace of elocution, the Commons were not to be diverted from their purpose, a vote being immediately passed for his accusation before the Lords, and a demand of his committal. On the following morning the message was delivered; but his Lordship had taken advantage of the interval to escape, and, first sending the Great Seal to the king, to sail for Holland. The articles against him were introduced to the Lords by Lord Falkland, and charged him with endeavouring to subvert the fundamental laws of England, and to introduce an arbitrary tyrannical government against law; and comprehended, besides others, his refusal to put the question as speaker; his soliciting the judges' opinions on ship-money when chief justice; and his framing and advising the king's declaration after the dissolution of the last parliament.[1]

From a passage in Lord Clarendon's work, originally suppressed, it appears that many of the ascendant party were not desirous of urging the charges against Lord Finch to extremity [2]; and their refraining from pressing for any further proceedings on the impeachment seems to warrant the assertion. His lordship remained quietly at the Hague, and the governing powers were content with receiving from him a composition of 7000*l*.[3] It does not appear when he returned to England, but he received two affectionate letters from Queen Henrietta Maria, in 1640, and Elizabeth, Queen of Bohemia, in 1655, showing their continued interest in him.[4] On Charles II.'s return to his throne, Finch was named in the commission for the trial of the regicides in October, 1660. Sir Orlando Bridgman, the lord chief baron, presided, but when Thomas Harrison in his defence asserted that the authority under which he acted was not usurped, but that it " was done rather in the fear of the Lord," he was interrupted by Lord Finch, who said,

[1] Parl. Hist. iii. 686—698.; Clarendon i. 310. [2] Clarendon, i. *525*.
[3] State Trials, iv. 18. [4] Archæologia, xxi. 474.

" Though my lords here have been pleased to give you a great latitude, this must not be suffered, that you should run into these damnable excursions, to make God the author of this damnable treason committed." In two or three of the other trials he also made some remarks.[1] He was then in his seventy-seventh year, which he did not live to complete, dying a month after on November 20, 1660. He was buried in the ancient church of St. Martin near Canterbury, in which parish his paternal seat, called the Moat, was situate; and a splendid monument to his memory was erected there by his widow.

However highly Lord Finch's talents and eloquence may have been spoken of, few have ventured to bear testimony to his independence as a judge or his wisdom as a statesman ; and the general character that has with apparent truth been assigned to him is that of an unprincipled lawyer and a time-serving minister.

He was twice married: first to Eleanore, daughter of Sir George Wyat of Boxley in Kent; and secondly to Mabella, daughter of Charles Fotherby, dean of Canterbury. As he left only a daughter (married to Sir George Radcliffe of the Privy Council of Ireland), the title became extinct.[2]

FOSTER, ROBERT.
Just. C. P. 1640.
See under the Reign of Charles II.

GATES, THOMAS.
Parl. B. E. 1648.
See under the Interregnum.

---

[1] State Trials, v. 986. 1025. 1045. 1067.
[2] Dugdale's Baronage, ii. 448. ; Hasted's Kent, xi. 162.

GODBOLT, JOHN.

PARL. JUST. C. P. 1647.

ABOUT 1604, the principal of Barnard's Inn gave a certificate to "the right worshipful the readers of Gray's Inn" that John Godbold of Toddington, Suffolk, was "admitted into the fellowship of Barnard's Inn the second day of May, and hath ever since his admittance very honestly and orderly used and behaved himself in the said house, and is a very good student, and hath done his exercises in learning for himself and others."[1] This, no doubt, was preliminary to his admission into Gray's Inn, which took place on November 16, 1604; where after the usual seven years' study, he was called to the bar, and in due time took his place at the bench table. He was elected reader there in autumn, 1627[2]; and soon appears in Croke's Reports with considerable practice. He received the dignity of the coif at the great call in 1636; and it must have been from his professional reputation, for there is no account of his interfering in the political troubles of the time, that, when the parliament took upon them to appoint the judges, he was selected by them to fill a vacant seat in the Common Pleas. This occurred on April 30, 1647[3], and he was immediately added to the commission to hear causes in Chancery.[4] He did not long retain his place, but died in the middle of the following year[5], the last case in his collection of Reports (published soon after his death) being decided on June 16, 1648. In 1684, one of his descendants lived at Hatfield-Peverell in Essex, but the family appears to be now extinct.[6]

[1] Barnard's Inn Book, ii. 6.　　　[2] Dugdale's Orig. 296.
[3] Whitelocke, 245.　　　[4] Journals.
[5] Woolrych's List, 44.　　　[6] Grandeur of the Law, 1684.

GREY, HENRY, EARL OF KENT.
PARL. COM. G. S. 1643. 1648.
See under the Interregnum.

GREY, WILLIAM, LORD GREY DE WERKE.
PARL. COM. G. S. 1648.
See under the Interregnum.

HARVEY, FRANCIS.
JUST. C. P. 1625.
See under the Reign of James I.

THE descendants of Sir Francis Harvey towards the end of the seventeenth century were residents in Suffolk[1]; but whether that was the native county of the judge does not appear. He is said to have commenced his legal studies at Barnard's Inn; he completed them at the Middle Temple, and was called to the bar of the latter society, of which he became reader in autumn, 1611.[2] Croke reports his name as an advocate in 1604; and on December 1, 1612 (at which time he resided at Northampton), he was chosen recorder of Leicester, with a fee of 5*l.* a year, and 20*s.* at every assize, with all his charges borne when he visited the borough on business.[3]

He attained the degree of the coif in Michaelmas, 1614; and on October 18, 1624, he was constituted a judge of the Common Pleas, on Sir W. Jones's removal from that court to the King's Bench. On one of his circuits he fined a whole jury 10*l.* apiece for giving perverse and wrongful acquittals in four different criminal cases; and in another, he showed some indignation on hearing an assize sermon at Norwich, in which the preacher alluded to the corruption of judges, say-

[1] Grandeur of the Law (1684).
[3] Rous's Diary, 24, 62.
[2] Dugdale's Orig. 219. 222.

ing in his charge to the grand jury, " It seems by the sermon we are all corrupt, but know that we can use conscience in our places as well as the best clergyman of all."[1]   He remained in that court till his death, which took place at Northampton in August, 1632.[2]

The Francis Harvey, who was treasurer of the Middle Temple in 1667, was probably his son.

HEATH, ROBERT.

CH. C. P. 1631.   JUST. K. B. 1641.   CH. K. B. 1642.

" UPPON the 20th day of May in the year 1575," says the chief justice in a short memoir of his life written a few months before his death, " I was borne at Brastid in Kent, of Robert Heath, gent., my father, and Jane his wife, my mother;" who was daughter and coheiress of Nicholas Poner.[3] Hasted says he was descended out of Surrey from John Heath of Limpsfield.[4]   He received the rudiments of his education at the free grammar school of Tunbridge, and at the age of fourteen was sent to St. John's College, Cambridge, where he remained for three years. He was then admitted of Clifford's Inn, and at eighteen he removed to the Inner Temple, where after ten years' study he was called to the bar in 1603.   In 1607 he was selected by his society to be reader of Clifford's Inn, and having performed that duty for two years, and acted as a practising barrister for several years more, he became a bencher of the Inner Temple in 1610, filling the post of reader there in the autumn in the next year, and that of treasurer in 1625.[5]

Of his studies or convictions during the greater part of this period no account is given.   He had the fortune to be a

---

[1] Borough MSS. Leicester.   [2] Croke, Car. 268.
[3] Presented by Evelyn Philip Shirley, Esq., to the Philo-Biblion Society.
[4] Hasted's Kent, iii. 152.   [5] Dugdale's Orig. 167. 171.

favourite of the favourite, Buckingham, for whose use he received by patent the profits of the King's Bench office; and thus ingratiated himself with the frequenters of the court. On the death of Richard Martin the recorder of London he was put up in opposition to James Whitelocke, and through the king's influence elected on November 10, 1618. This interference of the king did not, however, lessen " the especial love and favour" of the aldermen, for they, on his being chosen reader of his inn in the following July, presented him with 100l., two hogsheads of claret, and one pipe of canary.[1] The same patronage no doubt procured his nomination as solicitor-general on January 22, 1621; on which occasion he resigned the recordership, but was elected by the citizens to represent them in the parliament of that year. In it he was a frequent debater, trying to accommodate matters for the king, who knighted him, and retained him in his office during the rest of his reign.

Soon after Charles's accession, Heath on October 31, 1625, was promoted to the attorney-generalship. In the following May he had to bring articles of impeachment against the Earl of Bristol[2], in the nature of a cross-bill to the charges which the earl had made against the Duke of Buckingham, who at the same time was also impeached by the House of Commons. All these proceedings were stopped by the sudden and intemperate dissolution of the parliament. In the next year he had the invidious task of opposing the release of the knights who, having refused to contribute to the loan, had been committed to prison; and in this difficult duty he displayed much learning, ingenuity, and eloquence. In 1628, when the judges' refusal to bail or discharge them was taken up by parliament, Sir Robert Heath had again almost single-handed to maintain the argument against antagonists so powerful as Sir Edward Coke, Littelton, Selden, and Noy; and he did it with such

[1] City List of Recorders.   [2] Parl. Hist. ii. 80.

ability and courage, that though defeated he lost no credit by
his exertions.[1]   The violent termination of this parliament in
March, 1629, and the imprisonment of the members who forcibly detained the speaker in the chair at its close, led to other
proceedings in which Sir Robert Heath took a very prominent
part.   By the king's command, he obtained private opinions
of the judges upon certain abstract questions; and upon the
answers he obtained filed informations against the offending
members; and, on their refusing to plead, judgment of fine
and imprisonment was pronounced against them.   When the
conduct of the judges in this matter came to be canvassed by
the Long Parliament, Sir Robert Heath seems almost to have
escaped censure, as merely performing the duty which devolved upon him as the servant and advocate of the crown.
In the exercise of his functions as attorney-general he was so
zealous and active a partisan of the court, that the king could
not but appreciate his services.   On the death of Sir Nicholas
Hyde, and Sir Thomas Richardson being constituted chief
justice of the King's Bench in his room, Sir Robert was promoted to the vacant office of chief justice of the Common
Pleas on October 26, 1631[2], having been two days before invested with the coif; giving rings with the equivocal motto
— "Lex Regis, vis Legis."

The principal public act recorded while he was chief justice
of the Common Pleas was the prosecution in the Star Chamber against Henry Sherfield for breaking a superstitious glass
window in the church of Sarum, when, though it had been
instituted while he was attorney-general, on information, as
he stated, that the cause was much fouler than it appeared,
he advocated a lenient sentence in opposition to Laud and
other members of the council.[3]   This was in February, 1633,
and on September 14, 1634, he was discharged from his place

---

[1] State Trials, iii. 30. 133.   [2] Rymer, xix. 346.
[3] State Trials, iii. 540.

without any cause being assigned. His removal may perhaps owe its origin to his opposition to Land, and his disinclination to the extreme views which that prelate adopted in ecclesiastical matters. Hacket seems to insinuate as much when describing Laud's prosecution of Bishop Williams. He says: "Sir Robert Heath was displaced, and for no misdemeanour proved; but it was to bring in a successor, who was more forward to undo Lincoln, than ever the Lord Heath was to preserve him."[1] It was generally believed, however, that the question of ship-money, the writs to collect which were issued four days after the appointment of Sir John Finch as Heath's successor, had some connection with the change.[2] Anthony Wood, in his account of Noy, casually says that Sir Robert Heath was " removed from the Chief Justiceship of the *King's Bench* for bribery"[3]; but in his account of Heath himself he alludes in no way to his dismissal, and makes such mistakes in the courts to which he was appointed as to deprive his record of any value.[4] Whitelocke, who was not his friend, would not have omitted all notice of his removal could he have alleged such an imputation as the cause. Upon the foundation of Wood's loose statement merely, for no other can be cited, Lord Campbell makes this assertion: " The truth seems to be, that he [Heath] continued to enjoy the favour and confidence of the Government, but that a charge had been brought against him of taking bribes, which was so strongly supported by evidence, that it could not be overlooked, although no parliament was sitting, or ever likely to sit; and that the most discreet proceeding, even for himself, was to remove him quietly from his office."[5] Historians will be anxious for information of his lordship's authority for this statement; for they will be unwilling to suppose it to be

---

[1] Hacket's Bp Williams, ii, 118.   [2] Rushworth, ii. 253.
[3] Wood's Athen. Oxon. ii. 584.   [4] Wood's Fasti, ii. 45.
[5] Lord Campbell's Ch. Justices, i. 415.

gratuitous scandal, although it seems to be contradicted by the very act of the government that displaced him. In the next term after he was ousted from the bench he resumed his practice at the bar as junior serjeant[1], a privilege that the king would scarcely have granted, or that the fallen judge would have had the effrontery to ask, if his disgrace had been so notorious " that it could not be overlooked." That he was actually replaced on the bench, when the "parliament was sitting,"—a parliament, too, that was ready enough to find any blot in the king's appointments,— sufficiently shows the inconsistency of the charge. The chief justice himself says, in his memoir before cited, written when he was in sorrow, and just before his own death: " At the end of three years, I was on a sudden discharged of that place of chief justice, noe cause being then nor at any time since shewed for my removal."[2]

Not only was he allowed to practise, but in little more than two years he was again taken into the service of the crown, his patent as king's serjeant being dated October 12, 1636.[3] He is mentioned in that character not only in Croke's Reports, but in the government prosecution of the Rev. Thomas Harrison for falsely accusing Mr. Justice Hutton with high treason.[4] He continued at the bar for four years more, when he was replaced on the judicial seat on January 23, 1641, as a judge of the King's Bench, in the place of Sir William Jones; and was further favoured, on May 13, with the office of master of the Court of Wards and Liveries.[5] When the king retired to York, Sir Robert joined him there, and on June 10, 1642, addressed a letter to the House of Lords, informing them that he had " left the Parliament to go to the king at York as by oath and duty bound : " whereupon they

[1] Croke, Car. 375.   [2] Memoir, p. 21.
[3] Dugdale's Chron. Series.   [4] State Trials, iii. 1371.
[5] Rymer, xx. 448, 517.

resolved to the contrary, and that his staying at the parliament, being sent for from them, was not against his oath.[1] On
February 7, 1643, he was created doctor of civil law by the
university of Oxford; and on Sir John Bramston's removal,
the king, being then in that city, appointed Sir Robert chief
justice of the King's Bench in his place. Dugdale inserts
the date as October 31, 1643, on the authority of the memoranda of the clerk of the Crown, which cannot be supposed
to have been kept very regularly in such disturbed times; but
the appointment must have taken place some months before,
a letter being extant from the king to him as chief justice,
dated Oxford, " the fourth day of July in the nineteenth
yeare of our raigne " (1643), authorising him in the summer
assizes " to forbear those places whither you conceave you
may not goe, with convenient safety."[2] Clarendon says that
Bramston was removed because he stood bound by recogni-
sance to attend the parliament upon an accusation depending
there against him[3]: and this is confirmed by the " Autobiography of Sir John Bramston," published by the Camden
Society (p. 87), which fixes the date in October, 1642.

Several complaints were made to the parliament against
Chief Justice Heath and other judges who acted with him
on the circuit. First, for indicting the Earl of Northumberland and other peers and members of the House of Commons
for high treason at Salisbury, when the bill was not found;
and next, for condemning Captain Turpin, a sea-officer, on a
similar charge at Exeter, where he was executed in pursuance
of his sentence. On these charges, and for adhering to the
king, then in arms against the parliament, the Commons impeached them on July 24, 1644; but as the chief justice
never put himself in their power, he escaped trial. This,
however, did not prevent them from venting their enmity.

[1] Parry's Parliaments.   [2] Notes and Queries, 1st S. xii. 259.
[3] Clarendon, iii. 268.

On November 25, 1645, they passed an ordinance disabling him and four others from being judges, " as though they were dead; " and by another vote of October 24, 1648, they ordered that he should be excepted from pardon.[1] His estate was sequestered, but was recovered by his son Edward at the Restoration. According to his own relation, the parliament gave him liberty "either to exile himself into a foreign country, or to run the hazard of further danger."[2] Of course he never took his seat as chief justice in Westminster Hall; and the prothonotaries of the King's Bench, Henley and Whitwick, took advantage of the distractions of the times to appropriate to themselves the fees received for his use. They were brought to account by the chief justice's son in 1663, when, notwithstanding they pleaded the Statute of Limitations, they were forced by a decree in Chancery to refund the whole amount.[3]

Sir Robert fled into France in 1646, and survived his royal master just seven months, dying at Calais on August 30, 1649. His body was brought to England and entombed with that of his wife, who died nearly two years before him, under a stately monument in Brasted church.

Among his papers, now in the possession of his noble descendant, has been found a jeu-d'esprit on the twenty-four links of the collar of SS., each link representing some judicial attribute commencing with the letter S. It is wholly in his handwriting, and was probably composed as an amusement of his exile. It not only shows great ingenuity, but exhibits in the strongest light with what solemn responsibility the writer regarded the qualifications, the virtues, and the duties of a judge.[4] His short memoir also, written undoubtedly during his exile, gives pleasing evidence of an amiable and pious

---

[1] Whitelocke, 78. 96. 181. 345.; Parl. Hist. iii. 285.
[2] Memoirs, 22.   [3] W. Nelson's Reports, 75.
[4] Notes and Queries, 1st S. x. 357.

mind. It records that he married his wife on December 10, 1600, while yet a student, and that they had had a happy union of forty-seven years. She was Margaret, the daughter of John Miller, and by her he left one daughter, married to Sir William Morley, and five sons, Edward, John, George, Robert, and Francis. Some of his descendants became eminent in the law, among whom was Sir John Heath, of Brasted, attorney-general of the Duchy of Lancaster, whose daughter and heir, Margaret, married George Verney, fourth Lord Willoughby de Broke, and was the mother of the Hon. John Verney, master of the Rolls in the reign of George II., the grandfather of the present baron.[1]

HENDEN, EDWARD.

B. E. 1639.

THE old Kentish family of the Hendens is supposed to have originally resided on an estate bearing its name in the parish of Woodchurch in Kent. At a much later period the members of a branch of it lived at Benenden in its neighbourhood, and were clothiers there, in great repute. Sir Edward Henden, the baron, was descended from this branch, and purchased and settled at Biddenham-place in the same locality. He possessed also several manors in the county, and considerable property in and about Maidstone.

He was entered of Gray's Inn on April 27, 1586, and after passing through his legal studies there, his name appears as reader in Lent, 1614.[2] In Michaelmas, 1616, he was called to the degree of the coif. For the two and twenty years he was a serjeant he had an extensive practice, and earned so good a reputation as a lawyer that he was selected on January 22, 1639, to succeed Sir John Denham as a baron of the Exchequer[3], on which occasion he was knighted.

---

[1] Memoir; Wood's Fasti, ii. 45; Collin's Peerage, vi. 701.
[2] Dugdale's Orig. 296.   [3] Rymer, xx. 306.

When the parliament entered the field against the king they passed an ordinance assessing all who had not voluntarily contributed to the army, in such sum as the committee meeting at Haberdashers' Hall should deem reasonable, not exceeding a twentieth part of their estate. In December, 1643, the Commons applied to the Lords to rate Baron Henden, as an assistant to their Lordships; who accordingly assessed him at 2000*l.* for the twentieth part of his estate, to be employed for the defence of Poole and Lyme. The baron not obeying this order, the house, on the 23rd of the same month, directed proceedings against him, but as he was ill at the time it seems that they were not then taken, and that he died very shortly afterwards; the petition of his nephew and executor, on the 21st of the following February, being referred to the committee to do therein as they should think fit to end the business.[1] He was buried in the chancel of Biddenham church. Leaving no children, he bequeathed the bulk of his property to his nephew, Sir John Henden, whose descendants continued to reside in the mansion at Biddenham till it was alienated in the reign of George I.[2]

HOBART, HENRY.

CH. C. P. 1625.

See under the Reigns of James I.

HENRY VII.'s attorney-general, Sir James Hobart, was the great grandfather of this chief justice. He belonged to a family of ancient descent in Suffolk and Norfolk. His second son, Miles Hobart, who was seated at Plumsted in the latter county, died, leaving two sons, Thomas and John; the former of whom succeeded to the Plumsted estate, and mar-

---

[1] Lords' Journals, vi. 324. 328. 346. 350. 436.
[2] Hasted's Kent, iv. 311., vii. 132. 139. 175. 230., viii. 496. Hasted says that he died in 1662; but this is clearly a mistake.

ried Audrey, daughter and heir of William Hare of Beeston in Norfolk, Esq. By her he had two sons, Sir Miles and Sir Henry, the subject of the present sketch.

Henry having been admitted a member of Lincoln's Inn on August 10, 1575, was after a rather lengthened course, called to the bar on June 24' 1584.[1] In 1595 he was steward of Norwich[2], and in 1597 was returned to parliament as the representative for Yarmouth; for which place and for Norwich, he had a seat on several succeeding occasions. In 1591 he became a governor of his Inn, and reader there in Lent, 1608; an honour which was repeated two years afterwards, on the occasion of his being called serjeant by Queen Elizabeth; but, in consequence of her death, he was included in a new writ by King James.[3]

Having being knighted on the occasion, he was made attorney of the Court of Wards in 1605, being first exonerated from the degree of the coif; and on July 4, in the next year, he was created attorney-general, on the elevation of Sir Edward Coke. This office he held for above seven years, to the annoyance of Bacon, who served under him for six of them, and longed by his removal to take another step in promotion. Henry, Prince of Wales, made him his chancellor. In the case of the Post-nati, he of course took the part of the plaintiff[4]; and in the complaint raised by the Commons against Dr. Cowel's book, claiming the superiority of the civil to the common law, it is stated that Sir Henry "did very modestly and discreetly lay open the offence of the party and the dangerous consequence of the book."[5]

Modesty seems to have been his characteristic; and though a very learned, he was not by any means a sparkling lawyer. On the death of Sir Thomas Fleming the chief justice of the

[1] Black Book, v. 199. 359　　　[2] Blomefield's Norwich, i. 359.
[3] Dugdale's Orig. 254, 262.　　　[4] State Trials, ii. 609.
[5] Parl. Hist. ii. 1124.

King's Bench, when Bacon cunningly recommended that Coke should be removed to that court from the Common Pleas, and that the attorney should succeed to the latter, in order that he himself might be promoted to the attorneyship, he gives this account of Sir Henry : " The attorney sorteth not so well with his present place, being a man timid and scrupulous both in parliament and other business; and one that, in a word, was made fit for the late treasurer (Salisbury's) bent, which was to do little, with much formality and protestation."[1] Hobart accordingly received the appointment of chief justice of the Common Pleas on November 26, 1613.

, He presided in that court with great credit as a sound lawyer and upright judge for twelve years, and with so little imputation on his honesty and independence, as to form one óf the exceptions to the general subserviency of the bench. In delivering judgment against Wraynham for slandering Lord Bacon in a libel addressed to the king, he acknowledges the right of the subject to appeal to his majesty : " You may still resort to your sovereign for extreme remedy ; this is proper to a king, ' Cessas regnare, si cessas judicare;' for it is an inherent quality to his crown."[2] He was selected as chancellor to Prince Charles in 1617, and was obliged for the purpose of accepting the office to have his patent of chief justice revoked, and a new one granted, in order to enable him " to take fee and livery " from any one besides the king[3] ; and on the disgrace of Bacon, he was one of the first who was designated to succeed as lord chancellor ; no idea being entertained of the king's making choice of one then so inexperienced in law as Bishop Williams. But when Buckingham some years afterwards, wanted to persuade him to tell the king that the bishop was not fit for the place, because of

[1] Bacon's Works (Montagu), vii. 340.   [2] State Trials, ii. 1077.
[3] Croke, Car. 1.

his inability and ignorance, Hobart excused himself, handsomely saying, " My lord, somewhat might have been said at the first, but he should do the lord keeper great wrong that said so now."[1]

Before Hobart's elevation to the Common Pleas, King James had changed his knighthood into a baronetcy; he being one of those created on the institution of the order in May, 1611. King Charles on his accession renewed Sir Henry's patent of chief justice; but he survived King James only nine months, dying at his house at Blickling in Norfolk on December 26, 1625. He was buried under a fair monument in Christ Church, Norwich. His house in London was that at St. Bartholomew's, in which Lord Chancellor Rich resided in the reign of Edward VI.

Spelman says of him that he was " a great loss to the public weal;" Croke reports him as " a most learned, prudent, grave and religious judge;"[2] and there is an excellent character of him in the preface to 5 Modern Reports. His own Reports were published after his death, and are so well reputed as to have passed through several editions.

By his wife Dorothy, a daughter of Sir Robert Bell, of Beaupre Hall, Norfolk, lord chief baron under Elizabeth, he had no less than sixteen children, of whom twelve were sons. From Sir Miles his third son, who succeeded to the estates on the death of his brothers, descended Sir John, who in 1728 was created a peer by the title of Baron Hobart of Blickling; to which was added in 1746 the Earldom of Buckinghamshire.[3]

---

[1] Hacket's Bp. Williams, 201. [2] Croke, Car. 28.
[3] Collins's Peerage, iv. 362.

HUTTON, RICHARD.

Just. C. P. 1625.

See under the Reign of James I.

KING CHARLES, although Sir Richard Hutton declared the imposition of ship-money to be illegal, called him " the honest Judge ;" and although royal authority is seldom taken on this point, the people returned the same verdict. He was the second son of Anthony Hutton, of a good Yorkshire family residing at Penrith in Cumberland, and was born there about the year 1560. He was sent to Jesus College, Cambridge, where he devoted himself to the study of divinity; but being induced by his friends, among whom was George, Earl of Cumberland (who, on his death in 1605, left him 100 angels), to pursue the law as a profession, he became a member, first, of Staple Inn, in the hall of which his arms are emblazoned on the south window, and next of Gray's Inn, where he was entered in 1580, and called to the bar on June 16, 1586. He is mentioned in Croke's Reports as an advocate in 1595 ; and when James came to the crown, he was added to the list of those whom Queen Elizabeth, just before her death, had summoued to take the degree of the coif at Easter, 1603, and was then knighted.[1] In this character he was the leading counsel for the defendant in the case of the *Post-nati*.[2]

.. In 1608 he was made recorder of York[3]; and on the death of Mr. Justice Nicholls, Sir Richard Hutton was appointed to fill his place in the Common Pleas on May 3, 1617. Lord Chancellor Bacon's address to him on his being sworn in is memorable for the character it gives of him, and the advice it offers. " The king," it begins, " being duly informed of your learning, integrity, discretion, experience, means and repu-

---

[1] Fuller's Worthies, i. 237.; Wood's Ath. Oxon. iii. 27.; Dugdale's Chron. Ser.
[2] State Trials, ii. 609.　　　　　　　　　[3] Drake's York, 368.

tation in your country, hath thought fit not to leave you these talents to be employed upon yourself only, but to call you to serve himself and his people." Among the counsels he gave were " that you should draw your learning from your books, not out of your brain ; " — " that you should be a light to jurors to open their eyes, but not a guide to lead them by the noses ; " — " that your speech be with gravity as one of the sages of the law, and not talkative, nor with impertinent flying out to shew learning ; " — and particularly " that your hands, and the hands of your hands, I mean those about you, be clean, and uncorrupt from gifts, from meddling with titles, and from serving of turns, be. they of great ones or small ones."[1] Pity that his own precept was not followed by the lecturer as well as it was by his auditor.

On the accession of Charles I., Sir Richard Hutton was the eldest puisne judge of the court, and on the death of Chief Justice Hobart, so much confidence was placed in his learning and integrity, that the vacancy was not supplied for nearly a year; during which he presided as prime judge till Sir Thomas Richardson received the appointment.[2] On February 19, 1632, the office of keeper of the Great Seal of the Bishoprick of Durham was granted to him while the see remained in the king's hands[3]; which he held for four months. When Sir John Finch applied to each of the judges separately for their opinions with regard to ship money, Justice Hutton refused to subscribe; and although he afterwards signed the united opinion which they gave in favour of its legality, he declared, when Hampden's case came judicially before him in 1637, that he had so subscribed only for conformity with the majority; but that his private opinion was ever against it; and he gave his reasons, as he said, " with as much perspicuity as those imperfections which

[1] Bacon's Works (Montagu), vii. 270.   [2] Croke, Car. 56.
[3] Rymer, xix. 346.

attend my age will give me leave," why judgment ought not
to be given for the king.[1] However King Charles might
think it prudent to conceal his displeasure, there were some
among the clergy who were indignant at this denial, as they
called it, of the king's supremacy. Sir Richard, it seems,
had repeated his interpretation of the law in his charge to
the grand jury at Northampton; and Thomas Harrison, a
clergyman of that county, foolishly taking umbrage at this,
came to the bar of the Common Pleas, and cried out in a
loud voice, " I do accuse Mr. Justice Hutton of high treason." He soon suffered for his temerity. Being indicted for
the offence he was fined 5000l. and imprisoned, and required
to make his submission in all the courts at Westminster.
The only point of the story that does not tell to the judge's
credit, is that he also brought an action for damages against
Harrison, and recovered 10,000l.[2]

He lived not long after these events, dying in Serjeants'
Inn, Chancery Lane, on February 25, 1638-9, in the
seventy-ninth year of his age. He left a fair estate at Goldsborough in Yorkshire, and was buried at St. Dunstan's-in-
the-West. Croke describes him as " a grave, learned, pious
and prudent judge, and of great courage and patience in all
his proceedings."[3] He compiled " Reports of sundry Cases,"
which were published after his death.

Three sons of his are mentioned: Sir Richard, who was
killed on the king's side at Sherborne; Thomas, to whom
he left all his books in Serjeants' Inn; and Henry, who married Elizabeth the second daughter of John Cosin, Bishop of
Durham. He had also several daughters; and one of his
descendants was living at Goldsborough in 1684.[3]

---

[1] State Trials, iii. 844. 1191·   [2] Croke, Car. 503.   [3] Ibid. 537.
[4] Surtees's Durham, i. clxvi.; Collins's Peerage, viii. 456.; Wotton's Baronet.
i. 78.; Burke's Landed Gent. 901.; Grandeur of the Law (1684), 257.

HYDE, NICHOLAS.
Ch. K. B. 1627.

NORBURY, in the county of Chester, had belonged in regular descent to the family of Hyde, from the time of the Conquest. The third son of Robert Hyde of that place was Lawrence Hyde, who settled at West Hatch in Wiltshire, married Anne, daughter of Nicholas Sybill, Esq., of Chimbhams in Kent, and widow of Matthew Somerton, Esq., of Claverton in Somersetshire. This Lawrence died in 1590, leaving several sons and daughters. Sir Lawrence, his second surviving son, was an eminent lawyer, and became attorney-general to King James's queen; Henry, the third, was the father of the Earl of Clarendon; and Nicholas, the youngest, was the chief justice now to be noticed.

The age of Nicholas at his father's death does not appear; but he was left dependent on his mother, except an annuity of 30l. for life, bequeathed to him by his father. Admitted to the Middle Temple, he was called to the bar by that society, who elected him their reader in Lent, 1617, and their treasurer in 1626.[1] He had previously entered parliament in 1603 as member for Christchurch, Hants[2]; and he is first noticed in the Reports as an advocate in 1613. Though his professional progress is not recorded, he had sufficiently distinguished himself to be employed by the Duke of Buckingham in preparing his defence to the articles of impeachment prepared against him by the House of Commons in 1626.[3] The care and ingenuity evinced in that defence were so satisfactory to the duke, that on the removal of Sir Ranulphe Crewe, and the death of Sir John Davies his designated successor, Hyde, by the favourite's influence, was nominated chief justice of the King's Bench, though he had no claim

---

[1] Dugdale's Orig. 219. 221.   [2] Parl. Hist i. 974.
[3] Parl. Hist. ii. 167.; Whitelocke, 8.

from previous official employment; and the attorney and solicitor-general were passed over in his favour. To render his elevation more honourable, he was first made a king's serjeant; the date of the one being January 31, and of the other February 5, 1627 ;[1] and in the interim between the two he was knighted.

His sudden advance naturally excited remark and some jealousy, and was food for the wits of the bar. At the Bury assizes in the following Lent these lines on him and his four predecessors were repeated by Drue Drury almost in his hearing : —

> Learned Coke, curt Montague,
> The aged Lea, and honest Crew :
> Two preferred, two set aside,
> And then starts up Sir Nicholas Hyde.[2]

He presided in the court for four years and a half only, and had no easy time of it. He and the other judges had to justify themselves before the House of Lords for refusing to discharge the five gentlemen who were imprisoned for refusing to contribute to the loan.[3] He had also, in 1629, to adjudge the case of Stroud, Sir John Eliot, and the other members, for their violence to the speaker on the last day of the session. They were at first refused bail, unless they gave sureties for their good behaviour; which they refusing, some of them were tried and sentence pronounced upon them. For these proceedings, the judges in the commencement of the Long Parliament in 1640 were called to account, and their judgment reversed. Though a motion was made that the parties might have reparation out of the estates of Chief Justice Hyde and the rest of the court, the compensation appears eventually to have been granted out of the general revenue.[4] Long before this investigation took place Sir

---

[1] Rymer, xviii. 835.   [2] Walter Yonge's Diary, 101.
[3] Parl. Hist. ii. 291.   [4] State Trials, iii. 235—335.; Whitelocke, 38.

Nicholas was removed from the violence of the times. After taking a ride of fifty miles in a hot day, though "a spare, lean man of body, and of excellent temperate diet," he was seized with a fever, which, Lord Clarendon says, he got from the infection of some gaol in the summer circuit, and died at his house in Hampshire on August 25, 1631.

In the opinions given by him and his colleagues, in answer to the king's questions, they seem to have acted an independent part, and also on several other occasions, in refusing to stop the course of justice at the king's command. Sir Nicholas is said to have been mean in his person and bearing, and was so unostentatious that he rode his circuits on horseback, according to Sir Symonds D'Ewes, in a whitish-blue cloak, "more like a clothier or a woolman than a Lord Chief Justice." As an instance of his simplicity and want of observation, Serjeant Maynard reports a trial on an appeal of murder before him, interesting for the superstitious belief it records, in which he asked a witness how he knew "the print of a left hand from the print of a right hand?"[1]

But Croke and Whitelocke, his contemporaries and colleagues, and Lord Clarendon, his nephew, give evidence of the sterling points of his character. Croke calls him "a grave, religious, discreet man, and of great learning and piety."[2] Judge Whitelocke says that "he lived in the place with great integrity and uprightness, and with great wisdom and temper, considering the ticklishness of the times. He would never undertake to the King, nor adventure to give him a resolute answer in any weighty business, when the question was of the law, but he would pray that he might confer with his Brethren."[3] Lord Clarendon thus describes him: — "He was a man of excellent learning for that province he was to govern, of unsuspected and unblemished integrity, of an ex-

---

[1] Gent. Mag. July, 1851, p. 15., quoting a Day Book of Dr. Sampson.
[2] Croke, Car. 225.   [3] Rushworth, ii. 111.

emplar gravity and austerity, which was necessary for the manners of the time, corrupted by the marching of armies and by the license after the disbanding of them; and though upon his promotion from a private practiser of the law to the supreme judicatory of it, by the power and recommendation of the great favorite, of whose council he had been; yet his behaviour was so grateful to all the judges, who had an entire confidence in him, his service so useful to the king in his government, his justice and sincerity so conspicuous throughout the kingdom, that the death of no judge had in any time been more lamented."[1]

He married Margaret, daughter of Arthur Swayne, Esq., of Sarson, and left by her several children, whose descendants were settled at Marlborough and Hyde End in Berkshire.[2]

JERMYN, PHILIP,
PARL. JUST. K. B. 1648.
See under the Interregnum.

JONES, WILLIAM,
JUST. K. B. 1625.
See under the Reign of James I.

THE Joneses are an ancient family of North Wales, whose lineage is traced by the Welsh heralds from the princes and possessors of that country, and is equally honoured by claiming the judge as its descendant. Sir William Jones was the eldest son of William Jones, Esq., of Castellmarch in Carnarvonshire, where the family had long been seated. His mother was Margaret, daughter of Humphrey Wynn ap Meredith, of Hyssoilfarch, Esq. At the age of fourteen, he was sent from the free school of Beaumaris to the university of Oxford, where he pursued his studies at St. Edmund's Hall for five years, and then was entered of Furnival's Inn, to be

---

[1] Life of Clarendon, i. 3—13.   [2] Sir R. C. Hoare's Wilts.

instructed in the rudiments of law. After spending two years there, he removed to Lincoln's Inn, of which he was admitted a member on July 5, 1587, where, after the customary seven years' course, he was called to the bar on January 28, 1595[1], and became reader in Lent, 1616.[2] Although his name does not appear in any of the published Reports, he had acquired sufficient eminence in his profession to be selected in the following year for the chief justiceship of the King's Bench in Ireland. For this purpose he was called to the degree of serjeant on March 14, 1617, and knighted. Lord Bacon addressed him on the occasion, and after alluding to his " sufficiency every way," recommended him " in that great place in which you are to settle " to " take unto you the constancy and integrity of Sir Robert Gardiner; the gravity, temper and direction of Sir James Lea; the quickness, industry and dispatch of Sir Humphry Winch; the care and affection to the commonwealth, and the prudent and politic administration of Sir John Denham, and you shall need no other lessons."[3] It is curious that no less than three out of these his four predecessors in office were afterwards placed on the English bench, and that Serjeant Jones ultimately received the same honour.

After staying in Ireland for about three years, during which he was one of the commissioners of the Great Seal of that kingdom, on the vacancy in the office of lord chancellor, occasioned by the death of the Archbishop of Dublin, he resigned his seat in the King's Bench; and in the patent of his successor June, 1620, the services of Sir William are thus encomiastically alluded to. The king, while complying with his desire to be called from his charge, says, " he could wish, for the good of his service and his kingdom of Ireland, that a man so faithful, honest, and able would have affected

---

[1] Linc. Inn, Black Book, v. 410., vi. 9. [2] Dugdale's Orig. Jur. 255.
[3] Bacon's Works (Montagu), vii. 263.

z 2

to continue in that office longer."[1] On returning to England, he resumed his practice at the bar, his name appearing as an advocate in his own and Croke's Reports from Michaelmas, 1620, to the same term, 1621. In that term he was placed on the English bench as a judge of the Common Pleas, the first fine levied before him fixing the date[2], although his patent has not been found. He continued in that court for three years, during which he was also employed on a commission in Ireland ; and was then, on October 17, 1624, transferred to the King's Bench, where he remained for the rest of his life. He never went any other than the Oxford circuit.

In the great question, in 1628, as to the refusal of bail to the five gentlemen committed to prison for not contributing to the loan, Justice Jones, when called with his fellows before the House of Lords to assign his reasons for that judgment, adverted thus boldly, in his justification, to the antiquity of his house : " I am myself," said he, " Liber Homo, my ancestors gave their voice for Magna Charta. I enjoy that house still which they did. I do not now mean to draw down God's wrath upon my posterity ; and therefore I will neither advance the King's prerogative nor lessen the Liberty of the Subject, to the danger of either King or people."[3] What his view of the king's prerogative was may be judged by his joining in the opinion of the bench in favour of ship-money, and by the reasons he gave in support of that opinion in 1637, in Hampden's case[4]; but, however erroneous his view of the case might be, there is no doubt that his decision was founded on a conscientious opinion of its correctness.

By his death before the Long Parliament took up the question, he escaped the impeachment instituted against his colleagues who pronounced the same judgment. That event occurred at his house in Holborn, on December 9, 1640, in

[1] Law Off. of Ireland, 26. 88.   [2] Dugdale's Orig. 48.
[3] Parl. Hist. ii. 290.   [4] State Trials, iii. 844. 1181.

the seventy-fourth year of his age. He was buried under Lincoln's Inn chapel. Hearne describes him as " a person of admirable learning, particularly in the Municipal laws and British antiquities."[1] His " Reports of Special Cases," from 18 Jac. I. to 15 Car. I., which were not published till after his death, have a good reputation in Westminster Hall, and to distinguish them from those of Sir Thomas Jones, a judge in the reign of Charles II., they are cited as " First Jones's Reports."

At the age of twenty-one he married Margaret, eldest daughter of Griffith John Griffith, Esq., of Kevenamulch, by whom he left a numerous family of daughters. His only son, Charles, who was reader at Lincoln's Inn in Lent, 1640, died before him. He took a second wife, Catherine, daughter of Thomas Powys, of Abingdon, and widow of Dr. Hovenden, warden of All Souls' College, Oxford[2], but left no male issue by her.[3]

KENT, EARL OF. *See* HENRY GREY.

LANE, RICHARD.
CH. B. E. 1644. LORD KEEPER, 1645.

THE last lord keeper of the Great Seal of Charles I. was Richard the son of Richard Lane of Courtenhall, near Northampton, by Elizabeth, daughter of Clement Vincent of Harpole in the same county. He studied the law at the Middle Temple, and having been called to the bar it may be inferred that his early practice was in the Exchequer, from his Reports of Cases in that court from the 3rd to the 9th James I. 1605— 1612. He did not arrive at the post of reader to his inn till Lent 1630, nor to that of treasurer till 1637.[4] He had, how-

[1] Curious Discourses, ii. 448.   [2] Collins's Peerage, viii. 577.
[3] Wood's Ath. Oxon. ii. 673.; Preface to his Reports, 1675.
[4] Dugdale's Orig. 220. 222.

ever, so good a reputation in his profession as to be appointed
successor of Sir John Banks in the office of attorney-general
to the Prince of Wales in 1634.[1] When the House of Commons impeached the Earl of Strafford, Mr. Lane was assigned
to conduct the earl's defence, which he did so ably, especially
in the legal argument, showing that none of the facts alleged
against the earl were comprehended in the statute of treason,
that the Commons, seeing the great probability of the earl's
acquittal by the Lords, desisted from the trial, and effected
their malicious purpose by a disgraceful bill of attainder, which
by popular clamour was eventually passed.[2] Officially connected with the court, he of course joined the king at Oxford;
where, having been previously knighted, he was appointed Sir
Humphrey Davenport's successor as lord chief baron on January 25, 1644; having been invested with the serjeant's coif
two days before, and being created doctor of civil law by the
university six days afterwards.

The first duty that Sir Richard had to perform was to act
as one of the commissioners on the part of the king in treating
for an accommodation at Uxbridge, when he joined the other
lawyers in resisting the demand of the parliament to have the
militia entirely vested in them. There appearing no probability of satisfactorily settling this question, or that upon religion which was violently debated, the treaty was broken off
and the war proceeded.[3] In the course of the next year Lord
Lyttelton died, and within three days, on August 30, 1645,
the Great Seal was placed in the hands of Sir Richard as
lord keeper. The king, whose difficulties increased daily,
was at last obliged to escape from Oxford, and that city was
surrendered to the opposing army under General Fairfax on
June 24, 1646, under articles in which the lord keeper was
the principal party on the king's behalf. By one of them it

[1] Clarendon's Life, i. 67.   [2] State Trials, iii. 1472.
[3] Clarendon, v. 37. 60.

was provided that the Great Seal and all the other official seals should be left for the victors.[1]　Thus deprived of the insignia of his office, nothing remained to him but its name, which he retained during the remainder of the king's life. There is no evidence that his patent was renewed by Charles II., though he lived for nearly two years after that monarch's nominal reign began.　Like the king he became an exile from his native land, and died in 1650 in France; as appears by the commission, dated April 22, 1651, to his relict the Lady Margaret, to, administer to his personalty.　A somewhat improbable story is told that when he joined the king at Oxford he entrusted his chambers, his library, and his goods to his intimate friend Bulstrode Whitelocke; who, when they were applied for by the lord keeper's son, denied that he had ever known such a man as Sir Richard.[2]

LEEKE, THOMAS.
Cursitor B. E. 1642.

See under the Reign of Charles II.

LENTHALL, WILLIAM.
Parl. M. R. 1643.　Com. G. S. 1646.

LINCOLN, Bishop of.　*See* John Williams.

LYTTELTON, EDWARD.
Ch. C. P. 1640.　Lord Keeper, 1641.

More than a century had elapsed between the death of Judge Lyttelton, the eminent author of the Treatise on Tenures,[3] and the birth of his descendant, the chief justice and lord keeper of Charles I.　John Lyttelton, incumbent of Mounslow in Shropshire, who was the son of Thomas the youngest of the three sons of the judge, was the father of two sons, named

---

[1] Whitelocke, 210.　　[2] Wood's Fasti, ii. 63.　　[3] See Vol. IV. p. 436.

Thomas and Edward. Thomas's grandson, Sir Adam, of
Stoke Milburgh, was honoured with a baronetcy in 1642,
which failed in 1710 by the death without issue of Sir Thomas
Lyttelton, who was speaker in the parliament of 1698. Edward, seated at Henley, in Shropshire, became chief justice
of North Wales, was knighted, and married Mary, the daughter of Edmund Walter, chief justice of South Wales, and
sister to Sir John Walter, the distinguished lord chief baron
of the Exchequer in the reign of James I. The connection
of this lady with the law was somewhat remarkable; for,
besides being the daughter, the wife, and the sister of judges,
she was the mother of two; Edward, the eldest of her eight
sons being the subject of this memoir, and the seventh,
Timothy, becoming a baron of the Exchequer under Charles
II. William, another son, also, was a serjeant at law.[1]

Edward Lyttelton was born at Mounslow in 1589, and,
becoming a gentleman commoner of Christ Church in the
university of Oxford in the beginning of 1606, took his first
degree in arts on April 28, 1609.[2] At the Inner Temple, the
school in which his ancestors studied, he commenced his legal
career, and in due time was called to the bar. Lord Clarendon describes him as " a handsome and proper man, of a very
graceful presence, and notorious for courage, which in his
youth he had manifested with his sword. He had taken great
pains in the hardest and most knotty part of the law, as well
as that which was more customary; and was not only very
ready and expert in the books, but exceedingly versed in
records, in studying and examining whereof he had kept
Mr. Selden company, with whom he had great friendship,
and who had much assisted him; so that he was looked upon
as the best antiquary of the profession who gave himself up
to practice."[3] His early reputation in his profession is proved

---

[1] Wotton's Baronet. ii. 61.   [2] Wood's Fasti, i. 333.   [3] Clarendon, ii. 491.

by his being, on his father's death in 1621, appointed to suc-
eeed him as chief justice of North Wales.

Returned in 1626 to the second parliament of Charles I.,
he took an active part in the proceedings against the Duke
of Buckingham, arguing that common fame was a sufficient
ground for the house to act upon. It being so determined,
articles of impeachment were exhibited; but he was not one
of the managers selected to conduct it. In the midst of
the inquiry, the king, to save his favourite, dissolved the
parliament. When it met again in March, 1628, Lyttelton
was placed in the chair of the committee of grievances, and
on April 3 presented to the house their report, upon which
was founded the famous Petition of Right. In the subsequent conferences with the Lords, he ably enforced the resolutions, and replied to the objections of the crown officers
with temper and point. He was designated by the lord president in reporting the arguments, as " a grave and learned
lawyer;" and great must have been his elation when he heard
the king's answer to the petition, " Soit droit fait comme il
est désiré." On the dissolution of this parliament in the
following March, several members were imprisoned for their
violence in holding the speaker in the chair, while the protestation against Tonnage and Poundage was passed. On
their application to the court of King's Bench, Lyttelton
appeared for John Selden, who was one of those arrested,
and learnedly contended for his right to be discharged on
bail.[1] The well-known result of these arbitrary proceedings
has been related in another place.

Though a strenuous advocate for the liberty of the subject,
he had never exhibited any asperity in his language, nor
shown himself a violent partizan of those who opposed the
measures of the court. His learning and eloquence secured

---

[1] Parl. Hist. ii. 53. 239. 259. 319-323.   State Trials, iii. 85. 252.

him extensive professional employment, and naturally placed him in the rank of those lawyers destined for promotion. The king could not fail to see the benefits which would result from his services, and accordingly earnestly recommended him, on the death of Sir Heneage Finch, as recorder of the city of London, to which he was elected on December 7, 1631. About the same time, he was appointed counsel to the university of Oxford, and in autumn of the next year he arrived at the post of reader to the Inner Temple.[1] His popularity in London obtained for him on this occasion, a present from the aldermen of 100*l.*, two hogsheads of claret, and a pipe of canary.[2] It was not till October 17, 1634, that he received a further mark of the king's favour, when he was made solicitor-general in the room of Richard Sheldon, whom Clarendon calls "an old, useless, illiterate person," and was soon after knighted. This office he held above five years, and principally distinguished himself by his elaborate argument against Hampden in the case of ship money, in delivering which he occupied three days.[3]

While he held this office an extraordinary compliment was paid by his inn of court to the name of his illustrious ancestor. The solicitor-general having applied for a chamber, then vacant over his own, to be assigned to his kinsman, Mr. Thomas Lyttelton, "the whole company of the bench with one voice" not only granted his request, but desired that the "admittance should be freely without any fine, as a testimony of that great respect the whole society doth owe and acknowledge to the name and family of Lyttelton."[4]

On the elevation of Sir John Finch to the office of lord keeper, that of chief justice of the Common Pleas was conferred on Sir Edward Lyttelton on January 27, 1640, he having received the degree of serjeant nine days before.[5]

---

[1] Dugdale's Orig. 168.　[2] City List of Recorders.　[3] State Trials, iii. 923.
[4] Inner Temple Books ; Gent. Mag. Dec. 1856. p. 717.　[5] Rymer, xx. 380.

This, according to Clarendon, was an office "which he was wont to say, in his highest ambition, in his own private wishes, he had most desired;" but though it was the sphere "in which," says the same author, "he moved most gracefully and with the most advantage[1]," it was not his fortune to remain in it above a year. In the April following his appointment a new parliament was called, and after sitting barely three weeks was dissolved. Another, the Long Parliament, met in November, and one of its first inquiries was into the conduct of Lord Keeper Finch, who, dreading the consequences, fled the country. The Seal, being thus deserted, was delivered to Lyttelton (who had, by the recommendation of Strafford, been previously admitted into the Privy Council), with the title of lord keeper, on Jannary 18, 1641[2], and on the 18th of the following month he was created Lord Lyttelton of Mounslow. This advance did not add to his reputation or his peace. In the Common Pleas he had presided with great ability; in the Chancery he was only an indifferent judge. At the council and in parliament he felt himself out of his element, and was so disturbed with the unhappy state of the king's affairs that he fell into a serious illness, and was absent from his place for some months.

One of the first duties which the new lord keeper had to perform was to express the thanks of the Lords and Commons to the king for passing the act for triennial parliaments. Then came the impeachment and attainder of his friend, the Earl of Strafford, in behalf of whom he was prevented from pleading by his illness, the Earl of Arundel acting for him as speaker in the House of Peers.[3] Soon after, on May 18, the lord keeper was placed at the head of a commission to execute the office of lord high treasurer. On his resuming his seat he had the difficult duty of presiding during all the violent

[1] Clarendon, ii. 492.   [2] Croke, Car. 565.   [3] State Trials, ii. 956.

measures that occupied the house the remainder of that year
and the beginning of the next.   His conduct, while it could
not but be displeasing to the king, raising doubts of his
fidelity, was so satisfactory to the Commons, and so apparently compliant with their wills, that on their nomination
of lieutenants for the several counties they placed him at the
head of his native shire.[1]   In March, 1642, the king, offended
by the parliamentary proceedings, retired to York.   He had
been for some time suspicious of the lord's keeper's devotion
to him, and was particularly disgusted with his vote in favour
of the ordinance for the militia, and his arguments in support
of its legality.[2]   Lord Lyttelton, however, took an opportunity of explaining to Mr. Hyde (afterwards Lord Clarendon), who was secretly in the confidence of the king, that
he was in great perplexity how to act, that he had no person
to confer with or to confide in, and that he had given this
vote and others, which he knew would be obnoxious to the
king, for the purpose of disarming the rising distrust of the
Commons, and of preventing their proposed intention of
taking the Seal from him.   He thereupon planned with Mr.
Hyde that he would take advantage of the customary recess
of the house, between Saturday and Monday morning, to
send the Great Seal to the king, and himself to follow after.
This important service, as it was then deemed, was successfully effected, and on May 23 the lord keeper's escape was
reported to the Lords, who immediately ordered him to be
taken into custody; but at the end of the third day after
his departure he kissed the king's hand at York.[3]   This
statement would seem to be contradicted by his subsequent
letter to the Lords, in which he says that Saturday was *the
first time* that he ever heard of going to York, and that he
did so by the king's absolute commands.   He incloses an
affidavit showing his inability, from illness, to travel to

[1] State Trials, 1085.   [2] Whitelocke, 59.   [3] Clarendon, ii. 494—504

Westminster, as ordered; and at the same time proves the evasiveness of the excuse by "taking the boldness" to inform the Lords that he has the king's express commands upon his allegiance not to depart from him.   In another letter to Lord Willoughby he denies having voted for the militia ordinance; but his disavowal is contradicted, with circumstance, by the entry on the Journal, as well as by Lord Clarendon and Whitelocke.[1]   Such weakness of purpose, and such useless attempts to be well with both parties, sufficiently account for his not being respected by either.

It was not till a year afterwards that the parliament voted, That, if Lord Keeper Lyttelton did not return with the Great Seal within fourteen days, he should lose his place; and whatever should be sealed with that Great Seal afterwards should be void[2]: and the two houses passed an ordinance for a new Great Seal on November 10, 1643.[3]   The king was, at first, much dissatisfied with Lyttelton, whose hesitation and fears were rather annoying.   But Hyde convinced his Majesty of his lord keeper's fidelity, and prevented his being removed from his place, though he was not for some time entrusted with the actual custody of the Seal.[4]   According to the allegations of the Commons, it had been frequently in the hands of Mr. Porter, Sir George Ratcliffe, and others[5]: but this no doubt was in order to secure its safety, and to prevent its getting into the possession of the parliament.   Of Lyttelton's loyal devotion to the crown, all suspicion was at last removed.   On January 31, 1643, he received, with other of the king's adherents, the degree of doctor of the civil law from the university of Oxford[6]: in March he was again appointed first commissioner of the Treasury[7]: and on May 21, 1644, he was

[1] Parl. Hist. ii. 1319. 1366.   [2] Whitelocke, 70.
[3] Parl. Hist. iii. 180.   [4] Life of Clarendon, i. 146.
[5] Parl. Hist. iii. 178.   [6] Wood's Fasti Oxon. ii. 44.
[7] 4 Report, Pub. Rec. App. ii. 187.

actually entrusted with a military commission to raise a regiment of foot-soldiers, consisting of gentlemen of the Inns of Court and Chancery, and others. Of this regiment, the ranks of which were soon filled, he acted as colonel. Two centuries had elapsed since a keeper of the Seal and a soldier were united in the same person; and in the two centuries that have since passed, no other person has served the king in a like double capacity.

Notwithstanding this ebullition of zeal and spirit, Lyttelton was an altered man. The sad position of public affairs depressed him; he became melancholy, and the vigour of his mind and the strength of his body gradually decayed; so that he could not contend against an attack of illness, which carried him off on August 27, 1645. He was buried in the cathedral of Christ Church, Oxford, the place of his education, where his only daughter, Anne, erected a monument to his memory.

That he was a learned lawyer, powerful advocate, and an excellent judge; that in his private character he was highly esteemed; that he was incorrupt amidst corruption, and moderate among the violent; and that he never used power for the gratification of private malignity, nor for the prosecution of party purposes, both friends and enemies readily acknowledge. Desertion of the popular party for place, is somewhat harshly alleged against him. He had, as a member of parliament, manfully resisted the increasing encroachments upon the constitution; and when he had succeeded, as then appeared, in securing the liberty of the subject, and the parliament was dissolved, he became again a simple barrister. The country was then comparatively quiet, and he naturally received the gradual promotion to which his eminence as a lawyer entitled him. He had been already a Welsh judge; in 1631 he became recorder, in 1634 solicitor-general, and it was not till 1640 that he was selected as chief justice; and there is nothing in his conduct in either office that can justify the condemnation of the party in whose ranks he had fought the battle of freedom.   His subsequent career in his higher place must rather be blamed as weak than stigmatised as treacherous; and his flight with the Great Seal from the parliament, so dangerous, and, indeed, so fatal to himself, if he had been stopped, showed a degree of personal courage that must dissipate all doubts as to the principles by which he was guided.   He felt it to be his duty to resist the encroachments on the constitution, and he did resist them; he felt it equally to be his duty to support the sovereign when his power was threatened; and he flew to him for that purpose.   But he was not a man for the times he lived in.   He was not made for power; he could not cope with the spirits of the day; he was weak and wavering; and by endeavouring to be the friend of all parties, he experienced the usual consequence of being confided in by none. But he had dear friends on both sides who did not doubt his integrity.   Hyde, who knew him well, was his friend to the last.   Whitelocke, of the parliament side, always speaks kindly of him, and even in relating his flight calls him " a man of courage and of excellent parts and learning; " and, when in 1645 the Commons seized his books and manuscripts, Whitelocke induced them to bestow them on him, with the intention, he asserts, to restore them to the owner or his family, when " God gave them a happy accommodation." [1]

A volume of Reports in the Common Pleas and Exchequer, from 2 to 7 Charles I., was published with his name in 1683 ; but doubts have been raised as to their being of his composition.

His peerage died with him, as he left no surviving son to succeed him.   By his first wife, Anne, daughter of John Lyttelton of Frankley, he had a son and two daughters, who all died while infants.   His second wife was Elizabeth, one of

---

[1] Whitelocke, 172.

the daughters of Sir William Jones, the judge of the King's Bench, and widow of Sir George Calverley of Cheshire. By her he had an only daughter, Anne, who was married to her cousin, Sir Thomas Lyttelton, of Stoke Milburgh, Bart.[1]

MALET, THOMAS.
JUST. K. B. 1641.
See under the Reign of Charles II.

MANCHESTER, EARL OF. *See* E. MONTAGU.

MONTAGU, EDWARD, EARL OF MANCHESTER.
PARL. COM. G. S. 1646.
See under the Interregnum.

PAGE, JOHN OR WILLIAM.
CURSITOR B. E. 1638.

DUGDALE calls this baron William, and Rymer christens him John; and which is the real name has not been discovered, for there is no account of his birth, parentage, or education, or whether he was of any university or inn of Court, or had any practice or took any degree in law, before he is inserted in the Chronica Series as being appointed a baron of the Exchequer on October 29, 1638. That he was a cursitor baron there is no doubt, for he is never mentioned in the judicial proceedings of the court; and two years after his nomination, his name as baron appears in a commission to the lord treasurer and others, at a distance of five from the regular barons. In another commission, also, to the lord treasurer and barons of the Exchequer, two months afterwards, the four regular barons are mentioned without him, with the further expression, " to the Chief Baron and other

---

[1] Wood's Athen. Oxon. iii. 175.

the Barons of the Exchequer for the time being." He evidently succeeded Cursitor Baron Pagitt, who died in September, 1638; but only held his offiee for four years, dying suddenly on November 9, 1642.[1] One of his daughters married Bernard Walcot of Oundle in Northamptonshire.[1]

PAGITT, JAMES.

Cursitor B. E. 1631.

THE branch of the Pagitt family, to which the baron of the Exchequer belonged, was settled in Northamptonshire, where his great-grandfather, Thomas, is described of Barton-Segrave, and his grandfather, Richard, of Cranford. His father was Thomas Pagitt, an eminent lawyer, twice reader at the Middle Temple, and treasurer there in 1599.[2] His mother, Barbara Bradbury, died in 1583, and was buried in St. Botolph's, Aldersgate.[3] James was born about the year 1581, and received his legal education at the same Inn of Court as his father, and was called to the bar on November 26, 1602[4]; but never arrived at the dignity of reader. Apparently placed at an early age in the Exchequer, he is described as comptroller of the pipe in 1618[5]; and on October 24, 1631, he was raised to the office of a baron of the court.[6]

It is manifest, however, that this office was not that of one of the judicial barons. There was no vacancy among them at the time of his nomination; and during the whole of his career he neither took part in the business of the court, nor is ever mentioned in the conferences of the judges. He is not noticed as an advocate by the reporters; and not having been called to the degree of the coif, he could not go the circuits. Neither

---

[1] Dugdale's Chron. Ser.; Rymer, xx. 409. 433.; Peck's Desid. Cur. B. xiv. 19.; Burke's Landed Gentry, 1486.

[2] Dugdale's Orig. 218. 221.   [3] Maitland's London, 1076.

[4] Middle Temple Books.   [5] His 2nd wife's monument at Tottenham.

[6] Rymer, xix. 347. In Dugdale he is miscalled John.

was he ever knighted; an honour conferred on all the other members of the court. Anthony Wood calls him, " puisne baron of the Exchequer;"[1] the precise title given to Sir Thomas Cæsar, with the addition, " commonly called the Baron Cursitor."[2] To this latter offiee no doubt he was appointed, being conversant with the fiscal department of the Exchequer, as the successor to the second John Sotherton, of whom nothing is heard after Michaelmas, 1630.

Baron Pagitt died on September 3, 1638, at his house at Tottenham, in the church of which parish is a monument to his memory.

He married three wives, but had issue only by the first. She was Katherine, daughter of Dr. William Lewin, dean of the Arches, and died in 1628. The second was Bridget, daughter of Anthony Bowyer, of Coventry, draper, and widow of . . . . Moyse, of London. She died in 1626. The third was Mazaretta, daughter of Robert Harris, of Reading and Lincoln's Inn, who had previously had two husbands as he had had two wives ; viz., Richard Vaughan and Zephaniah Sayers, both of London. She died in 1666, aged eighty-eight.

Besides two daughters, he left two sons. 1. Justinian, of Hadley, Custos Brevium of the King's Bench, and afterwards knighted, who had a large family. 2. Thomas, a lawyer, who was a great friend to Elias Ashmole, whose mother was sister to the baron's second wife, Bridget.

" Old Father Ephraim Pagitt, above 40 years Rector of St. Edmond, Lombard Street, which, it is said, upon the breaking out of the civil war, he was forced to quit merely for quietness sake," was the son of Eusebius Pagitt, the brother of the baron's father.[3]

---

[1] Ath. Oxon. iv. 354.   [2] Dugdale's Orig. 149.

[3] Oldfield's and Dyson's Hist. of Tottenham, 48. ; Ashmole's Antiq. of Berks, iii. 88. ; Wotton's Baronet. ii. 33. ; with additional information kindly communicated by Arthur Pa et, Esq. of Cranmore Hall, Shepton Mallet.

PHESANT, PETER.

PARL. JUST. C. P. 1645

See under the Interregnum.

PRIDEAUX, EDMOND.

PARL. COM. G. S. 1643.

DESCENDED from an ancient and honourable family, which traces its lineage as far back as the Norman conquest, when it was seated in Prideaux-castle in Cornwall, Edmond Prideaux was the second son of an eminent lawyer of the same name, by Catherine, daughter of Piers Edgecombe, Esq., of Mount Edgecombe in Devonshire. The father in 1622 received from King James the dignity of a baronet, which survives at the present day.[1]

Edmond was born at his father's residence at Netherton, near Honiton, and seems to have received his education in the university of Cambridge, and to have taken his master's degree there; since, some years after, in July 1625, he was admitted *ad eundem* at Oxford. His legal course is traced with greater certainty; having been entered as a student at the Inner Temple on May 12, 1616, and been called to the bar on November 23, 1623.[2] His name does not appear in the Reports of Charles's reign, his practice being chiefly in Chancery; but at one time he was recorder of Exeter.[3] The electors of Lyme-Regis in Dorsetshire returned him in 1640 as a member of the Long Parliament, where he took the popular side, and subscribed in June, 1642, 100*l.* towards its defence.[4] Though he did not mix much in the debates, he was evidently looked upon as an active partizan; for when the two houses adopted a Great Seal of their own, he was one of the four members of the House of Commons, who with two

[1] Wotton's Baronet. i. 517.
[2] Inner Temple Books.
[3] Wood's Fasti, i. 424., ii. 66.
[4] Notes and Queries, 1st S. xii. 359.

peers were nominated commissioners. The ordinance appointing them was dated November 10, 1643. He filled the post
for nearly three years; the parliament then changing the custody of the seal and placing it in the hands of the speakers of
the two houses on October 30, 1646. While holding this
offiee he still kept his place in the House of Commons, and
was employed in 1644 to urge their reasons for passing the
ordinance for secluding such members of both houses as had
deserted the parliament. He was also named as one of the
commissioners who assembled at Uxbridge in January, 1645,
to negotiate a treaty of accommodation with the king. On
his removal from the Great Seal the Commons ordered that,
as a mark of honour and of their acknowledgment of his services, he should practise within the bar, and have precedence
next after the solicitor-general.[1]

Prideaux then resumed his professional practice till 1648,
when the parliament, on filling up the vacancies on the bench,
named him solicitor-general on October 12, and he was sworn
in on November 25. When he saw, however, what proceedings were adopted for taking the king's life, it is evident that
he threw up the office ; for on Charles's trial in the succeeding January William Steele acted as attorney, and John Cook
as solicitor-general[2] : and also on the subsequent trials of the
Duke of Hamilton and others.[3] That he lost no favour with
the parliament by his conduct in avoiding these trials is apparent from his receiving the appointment of attorney-general
on the 9th of the following April; and from his retaining it
during the remainder of his life, through all the different
changes that took place in the government; — under the
Council of State; under all the three parliaments of Cromwell; under that of Richard his son; and again under the
Rump Parliament. During the whole of this time he con-

---

[1] Journals; Whitelocke, 92. 125. 226.   [2] Whitelocke, 342. 357. 368.
[3] State Trials, iv. 1167. 1209.

tinned member for Lyme Regis.[1]   The dignity of baronet was conferred upon him on May 31, 1658, " in respect of his voluntary offer for the mainteyning of 30 foot-souldiers in his Highnes army in Ireland."[2]   He survived Cromwell about a year, dying on August 19, 1659.

Whitelocke describes him as " a generous person, and faithful to the Parliament's Interest.   A good Chancery lawyer." This is not great praise ; and it seems that he was equally faithful to his own interest.   Besides his practice at the bar, which was worth about 5000l. a year, he was postmaster for all the inland letters, an offiee which, at sixpence a letter, is said to have netted him 15,000l. a year.[3]   No wonder, therefore, that he made a large fortune, and that he was enabled to purchase Ford Abbey in the parish of Thorncombe, Devon, and to build on its ruins a noble mansion.

He married two wives ; the first was a daughter of —— Collins, Esq., of Ottery St. Mary in Devonshire, by whom he had no children ; the second was the daughter and coheir of —— Every, Esq., of Cottey in the county of Somerset, by whom he left an only son, also named Edmond, whose education was superintended by Mr. (afterwards Archbishop) Tillotson.   Edmond took his wife's name of Fraunceis, and left an only daughter, who married Francis Gwyn, Esq., of Lansanor in Glamorganshire ; in the possession of whose representatives the Prideaux estates are still remaining.[4]

REEVE, EDMUND,

Just. C. P. 1639.

EDMUND REEVE was of a Norfolk family, and is rightly claimed by the society of Barnard's Inn as having commenced

---

[1] Whitelocke, 394. ; Parl. Hist. iii. 1429. 1480. 1532.
[2] 5 Report Pub. Rec. App. 273.   [3] Parl. Hist. iii. 1606.
[4] Wotton's Baronet. i. 513. ; Hasted's Kent, xii. 27.

his legal studies there.[1]   He completed them at Gray's Inn, where he was admitted a member on October 8, 1607, and attained the post of reader in autumn, 1632.[2]   His arguments as a barrister are not reported by Croke till 1629 ; but it may be presumed that he was a prosperous lawyer in 1624, when, in conjunction with Mr. Francis Bacon, also afterwards raised to the bench, he repaired the font of St. Gregory's church at Norwich.[3]   He was called serjeant on May 30, 1636 ; and on the death of Mr. Justice Hutton was promoted to the bench of the Common Pleas, his patent being dated March 24, 1639.[4]

In the propositions made to the king in February, 1643, he was one of the judges whom the parliament requested to be continued; and in Michaelmas Term of that year he sat alone in his court at Westminster, when the king's proclamation to adjourn it to Oxford was delivered to him.   In subservience to the parliament he caused the apprehension of the messenger, who was tried by a council of war, and condemned and executed as a spy.[5]   The judge retained his seat till his death, on March 27, 1647 ; when his remains were interred in the church of Estratuna, in Norfolk.[6]   Lord Clarendon speaks of him as " a man of good reputation for learning ; who in good times would have been a good judge: " and represents him as giving some prudent counsel to the king on his coming to Leicester during the assizes in July, 1642.[7]

Phillips states that Sir George Reeve of Thwaite in Suffolk (who obtained a baronetcy in 1663, which failed about 1688 by the death of his son without issue), was descended from him.[8]

---

[1] Barnard's Inn Book, i. p. 16.
[2] Gray's Inn Books.
[3] Blomefield's Norwich, ii. 274.
[4] Rymer, xx. 381.
[5] Clarendon, iii. 407., iv. 342.
[6] Gent. Mag. lxxxviii. p. i. 396.
[7] Clarendon, iii. 145—149.
[8] Grandeur of the Law (1684), 87.

RICHARDSON, THOMAS.

CH. C. P. 1626.   CH. K. B. 1631.

DR. THOMAS RICHARDSON, a clergyman of Mulbarton, Norfolk, was the father of the chief justice, who was born at Hardwick in the same county on July 3, 1569. His place of early education is not recorded, but on March 5, 1587, he was admitted a member of Lincoln's Inn, and was called to the bar on January 28, 1595.[1] Though he is not introduced into the Reports till Hilary, 1612, it is evident that he had long acquired some eminence in his profession, for he had been elected recorder, first of Bury, and afterwards of Norwich; having been previously under-steward of the dean and chapter of that cathedral.[2] He was appointed reader of Lincoln's Inn in Lent, 1614, on occasion of his being called serjeant; which degree he took in the following Michaelmas.[3] His next advance was to be chancellor to the queen; and soon after her death, being elected member for St. Albans, he was chosen speaker of James's third parliament, which met in January, 1621, and was remarkable for the proceedings which resulted in the disgrace of Lord Chancellor Bacon; against whom Mr. Speaker Richardson had to demand the judgment of the Lords. During this parliament he received the honour of knighthood; and after two noisy sessions, in which he prudently abstained from any prominent interference, his duties as speaker were terminated by its dissolution in December following.[4] He was not replaced in the speaker's chair in the next parliament; but on February 20, 1625, he received the appointment of king's serjeant.

On the place of lord chief justice of the Common Pleas becoming vacant by the death of Sir Henry Hobart at the end of that year, eleven months were allowed to pass before it was filled up. It was then given to Sir Thomas Richardson on

[1] Black Book, v. 410., vi. 9.
[2] Blomefield's Norfolk, i. 684.
[3] Dugdale's Orig. 255.; Chron. Ser.
[4] Parl. Hist. i. 1181—1371.

November 22, 1626; not without suspicion that its acquisition cost him 17,000*l*.[1] His marriage in the next month with his second wife Elizabeth, daughter of Sir Thomas Beaumont of Staughton in Leicestershire, and widow of Sir John Ashburnham[2], sister of the Duke of Buckingham's mother, more probably accounts for the elevation.[3] When, two years afterwards, the duke was assassinated, Sir Thomas, on a question put to him by the king, whether the murderer might not be put to the rack, had the gratification to convey the judges' unanimous opinion that torture was not known or allowed by the law. On two or three other occasions he showed himself moderate in his sentences and independent in his principles[4]: but he was considered by the parliament to be a favourer of the Jesuits.[5] After presiding for five years in the Common Pleas, he was removed, on October 24, 1631, to the chief justiceship of the King's Bench, where he sat during the remainder of his life. He died on February 4, 1635, at his house in Chancery Lane; and was buried in Westminster Abbey, where his monument may still be seen.

Although esteemed a good lawyer, he was not respected on the Bench. Evelyn calls him "that jeering judge;"[6] and no doubt he carried his inclination to humour and jocularity too much into court. Fuller had not a more favourable opinion; for in treating of him he says, " coming now to our own times . . . . seeing many ready to carp, it is safest for me to be silent[7]:" a cautious reserve, which he does not practise with regard to other contemporaries of whom he can speak in praise. The chief justice was inclined to the Puritans. His sentence against Sherfield for breaking a painted glass window was more lenient than that of other members of the court; and he made an order while on the Somersetshire circuit, to sup-

---

[1] Walter Yonge's Diary, 97. [2] Collins's Peerage, iv. 253.
[3] For an account of the Wedding Dinner, *see* Notes and Queries, 1st S. i. 99.
[4] State Trials, iii. 359. 371—374. [5] Parl. Hist. ii. 475.
[6] Evelyn's Diary, i. 10. [7] Fuller's Worthies, ii. 130.

press wakes and other pastimes on Sundays. For this the bishops, who considered it an intrusion on their power, encouraged Archbishop Laud to complain; and the chief justice received a reprimand from the Council.[1] Even then he could not refrain from joking; as he passed out he declared, that "the lawn sleeves had almost choked him." To remove, perhaps, all suspicion of his principles, he was as violent and absurd as any of his colleagues in the Star Chamber, in the unjustifiable sentence pronounced shortly after against William Prynne for writing his "Histrio-mastix."[2] And upon Prynne's being brought before the council on a subsequent occasion, and the question being, whether he might go to church and be allowed books, the chief justice, not being able to restrain his joke, said, "Let him have the Book of Martyrs, for the Puritans do account him a martyr."

While attending at the assizes at Salisbury, a prisoner, whom he had condemned to death for some felony, threw a brickbat at his head; but, stooping at the time, it only knocked off his hat. On his friends congratulating him on his escape, he said: "You see now, if I had been an upright judge, I had been slaine."[3] The additional punishment upon this offender is thus curiously recorded by Chief Justice Treby, in the margin of Dyer's Reports, p. 188, b.: —

"Richardson, C. J. de C. B. at Assizes at Salisbury in Summer 1631, fuit assault per Prisoner la condemne pur Felony; — que puis son condemnation ject un Brickbat a le dit Justice, que narrowly mist. Et pur ceo immediately fuit Indictment drawn pur Noy envers le Prisoner, et son dexter manus ampute et fixe al Gibbet, sur que luy mesme immediatement hange in presence de Court."

He could not resist joking even with a witness on a trial. In a case between two parties, where one coming upon the other's land without leave for the purpose of hawking, the

---

[1] Whitelocke, 17.   [2] Rushworth, ii. 234. 248.

[3] Anecdotes and Traditions (Camden Soc.), 53.

owner provoked him so much by his rude language, that he horsewhipped him and spit in his face. The chief justice said to a witness of the assault, "Friend, I forgot to ask thee one question of much importance in this cause; whether did the defendant *hawke* before he spit, or spit before he *hawked?*" Another time, seeing an attorney over-busy in the court, he called him to him, and asked him his name; and being told it was Rapier, he said, "Well that's something to the point yet; but what profession?" "An attorney."—"An attorney," said the judge, seeing he was in a light-coloured suit, "I'm ashamed on't. Well, sirrah, unless you get an handsomer coloured scabbard, and speedily, I'll scour your blade for you, and that thoroughly too."

The natural consequence of this habit was that he lost the respect of all, even of his servants. One of them, whom he reprimanded for being at a tavern, saying, "I saw you well enough, sirrah, at the window to day," had the impudence to answer, "I am sorry at my heart that I did not see you, for if I had, I would have given you a quart of sack." And one day, at the time he was a barrister, asking a merry carman "why his fore horse was so lusty and pampered, and all the rest such lean jacks?" the man replied, "Why, the reason is very plain; for my fore horse is the counsellor, and all the rest are his poor clients."[1]

By his first wife, Ursula, daughter of John Southwell, Esq., of Barham Hall in Suffolk, he had a large family. His second wife, Lady Ashburnham, brought him no issue. She, in 1628, Sir Thomas being then chief justice of the Common Pleas, was created a baroness of Scotland, by the title of Lady Cramond, with remainder to his children.[2] None of his sons surviving her ladyship, his grandson, on her death in 1651,

---

[1] Harl. MSS. 6395.

[2] A similar instance occurred in our own time; the wife of Sir John (afterwards Lord) Campbell, then attorney-general, and since lord chief justice, having been raised to the peerage by the title of Lady Stratheden.

ROLLE, HENRY.

Parl Just. K. B. 1645; Ch. K. B. 1648.

See under the Interregnum.

St. JOHN, OLIVER, Earl of Bolinbroke.

Parl. Com. G. S. 1643.

OLIVER St. JOHN, fourth Lord St. John of Bletsoe, succeeded his father in September, 1618. He was created Earl of Bolinbroke by King James I. on December 28, 1624, and is no otherwise famous than for being one of the very few peers (who, Wood says, were " all of the presbyterian dye ") remaining with the parliament after Charles I. retired to York, and concurring with the House of Commons in the violent votes and ordinances then passed. It was from this contraction of choice rather than from any special ability in him, that he was selected, in 1643, as one of the two members of the House of Lords, to be united with four commoners, in whom the custody of the new Great Seal was to be placed. They were accordingly appointed commissioners on November 10. He occupied this position about two years and a half, and died in possession of it in June or July, 1646, the Earl of Salisbury being nominated in his place on the 3rd of the latter month.

The title was held by his two grandsons in succession; and upon the death of the last without issue in 1711, the earldom became extinct, but the barony of St. John of Bletsoe survived, and still flourishes.[2]

St. JOHN, OLIVER.

Parl. Com. G. S. 1643. Ch. C. P. 1648.

See under the Interregnum.

---

[1] Blomefield's Norfolk, i. 684 ; Collins's Peerage, iv. 253.

[2] Dugdale's Baronage, ii. 398 ; Wood's Athen. iii. 134. ; Journals.

SALISBURY, Dean of.   *See* J. Williams.

SALISBURY, Earl of.   *See* W. Cecil.

SOTHERTON, JOHN.
Cursitor B. E. 1653.
See under the Reign of James I.

There are three barons of the Exchequer of the name of
Sotherton, two of whom, John and Nowell, have been already
mentioned. The former of these, who died in 1605, aged eighty,
was probably father of the baron now to be noticed, by his
second wife, Maria, daughter of Edward Woton, M.D.[1] In
Dugdale's "Chronica Series," this John Sotherton is entered as
baron on 24th October, 1610; and in his "Origines Juridi-
ciales," p. 149, he is allowed by an order of the Inner Temple
of the 6th of November following, to "have his place at the
Bench Table above all the Readers in such sort as Sir Thomas
Cæsar, Knight, late Puisne Baron of the Exchequer, had."
This proves that he had not been a reader to the society, and
that he was not of the degree of the coif, because if he had
been, he would no longer have been a member of that house,
but of Serjeants' Inn. On December 5, he was one of the
commissioners with the lord mayor who tried Mackalley's
case at the Old Bailey[2]; but as he is never mentioned as
sitting in the Exchequer Court, nor as joining in the conferences of the other judges during the remainder of James's
reign, it would seem, in connection with the above facts, that
he held the office which is now called cursitor baron. This
impression derives greater weight from the fact that in a
special commission to inquire into defective titles, issued in
1622, he is named after the attorney-general, though two
other barons of the Exchequer, Denham and Bromley, are

[1] Stow's London, 332.   [2] 9 Coke's Rep. 62.

inserted previous to that officer. The same order of precedence is preserved in another commission in the following year on the same subject : and in a commission relative to nuisances in London in 1624, several knights and the recorder of London intervene between the other barons and him.[1]

The same remark applies also to the reign of Charles, in which he lived several years. The Reports never mention him but once, and then only as transacting business which was "of course" (cursitor). In the year 1630, the plague raging in London, Michaelmas Term was adjourned from one return to another ; and it is recorded that the essoigns of one of them was kept by Mr. Baron Sotherton[2], which was a mere formality. He died or resigned in the course of the next year, his successor, James Pagitt, being appointed on October 24, 1631.

He married Elizabeth, widow of Sir John Morgan of Chilworth, Surrey.[3]

TANFIELD, LAURENCE.
Ch. B. E. 1625.
See under the Reign of James I.

GAYTON in Northamptonshire was the residence of this family, and Francis Tanfield of that place was the father of the judge.[4] Laurence Tanfield, destined to the law, after passing through the usual course of the Inner Temple, of which he was admitted a member in 1569, became reader there in Lent, 1595.[5] He had long before acquired professional fame, for the Reports introduce his name as an advocate as early as 1579. On January 28, 1603, he received a summons to take upon him the degree of the coif in the following Easter; but Queen Elizabeth dying before that time,

---

[1] Rymer's Fœd. xvii. 388. 512. 540.   [2] Croke, Car. 200.
[3] Manning and Bray's Surrey, ii. 118.   [4] Wotton's Baronet. ii. 173.
[5] Dugdale's Orig. Jur. 166.

a new writ was issued by King James with the same return. He was member of the first parliament in that reign; and on January 13, 1606, he was constituted one of the judges of the King's Bench in the room of Mr. Justice Gawdy. He did not long remain in that position, being advanced on June 25, 1607, to the offiee of chief baron of the Exchequer, over which court he presided with much credit for integrity, independence, and learning during the remainder of his life. In the public acts of his time in which was he engaged, viz. in the case of the Post-nati, the proceedings against the Countess of Shrewsbury for contempt, the trial of the Countess of Somerset for the murder of Sir Thomas Overbury, and the prosecution of Mr. Wraynham for slandering Lord Chancellor Bacon, no record is preserved of the part he took, except with regard to the latter, in which the judgment he pronounced is distinct and impressive.[1]

That he was a favourite with his contemporaries may be inferred from the name of his residence in the Temple, theretofore called Bradshaw's Rents, being changed to Tanfield Court in compliment to him.[2] He survived King James about a month, and dying on April 30, 1625, was buried under a costly monument in Burford church, Oxfordshire.[3] He had purchased the Priory there with the manor of Great Tew and other lands, which he left to his only daughter Elizabeth, who married Sir Henry Cary of Aldenham, first Viscount Falkland; and Lucius Cary, the second viscount, whose virtues are so eloquently celebrated by Lord Clarendon, was her son. Burford Priory afterwards became the property of Sir William Lenthall.[4]

[1] State Trials, ii. 96. 609. 770. 952. 1076.; Dugdale's Chron. Ser.
[2] Dugdale's Orig. 146.   [3] Gent. Mag. lxiv. 1196.
[4] Clarendon's Life, (ed. 1827.) i. 42.; Wood's Ath. Oxon. iii. 604.

TOMLINS, RICHARD.

PARL. CURS. B. E. 1645.

See under the Interregnum.

TREVOR, THOMAS.

B. E. 1625.

THOMAS TREVOR was the youngest of five sons of John Trevor, Esq., of Trevallyn in Denbighshire, of an ancient and noble Welsh family, by Mary, daughter of Sir George Bruges of London.   The second of these sons, Sir John, was the ancestor of the first Lord Trevor, chief justice of the Common Pleas in the reigns of Queen Anne and George I. Thomas was born July 6, 1586, and having lost his father when three years old, was brought up to the law, being the first of the family who adopted that profession.   He was admitted a member of the Inner Temple, and became reader there in autumn 1620.[1]   He was soon after knighted, and made solicitor to Prince Charles, who, when he ascended the throne, called him to the degree of the coif, and nominated him one of his serjeants on April 8, 1625.   On the 12th of the following month he was advanced to a seat of the Exchequer[2], in the place of Baron Snigge, who died in the last reign.

Nothing is told of him for the first ten years of his judicial life, except that at the Bury assizes trying a cause about wintering of cattle, and thinking the charge immoderate, he said, " Why, friend, this is most unreasonable ; I wonder thou art not ashamed, for I myself have known a beast wintered one whole summer for a noble."   " That was *a bull*, my lord, I believe," retorted the man, to the infinite amusement of the auditory.[3]

[1] Dugdale's Orig. Jur. 167.   [2] Rymer, xviii. 637.
[3] Anecdotes and Traditions (Camden Soc.), 79.

But more serious matters soon occupied him. The imposition of ship money was attempted, and Baron Trevor united with the rest of the judges, in 1636, in subscribing a joint opinion in favour of its legality, which he afterwards supported in a most foolish inconclusive speech in the case of Hampden.[1] On the meeting of the Long Parliament, in 1640, proceedings were commenced against him and five of the other judges, who were eventually impeached for the judgment they had delivered. Trevor was sentenced to imprisonment and a fine of 6000*l.*, but upon payment he was discharged and permitted to resume his duties. In 1643 the king had issued proclamations to adjourn the term from Westminster to Oxford, but as these had been hitherto fruitless "for want of the necessary legal form of having the writs read in court," the judges at Oxford could not proceed to business there till that formality had been observed. The parliament, having then assumed the sovereign power, had published orders to the contrary; yet the king, thinking that the judges remaining in London would obey him rather than the parliament, sent messengers in Michaelmas Term with directions to deliver them the writs. There were only three judges then sitting in London; Justice Bacon in the King's Bench, Justice Reeve in the Common Pleas, and Baron Trevor in the Exchequer. The two latter were served, but immediately ordered the apprehension of the messengers, who, being tried by a council of war, were condemned as spies, and one of them was actually executed as an example. The fears that then influenced Trevor seem to have been dispersed by the tragic termination of the king's life. On February 8, 1649, he was one of the six judges who boldly refused to accept the new commission offered them by the then ruling powers.[2]

He lived nearly eight years after his retirement, and dying

---

[1] State Trials, iii. 1152.
[2] Clarendon, iv. 287. 342.; Whitelocke, 47. 76. 378.

on December 21, 1656, was buried at Lemington-Hastang in Warwickshire, the manor of which belonged to him.

He was twice married: first, to Prudence, daughter of Henry Butler, Esq.; and, secondly, to Frances, daughter and heir of Daniel Blennerhasset, Esq., of Norfolk. He survived both these ladies, who were buried in St. Bride's, London. An only son he had by the former, named Thomas, was created a baronet in 1641, but dying without issue in 1676, the title became extinct, and the estate was bequeathed by him to Sir Charles Wheler, baronet, the grandson of Mr. Baron Trevor's sister. This family still enjoy the estate, and preserve the memory of the donor by the use of his name.[1]

VERNON, GEORGE.

B. E. 1627. Just. C. P. 1631.

DESCENDED from the noble and ancient family of Vernon in Normandy, which established itself in this country at the Conquest, Sir George Vernon was the son of Sir Thomas Vernon of Haslington in Cheshire and his wife Dorothy, the daughter of William Egerton, Esq., of Betley. Nothing is related of him till he became a member of the Inner Temple in 1594. He was called to the bar by that society in 1603, and was elected autumn reader in 1621.[2] His name does not appear in the Reports, but on July 4, 1627, he was raised to the degree of the coif, an honour which Judge Whitelocke states that he paid for,—*dedit aurum*.[3] In four months, no doubt as part of the bargain, he was made a baron of the Exchequer, his patent being dated November 13. After remaining in that court three years and a half, he was removed to the Common Pleas on May 8, 1631, to supply the vacancy made by

---

[1] Collins's Peerage, vi. 294., where Sir Thomas is mistakingly described as a judge of the Common Pleas, and chief baron of the Exchequer. Stow's London, 875. ; Wotton's Baronet. iii. 143.

[2] Dugdale's Orig. 168.   [3] Bacon's Works (Montagu), xvi. cccix.

Judge Davenport's appointment as chief baron of the Exchequer.[1] In the great case of ship money in 1637 he abstained from stating his reasons on account of his want of health; but delivered his opinion not only in favour of the charge, but also asserting that a statute derogatory from the prerogative did not bind the king, and that the king might dispense with any law in cases of necessity.[2] For these ultra sentiments Sir George Vernon escaped the retribution which in the parliament of 1640 visited those of his colleagues who pronounced a similar judgment, by his death, which occurred on December 16, 1639, at his chambers in Serjeants' Inn, Chancery Lane. He was buried in the Temple church. Croke, his brother judge, describes him as being "a man of great reading in the Statute and Common Law, and of extraordinary memory;" but says nothing of his integrity or independence.[3]

His first wife was Jane, daughter of Sir George Corbett of Morton Corbett in Shropshire. By her he had an only daughter and heir, Muriel, who was married to his relative Henry Vernon of Sudbury in the county of Derby, the great-grandfather of the first Lord Vernon; a title which still exists in their descendants.[4] Of Sir George's second wife nothing is known, except that she produced no issue.

WALTER, JOHN.

Ch. B. E. 1625.

EDMUND WALTER of Ludlow in Shropshire, the father of the chief baron, was an eminent counsel in the reign of Queen Elizabeth, and chief justice of South Wales. He was descended from the ancient family of Walter of Warwickshire, an offshoot of the Norman baronial line to which

---

[1] Rymer xix. 348.   [2] State Trials, iii. 1125.
[3] Croke, Car. 565.   [4] Brydges's Collins's Peerage, vii. 399. 406.

Theodore and Hubert Walter belonged.[1] By his first wife, Mary, the daughter of Thomas Hackluit, Esq. of Eyton in Herefordshire, he had four sons and three daughters.

John Walter, the second son, was born at Ludlow in 1563; and after completing his education at Brazenose College, Oxford, was admitted a member of the Inner Temple on April 24, 1583. In 1590, he was called to the bar, and became reader there in Lent, 1607.[2] Previously to this time he had sufficient reputation as a barrister to be employed with Serjeant Altham and Mr. Stevens, before the council and the judges, in defence of the rights and privileges of the Court of Exchequer. For this service he received on March 13, 1605, "in reward for his pains and attendance," 13*l*. 6*s*. 8*d*.; and in the next year he was paid 10*l*. for the pains he took as counsel before the Peers in defending the King's title to Alnage.[3] He was also counsellor for the university of Oxford, and received from it on July 1, 1613, the degree of M.A. In the same year he was selected as attorney-general to Prince Charles, and was knighted on May 18, 1619. He still held this place, when on a brief being sent to him against Sir Edward Coke, then prosecuted by the court, he had the courage to decline it, saying, " Let my tongue cleave to the roof of my mouth, when I open it against Sir Edward Coke."[4] This generous conduct, forming such a contrast with Bacon's on a similar occasion, did not prevent his advancement. Immediately on Charles's coming to the crown he appointed Sir John Walter one of his ser-, jeants; and on the death of Sir Laurence Tanfield, a month after, he raised him to the chief seat in the Exchequer; his patent being dated on May 12, 1625.[5]

The new chief baron, however, did not answer the king's

[1] *See* vol. i. 423.; vol. ii. 123.   [2] Inner Temple Books.
[3] Devon's Issues of Exch. 32. 64.   [4] Brit. Biog. iv. 179.
[5] Rymer, xviii. 638.

expectations. He was too independent and too honest to suit the royal will. For some cause or other, which is not precisely described, the king was dissatisfied with his conduct, and would have discharged him, had he submitted to be thus thrown aside. But he alleged that by his patent he held his office " quamdiu se bene gesserit," and he refused to retire without a *scire facias* to show " whether he did bene se gerere, or not ; " a course which the king did not think proper to adopt, but was obliged to be contented with forbidding him to sit in court. Before this event had taken place, viz. on February 14, 1628–9, he and the other barons had given the somewhat equivocating answer to the House of Commons for refusing to deliver back the goods seized for tonnage and poundage.[1] But the immediate cause of his disgrace was said to be that he disagreed with the rest of the judges as to the legality of proceeding criminally against a member of parliament for acts done in the House.[2] Sir W. Jones says he received his prohibition to sit in court in the beginning of Michaelmas Term, 1630; and that he forbore till he died.[3] The interval between the two events was but short, for his decease took place on November 18, at his house in the Savoy ; to the poor of which place he left 20*l.* He was buried in the church of Wolvercote near Oxford ; where there is a splendid monument to him and his two wives.[4]

His contemporary Judge Croke describes him as " a profoundly learned man, and of great integrity and courage ; "[5] and Fuller joins his testimony to the same effect, adding that he " was most passionate as Sir John, most patient as Judge Walter ; " and that such was his gravity, that once when Judge Denham said to him, " My Lord, you are not merry," he answered, " Merry enough for a judge."[6] In the year

---

[1] Parl. Hist. ii. 472.   [2] Whitelocke, ii. 16.
[3] Sir W. Jones's Reports, 228.   [4] Wood's Fasti Oxon. i. 355.
[5] Croke, Car. 203.   [6] Fuller's Worthies, ii. 260.

after his elevation he obtained a curious licence for himself and his wife, and any four friends invited to his table, to eat meat on the prohibited days, on payment of 13s. 4d. per annum to the parish where he resided.[1]

His first wife was Margaret, daughter of William Offley, Esq., an eminent London merchant; his second was Anne, daughter of William Wytham, Esq., of Leastone in Yorkshire, and relict of Sir Thomas Bigges of Lenchwike in the county of Worcester, baronet. By the latter he left no issue; but by the former he had four sons and four daughters. His eldest son was created a baronet in 1641, but the title became extinct in 1731.[2]

WESTMINSTER, DEAN OF. *See* J. WILLIAMS.

WESTON, JAMES.
B. E. 1631.

JAMES WESTON was the nephew of Sir Richard Weston, the judge of the Common Pleas in the reign of Queen Elizabeth, being the third son of James Weston, of Lichfield (the judge's brother), who died in 1589. His mother, Margeria, daughter of Humfrey Lowe of Lichfield, died in 1587. He was then very young; but three years after his father's death he was entered of the Inner Temple, where, having been called to the bar in 1600, he attained the post of reader in autumn 1618.[3] He was summoned to take the degree of serjeant on March 19, 1631, evidently for the purpose of being made a baron of the Exchequer; to which office he was appointed on the 16th of the following May[4], and knighted,

[1] Rymer, xviii. 309.
[2] I am indebted for much information relative to this family to the kindness of Robert Edmond Waters, Esq. This mode of spelling the name is adopted by some branches.
[3] Inner Temple Books.
[4] Rymer, xix. 256. 348.

probably through the interest of his relative Lord Weston. His career as a judge was of very short duration, for in the vacation between Michaelmas, 1633, and Hilary, 1634, he died in his chamber in the Inner Temple, being described by Croke as a "wise and learned man, and of courage."[1]

By his wife Maria, daughter of William Weston, Esq., of Kent, he had an only daughter, who married Nicholas, son of Sir Nicholas Bacon, Bart., of Redgrave, Suffolk.[2]

WESTON, RICHARD.

B. E. 1634.

OF the same family as Richard Weston, the judge of the Common Pleas in the reign of Elizabeth, and the last-mentioned Sir James Weston, the baron of the Exchequer, who were both descended from John Weston of Rugeley, this Richard Weston was the son of Ralph Weston of Rugeley, the grandson of John, by Anna, daughter and heir of George Smith, of Apleton in Lancashire.

Like his relative, he pursued his legal studies in the Inner Temple, where he was elected reader in autumn, 1618.[3]   On May 25, 1632, he became a judge on the Welsh circuit; and on Sir James Weston's death he was appointed, no doubt by the interest of Lord Weston, to succeed him as baron of the Exchequer, his patent for that office being dated April 30, 1634; the degree of the coif having been conferred upon him a few days before.[4]   He thereupon received the honour of knighthood.   In his argument in favour of ship-money, which was delivered four years after, though it evinced some learning, he was more technical than conclusive.[5]   He was consequently one of the six judges who were impeached by the Long Parliament in 1641, and though he was not

[1] Croke, Car. 339.   [2] Erdeswicke's Staffordsh. (Harwood), 136.
[3] Dugdale's Orig. 168.   [4] Rymer, xix. 433. 528. 607.
[5] State Trials, iii. 1065.

brought to trial, he was, by a vote of the Commons on October 24, 1645, disabled from being a judge "as though he was dead."[1]

He lived till March 18, 1651, leaving by his wife Katherine a son, Sir Richard, who joined the army of Charles I., and was slain in the Isle of Man. He had also another son named Ralph, and a daughter Elizabeth.[2]

WHITELOCKE, BULSTRODE.
PARL. COM. G. S. 1648.
See under the Interregnum.

WHITELOCKE, JAMES.
JUST. K. B. 1625.
See under the Reign of James I.

THE younger son of an ancient and respectable family, seated at the Beeches, near Oakingham, in the county of Berks, Richard Whitelocke was brought up to commercial pursuits, and became a merchant in London. By his wife Joan, the daughter of John Colte of Little Mundem, Herts, and widow of . . . . Brockhurst, he had two sons, twins, who were born on November 23, 1570, a few months after their father's death. The youngest of these posthumous children was James, the future judge.

He was educated at Merchant Taylors' School, whence he was elected a scholar of St. John's College, Oxford, in 1588, and eventually became a fellow. He took the degree of bachelor of civil law in 1594, and held his fellowship till June, 1598, residing principally at the university. During the same period, however, he kept his terms at the Middle Temple, to which society he was admitted in March, 1592, having previously spent a year of preparation at New Inn; and after the usual term of probation, he was called to the

---

[1] Whitelocke's Mem. 47. 181.   [2] Erdeswicke's Staffordsh. 136.

bar on October 24, 1600.[1]   Not only did his college appoint
him steward of their lands, but he soon obtained an honourable and profitable practice; and going the Oxford circuit,
he was elected recorder of Woodstock, for which borough he
was returned member in 1609, to the parliament which was
dissolved in 1611.

It was probably some freedom of language in which he indulged in that parliament that excited the king's displeasure;
for it is difficult otherwise to understand the reason of his
prosecution in 1613.   His "simply giving a private verbal
opinion as a Barrister," as the charge is generally represented,
is too absurd and incredible even for those arbitrary times.
From the whole tenor of the Attorney-General Bacon's
speech, and weak enough it was, it would rather appear that
Whitelocke had urged in court an elaborate argument, contending that some commission which the king had issued was
not strictly according to law — an argument which any counsel might assuredly use, whether by private opinion or in open
court, without blame, if he did it in a decent and unobtrusive
manner.   The account, however, is very slight, and the cause
is left in much uncertainty.   Little more is known than that
he was taken before the council, and committed to the Fleet,
in May, 1613, that he was heard in June, and upon making
his submission, was discharged from custody.   His son, in a
speech to the Long Parliament, publicly and without contradiction attributed his father's imprisonment to "what he said
and did in a former Parliament."[2]

That this incident had no injurious effect on his character
is evidenced by the fact that in the short parliament that met
in April, 1614, to be dissolved in June, he was not only returned for Woodstock, but for Corfe Castle also.   But the
court cloud still hovered over him; for on the death of Richard

[1] Middle Temple Books.
[2] Bacon's Works, vii. 381.; State Trials, ii. 765.; Whitelocke, 39.

Martin, the recorder, in 1618, he was opposed in his endeavours to obtain the place by the king's influence being exerted
against him in favour of Robert Heath, who was elected. In
autumn, 1619, he was chosen reader of the Middle Temple,
and took for his subject the Statute 21 Henry VIII. c. 13,
his reading upon which is now preserved in MS. in the Ashmolean Museum at Oxford. He again represented Woodstock in James's third parliament, in 1621.

In the meantime his political offences had been atoned for
or overlooked. On June 18, 1620, he was called serjeant,
and, on the 29th of the following October, was knighted, and
made chief justice of Chester. Sir Thomas Chamberlayne,
whom he succeeded, was promoted to a judgeship of the King's
Bench, but in four years resumed his post on the Welsh Circuit, and Sir James Whitelocke was appointed a judge of the
King's Bench in his room on October 18, 1624[1], a few months
before King James's death.

His patent was renewed by Charles; and, as junior judge,
he had in the first year to adjourn Michaelmas Term to
Reading on account of the plague then raging in London.
The state of that city, and the terror of those who approached
it, are depicted by his son in his description of the judge
going from his house in Buckinghamshire, and arriving early
the next morning at Hyde Park Corner, " where he and his
retinue dined on the ground, with such meat and drink as
they brought in the coach with them, and afterwards he drove
fast through the streets, which were empty of people and
overgrown with grass, to Westminster Hall, where the officers
were ready, and the Judge and his company went strait to
the King's Bench, adjourned the court, returned to his coach,
and drove away presently out of town."[2] He retained his
place till his death; and in the seven years that intervened,
the two great cases of *habeas corpus* came before the court.

[1] Dugdale's Orig. 219.; Chron. Ser.   [2] Whitelocke's Mem. 2.

For the first judgment, which was against those who refused to contribute to the loan, he and the other judges gave their reasons to the Lords in the next parliament[1], which led to the Petition of Right. On the second, when the court refused to discharge the members imprisoned for their conduct in the previous parliament, without sureties for their good behaviour, and afterwards, upon their refusing to plead, fined and imprisoned them, the judges were called to account by the Long Parliament. On a motion that reparation should be made out of their estates, Judge Whitelocke, who had been long dead, on the representation of his son, confirmed by several other members, that he was of the same opinion with Judge Croke, was excused from censure.[2]

Judge Whitelocke died on June 22, 1632, at his house at Fawley in Bucks, which, with the manor, he had bought sixteen years before, and was buried there with his wife, who died a year before him, under a stately monument erected by his son. Though an advocate for the rights of the people, he was a conscientious supporter of the king's prerogative. King Charles said of him " that he was a stout, wise, and learned man, and one who knew what belongs to uphold magistrates and magistracy in their dignity ;" and even designed him for the place of lord chief baron on the retirement of Sir John Walter; but Sir Humphry Davenport was appointed instead of him. All authorities allow him to have been an able lawyer and a deeply learned man. Of his skill in the Latin tongue he gave a remarkable proof when sitting as judge of assize at Oxford. Some foreigners of distinction coming into court while he was addressing the grand jury, " he repeated the heads of his charge to them in good and elegant Latin, and thereby informed the strangers," his son adds, " of the ability of our judges, and the course of our

---

[1] State Trials, iii. 161.   [2] Whitelocke's Mem. 39.

proceedings in law and justice."[1] He was an excellent gene-alogist, and was not only deeply versed in Jewish history, but conversant with that of his own country; being one of the early members of the Society of Antiquaries in the reign of Elizabeth, to which he contributed papers on the "Antiquity of Heralds," of "Places for the Students of the Law," and of "Lawful Combats in England."

His wife, whom he married in 1602, was Elizabeth, eldest daughter of Edward Bulstrode of Bulstrode in Upton, Esq., and Cecilia, daughter of Sir John Croke, of Chilton, so that he was closely connected with both the Judges Croke. Besides two daughters, he had only one surviving son, Bulstrode Whitelocke, who will be noticed as lord commissioner of the Great Seal under Cromwell.[2]

WIDDRINGTON, THOMAS.

PARL. COM. G. S. 1648.

See under the Interregnum.

WILDE, JOHN.

PARL. COM. G. S. 1643. CH. B. E. 1648.

See under the Interregnum.

WILLIAMS, JOHN, DEAN OF SALISBURY AND WESTMINSTER, BISHOP OF LINCOLN, and ARCHBISHOP OF YORK.

LORD KEEPER, 1625.

See under the Reign of James I.

JOHN WILLIAMS, the youngest of five sons of Edmund Wil-liams, Esq., a gentleman of an ancient Welsh family, by Mary, the daughter of Owen Wynne, Esq., was born at Abercon-way in Carnarvonshire, the residence of his father, on March

---

[1] Whitelocke's Mem. 11. 17.; Sir W. Jones's Reports, 230.
[2] Hearne's Curious Discourses, i. 55. 78., ii. 190. 389. 447.

25, 1582. From the grammar school of Ruthin, where he received the rudiments of his education, he was removed in 1598 by his relative Dr. Vaughan, afterwards Bishop of London, to St. Johu's college, Cambridge. There he pursued his studies so diligently, taking it is said but three hours' sleep out of the twenty-four, and acquired such commendation for his proficiency, that when he commenced bachelor of arts in 1603 he was immediately elected fellow of his college. His degree of master he took in 1605, and about the same time was admitted into clerical orders, for in a letter written in that year to his relation Sir John Wynne of Gwydir he speaks of a small benefice he had got[1], which Hacket, his biographer, supposes to have been Fakenham. He soon after was called to preach before the king at Royston; and was so much admired for his learning and eloquence that Lord Chancellor Ellesmere in 1611 appointed him one of his chaplains. In the next year he became proctor to the university, and, though he performed its duties with general applause, he incurred the enmity of the Vice-chancellor, Dr. Gouch, by the activity and earnestness he displayed in the elections of the headship of St. John's and the chancellorship of the university; both of which became vacant in his year of office.[2] At its termination he resumed his position as chaplain, and sat in the convocation of 1613 as one of the archdeacons of Wales. The livings of Walgrave and Grafton-Underwood in Northamptonshire were soon presented to him, to which were added a residentiaryship in Lincoln cathedral, and a choral place in those of Peterborough, Hereford, and St. David's. Increasing in favour, he was treated with the greatest confidence by the lord chancellor, who frequently discussed with him the causes before the court; entrusted him during his illness with various messages on state affairs to the king; and, just previous to his death in 1616, presented him with his manuscript collections

---

[1] Yorke's Royal Tribes of Wales, 149.   [2] Ibid. 153.

for the regulation of parliament and the council board, and the different courts over which he presided, as "tools to work with:"—a legacy of which Williams soon learned the value. Bacon offered to retain him in his service, but he declined the honour, and was forthwith, by the king's order, sworn one of the royal chaplains. In 1617 he disputed in the schools for his doctor's degree, on the occasion of the Archbishop of Spalato's visit to the university.

From this time, except when duty called him to the court or to his canonry, he resided on his living at Walgrave; until in September 1619 he was presented with the deanery of Salisbury. In his personal attendance on the king, from being at first conversed with for his learning and his wit, he came by degrees to be consulted for the wisdom of his counsel. He ingratiated himself with Buckingham by forwarding the favourite's marriage with Lady Katherine Manners, and converting her from the Romish faith. Thus favoured, he was advanced on July 12, 1620, to the deanery of Westminster: and when the parliament that met in the following January began to cry out against the oppressions of the people, and to proceed against Sir Giles Mompesson and other offenders, Buckingham, who feared that he himself might be hit, and the king, who knew not where the bolt might fly, appealed for advice to the dean. He gave them this counsel: " Swim with the tide, and you cannot be drowned; . . . Throw the cormorants overboard in the storm; . . . Cast all Monopolies and Patents of griping projections into the Dead Sea after them; . . . Damn all these by one Proclamation, that the world may see that the King, who is the Pilot that sits at the helm, is ready to play the pump to eject such filth as grew noysome to the nostrils of his people." Acting on this advice the storm passed over with only one other victim, Lord Chancellor Bacon.

Hacket with regard to this event exhibits a somewhat sus-

picious reserve, stating merely the fact of Bacon's downfall,
and the dean's surprise at his own elevation.   There seems,
however, to be no sufficient ground for charging Williams
with assisting in the chancellor's disgrace, and still less with
advising the king and Buckingham to prevent him from defending himself.   Any defence was hopeless, and Williams's
recommendation not to dissolve the parliament for the purpose
of stopping the proceedings, appears to have been as honestly,
as it was wisely, offered.   Ben Jonson, whose partiality for
Bacon is evident more than once in his works, both in prose
and verse, would scarcely have addressed a complimental epigram to Williams on his removal from the Seal[1], had he been
suspected of any underhand or unfriendly dealing towards
Bacon.

The Seal, for the next two months, was placed in the hands
of commissioners; and, according to Hacket, the dean was consulted as to the different candidates for the office, and was himself selected by the king and Buckingham in preference to
all of them without any application on his own behalf.   The
latter fact is confirmed by the record itself, which, in stating
his appointment on July 10, 1621, as lord keeper, adds, "præ-
ter suam expectationem."   In the previous month he had been
sworn of the Privy Council, and designated for the bishoprick
of Lincoln.   His consecration was delayed by the unfortunate
occurrence which happened to Archbishop Abbot in acci-
dentally killing a man while aiming at a buck; and at last,
in consideration of the lord keeper's scruples, that ceremony
was performed by four bishops on November 11.   Being allowed to retain his deanery, his canonry in Lincoln Cathedral,
and his living of Walgrave, he was fairly subject to the remark
made of him, " that he was a perfect diocese in himself, being
at the same time Bishop, Dean, Prebendary, and Parson."
He took his seat in the Court of Chancery on October 9, the

---

[1] Gifford's Ben Jonson, viii. 452.

first day of Michaelmas Term [1], no ecclesiastic having presided there since Archbishop Heath in the reign of Queen
Mary.

In the performance of his legal functions he supplied his
want of knowledge of the rules of the court by obtaining the
frequent assistance of two of the judges. His industry was
extraordinary, leaving him scarcely any leisure; and though
he was in the habit of checking any unnecessary argument,
he became soon a general favourite with the bar. At first
some of the advocates endeavoured to take advantage of his
inexperience, and one of them, to puzzle him, " trouled out a
motion crammed like a granado with obsolete words, coins of
far-fetched antiquity, which had long been disused." The lord
keeper, nothing baffled, answered him " in a cluster of most
crabbed notions, picked out of metaphysics and logic, as cate-
gorematical and syncategorematical, and a deal of such drum-
ming stuff; " so ˙that the motioner was foiled at his own
weapon, and well laughed at by the court.

In the Star Chamber he was ever merciful in his judgments,
and where they were heavy for the sake of example, he inter-
ceded with the king to lighten the penalty. He would not
only with soft words turn away wrath, but would often venture on a facetious jest to pacify the royal displeasure. By
his leniency he incurred by turns the suspicions of the anta-
gonistic religious parties; at one time being stigmatised as a
favourer of Roman Catholics, and at another as one of the
Puritans. The former charge may be answered by his opposition to the erection of Titular Popish Prelates in the kingdom; and the latter, by his addition of four scholars to
Westminster College, with a liberal endowment to St. John's
College, Cambridge, and two fellowships to be chosen out of
them, with four rich benefices for their ultimate provision.

In the parliaments over which he presided, his speeches were

---

[1] Rymer, xvii. 297. 312. 320.

marked with ingenuity and wit; the customary flattery to the king not being altogether omitted, but more delicately administered. In his address to that which met in February, 1624, he alluded to his Majesty's speech thus : " A Lacedemonian being invited to hear a man that could counterfeit well the notes of a nightingale, put him off with these words, ' I have heard the nightingale herself.' And why should you now be troubled with the croaking of a chancellor, that have heard the loving expressions of a most eloquent king?"

But the brightness of his fortune began to be obscured. The fickleness of Buckingham, and his jealousy of the reliance shown by the king on the lord keeper's judgment, with probably, too, his displeasure at Williams's occasional insubjection to his will, were soon exhibited in his attempts to sink the man whom he had - aided to raise. His favour had been transferred to Bishop Laud; and taking pretended offence at some of the lord keeper's proceedings, and indignant at some expressions of confidence which the king had used, all the cunning of the duke was exerted to hasten Williams's ruin. It was ineffectual, however, during the life of King James, who, appreciating his keeper's loyalty and prudence, and admiring his learning and wit, acted steadily as his friend, and preserved him in his office to the end of his reign. But some of the ill effects of the want of the favourite's countenance could not fail to be experienced. As soon as it was perceived that Buckingham's eye began to look frowningly on the lord keeper, disappointed suitors were ready to complain of his decrees, and accusations accumulated against him in both houses of parliament. He triumphed over them all. The Commons dismissed seven and thirty in one day, and the Lords punished one with the pillory for slander.[1] King James died in March, 1625, and Williams preached his funeral sermon, drawing a parallel between him and Solomon.

---

[1] Parl. Hist. i. 1399.

Though King Charles, on his father's death, retained Williams as lord keeper, the latter soon felt the instability of his position. Buckingham was more than ever resolved to effect his ruin, and endeavoured to induce Chief Justice Hobart to complain of his unfitness for his place on account of his ignorance and inability. The honest judge, though tempted with the promise of the post on Williams's removal, answered, "My Lord, somewhat might have been said at first; but he should do the Lord Keeper great wrong, that said so now." Buckingham was not easily thwarted. The king was already prejudiced against Williams, and the grave advice which he gave to his majesty and the favourite not to quarrel with the parliament, completed his disfavour. The Seal was taken from him on the 25th of October, and placed in the hands of Sir Thomas Coventry.

There was a kind of reconciliation with Buckingham just before his assassination in 1628; but Bishop Laud, whom Williams had formerly befriended, then became his bitter enemy, under the supposition that he was a promoter of the Petition of Right, and, what was considered worse, an encourager of the Puritans. Continuing thus in disgrace at court, vexatious complaints were made against him, all of which failed in their object until 1637, when his enemies succeeded in procuring a conviction in the Star Chamber for a pretended offence committed nine or ten years before, in having revealed the king's secrets, and on a false accusation of tampering with the witnesses; for which he was sentenced to pay a fine of 10,000*l.*, to be imprisoned, and to be suspended from his ecclesiastical functions.

This sentence was executed with the greatest rigour. His property was wantonly despoiled under pretence of raising his fine, his person was incarcerated for three years and a half, and his desire to offer submission was met by the demand of such degrading and ruinous terms that he felt compelled to

reject them.   He only procured his liberation at last by presenting a petition to the House of Lords in November, 1640,
detailing his grievances and demanding his writ.   On his discharge he forgot his personal complaints in the distress of the
State, and boldly stood up for his order and the monarchy.
His conduct of course pleased as much as it surprised the
king, who not only erased all memorial of the proceedings
against him, but admitted him to his favour, took counsel of
him in the difficulties that surrounded the throne, and on
December 4, 1641, translated him to the Archbishoprick of
York.

The cry against the bishops at that time ran high; and
twelve of them, of whom the archbishop was at the head,
were soon after his translation committed to the Tower under
a ludicrous accusation of high treason for presenting a petition
to the Peers, complaining that the mob prevented their access
to the House, and declaring that whatsoever was done there
during their forced absence was invalid and of none effect.
The act excluding the bishops from parliament having passed
during their confinement, the prosecution dropped, and the
archbishop and his colleagues were released, after being detained for eighteen weeks, in the course of which Williams
was reconciled to Archbishop Laud, then an inmate of the
same prison.

Retiring to his diocese, the archbishop was soon obliged
hurriedly to leave his castle of Cawood, in consequence of
the advance of Sir John Hotham's son against it; and after
having supplied the king with what aid in men and money he
could, he fled to his native country, where he exerted himself
to defend the royal cause.   After fortifying Conway Castle
at his own expense, he attended the king at Oxford, where he
is said to have cautioned his majesty particularly against
Cromwell, and to have urged his being either won by great
promises or cut off by stratagem.   His subsequent advice to

the king to submit to the parliament on terms not being relished, he returned to Conway Castle, in the government of which he was superseded the year after by Sir John Owen, under a commission from Prince Rupert. Those who had deposited their money and jewels there were refused restitution, and the archbishop's appeal to the king on their and his own behalf was slighted; so that when Colonel Milton with an overpowering force came into the country on the part of the parliament, they represented their case to the colonel, and, upon his promise to restore to them their property, agreed to assist him in obtaining possession. In doing this they were aided by the archbishop, whose conduct on the occasion subjected him to the imputation of having deserted the king and assisted the rebels. He defended himself by asserting that, as the king's cause in Wales was past hope, he was justified in obtaining the restoration of the property of his friends, and in making the best terms he could for his countrymen's immunities.

"From the fidelity of the king he never," says Bishop Hacket, "went back an inch;" and when the last scene of the tragedy was over, he deeply mourned his royal master's death in solitary retirement; his cheerfulness forsook him, and he seldom spoke. He survived the king little more than a year, and died on his birthday, March 25, 1650, at Glodded, in the parish of Eglwysrose, Carnarvonshire, the house of his kinswoman, Lady Mostyn. His body was removed for burial to the church of Llandegai, where his nephew and heir, Sir Griffith Williams, erected a monument to him, to which his former chaplain, Bishop Hacket, supplied the inscription.

It is difficult to form a just estimate of the character of any individual who lived in the times during which Archbishop Williams flourished. Men's passions were so strong, their prejudices so great, and their animosity against opposite

opinions so violent, that acts in themselves indifferent were
frequently misinterpreted, and what was lauded by one party
was abused by the other.   Clarendon and Heylin, enemies of
the archbishop, look with a jaundiced eye on his whole career;
and Bishop Hacket, his chaplain and friend, and Wilson the
historian, give perhaps too partial a colouring to everything
he did; so that entire reliance is not to be placed on either.
The weight of evidence, however, clearly preponderates in
his favour; though it must be allowed that, as a counsellor
of state, he was too much of a temporiser, and no excuse can
justify the casuistry with which he recommended Charles to
consent to Strafford's death.   But he was honest and sincere,
and generally wise, in the advice which he offered; and to
the monarchs whom he served he was faithful and true.

In person he was dignified and comely; in manner affable
and kind; and though in temper he was warm, as most Welsh-
men are, yet his anger was quickly mollified; and, notwithstanding the oppressions which he suffered, he showed
no wish for revenge.   He was laborious in the performance
of his duties, both political and clerical, and refined in the
choice of his relaxations; music, in which he was a proficient,
being his delight.   His learning was undoubted; and his
eloquence, according to the fashion of the times, was superior
to that of most of his contemporaries, his allusions and illus-
trations being more apt and ingenious, and his wit more
lively and delicately pointed.   He was profusely hospitable
in his household, and liberal to learned poverty; and the
sums which he expended in repairing Westminster Abbey,
and in building the library at St. Johu's College, Cambridge,
and the chapel at that of Lincoln, in Oxford, witness his
generous munificence.

His works were principally on clerical subjects, but that
which excited the most observation was entitled, "The
Holy Table, Name, and Thing," published in opposition to

the innovations introduced by Archbishop Laud, which Bishop Warburton commends as abounding in wit and satire.[1]

YELVERTON, HENRY.

JUST. C. P. 1625.

TWO members of this family have already been noticed as occupying judicial seats, Sir William, and Sir Christopher Yelverton, judges of the King's Bench, the first in the reigns of Henry VI. and Edward IV., the last in that of James I.[2] Sir Henry Yelverton was the eldest son of the latter, by his wife Margaret, daughter of Thomas Catesby, Esq., and was born, as some say, at his father's seat at Easton-Mauduit in Northamptonshire; or, as others assert, at Islington near London, on June 29, 1566. He was educated in the University of Oxford, but Auth. Wood does not state at what college; and then became a member of Gray's Inn, where his ancestors had pursued their legal studies. Having been in due course called to the bar, he attained the honour of being reader to the society in Lent, 1607.[3] But long before that time, he had been elected recorder of Northampton, and is mentioned frequently in Coke's, and Croke's, and his own Reports from 1602.

To the first parliament of James I. he was returned as member for Northampton; and as a representative of the people, he took an independent, but not a factious part. He supported the subsidy, but advocated its gradual, instead of its immediate payment, and in all questions brought before the house, he freely expressed his real opinions, without considering whether they were acceptable to either party, and without weighing over nicely the expressions with which he urged them. But he was popular as an advocate, and con-

[1] Lives of the archbishop, by Bishop Hacket and A. Philips; Clarendon's Rebellion; and Heylin's Reformation (Robertson).

[2] See Vol. IV. p. 461.; and ante, p. 203.   [3] Dugdale's Orig. 296.

sequently had professional enemies jealous of his fame. His
plain dealing and the freedom of his language were accordingly misrepresented at court, and phrases were singled out
of his speeches to prove that he hated the Scotch, and had no
respect for the king. These reports gradually made their way
to James's ear; and Yelverton found after some time that he
was looked upon with a suspicious and unfriendly eye, not
only by his sovereign, but by the Scotch nobles around him.
George Hume, Earl of Dunbar, the lord treasurer of Scotland,
took offence, when a question arose in parliament as to the confirmation of certain land granted to the earl on the confines of
Scotland, contiguous to Lord Hume's land on the confines of
England, at Yelverton's using the cumulative words " *Humus
super humum*," conceiving they were intended as a personal
reflection. The king also felt himself grievously offended,
because one of Yelverton's arguments for the naturalization
of Lord Kinloss was, that he was not all Scot, but half
English; and he was " much enraged " that on another occasion Yelverton had said, " that he would weigh the king's
reasons as he did his coin." It was natural, therefore, that
a man, all whose intentions were loyal, should be desirous of
understanding and explaining the charges made against him;
and Yelverton took the straightforward course of seeking an
interview, both with the earl and the king. This he effected
through the means of the Lady Arabella and the lord chancellor of Scotland, the Earl of Dunfermlin; and he gives a
very interesting and curious account of his interviews, in
which he was successful in satisfying both. He stated that
so far from opposing the union, he refused the employment,
when assigned, to argue the case of the Post-nati on the part
contrary to his majesty's desire. The whole transaction of
the reconciliation is very creditable to all the parties. The
grounds of complaint are openly avowed, and the ingenious
justification generously admitted. No unfair compromise of

principle is demanded or promised, and on a subsequent visit to Robert Cecil, the lord treasurer, that nobleman says that he shall assure himself that Yelverton, to please the king, will not speak against his conscience.[1]　These scenes were enacted in January, 1609–10, and nothing can better prove that they were not intended, and did not operate, to restrain Yelverton from expressing any views he might have with regard to pending discussions, than his composition, a few months after, of a learned and unanswerable argument against the impositions of the crown on merchandise, without the assent of Parliament.[2]　This argument, though written at the time, was not published till 1641, eleven years after the author's death.

Yelverton had to wait nearly four years before he reaped any fruits of his reconciliation with the king.　His father, the judge, died in 1612; and on October 29, 1613, through the patronage of Carr, Earl of Somerset, he was made solicitor-general, and knighted ten days after.　In little more than two years, the earl was indicted for the murder of Sir Thomas Overbury; but Sir Henry, though this was a state prosecution, and he held an office under the crown, is said to have declined to appear against his patron; and he is not recorded as having taken any part in the trial.　Bacon, who was the attorney-general at the time, must have felt this courageous refusal as a reflection on his own conduct with regard to the Earl of Essex, especially as it was not visited by any evil consequences, such as he had pretended to fear. Yelverton had always acted a friendly part towards Bacon. When the House of Commons showed some hesitation in allowing the attorney-general to sit as a member, Yelverton

---

[1] This narrative is given in Archaeologia, vol. xv. p. 27–52., communicated by James Cumming, Esq., F.S.A., who has not stated from what source he obtained it.

[2] State Trials, ii. 478.

came to the rescue and Bacon was admitted; and when Bacon had become lord keeper, and had got into temporary disgrace both with the king and Buckingham for his interference in respect to the marriage of Sir John Villiers with Sir Edward Coke's daughter; Yelverton, who had succeeded as attorney-general on March 12, 1617, wrote him a letter of excellent advice how to act under the circumstances.[1]   But whether Bacon was offended at Sir Henry for not following his example in pleading against the Earl of Somerset, or for his presumption in offering counsel to his superior, or more probably because he wished to ingratiate himself with Buckingham, he frequently speaks injuriously of Yelverton in his correspondence with that nobleman.[2]   Yelverton was no favourite with the duke, who was prejudiced against him from his connection with Somerset, from his being suspected of implication in Bacon's interference in regard to the marriage, and particularly from his declared independence of the duke's protection.   Judge Whitelocke gives a curious account, which he had from Yelverton's own mouth, of the "manner of his coming to the place" of attorney-general.   Though pressed by the courtiers to apply to Buckingham, who "was agent to another, and did crosse him," he refused "to deal with him about it nor speak to him," but protested "he would leave it to the king, who he knew had judgment enough to chuse his own servants."   At last Buckingham sent to him to bring his warrant, and expostulated with him that he had not used his help, telling him that he looked not for any recompence, though Sir James Ley had offered 10,000l. for the place.   Yelverton protested to Whitelocke, "that he neither gave to the erl, or to any other subject in the kingdom, one farthing to cum to the place, . . . but when the businesse was done, he went privately to the king, and told him he did acknowledge how like a good master and worthye

---

[1] Bacon's Works (Montagu), xii. 331.   [2] Ibid. 263, 264, 265. 387.

prince he had dealte with him; and although there was never mention, speech, or expectation of anything to be had for his having of this place, but he came to it freely, yet out of his duty he wolde give him 4000*l.* reddye money. The king," proceeds the relation, " tooke him in his armes, thanked him, and commended him muche for it, and told him he had need of it, for it must serve even to buy him dishes."[1]

One of the first public duties Yelverton was called upon to perform, was to pray an order of the court for execution of Sir Walter Raleigh, on the judgment pronounced against him fifteen years before; and the language in which he did it forms a strong contrast with that adopted by Sir Edward Coke on his trial.[2]

He held his office for three years supported by the favour of the king; but Buckingham, whom he further displeased by his opposition to some of the illegal patents which were afterwards the subject of enquiry, was resolved to remove him. An opportunity was at last found. A new charter had been granted to the city of London, into which the at- torney-general was charged with having introduced certain clauses not comprehended in the king's warrant. Yelverton's submission not being considered satisfactory by the council, they recommended that he should be sequestered and pro- ceeded against in the Star Chamber.[3] He was accordingly superseded on June 27, 1620, and the proceedings in the Star Chamber commenced, in which Yelverton cleared himself of any corruption, but acknowledged himself guilty through ignorance; and Bacon making a jesuitical speech against him, and Coke pressing him hard, he was sentenced to imprison- ment during pleasure, and to a fine of 4000*l.* Bacon's letters, and his expression " how I stirred the court, I leave it to

---

[1] Whitelocke's Liber Famelicus, in Bacon's Works (Montagu), xviii. cccviii.
[2] State Trials, ii. 33.   [3] Bacon's Works (Montagu), xii. 266.

others to speak," show his mean endeavours to aid Buckingham's inveteracy.[1] Yelverton was committed to the Tower, and while there, the parliament by which Bacon was condemned met. In the course of their investigations into the grievances of patents, the Commons implicated Yelverton; who, in his answer to the Lords, cleared himself from the charge, boldly asserting his innocence, and attributing his present imprisonment to the course which he had taken in the Patent of Inns. The king thereupon took the matter up, and though in his speech he acquitted Sir Henry, who he acknowledged disliked and resisted the proceedings intended against the innkeepers, yet, because in his defence he had inferred that " all the punishment upon him was for his good service done to his majesty," he called upon the lords " who are able to do him justice, to punish Sir Henry Yelverton for his slander." Yelverton, on being afterwards brought up again, made this inference more clear, by directly charging Buckingham with being " ready, upon every occasion, to hew him down," and with threatening that he " should not hold his place a month, if he did not conform himself in better manner to the Patent of Inns," and by roundly asserting, " that he suffered unjustly by his lordship's means." This was naturally deemed an aggravation of his offence, and on May 16, 1621, he was sentenced to be imprisoned, and to pay 10,000 marks to the king, and 5000 to Buckingham, who immediately remitted his part of the fine, and the prince and the lords agreed to move his majesty to mitigate the other.[2]

He did not long continue a captive in the Tower. It is related that Buckingham came to him there in disguise, and from the result of the interview (the very improbable details of which Sir Anthony Weldon professes to give), he made

---

[1] Bacon's Works (Montagu), xii. 446-449.
[2] Parl. Hist. i. 1232-1235. 1243-1248. 1255-1259.

his peace, and procured his immediate release.[1] He resumed his practice at the bar in the following Michaelmas Term, when his name appears in Croke's Reports, and for the remaining four years of the reign.

That the reconciliation was complete is apparent from the fact that, within six weeks after King Charles came to the crown, Buckingham procured for him a seat on the bench of the Common Pleas, not to supply any vacancy, but in addition to the court as a fifth judge. He received his patents as serjeant on April 30, and as judge on May 10, 1625; and, according to Bishop Hacket, there were rumours of his being made lord keeper by the removal of Lord Coventry, which was only prevented by the assassination of the Duke.[2] What foundation there was for these rumours cannot now be known; but within eighteen months of the duke's murder, Sir Henry's own career was closed by his death on January 24, 1630, at his house in Aldersgate Street. His remains were removed for interment in the church of Easton-Mauduit, where a monument is placed with recumbent effigies of himself and his lady.

He was much respected and admired by his contemporaries, for his eloquence, his courage, his integrity, and his learning. His reputation as a lawyer was very great, and was not diminished by the subsequent publication, by Sir W. Wylde, of his "Reports of Special Cases." Cecil, Earl of Salisbury, at an early period of his career, gave this testimony of him to his face. "Indeed, I must say your father's education of you, that have made you so lively resemble himself, for you have good elocution and sound reason, whereby the apprehension of them that hear you is made more active, and so hath your father, which is a great merit in the professors of the law."[3]

---

[1] Court of James (1650), 157.   [2] Life of Bishop Williams, ii. 19.
[3] Archaeologia, xv. 51.

He married Margaret, daughter of Robert Beale, Esq., clerk of the council to Queen Elizabeth, who had the unpleasant duty of reading the warrant for the execution of Mary Queen of Scots, at the scaffold on which she suffered. He left several children, the eldest of whom, Christopher, was created a baronet in 1641, and was succeeded in the title by his son, Sir Henry, who married Susan, in her own right Baroness Grey de Ruthyn. Their two sons, Charles and Henry, successively came to this title, and the latter of whom being created Viscount Longueville in 1690, his son received the earldom of Sussex in 1717. These two additional titles failed by the death of the third earl in 1799 without male issue; but the barony of Grey de Ruthyn descended to Henry the son of his daughter Barbara, by Edward Thoroton Gould, Esq. He took the name of Yelverton, and his daughter now enjoys the title, together with that of Baroness Hastings of Ashley.[1]

YORK, Archbishop of. *See* J. Williams.

[1] Wood's Ath. Oxon. ii. 476.; Collins's Peerage, vi. 624.

INTERREGNUM

Of 11 years, 2 months, and 29 days; from January 30, 1649,
to May 29, 1660.

SURVEY OF THE PERIOD.

THE interval of little more than eleven years that elapsed
between the decapitation of Charles I. and the restoration of
his son, though generally called the Commonwealth of England, was signalised by no less than eight changes in the
government of the country.

I. That adopted on the king's death was a republic, without
any king or House of Lords, under the nominal rule of the
House of Commons and a Council of State. The style or
title assumed was " The Parliament of the Commonwealth of
England ; " the *teste* of the writs was in the name of the
" custodes Libertatis Angliæ, authoritate Parliamenti ; " and
indictments were framed " contra pacem publicam." This
system lasted for four years and nearly three months.

II. After the parliament had been violently expelled by
Cromwell on April 20, 1653, he exercised absolute power as
lord general of the army, and on July 4 he called together, as
a convention or parliament, a certain number of persons nominated by himself, to whom " the great charge and trust of
the peace, safety, and good government of the commonwealth was committed," according to the language of the summons. This trust they executed by surrendering back their
powers to him from whom they had received them, on the

12th of the next December; thus ending the second form of government after about eight months' continuance.

III. The government was then declared to be and reside in *one person* and the people assembled in parliament, and Cromwell received the title of " Lord Protector of the Commonwealth of England, Scotland, and Ireland " for life. The offiee was to be elective and not hereditary; and he was to be assisted by a council of twenty-one, and a parliament of 460. The first parliament under this new regime met on September 3, 1654, but not being sufficiently compliant with the protector's will, he dissolved them in the following January, and called another in September, 1656, in which he prevented the entry of any unyielding members, by requiring all who were elected to be armed with a certificate of approval by his council. Having thus got rid of more than ninety stiff-necked representatives, the Protector's influence over a majority of the remainder was unbounded. They offered him the title of king, which he, upon a broad hint from the army, most reluctantly refused. Thereupon they proposed a new settlement of the government, which was adopted on May 25, 1657,—this limited protectorate having lasted three years and five months.

IV. By the new constitution Cromwell was again appointed lord protector and chief magistrate, with exclusive authority and power to appoint his successor, and to nominate not exceeding seventy, nor less than forty, members of what was called " the other House." By virtue of this power he created sixty-three peers; but the Commons, quarrelling as to the appellation to be given to the " other House," Cromwell dissolved them on February 4, 1658. He died on the 3rd of the following September, his reign under this constitution having lasted only one year and little more than three months.

V. Richard, his son, was then proclaimed protector under

the same settlement; but at the end of eight months he dissolved the parliament he had summoned; and soon after was dismissed from his offiee.

VI. The Long Parliament resumed its sittings on May 7, 1659, and those members who were in it when it was expelled by Cromwell continued to meet for nearly five months, when on October 13 they were again ejected.

VII. The army then assumed the government, and appointed what they termed a Committee of Safety, which in its turn by the influence of General Monk was contemptuously discarded, after ruling for two months, and

VIII. The Long Parliament was again restored on December 26, 1659. After being obliged by Monk to admit the members who had been formerly excluded as malignants, and sitting for nearly three months more, they dissolved themselves on March 16, 1660.

The Convention Parliament met on April 25, and prepared the way for the peaceful restoration of Charles II.

In most of these changes the reappointment of official and judicial officers was required, and in some of them new oaths were imposed. This will account for the frequent alterations occurring in the courts of justice during this short period, by the removal of some of the judges, and the substitution and transfer of several, and the refusal of others to act.

In Chancery Richard Keeble was removed from the custody of the Great Seal when Oliver Cromwell became Protector; and Whitelocke and Widdrington were displaced by the Protector's authority. When Richard succeeded his father, Whitelocke was restored, but went out on Richard's dismissal; and the Long Parliament on its recall appointed new commissioners, superseded in turn on the subsequent changes.

In the Upper Bench two chief justices resigned, — Rolle from a disinclination to go to the lengths that Cromwell desired; and Glynne on the return of the Long Parliament. Of the puisne judges, Nicholas was removed by the Protector to the Exchequer, and restored by the parliament, which had first appointed him, to his original court. Newdigate was turned out by the Protector for " not observing his pleasure," notwithstanding the " quamdiu se bene gesserit " of his patent; but was again restored by the same power, and was eventually made chief justice on Glynne's resignation.

In the Common Pleas, Peter Warburton was transferred from this court to the Upper Bench. Edward Atkyns, appointed by the Long Parliament, retired when it was turned out by the army; and Matthew Hale, induced to take a seat on the bench by Cromwell, upon the death of the Protector refused a new commission from Richard his successor.

In the Exchequer, Chief Baron Wilde was removed without any cause assigned when Cromwell became Protector, but was restored to his place seven years afterwards by the Long Parliament by whom he had been first nominated. Baron Nicholas was reinstated in his original seat on the Upper Bench by the Long Parliament on its last restoration, to make room for Francis Thorpe, who had five years before been dismissed by Cromwell for non-compliance with his commands; and Baron Hill was transferred to the Upper Bench at the same time to make up the complement of judges there; which just before the return of Charles II. was three in each court, including the chief.

It has been customary to take the names of the judges and the order of their appointment from " Whitelocke's Memorials." But his diary is necessarily deficient in this information while he was engaged in his Swedish Embassy, from November 6, 1653, to June 30, 1654, during which Cromwell became protector, and made several changes. Some confusion also arises from his noticing some judges as if they were newly appointed on one or other of the changes of government, when they only received the customary new patent. From the Reports of the time, however, though very few in number, and from various other sources, it is hoped that these deficiencies have been supplied, and that the list now offered gives the succession on each bench with as much accuracy as can now be attained.

The salary to each of the judges was 1000*l.* per annum, being the same as that of the lords commissioners of the Great Seal; and by an ordinance of January 27, 1652, they were prohibited from taking any fee, perquisite, or reward, either by themselves or their servants.[1]

The sittings of the court were early, and the judges were sometimes kept to a late hour. One cause, Colt *v.* W. Dutton, occupied them from eight in the morning till eight at night.[2]

COMMISSIONERS OF THE GREAT SEAL.

AT the end of the reign of Charles I., the commissioners who had been previously appointed by parliament were: —

1649. Jan. 29.   HENRY GREY, EARL OF KENT,
WILLIAM GREY, LORD GREY DE WERKE,
SIR THOMAS WIDDRINGTON, and
BULSTRODE WHITELOCKE,
who remained in office little more than a week after Charles's death.

Feb. 8.   BULSTRODE WHITELOCKE,
JOHN L'ISLE, and
RICHARD KEEBLE,
then succeeded, and continued till Oliver Cromwell became protector: soon after which,

1654. April 5.   BULSTRODE WHITELOCKE,
SIR THOMAS WIDDRINGTON, and
JOHN L'ISLE,
were entrusted with the Seal. The protector removed the two first of these, and placed it in the hands of

---

[1] Whitelocke, 520.   [2] 2 Siderfin, 3.

1656. June 15.   NATHANIEL FIENNES, and
                 JOHN L'ISLE,
           who retained it during the rest of Oliver's life.   The Pro-
           tector Richard granted a new commission to
1659. Jan. 22.   BULSTRODE WHITELOCKE,
                 NATHANIEL FIENNES, and
                 JOHN L'ISLE;
           and they remained till the Long Parliament, on its revival,
           appointed
      May 14.   WILLIAM LENTHALL, M.R., the speaker,
           for about three weeks; and then,
      June 3.   JOHN BRADSHAW,
                 THOMAS TYRRELL, and
                 JOHN FOUNTAINE.
           But upon the second expulsion of the Long Parliament
           the Committee of Safety nominated
1659. Nov. 1.   BULSTRODE WHITELOCKE, sole keeper.
           He kept it till the Long Parliament met again; who
           delivered it for a few days to
1660. Jan. 13.   WILLIAM LENTHALL, M.R., their speaker,
           and then appointed new commissioners, viz.,
      „   17.   SIR THOMAS WIDDRINGTON,
                 THOMAS TYRRELL, and
                 JOHN FOUNTAINE.
           On the meeting of the Convention Parliament,
      May 5.   EDWARD MONTAGU, EARL OF MANCHESTER,
           was added to these; and the Seal remained in the pos-
           session of these four commissioners till it was defaced and
           broken by the House of Commons, on May 28, the day
           before the return of the king.

During all these changes, commissions were issued to the master of the Rolls, with some of the judges and masters in Chancery, to hear causes in the absence of the lords commissioners.

Whitelocke says that the commissioners " found their meetings to be more convenient out of Term and in the afternoons in the Middle Temple Hall, both for them and the counsel." [1]

---

[1] Whitelocke, 388.

MASTER OF THE ROLLS.

WILLIAM LENTHALL, during the whole period from the death of Charles I. to the restoration of Charles II., kept possession of this office.

MASTERS IN CHANCERY.

William Lenthall, M.R. -	1649 to 1660
Edward Leech -	1649 to 1652
John Page -	1649 to 1655
Sir Thomas Bennett, LL.D. -	1649 to 1660
Robert Aylett, LL.D. -	1649 to 1655
William Child -	1649 to 1659
Sir Justinian Lewen, LL.D. -	1649 to 1651
John Sadler -	1649 to 1656
Arthur Duck, LL.D. -	1649 to 1650
Edwin Rich -	1649 to 1660
William Hakewell -	1649 to 1652
Edward Eltonhead -	1649
John Bonde -	1650 to 1655
Robert Keilway -	1651 to 1660
Thomas Estcourt -	1652 to 1660
Nathaniel Hobart -	1652 to 1660
Arthur Barnardiston -	1655
William Harrington -	1655 to 1660
William Glasscocke -	1655 to 1659
Edmund Gyles -	1655 to 1660
Thomas Bulstrode -	1656 to 1660
Robert Warsup -	1659 to 1660
William Eden -	1659 to 1660

Some of these were removed in consequence of an ordinance of May 2, 1655, limiting the number to six. The six clerks were reduced to three; and the office of registrar was no longer to be executed by deputy, but four were appointed.

The Great Seal and its emblems shared in the variations of the revolution. The Seal which had been substituted by the parliament for that which Lord Lyttelton took away to Oxford in 1642, and which it imitated in all its insignia and inscriptions, was, immediately after the death of the king, brought into the House of Commons, and there broken up, and the pieces given to the two commissioners, Widdrington and Whitelocke, to be disposed of at their pleasure.

The Seal adopted by the Commonwealth, which had been previously ordered, was then delivered to the new commissioners. The order in the journals describes that it shall be " graven with the addition of the kingdom of Ireland and of Jersey and Guernsey together with a map of England, and in some convenient place on that side the arms by which the kingdoms of England and Ireland are differenced from other kingdoms. — That on the map side of the Great Seal the Inscription shall be ' The Great Seal of England, 1648.' — That the inscription on the other side of the Seal, on which the Sculpture of the House of Commons is engraven, be this, viz. ' In the first year of freedom by God's blessing restored, 1648.'" Whitelocke adds that the design was the fancy of Mr. Henry Martin.[1]

In December, 1651, another new Great Seal was delivered to the commissioners by the parliament, which seems in no respect to have differed from the former, except that the date was altered to 1651, and the "first year" to the "third year;" but it was far more elaborately engraved.

On the expulsion of the House of Commons in 1653, there was no alteration in the Great Seal; and in the Barebone's Parliament, soon after summoned, a bill was brought in and nearly carried for taking away the Court of Chancery.

The Great Seal of the Protectorate, after Cromwell's second investiture in May, 1657, is thus described in Prestwich's " Respublica : "—" A large circle, having thereon the protector bare headed, mounted on mareback, attired in a short coat or jacket of mail, over which was a military sash, placed over his right shoulder and under the left arm, tied

---

[1] Journals; Whitelocke, 367, 380.

behind; pendant to his left side, a large and broad sword, his right hand grasping the head of a truncheon, which he holds before him, one end resting on the pommel of the saddle, his left hand holding the bridle. Behind, on the space on the sinister side, and near the top, was a civic shield, with four quarters; the first and fourth, with the Cross of St. George for England; 2d. the Saltier or Cross of St. Andrew for Scotland; and 3d. the Harp of King David for Ireland. On the margin of this side the seal these words, ' Olivarius, Dei Gra. Reip. Angliæ, Scotiæ, et Hiberniæ, &c. Protector.' On the other side the like arms as that for proclamations, only with this difference, the mantling lamberquin'd with four doublings or folds; on the margin, ' Magnvm Sigillvm Reipub. Angliæ, Scotiæ, et Hiberniæ.' "[1]

When the Long Parliament resumed its sittings in May, 1659, they ordered that a new Great Seal should be prepared according to the form made in 1651. This seems to have been used, even after the meeting of the Convention Parliament and the proclamation of Charles II., up to the day before the king's return, when it was "defaced by a smith" in the House of Commons, and the pieces given to the late commissioners as their fee.[2]

With the abolition of the monarchy the name of King's Bench became inapplicable and obnoxious. The court which was so called received the designation of the Upper Bench, and the oath of the judges was no longer to be taken in the name of the king, but in that of the people.

CHIEF JUSTICES OF THE UPPER BENCH.

HENRY ROLLE, named three months before the king's death, was the first chief justice. He occupied the seat for the next six years, when, on his resignation, Cromwell appointed

---

[1] Burton's Diary, ii. 515.　　　[2] Journals; Parl. Hist. iii. 1551, 1556.

JOHN GLYNNE, serjeant at law and late recorder of London, on June 15, 1655. He resigned the place soon after the return of the Long Parliament, who supplied it by the promotion of

RICHARD NEWDIGATE, one of the judges of the same court, on January, 1660. He continued to preside till Charles's return in May.

JUSTICES OF THE UPPER BENCH.

OF the three puisne judges who were in office at the death of the king, two, Francis Bacon and Samuel Browne, refused to act, one only consenting to exercise his functions under the new government, viz.:—

> 1649. Feb. Philip Jermyn.
> June 1. Robert Nicholas.
> Richard Aske.
> 1654. June 2. Richard Newdigate, loco R. Nicholas.
> Newdigate was removed the next year, but restored in 1657.
> 1655. June. Peter Warburton, loco P. Jermyn.
> 1660. Jan 17. Robert Nicholas, loco P. Warburton.
> Roger Hill, loco R. Aske.
> The judges of this court at the time of the Restoration, were—
> Richard Newdigate, chief justice,
> Robert Nicholas. Roger Hill.

CHIEF JUSTICE OF THE COMMON PLEAS.

OLIVER ST. JOHN, the chief justice at the death of the king, was continued in his place, and retained it till the restoration of Charles II.

JUSTICES OF THE COMMON PLEAS.

THOMAS BEDINGFIELD and Richard Cresheld, two of the

former judges of this court, refused to be resworn. The
remaining one was —

1649.   Feb.   Peter Phesant.
        June 1.   John Puleston.
                  Peter Warburton.
        Oct. 19. Edward Atkyns, loco P. Phesant.
1654.   ?   Matthew Hale, loco (?)J. Puleston.
        June 2.   Hugh Wyndham, loco P. Warburton.
1659.   May 15.   John Archer, loco M. Hale.
1660.   Jan. 17. Edward Atkyns, retired.
                  The judges of the Common Pleas who were in office
                  when Charles II. returned, were —
                        Oliver St. John, chief justice,
                  Hugh Wyndham,   John Archer.

Chief Barons of the Exchequer.

JOHN WILDE kept his place as lord chief baron, to which
he had been appointed in the October previous to the death
of Charles I., till Cromwell became protector, in December,
1653. The office then remained vacant for above a year, when

WILLIAM STEELE, formerly attorney-general to the Commonwealth, and then recorder of London, was sworn chief
baron on May 28, 1655. In the next year, on August 20,
he was made lord chancellor of Ireland, and there was no
other chief baron for nearly two years.

SIR THOMAS WIDDRINGTON, serjeant at law, who had
been one of the commissioners of the Great Seal, was appointed on June 26, 1658. On his restoration to the com-
missionership of the Great Seal,

JOHN WILDE was replaced on January 17, 1660, and
presided in the court till the Restoration.

Barons of the Exchequer.

TWO also of the old barons of this court, Thomas Trevor

and Edward Atkyns, declined to hold office after the king had been beheaded. There only remained—

1649.	February.	Thomas Gates.
		Richard Tomlins, cursitor Baron.
	June 1.	Francis Thorpe.
		Alexander Rigby.
1654.	January.	Robert Nicholas, loco T. Gates.
	June 2.	Richard Pepys, loco A Rigby.
1655.	?	John Parker, loco F. Thorpe.
1657.	Before Easter.	Roger Hill, loco R. Pepys.
1660.	Jan. 17.	Francis Thorpe, loco R. Nicholas.
		Roger Hill, transferred to Upper Bench.

At the restoration of Charles II., he found the court thus constituted : —

John Wilde, chief baron,

Francis Thorpe,   John Parker.

Richard Tomlins, cursitor baron.

TABLE OF THE LORD COMMISSIONERS OF THE GREAT SEAL AND MASTER OF THE ROLLS.

DATE.	LORDS COMMISSIONERS.	MASTER OF THE ROLLS.
1649, Feb. 8	Bulstrode Whitelocke John L'Isle Richard Keeble	William Lenthall.
1654, April 5	Bulstrode Whitelocke Sir Thomas Widdrington John L'Isle	
1656, Jan. 15	Nathaniel Fiennes John L'Isle	
1659, June 22	Bulstrode Whitelocke Nathaniel Fiennes John L'Isle	
May 14	William Lenthall, M. R.	
June 3	John Bradshaw Thomas Tyrrell John Fountain	
Nov. 1	Bulstrode Whitelocke	
1660, Jan. 13	William Lenthall, M. R.	
17	Sir Thomas Widdrington Thomas Tyrrell John Fountain	
May 5	Edward Montagu, Earl of Man- chester, added to the last three	

King Charles II. returned to England on May 29, 1660.

TABLE OF THE CHIEF JUSTICES AND JUDGES OF THE UPPER BENCH.

DATE.	CHIEF JUSTICES.	JUDGES OF THE UPPER BENCH.		
1649, February	Henry Rolle	Philip Jermyn		
June 1	—	—	Robert Nicholas	Richard Aske.
1654, January	—	—	transferred to Ex	—
June 2	—	—	Richard Newdi-gate	—
1655, March 18	—	died	—	—
June	—	Peter Warburton.	dismissed	—
15	John Glynne	—	—	—
1656, June 23	—	—	—	died.
1657, before Mich.	—	—	restored	
1659, before Trin.	—	died	—	
1660, Jan. 17	Richard Newdi-gate	Robert Nicholas	made Ch. J.	Roger Hill.

TABLE OF THE CHIEF JUSTICES AND JUDGES OF THE COMMON PLEAS.

DATE.	CHIEF JUSTICE.	JUDGES OF THE COMMON PLEAS.		
1649, February	Oliver St. John	Peter Phesant		
June 1	—	—	John Puleston	Peter Warburton.
Oct. 1	—	died	—	—
19	—	Edward Atkyns	—	—
1654, ?	—	—	Matthew Hale	—
June 2	—	—	--	Hugh Wyndham.
1658, Sept.	—	—	retired	—
1659, May 15	—	—	John Archer	—
1660, Jan. 17	—	retired	—	—

TABLE OF THE CHIEF BARONS AND BARONS OF THE EXCHEQUER.

DATE.	CHIEF BARONS.	BARONS OF THE EXCHEQUER.			CURSITOR BARON.
1649, January	John Wilde	Thomas Gates	Francis Thorpe	Alexander Rigby	Richard Tomlins.
June 1	—	—	—	died	—
1650, ugust	not reappointed.	died	—	—	—
1654, January	—	Robert Nicholas	—	Richard Pepys	—
June 2	—	—	dismissed	—	—
1655, May 1	William Steele	—	John Parker	—	—
28	—	—	—	—	—
?	—	—	—	—	—
June	made Ld. Chan. of Ireland.	—	—	made Ch. J. in Ireland	—
1656, August 20	—	—	—	—	—
1657, before Easter	Thomas Widdrington	—	—	Roger Hill	—
1658, June 26	—	—	—	—	—
1660, Jan. 17	John Wilde	Francis Thorpe	—	transferred to U. B.	—

The people showed no inclination to be satisfied with the decisions of the courts, and were often greatly inconvenienced by the delay of justice. In November, 1652, Whitelocke complains that the business of the Chancery "was full of trouble, and no man's cause came to a determination, how just soever, without the clamour of the Party against whom Judgment was given." The expulsion of the parliament put a stop for a time to legal business; and in the following October the hearing of causes in Chancery was suspended for a month, while the bill for the suppression of the court was under discussion.[1] In the summer of 1654 the assizes were delayed by an ordinance of council that none of the judges should go out of town till further order; and in the disordered state of the nation, after the return of the Long Parliament, there were no less than three terms lost; all writs, fines, and assurances were stopped, and there was danger of having no assizes. These were given as reasons for using the Seal of the commonwealth, just before the return of the king[2]; and it is clear they were well-founded, for all the circuits for the Lent assizes had been put off, and commissions of Oyer and Terminer to clear the gaols had been issued to the justices of the peace for the several counties, thus leaving the civil causes without trial[3]; and an order was issued for putting off Easter term.[4]

For some time after the death of the king the law and its professors were very unpopular. So many of the profession had sided with the king till his death, and were known still to retain monarchical principles, that the parliament in October, 1649, made an order "that all such persons as were heretofore judges, and likewise all serjeants at law, counsellors, doctors of the civil lawe, attorneys, clerks, and solicitors in the respective courts, who have beene against the Parlia-

---

[1] Whitelocke, 548. 555. 567.   [2] Council Books; Journals.
[3] Mercurius Politicus, No. 609.   [4] Mercurius Publicus, No. 19.

ment, and adherent to or beene ayding and assisting to the
Enemy, be removed from their chambers respectively within
either of the Serjeants' Innes, or any of the Innes of Court
or Chancery, and from the Doctors' Commons."[1]   In the next
month also, " There was a great peek against the Lawyers,
insomuch as," according to Whitelocke, " it was again said,"
as it had been formerly, ' That it was not fit for Lawyers
who were Members of Parliament (if any Lawyers ought to
be of the Parliament) to plead or practise as Lawyers during
the time that they sit as Members of Parliament.' "   Upon
which the memorialist made a learned speech in their defence,
and by his eloquence stifled the opposition.[2]

Gratitude is due to the parliament for the suggestion of some
improvements of the law, which were afterwards adopted.
One of their greatest and most beneficial innovations in the
proceedings of the courts, was the introduction of English
into all the process and pleadings ; and Style reports that
the first rule in the Upper Bench made in English was in
Easter term, 1651, in a cause between White and Kibble-
white.[3]

ATTORNEY-GENERAL.

1649.	February.	William Steele.
	April 9.	Edmond Prideaux, till his death ; receiving new Patents from the protectors, Oliver and Richard, in 1653 and 1658.
1659.		Robert Reynolds, till the Restoration.

SOLICITOR-GENERAL.

1649.	February.	John Cook.
1650.		Robert Reynolds.
1654.	May 24.	William Ellis.

[1] Journals.   [2] Whitelocke, 430.   [3] Style's Reports. 261.

SERJEANTS-AT-LAW.

It may be as well to repeat here the names of those serjeants who were called by the parliament in the October before the king's death.

The added initials mark the Inn of Court to which they belonged; and those who became judges are distinguished by a *

1648
* Thomas Widdrington (G.),
* Thomas Bedingfield (G.),
* Richard Keeble (G),
* Francis Thorpe (G.),
* John Bradshaw (G.),
* Oliver St. John (L.),
* Samuel Browne (L.),
* John Glynne (L.),
  Erasmus Erle (L.),
* Bulstrode Whitelocke (M.),
  William Conyers (M.),

1649.
* Peter Warburton,
* Alexander Rigby,
? Evan Seys.

1654.
* Richard Pepys (M.),
  Thomas Fletcher (L.),
* Matthew Hale (L.),
* William Steele (G.),
* Richard Newdigate, (G.),

1655. * Roger Hill (I.),
1656.   William Shephard,
1658. * John Fountaine (L.),
1659. * Thomas Tyrrell (I.),
      — Steel,
?   Thomas Waller,
      — Wroth,
      — Finch,

* John Puleston (M.),
  Thomas Chapman (I.),
* Thomas Gates (I.),
  William Littleton (I.),
  William Powell (L.),
  John Clerke (L.),
  John Eltonhead (M.),
* Robert Nicholas (I),
* John Parker (G.),
  Robert Bernard,
  Robert Hatton (M.).
* Richard Aske (I.).

  Thomas Twisden (I.),
* Hugh Wyndham (L.),
* John Maynard (M.),
  Unton Croke (I.).

* John Archer (G.).
  — Lynne,
  John Corbet.
  — Hyde.

SERJEANTS FOR THE COMMONWEALTH.

1650. * Thomas Widdrington (G.),
1654. * John Glynne (L.),
1658. * John Maynard (M.).

John Green (L.).
Erasmus Erle (L.).

SERJEANTS' INN, FLEET STREET.—In October, 1649, the parliament ordered that the contractors for the sale of the lands of the late deans and chapters should " forbear to contract with any person for sale of . . . Serjeants' Inne in Fleet Street, where divers of the Judges and Serjeants at Lawe have for a long time resided, and still reside, until the residue of the said lands shall be contracted for and sold."

SERJEANTS' INN, CHANCERY LANE.—The rector of St. Dunstan's was accustomed to receive a gratuity of 3s. 4d. for each judge and serjeant of this house, which in the early entries is called indifferently "for his Tithes," and " Tenths." There was a curious custom attached to the payment. In the application by the rector in Easter term, 1653, giving notice of a sermon on Ascension Day, and claiming the above sum " in lieu and satisfaction of all manner of Dues and Duties ecclesiastical whatsoever to the rector on reasonable request," he acknowledges that it " was and is of ancient Custom and Duty to present the Society upon Ascension Eve yearly with a good dish of fresh Fish ready dressed, as of Lobsters, Plaice, or some other choise fresh Fish, and with a Bottle of French Wine, White, or Claret of the best."

COUNSEL.

THE initials show the courts to which those who became judges were first appointed : —

— Adams,	— Bernardiston,	— Deves,
— Allen,	— Boynton,	— Dormer,
J. Archer, C. P.,	J. Bradshaw, Com.G.S.,	— Edgar,
R. Aske, U. B ,	E. Bulstrode,	W. Ellis,
R. Atkyns,	— Carew,	J. Eltonhead,
W. Ayloff, K. B.	T. Chapman,	E. Erle,
— Babington,	C. Chute,	S. Evre,
F. Bacon,	J. Clerke,	— Fell,
N. Bacon,	J. Coke,	H. Finch, L. K.,
— Baldwin,	W. Conyers,	T. Fletcher,
— Barry,	J. Corbet,	J. Fountaine, Com. G.S.,
F. Bernard,	U. Croke,	— Foxwist,

— Freeman,	— Manley,	W. Steele, Ch. B. C.
G. Gerrard, M. R.,	J. Maynard, Com. G. S.,	— Stephens,
— Gibs,	— Merrifield,	— Thomas,
J. Glynne, Ch. U. B.,	W. Montagu, Ch. B. E.,	F. Thorpe, B. E.,
J. Green,	— Moseley,	— Trever,
— Griffith,	R. Newdigate, U. B.	— Tucke,
M. Hale, C. P.,	R. Nicholas, U. B.	C. Turner,
B. Hall,	— Norbury,	J. Turner,
T. Hardres,	— Panel,	T. Twisden, K. B ,
A. Harris,	J. Parker, B. E.,	T. Tyrrell, Com. G. S.,
R. Hill, B. E.,	— Parsons,	— Vaughan,
— Holhead,	R. Pepys, B. E.,	— Walker,
— Hooper,	W. Powell,	G. Waller,
B. Hoskins,	— Powis,	P. Warburton, C. P.,
— Howell,	E. Prideaux,	— Webb,
— Hurst,	— Proby,	B. Whitelocke, Com. G. S.,
R. Hyde,	— Reeves,	T. Widdrington, Com.
E. Johnson,	R. Reynolds,	G. S.,
E. Jones,	A. Rigby, B. E.	— Wild,
W. Jones,	— Scrogg,	— Williams,
— Latch,	J. Sedgwick,	— Wilmot,
— Lechmere,	E. Seys,	— Wroth,
W. Littleton,	— Shaftoe,	— Wylde,
L. Long,	R. Siderfin,	H. Wyndham, C. P.,
— Lynne,	— Starkey,	W. Wyndham, K. B.
T. Manby,	— Steel,	— Yard.

During the troubles of this period, the regular exercises of the inns of Court were greatly interrupted, and the readings discontinued. In June, 1657, Cromwell's parliament ordered " that it be recommended to his Highness and the Council, to take some effectual course upon advice with the Judges, for reforming the Government of the Inns of Court . . . and also for reviving the readings in the several Inns of Court, and the keeping up of exercise by the students there."[1] Few and short are the entries found of any of these societies.

INNER TEMPLE.—The only account of this inn during this eventful period is that Brick Buildings, between Inner Temple Lane and Hare Court, were erected in 1657.[2]

---

[1] Burton's Diary, ii. 313. [2] Dugdale's Orig. 147.

MIDDLE TEMPLE. — This society seems also to have employed its leisure, anticipating more peaceful times, in erecting "a good fair fabrick" in Middle Temple Lane, in 1653, and "a very large, high, spacious brick building in Essex Court," in 1656.[1]

GRAY'S INN. — This society took advantage of the times to relieve themselves from the payment of the rent of 6*l*. 13*s*. 4*d*. to the crown, by purchasing it of the commissioners of the commonwealth in 1650 for 86*l*. 19*s*. 10*d*.; but the sale was repudiated when legitimate government was restored.[2]

BARNARD'S INN. — That attorneys and students usually wore gowns when attending the courts at Westminster appears from an order of this inn in 1658, that no companion shall come into the hall of the society at dinner or supper time without such gowns. Disorderly meetings held by the young gentlemen of the house under the name of "initiations," were prohibited under a penalty of 40*s*.

By the orders in the reign of James I., attorneys and solicitors were expressly excluded from each of the four inns of Court; and by the renewal of the prohibition under Charles I. in more stringent terms, it appears to have been sometimes evaded. The admission of this branch of the profession into the inns of Chancery seems to have been gradually recognised; and in Michaelmas, 1654, by a rule of the Court of Upper Bench, it was made absolutely indispensable for every member of it to be admitted in one of the inns of Court or Chancery. It declares " That all officers and attorneys of this court be admitted of some Inn of Court or Chancery, at the beginning of Hilary Term next, or in the same term wherein they shall be admitted officers or attorneys, and be in commons one week in every Term, and take chambers there, &c., under pain of being put out of the Roll of Attorneys."[3]

---

[1] Dugdale's Orig. 100.   [2] Report on Inns of Court, 1855, p. 76.
[3] Adolphus and Ellis, 19.

BIOGRAPHICAL NOTICES

OF

THE JUDGES IN THE INTERREGNUM.

ARCHER, JOHN.

Just. C. P. 1659.

See under the Reign of Charles II.

ASKE, RICHARD.

Just. U. B. 1649.

RICHARD ASKE belonged to a younger branch of an ancient Yorkshire family settled at Richmond. His grandfather Robert Aske of Aughton was high sheriff of the county in 1588; his father was John Aske of the same place, and his mother was Christiana, daughter of Sir Thomas Fairfax of Denton, knight.[1] Richard, when he was admitted a member of the Inner Temple on Jannary 27, 1606, was described as of Rides Park in that county.. He was called to the bar on January 29, 1614, but did not reach the post of reader till Lent, 1636.[2] His connection with the Fairfaxes — for besides his mother, two of his father's sisters had married into that family — probably introduced him to the notice of the parliamentary leaders. He was employed by Mr. Stroud, one of the imprisoned members in 1629, to argue against the return to the *habeas corpus*.[3] On October 18, 1643, the Commons

---

[1] Whittaker's Richmondshire, i. 216.; Harl. MSS. 1394. 1487.
[2] Inner Temple Books.   [3] Rushworth, i. App. 18.

specially recommended him to the lord mayor and aldermen of London to be elected one of the four pleaders; and in June, 1644, both houses presented him with the valuable office of coroner and attorney of the king in the King's Bench.[1]   He was next selected as junior counsel on the trial of King Charles; and on June 1, 1649[2], as a reward for his pains, the parliament nominated him one of the justices of the Upper Bench, making him a serjeant for the purpose.[3] For a short time in June, 1655, he was the only judge in the court[4]; and on the 23rd day in the same month in the following year his death is recorded.[5]

ATKYNS, EDWARD.
Just. C. P. 1649.
See under the Reigns of Charles I. and II.

BRADSHAW, JOHN.
Com. G. S. 1659.

THE parentage of John Bradshaw has been the subject of some uncertainty, arising partly from his leaving no immediate descendants, but principally from the disrepute that attached to his name as the president of the court that condemned Charles I. to the block. It is now satisfactorily established that he was a younger son of Henry Bradshaw of Marple Hall, in a township of that name in the parish of Stockport in Cheshire, descended from a family of considerable respectability in Derbyshire, and that his mother was Catherine, daughter and coheir of Ralph Winnington, Esq., of Offerton.

Born at Marple in 1602, and baptised in the parish church of Stockport on December 10 in that year, he received his

---

[1] Com. Journ. iii. 280. 521. 535.
[2] State Trials, iv. 1054.
[3] Whitelocke, 405.
[4] Style's Reports, 452.
[5] Peck's Desid. Cur. B. xiv. 29.

education first at the free school there, and then at Bunbury and Middleton, to all of which he bequeathed large sums for their endowment. Designed for the law, he commenced his legal studies at Gray's Inn on March 15, 1620, and was called to the bar on April 23, 1627, and to the bench of that society on June 23, 1645 [1], when appointed judge of the Sheriffs' Court in London. He probably acted for some years as a provincial counsel, as he lived at Congleton, and served the offiee of mayor there in 1637, and was afterwards high steward [2]; and at one time of his life he resided in Bradshaw Hall in Bolton, on a stone over the door of which his family arms remain. [3]

In the year 1643 he became a candidate for the offiee of one of the judges of the Sheriffs' Court of the city of London, then vacant, his antagonists being Richard Proctor and William Steele, afterwards chief baron. The right of election was claimed by both the Courts of Aldermen and Common Council, and Bradshaw was chosen by the latter on September 21, and sworn in on the 24th. [4] Immediately afterwards the Court of Aldermen elected Proctor, who thereupon brought an action in the King's (afterwards the Upper) Bench, which, however, did not come to a final hearing till February, 1655, when the right was determined to be in the Common Council, with whom it has ever since continued. Bradshaw, in the meantime, had performed the duties of the offiee, for in February, 1649, he was permitted to appoint a deputy at Guildhall " in regard of his employment in the High Court." [5]

Clarendon says he was " not much known in Westminster Hall, though of good practice in his chamber and much employed by the factious." [6] The absence of his name from all the Reports seems to confirm this account. The earliest men-

[1] Gray's Inn Books.   [2] Gent. Mag. lxxxviii. i. 328.
[3] Baines's Lancashire, i. 540.   [4] Com. Council Bks. xl. 74, 75.
[5] Whitelocke, 377.   [6] Clarendon, vi. 217.

tion of him is in October, 1644, when he was assigned as one of
the counsel against Lord Macguire for the rebellion in Ireland[1]; and he probably assisted Prynne in his argument to prove
that Irish peers were amenable to trial by an English jury.
In December he was appointed high sheriff of Lancashire.[2]
He next appears in the following year as leading Lilburn's
appeal to the House of Lords for reparation against the iniquitous sentence of the Star Chamber in 1638[3]; and in the
discussions which arose in the two houses in 1646, as to placing the custody of the Great Seal in commissioners who were
not members of parliament, he was among those voted by
the Commons, but objected to by the Lords.[4]   The appointment of chief justice of Chester, however, was given to him
in March, 1647 ; in June he was retained as one of the
counsel to assist in the prosecution of Judge Jenkins ; and
on October 12, 1648, he was included in the batch of serjeants then made by the parliament.[5]

When the Lords rejected the ordinance for the trial of the
king, and the Commons determined to proceed without their
concurrence, the names of the peers and judges who had
been appointed were struck out of the commission, and those
of Bradshaw, Nicholas, and Steele were substituted ; and
Bradshaw was dignified with the title of lord president of the
so-called high court of justice.[6]   The selection of a man of
so little weight in his profession can only be accounted for
by the supposition that the concocters of the tragedy could
not prevail on any of the more eminent lawyers to undertake
the obnoxious service ; and that they had discovered in
Bradshaw a nature exactly suited to their purpose — bold
and resolute, with a small organ of veneration, and a great
lack of modesty, and not encumbered with any nice delicacy

[1] Whitelocke, 106.   [2] Godwin's Commonwealth, ii. 79.
[3] State Trials, iii. 1347.   [4] Journals ; Whitelocke, 224.
[5] Whitelocke, 238. 240. 255. 342.   [6] Ibid. 366. 368.

of feeling. Whitelocke and Widdrington had refused the commission; neither Rolle nor St. John, the two chief justices, nor even Chief Baron Wilde, could be entrusted to obey their behest; and their own law-officer, Prideaux, either from objections on his part, or want of confidence on theirs, was displaced, while creatures of their own were appointed temporary attorney- and solicitor-general to conduct the charge. The trial began on January 20, 1649; and Bradshaw's conduct throughout its continuance fully answered the description of Clarendon, that he administered the office " with all the pride, impudence, and superciliousness imaginable."[1] Whatever may be the differences of opinion on the material point of the trial — and great will be the differences among men — no doubt can be entertained that it was ordained by usurped authority, that its end was determined before its commencement, that its proceedings were illegal and undignified, and that the conduct of the president was insolent and overbearing. During the sittings of the court, lodgings were provided for him at Sir Abraham Williams's house in New Palace Yard, and all provisions and necessaries were ordered to be supplied. He was treated with all the forms of judicial state; decorated with a scarlet robe, a sword and mace were borne before him, and twenty gentlemen were appointed to attend him with partizans. When, after a long speech, he had pronounced the sentence, he was the first to sign the warrant for execution. But, however willing an instrument, he was not altogether a free agent; for all that he did, and almost all that he said, seems to have been directed and dictated by the majority of the commissioners, consisting of the king's most determined enemies.[2] In the subsequent trials of the Duke of Hamilton, the Earl of Holland, and others, he was continued lord president of the court; and the dean's house at Westminster was given to him for

[1] Clarendon, vi. 218.　　　[2] State Trials, iv. 1008—1154.

ever for his residence and habitation, with a donative of
5000*l.* He became one of the council of state, and, being
elected its president, is noticed by Whitelocke for his lengthened arguments, and the inconvenience they occasioned. A
vote to settle 2000*l.* a year in lands out of the Earl of St.
Alban's and Lord Cottington's estates on him and his heirs
was passed; and his appointment of chief justice of Chester
was renewed, to which the chancellorship of the duchy of
Lancaster was afterwards added.[1]   He does not seem to have
acted as lord president of the high court of justice beyond
1650, Serjeant Keeble presiding in 1651, and Serjeant L'Isle
in 1654.[2]

Bradshaw was a staunch republican, and looked with a
jealous eye on Cromwell's attempt to gain the sole authority.
When the ambitious general ejected the Long Parliament on
April 20, 1653, and came to the council of state to put an
end to its sitting, Bradshaw, who still presided, rose and
boldly addressed him in these words: — " Sir, we have heard
what you did at the House in the morning, and before many
hours all England will hear it; but, sir, you are mistaken to
think the Parliament is dissolved, for no power under heaven
can dissolve them but themselves; therefore take you notice
of that."[3]   He was not, of course, one of the members selected
by the general to sit in what was called Barebone's Parliament; but in it an act was passed for continuing in him the
jurisdiction of the county of Lancaster.[4]   Cromwell, when
he became protector, summoned him to the council, and required him to take out a new commission for his office of
chief justice of Chester; but he refused to do so, alleging
that he held that place by a grant from the parliament of
England, to continue *quamdiu se bene gesserit;* and whether
he had carried himself with that integrity which his com-

---

[1] Whitelocke, 390. 414. 420. 529.   [2] State Trials, v. 43. 518.
[3] Ludlow, 195.   [4] Whitelocke, 565.

mission exacted of him, he was ready to submit to a trial by twelve men to be chosen by Cromwell himself. Cromwell was silenced, and, though an order was actually signed dismissing him from the offiee, did not think it safe to prevent him from proceeding on his circuit.[1] In Cromwell's parliament of 1654 Bradshaw was elected member for Cheshire, notwithstanding the protector's attempts to keep him out, and distinguished himself against the court party in the debate whether the government should be in one single person and a parliament.[2] That parliament was soon dissolved; and on summoning another in September, 1656, Cromwell was more successful in his efforts, and Bradshaw was not returned. The distaste between them continued to increase, and Bradshaw was omitted from the list of peers nominated by the protector.

On the death of Cromwell, Bradshaw was returned for Cheshire to Richard's parliament of January, 1659. With its dissolution in April, the protectorate terminated from mere imbecility, and the remnant of the Long Parliament, nicknamed the Rump, resumed its sittings. Bradshaw, a determined commonwealth's-man, was named on the council of state[3], and on June 3 was appointed one of the commissioners of the Great Seal, in conjunction with Tyrrell and Fountaine. He had been for eight months suffering from the ague, and was then in the country. His attendance, therefore, was dispensed with at that time; but in July 22 he took the oaths in the house.[4] Ere four months had elapsed this Rump was again dismissed by the army, and Bradshaw, still sick and suffering, attended in the council of state, and almost with his last words expressed "his abhorrence of that detestable action," as he called it.[5] He then withdrew, and

---

[1] Ludlow, 240—244.; Godwin, iv. 270.   [2] Parl. Hist. iii. 1428. 1445.
[3] Ludlow, 261. 277.   [4] Whitelocke, 680. 681.   [5] Ludlow, 307.

survived the scene about a fortnight, dying on October 31[1], with the declaration that if the king were to be tried and condemned again, he would be the first man that should do it. His death occurred in the Deanery at Westminster, and he was buried with great pomp in the abbey, his funeral sermon being preached by John Rowe.[2] On the restoration of Charles II. his body, and those of Cromwell and Ireton, which had been deposited in the same place, were disinterred, and, with every mark of obloquy, were dragged on sledges to Tyburn, where they were hanged on the several angles of a triple gibbet, then beheaded, their trunks thrown into a hole under the gallows, and their heads exposed on poles at top of Westminster Hall.[3]

The partisans of the royal and the republican party of course differ essentially in their estimate of Bradshaw's character. The laudation of it during his life by Milton [4] (whom he had patronised, and to whom he bequeathed 10*l.*[5]), is too exaggerated, and Clarendon's description of him after his death is perhaps too severe. Whitelocke's (with whom he was evidently no favourite) is pithy, and nearer the mark: " A stout man, and learned in his profession, no friend to monarchy." The best part of his character is his consistency ; for he showed as much resistance to the semblance of royalty as to the reality, opposing the usurpation first of Cromwell, and then of the army, as firmly as he had stood against the king.

FIENNES, NATHANIEL.

Com. G. S. 1655.

THE Great Seal having in former times been occasionally en-trusted to members of the military profession[6], Cromwell no

---

[1] Whitelocke, 686.   [2] Wood's Ath. Oxon. iii. 1129.
[3] Harris's Lives, iii. 520.   [4] Defensio pro propulo Anglic. (1651.)
[5] Bradshaw is stated to have been a kinsman of Milton, by the mother's side.
[6] See Bousser, vol. iii. 400.; De la Pole, Scrope, Segrave, Beaufort, and Nevill, vol. iv. 70. 80. 86. 151. 844.

doubt considered that he might follow the precedent when he appointed Colonel Nathaniel Fiennes to be one of his lords commissioners.   But from the disgrace that the colonel had previously incurred, the lawyers might well congratulate themselves that he had no claim to be regarded as a brother.

He was the second son of William, Lord Say and Sele, who was created a viscount in 1624, and who became a great supporter of the discontented party, by Elizabeth, daughter of John Temple, Esq., of Stowe in Buckinghamshire.   He was born about 1608 at Broughton in Oxfordshire, and after receiving the rudiments of his education at Winchester, was admitted in 1624 fellow of New College, Oxford, as founder's kin.[1]   He remained there about five years, and then spent some time abroad, " in Geneva and amongst the cantons of Switzerland, where," says Clarendon, " he improved his disinclination to the church, with which milk he had been nursed."   From his travels he returned through Scotland in 1639, at the time of the tumults there, which he assisted in fomenting.[2]

In 1640 he was elected a member of the Long Parliament as representative for Banbury, close to the place of his birth, and soon became a leader of the party called " root and branch."   He strongly supported the bill against the bishops, and so little had the consequences been considered that, in a conversation with Clarendon, in answer to the question, what government they meant to introduce instead, he said, " There would be time enough to think of that."[3]   He was appointed of the committee to attend the king on his journey to Scotland in 1641.[4]   When the parliament took up arms in the following year, Fiennes not only undertook to find one horse and bring 100*l.* in money as his subscription towards the

[1] Wood's Athen. Oxon. iii. 877.   [2] Clarendon's Rebellion, i. 325. 510.
[3] Ibid. i. 410.; Life, i. 90.   [4] Rebellion, i. 494.

cause[1], but accepted a commission of colonel of their forces.
His first exploit, the defeated attempt to surprise Worcester[2],
did not speak much to the credit either of his courage or
military skill; and his conduct at Bristol, the governorship of
which was entrusted to him in April, 1643, confirmed the
bad impression he had made.   Professing great zeal for the
parliament, he had removed the former governor on suspicion
of disaffection, and had condemned and executed two principal citizens on the charge of plotting to give up the place
to the king; and yet, after laying in stores of ammunition
and provisions sufficient to sustain a siege of three months,
no sooner had Prince Rupert invested the city, than, after a
slight show of resistance, he demanded a parley, and surrendered it to the royalists, to the great advantage of their cause
in the west, and the infinite discouragement of the parliamen-
tarians.

On the colonel's return to parliament " every one looked
strangely on him with a discontented aspect," so palpably
showing their suspicion of either treachery or cowardice, that
he felt it necessary to make his apology openly in the house,
concluding with a desire that his conduct might be examined
by a council of war.   This relation being published by himself was answered and exposed by Mr. Walker and Mr.
Prynne, in a book called "Rome's Masterpiece;" for the
publication of which the writers were summoned before the
council to make good their accusation.   The consequence was
that Colonel Fiennes was called upon to defend himself; and
after a solemn trial conducted most ably by Mr. Prynne, which
by reason of frivolous obstacles and objections raised by the
colonel lasted no less than nine days, he was convicted by the
council of war, and condemned to lose his head.   The sentence, however, was not put in execution; by his family interest and connections, and perhaps by the consideration of his

---

[1] Notes and Queries, 1st Ser. xii. 338.   [2] Rebellion, iii. 234. 625.

great civil ability, and the eminent services and zeal he had previously shown in the cause, the general was induced to grant him a pardon. His military career, for which he was totally unfitted, thus ended in infamy, and he quitted the kingdom to cover his disgrace.[1]

Returning after some years' retirement, he resumed his attendance in parliament and almost his former ascendancy. He was one of the committee formed for the safety of the kingdom in January, 1648[2]; and on the 1st of the following December he made a speech in favour of receiving the king's answers from the Isle of Wight as satisfactory. In cousequence he was, a few days after, one of the first victims of Pride's Purge, and, after being imprisoned for a short time, was secluded from the house.[3]

In the parliament which Cromwell called after he was declared protector in September, 1654, he was elected one of the members for Oxfordshire. Though he of course subscribed the recognition of the protector's authority, and was one of the committee for the enumeration of damnable heresies, his name does not appear in Goddard's account as taking any part in the debates of that parliament, which was dissolved in January, 1655, without passing a single act.[4] In the following May, Fiennes was a commissioner of the protector's Privy Seal, with an allowance of 20s. a day; and on June 16 he had an additional grant of 63l. 5s. a year, nominally as a member of the council[5], but really as lord commissioner of the Great Seal, to which he had been appointed on the day before, on the secession of Whitelocke and Widdrington, when they refused to carry into effect the ordinance concerning the Chancery. L'Isle was his colleague, and Whitelocke says that Fiennes never had experience in mat-

---

[1] State Trials, iv. 185—298. ; Rebellion, iv. 141. 343. 611.

[2] Whitelocke, 286.   [3] Parl. Hist. 1143. 1248.

[4] Introd. to Burton, cxiv.   [5] 4 Report, Pub. Rec. App. ii. 193.

ters of that nature, and L'Isle had no knowledge but what he acquired by accompanying the late commissioners.[1]

Fiennes is said to have been the author of the declaration issued by Cromwell in the following October, vindicating the severity with which he had treated all the royalists, making them suffer in money or in person for the plots against him, whether they were implicated in them or not.[2] In Jannary, 1656, he was united with Whitelocke and others in the nego- tiation of the treaty with the Swedish ambassador. The next parliament, which met on September 17, and to which he was returned for the university of Oxford, confirmed him and L'Isle as commissioners of the Great Seal.[3] In the en- deavour to remove the scruples which Cromwell professed to assuming the title of king, he was one of the principal speakers. This attempt being set aside, he bore the Seal at the solemn ceremony of the re-inauguration in June, 1657.[4] Un- der the new constitution he was appointed one of Cromwell's lords ; and, on the protector's death in 1658, assisted in pro- claiming Richard as his successor, and was reinstated in the custody of the Great Seal, with his former colleague and Bulstrode Whitelocke.[5] In the list of the members of the parliament called by Richard in Jannary, 1659, the name of Nathaniel Fiennes appears as member for Banbury[6], which, as he was a member of the " other house," either must be a mistake, or some other person of the same name must be in- tended. He is not only mentioned as lord keeper in Richard's speech on the first day, as about to address the parliament on certain matters untouched by him[7], but is named in April as going up to the bar of the " other house " to receive a decla- ration from the Commons.[8] In his oration at the opening of

[1] Whitelocke, 627.

[2] Harris's Lives, iii. 432—435.

[3] Whitelocke, 632—649. 653.

[4] Parl. Hist. iii. 1498. 1515.

[5] Whitelocke, 666. 675. 676.

[6] Parl. Hist. iii. 1533.

[7] Parl. Hist. iii. 1540.

[8] Whitelocke, 677.

the parliament, after Richard had finished speaking, he exceeded even Bishop Williams's famous address, by commencing it with the remarkable expression, "What shall a man say after a king?"[1]   Soon after the dissolution of the parliament on April 22, Richard's authority ceased, and with it Fiennes's office, the Long Parliament, which met again on May 7, appointing other commissioners.[2]

On the king's return, Fiennes retired to his country seat at Newton Tony in Wiltshire, where he died on December 16, 1669, and was buried in the church there, with a monument to his memory. However that memory might be cherished by his friends and family, the only claim to admiration by the public would be his undoubted talent and eloquence, of which his published speeches afford ample evidence; but in regard to his conduct either as a soldier or civilian, tainted in the former as it must ever remain with the suspicion of treachery and the imputation of cowardice, and exhibiting in the latter so many proofs of changeableness and timeserving, he cannot but be held in the lowest estimation.

He married twice. His first wife was Elizabeth, daughter of Sir John Eliot of Port Eliot in Cornwall, by whom he had a son; and his second was Frances, daughter of Richard Whitehead, Esq., of Siderley, Hants., by whom he had three daughters. His son William, by the death of his first cousin without male issue, became third Viscount Saye and Sele, and the title remained in the family till 1781, when the viscounty became extinct, but the ancient barony survived in Thomas Twistleton, descended from the daughter of the eldest son of the first viscount.[3]

[1] Noble's Cromwell, i. 179.   [2] Whitelocke, 678.
[3] Noble; A. Wood, ut suprà; Nicholas's Synopsis.

FOUNTAINE, JOHN.

COM. G. S. 1659, 1660.

ALTERNATELY a royalist and parliamentarian, this lawyer was commonly called Turncoat Fountaine. Anthony Wood is evidently mistaken in describing him as the son of William Fountaine of Seabrooke in Buckinghamshire, and most probably so in stating that he was the man, who, after being entered of Lincoln College, Oxford, was removed to Corpus Christi, and took his two degrees of B. A. and M. A. in 1634 and 1637.[1] A monumental inscription in the church of Salle in Norfolk proves him to have been the eldest son of Arthur Fountaine of Dalling in that county, one of the sons of another Arthur Fountaine of Salle. His mother was Anne, the daughter and heir of John Stanbow.[2] The Lincoln's Inn Books confirm this description, and record his admission to that house on October 30, 1622; and his call to the bar on June 21, 1629. A. Wood seems to have confounded a member of another family of the same name settled in Bucks with the serjeant; for it is not very likely that any one would take his academical degrees five and eight years after he had become a barrister.

When the civil war broke out in 1642, John Fountaine showed his devotion to the crown by refusing to contribute to the subscription required by the Parliament; whereupon the House of Commons committed him " to the Gatehouse " on October 12; and Whitelocke in stating the fact adds, " but, afterwards, he and many others refused, and again assisted on both sides, as they saw the wind to blow."[3] Three days after

---

[1] Fasti Oxon. i. 473. 497.

[2] Exemplified pedigree in Heralds' Coll. Norfolk, ii. 82.

[3] Com. Journ. ii. 804; Whitelocke, 63. The " Mr. Fountayne," mentioned in Notes and Queries, 1st Ser. xii. 359., as promising to "bring in one horse" to the subscription, was Thomas Fountaine, M.P. for Wendover, in Bucks, who died about 1646.

his committal he had liberty for four days, "to go with his keeper to bury his wife;" and a short time after he was allowed to go, similarly attended, "to serve God at St. Margaret's, Westminster." He was still in confinement on December 20, when his petition to be bailed was refused.[1] His discharge from custody was probably granted on condition of his leaving London; for Clarendon mentions him in 1645, as assisting and counselling Sir John Stawel in forming the Association of the four Western Counties, and calls him a "lawyer of eminency, who had been imprisoned and banished London for his declared affection to the crown."[2]

As long as the royal cause prospered, Fountaine remained its staunch adherent; but as soon as he considered it was hopeless, he deserted Oxford, and went over to the enemy under Colonel Rainsborough at Woodstock. The colonel announced his "coming in," and his being then at Aylesbury, to the Commons, who, evidently distrusting him, ordered that he "should be sent prisoner to Bristol, and that Major-General Skippon should take care to keep him in safe custody."[3] During the fortnight he was at Aylesbury, he published a "Letter to Dr. Samuel Turner concerning the Church and its Revenues," urging him to advise the king for the sake of peace, and to "save what is left," to concede all the parliament required, bishops and church lands, and all.[4] Dr. Richard Steuart wrote an answer[5], in which he calls the writer "an Oxford Londoner," and reminds him, in reference to his profession of "reason and honesty," of a sentence he was wont to utter, that "when vessels do once make such noises as these, 'tis a shrewd sign they are empty."

On his release he appears to have remained quiet for the

---

[1] Com. Journ. ii. 810. 832. 896. [2] Rebellion, v. 86.

[3] Com. Journ. 25 April, 1646; Whitelocke, 202.

[4] This pamphlet is in the British Museum, catalogued under the title "Turner, Samuel."

[5] Wood's Athen. Oxon. iii. 297.

next six years, and so far to have satisfied the parliament as to be appointed in January, 1652, one of the committee of persons, not members, to take into consideration what inconveniences existed in the law, and to suggest remedies. His name, however, was not at first proposed, and was only at last adopted after a close division, occasioned probably by a remembrance of his former delinquency; from which he was not fully cleared till March, 1653; compounding for his estate at 480*l.*[1] Although he does not appear in the few Reports of legal proceedings during that period, he must have acquired some reputation as a lawyer, as he was made a serjeant at law on November 27, 1658, in the short reign of the Protector Richard.

The Long Parliament, on its restoration, selected him on June 3, 1659, for one of the three commissioners of the Great Seal for five months; the other two being John Bradshaw and Thomas Tyrrell, his brother-in-law. Before that term expired the Committee of Safety superseded the commission, and on November 1 entrusted the Seal to the sole keeping of Whitelocke. Fountaine, however, was replaced on January 17, 1660, on the Long Parliament again resuming the government, and with his colleagues continued in possession of the Seal, till its commonwealth emblems were defaced, and the Broad Seal of the monarchy restored. On the return of Charles II., he resumed his old political creed, and was immediately confirmed in his degree of the coif.[2]

Pursuing his profession, he resided in Boswell Court, and survived the Restoration eleven years. He died on June 4, 1671, in the seventieth year of his age, and was buried at Salle, the seat of his ancestors. The name of his first wife, who died in 1642, is not given. By her he had two sons and a daughter. By his second wife, Theodosia, daughter of Sir

[1] Whitelocke, 520.; Com. Journ. vii. 69. 71. 73. 268.; Dring's Catal.

[2] Noble, i. 438.; Whitelocke, 680. 693.; 1 Siderfin, 3.

Edward' Harrington of Ridlington, Bart., whom he married in 1649, he left one son and one daughter. One of his grand-daughters was the mother of the first Viscount Galway ; and, though the commissioner had written against the church, two others became the wives of bishops, one of Simon Patrick, bishop first of Chichester, and then of Ely ; and the other of Thomas Sherlock, master of the Temple, bishop successively of Bangor, Salisbury, and London. His descendants, among whom was another churchman, Dr. John Fountaine, Dean of York, now reside at Melton, in Yorkshire, where there is a portrait of the serjeant.

GATES, THOMAS.

B. E. 1649.

See under the Reign of Charles I.

WHETHER this judge was connected by relationship with Sir Thomas Gates, who in 1606 was united with Richard Hackluyt and other adventurers in planting the first colony of Virginia[1], is uncertain ; but the period of his death, which was about 1588, makes it not improbable. He is described as of Churchill in the county of Oxford in his admission to the Inner Temple, which took place on January 1, 1606–7. Having been called to the bar January 29, 1614–15[2], he was elected reader to that society in autumn, 1635. As his name is never mentioned in the Reports, there seems nothing but his politics to induce the Long Parliament (of which he was not a member) to recommend him to be called serjeant, and to be made a baron of the Exchequer. This however they did on October 12, 1648, and he was sworn in the following month. He accepted a renewal of his commission on the death of the king ; and was excused from

[1] Wood's Athen. Oxon. ii. 187. [2] Inner Temple Books.

riding the next summer circuit by reason of his sickness.[1] His death on August 19, 1650, at the age of sixty-three, was occasioned by an infection taken at Croydon while engaged in his judicial duties; and he was buried in the Temple Church.[2]

He left a daughter who was married to John Lane, Esq., of Perivale in Middlesex, where there is a tablet to her memory in the church.

GLYNNE, JOHN.

Ch. U. B. 1655.

THE genealogy of this family commences in the year 843 with Cilmin Droed-tu, one of the fifteen tribes of North Wales. Without going through the pedigree it is enough to say that the future chief justice was the eldest son of Sir William Glynne, knight, of Glyn-Llivon in Carnarvonshire, by Jane daughter of John Griffith, Esq., of Carnarvon.[3] John Glynne was born in 1602 at the ancient seat of his ancestors. He had the advantage of being educated at Westminster school, and afterwards at Hart Hall, (now part of New College) in the university of Oxford, whither he went at Michaelmas, 1620, and remained three years.[4] During this time he had kept his terms at Lincoln's Inn, of which he was admitted a member on January 27, 1620, and having been called to the bar on June 24, 1628, he got quickly into practice, for he appears in Croke's Reports in Hilary Term, 1633.

On August 7, 1638, he received a grant of the office of keeper of the writs and rolls in the Common Pleas in reversion[5], a place of considerable profit. Having been previously appointed high steward of Westminster, he was elected representative for that city in both the parliaments that met in

---

[1] Dugdale's Orig. 168. 179.; Whitelocke, 342, 378. 411.
[2] Peck's Desid. Cur. B. xiv. 23.   [3] Wotton's Baronet. iii. 289.
[4] Wood's Athen. Oxon. iii. 752.   [5] Rymer, xx. 300.

1640. In the first of these he was a silent member: but in the last, the Long Parliament, he showed himself to be an active partisan of the discontented party. He took a prominent part in the prosecution of the Earl of Strafford; and one of the arguments he used to prove that the multitude of the earl's minor offences amounted to high treason, was "Raine in dropps is not terrible, but a masse of it did overflow the whole world." In all the proceedings his reasoning was inconsequential and his conduct harsh and inhuman. He was one of the committee to prepare the votes condemnatory of the canons, and to draw up a charge against Archbishop Laud[1], and was the messenger from the Commons with a charge of high treason against the bishops who had signed a protestation against the Lords' proceeding in their absence.[2] He reported likewise from the committee upon the proceedings against Sir John Eliot and others, who were imprisoned and condemned to pay various fines for their conduct in the parliament of 1629; and was also selected to report relative to the army plot which was to overawe the House. He supported and spoke in favour of the remonstrance on the state of the kingdom, the carrying of which had so great an effect in widening the breach with the king[3]; and he published a speech, delivered by him in January, 1642, strenuously vindicating the privileges of the Commons on the occasion of the king's unadvised attendance at the House, and demanding the delivery of the five members whom he had caused to be accused of high treason.[4] He next accepted a commission of deputy lieutenant under the militia ordinance in May[5]; and further showed his zeal in the cause by subscribing in June 100l. in money or plate, together with the maintenance of a horse, for the defence of the parliament.[6]

[1] Verney's Notes, 44. 84.
[2] Whitelocke, 53.
[3] Verney's Notes, 102. 110. 125.
[4] Parl. Hist. ii. 1023.
[5] Whitelocke, 59.
[6] Notes and Queries, 1st Ser. xii. 358.

His active zeal will account for his being elected on May
30, 1643, recorder of London, in the place of Serjeant
Phesant, who had held the offiee not quite a month.[1] In the
next year he assisted at the Assembly of Divines, and had the
thanks of the house for his speech on the Jus Divinum.[2]
In all the questions discussed he was a popular debater, but
stoutly opposed the self-denying ordinance.[3] No unwilling
sharer in the forfeited spoils of the loyalists, the small were
as welcome as the great; and he did not disdain a grant of
the books of Mr. Vaughan of Lincoln's Inn[4], at the time he
was being gratified with the clerkship of the Petty Bag,
worth 1000l. a year.

The Presbyterian party, with which he was connected,
becoming jealous of the army, took measures in June, 1647,
for its being disbanded. Sir Thomas Fairfax counteracted
this attempt by bringing a charge in the name of the army
against eleven of the opposing leaders, including Glynne,
and insisting on their being sequestered from their attendance
on the house. Though the Commons at first resisted the
interference, the accused members, upon the army's advance towards London, thought proper to withdraw. This
was quickly followed by their impeachment, their expulsion
from the house, and the attempt to place Mr. Steele as
recorder instead of Glynne. After a year's bye-play, resulting in the discharge of the accused, and their being
restored to their seats, the farce concluded, having answered
its purpose of getting rid for the time of the popular opponents of the army and their plans.[5] Glynne was readmitted
on June 7, 1648, and was so entirely restored to confidence as to be appointed in the following September one of
the commissioners to treat with the king in the Isle of Wight;

---

[1] City List of Recorders, 12'   [2] Whitelocke, 110.
[3] Clarendon, v. 89.   [4] Whitelocke, 177.
[5] State Trials, iv. 857—922.; Whitelocke, 253—310.

and while engaged in that service to be named, on October 12, a serjeant at law.[1]   In December, however, he was one of the victims of Pride's Purge, by the vote of the Rump repealing the previous revocation of the proceedings against the eleven impeached members[2]; which, so far from being detrimental to him, turned out to his future advantage, by relieving him from all implication in the murder of the king.

After that event another attempt was made to deprive Glynne of the recordership, on the pretence that as a serjeant at law he was no longer qualified; although Phesant, the last recorder, was a serjeant when elected.   He refused to retire on the ground stated, but the next week he tendered his resignation as his own voluntary act, and the city thereupon presented him with 300*l.* as a gift.[3]   Steele, for whom the parliament wished to provide in consequence of his services on the king's trial, was immediately elected recorder.

Glynne's party having now lost all power, he soon after showed an inclination to side with that of Cromwell, who, willing enough to encourage his advances, made him, on becoming protector, his serjeant.   In this character he appeared in the high court of justice[4], and went the Oxford circuit as a judge in 1654.[5]   In the same year he received the appointment of chamberlain of Chester[6], and was returned member for Carnarvonshire in Cromwell's parliament of September; in which he seems to have been extraordinarily silent. In April, 1655, he presided at the trial of Colonel Penruddock for the rising in the west, when the judges were seized at Salisbury[7]; and on July 15, when Chief Justice Rolle, who had refused to be concerned in that trial, had retired, was put into his place as chief justice of the Upper Bench.[8] This position, there being then no House of Lords, did not

[1] Whitelocke, 334. 342.
[2] City List of Recorders, 12, 13.
[3] Athen. Oxon. i. xxiii.
[4] State Trials, v. 767.
[5] Parl. Hist. iii. 1247.
[6] State Trials, v. 518.
[7] Ibid. iii. 604.
[8] Style's Reports, 452.

disqualify him from sitting for Flintshire in Cromwell's next parliament of September, 1656. He supported Alderman Pack's motion to offer Cromwell the title of king, and, being one of the committee to forward the application, in a round-about inconclusive speech he endeavoured to remove the protector's scruples, by arguing that the kingly office is essential to our constitution.[1] He cunningly published his speech as a pamphlet on the king's return, under the title of " Monarchy asserted to be the best, most ancient, and legal form of Government." In the new constitution which followed, he accepted a seat in Cromwell's House of Peers.[2]

The protector died on September 3, 1658, and Glynne was continued chief justice by Richard, on whose removal and the return of the Long Parliament, with a prophetic glance at the political horizon, he resigned his chief justiceship. In the new parliament, called the Convention Parliament, that met on April 25, 1660, he was returned for the county, and his son for the town, of Carnarvon[3], and played his cards so adroitly, that, on the arrival of Charles II. in England, he was included in the first batch of serjeants, being those who had been appointed irregularly by the parliament. On November 8, in the same year, all bygones forgotten, he was made, according to Anthony Wood, "by the corrupt dealing of the then Lord Chancellor" (Clarendon), the king's serjeant[4], and was knighted. He and Maynard, who also attained the same rank, were both employed in the crown prosecutions that followed, and divided the shame of appearing against Sir Harry Vane, their old coadjutor and friend.[5]

Charles's coronation took place on April 23, 1661; and the account given by Pepys of an accident on the occasion shows the feeling that existed in regard to the two legal

[1] Parl. Hist. iii. 1432. 1483. 1498.; Harris's Lives, iii. 472.

[2] Whitelocke, 666.　　　　[3] Mercurius Publ., No. 15.

[4] Siderfin, 3.　　　　[5] Burton's Diary, iii. 175. 182.

renegadoes: "I have not heard of any mischance to any body through it all, but only to Serjeant Glynne, whose horse fell upon him yesterday and is like to kill him, which people do please themselves to see how just God is to punish the rogue at such a time as this, he being now one of the king's serjeants, and rode in the cavalcáde with Maynard, to whom people wish the same fortune." That the hostile impression was not confined to the courtier, is proved by Butler's immortalising their names in the following couplet:—

> "Did not the learned Glynne and Maynard
> To make good subjects traitors strain hard?"

He continued in the practice of his profession till his death, which occurred at his house in Portugal Row, Lincoln's Inn Fields, on November 15, 1666. He was buried in his own vault under the altar in St. Margaret's, Westminster.

The reputation of his wealth was no doubt founded in truth; for, besides his professional gains, the places which he enjoyed must have brought him considerable profit. He was undoubtedly an able lawyer, and in his judicial character, as between man and man, was just and impartial. Siderfin states that his plainness and method in arguing the most intricate case were such that it was made clear to the comprehension of every student.[1] But here his praise must end. As a politician, though the cunning with which he joined all the ruling powers in turn may be admired, who but must despise his various tergiversations?

Sir John was twice married. His first wife was Frances, daughter of Arthur Squib, Esq., for whom he procured the place of Clarencieux herald, worth 400l. a year, and who afterwards became one of the tellers of the Exchequer. His second was Anne, daughter and coheir of John Manning, Esq., of Cralle in Sussex. By both he left children. His eldest

[1] Siderfin, 159.

son, William (by his first wife), was, during his father's life, created a baronet on May 20, 1661, and his successors still enjoy the title.

GREY, HENRY, EARL OF KENT.
COM. G. S. 1649.
See under the Reign of Charles I.

HENRY GREY, the tenth Earl of Kent of that family, succeeded to the title on the death of his father, Anthony, in 1643, and had not long taken his seat among the peers before he was substituted for the Earl of Rutland in the commission from the parliament for the custody of their Great Seal. Clarendon says, " The Earl of Rutland was so modest, as to think himself not sufficiently qualified for such a trust: . . . whereupon they nominated in his room the Earl of Kent, a man of far meaner parts, who readily accepted the place." Indeed, the number of lords who attended the parliament was so small, that their choice of the two who were to represent them was very limited.[1] Oliver, Earl of Bolinbroke, was the other peer; and they and the four commissioners of the Commons' house entered on their new office on November 10, 1643. The only change that took place during three years was the appointment of the Earl of Salisbury on the death of the Earl of Bolinbroke. The seal was taken from them on October 30, 1646, and given to the speakers of the two houses.[2]

In December, 1647, the earl was one of the lords commissioners to take the four bills to the king at the Isle of Wight, and had to bring them back with the king's refusal to assent to the destruction of the royal authority which they involved. He was renominated on March 15, 1648, chief commissioner of the Seal, in conjunction with another lord and two commoners; who continued in office till the death of the king;

---

[1] Rebellion, iv. 340. 403.   [2] Journals.

not one of them approving or taking any part in the tragic event. With that the power of the lords who were commissioners virtually terminated, but they remained in office till the Commons on February 6, 1649, voted the abolishment of the House of Peers, and two days after put the seal into other hands.[1]

So ended the earl's political career. He died in 1651: and the title descended to his son and grandson, the latter of whom was created a duke, but dying in 1740 without male issue, these titles became extinct. A marquisate De Grey, which he also obtained, lasted till 1797, and the daughter of the last survivor was created in 1816 Countess de Grey with remainder to her nephew, who now enjoys that Earldom.

GREY, WILLIAM, Lord Grey de Werke.

Com. G. S. 1649.

See under the Reign of Charles I.

Sir William Grey, a baronet of 1619, was advanced to the peerage in 1624 by the title of Lord Grey of Werke in Northumberland. From the commencement of the civil war he was an active partisan of the parliament, and one of the few peers that remained in the House of Lords while the rest joined the king. When Lord Fairfax suffered a defeat in the north, and the parliament were desirous to send to the Scots to assist them, Lord Grey on being named one of the deputation refused to go, and was committed to the Tower; but making his peace he was soon after selected by the lords as their speaker, in the absence of the lord keeper. In 1648, when the parliament were appointing commissioners of the Great Seal, Lord Grey of Werke was at the Lords' request added to them by an ordinance dated March 15. He per-

---

[1] Whitelocke, 283. 286. 295. 369. 377, 378.

formed the duties attached to his office for nearly eleven months; the last few days being after the king's death; in the planning or execution of which fearful event he is not charged with concurring. With the abolition of the House of Lords of course his office ceased; but he consented to be nominated on the Council of State.[1]

He survived the restoration of Charles II. more than fourteen years; and died in July 1674. His title, after being held by his son and two grandsons, became extinct in 1706, together with the Earldom of Tankerville, which had been granted in 1695 to the elder grandson; but which was revived a few years after, in favour of Charles Bennet, second Lord Ossulston, who had married the earl's daughter and heir. Their descendants still enjoy the title.[2]

HALE, MATTHEW.

Just. C. P. 1654.

See under the Reign of Charles II.

HILL, ROGER.

B. E. 1657?. Just. U. B. 1660.

ROGER HILL belonged to a very ancient Somersetshire family, which had flourished at Hounston in that county from the time of Edward III. In the reign of Henry VIII. it was seated at Poundsford near Taunton, where William Hill, the father of the Baron, lived and died in 1642. His mother was Margaret or Jane, daughter of John Young of Devonshire. Roger was born at Colliton in the latter county, at the residence of his father's sister, Mrs. Sampson, on December 1, 1605[3]; and when he was little more than eighteen he

---

[1] Clarendon, iv. 153. 368. 415.; Whitelocke, 295. 377. 381. 488.

[2] Dugdale's Baronet. ii. 449.; Nicolas's Synopsis.

[3] To Albert Way, Esq. F.S.A., a descendant of the family, I am indebted for these particulars, as well as for many other proofs of his obliging disposition to assist me in this work.

commenced his legal studies at the Inner Temple, to which society he was admitted on March 22, 1624. He was called to the bar on February 10, 1632, and became a bencher on June 10, 1649.[1]

In March, 1644, he was the junior of the five counsel em-ployed against Archbishop Laud, who, in allusion to the senior four being the only spokesmen, calls him " Consul Bibulus."[2] In the next year he was returned to the Long Parliament as member for Bridport, in the place of one of its former representatives, disabled for adhering to the king.[3] One of the first fruits of his siding with the popular faction was the grant to him in 1646 of the chambers of Mr. Mostyn and Mr. Stampe in the Temple.[4] Though named in the commis-sion for the king's trial he never sat on it.

Cromwell made him a serjeant at law on June 29, 1655, and in Easter Term, 1657, he is mentioned in Hardres' Re-ports as a baron of the Exchequer. In that character he as-sisted at the ceremony of investiture of the protector in June, 1657; and as one of the judges-attendant on Cromwell's House of Peers, he delivered a message from them to the Commons in the following January.[5] In the summer of 1658 he went the Oxford circuit with Chief Justice Glynne, an account of the proceedings in which, " writ in drolling verse," was published soon after.[6] When the commonwealth was re-stored by the removal of Richard Cromwell and the return of the Long Parliament, Baron Hill resumed his place as a mem-ber[7]; and on January 17, 1660, he was transferred from the Exchequer to the Upper Bench[8], where his name appears as a judge in Hilary Term in Siderfin's Reports.

The author of " The Good Old Cause " says that the par-

---

[1] Inner Temple Books.

[2] Wood's Athen. Oxon. iii. 130.

[3] Parl. Hist. ii. 608.

[4] Whitelocke, 201.

[5] Burton's Diary, ii. 340. 512.

[6] Wood's Athen. Oxon. iii. 754.

[7] Parl. Hist. iii. 1548.

[8] Whitelocke, 693.

liament granted him the Bishop of Winchester's manor of
·Taunton Dean, worth 12,000*l.* a year, on the determination of
the estate for lives [1]; which he, of course, was not allowed to
retain when the bishops were replaced at the Restoration. At
that period he escaped the censure of the king, but being one
of the Rump Parliament he had not the same favour shown
to him as most of the other serjeants of the commonwealth
experienced, in being confirmed in their degree. He survived
Charles's return for seven years, during which he married his
third wife, who brought him an estate at Alboro' Hatch in
Essex, where he died on April 21, 1667, and was buried in
the Temple Church.

He married three times: first, in 1635, Katherine, daughter
of Giles Green of Allington in the Isle of Purbeck, who died
in 1638, leaving a son and daughter; secondly, in 1641, Abigail, daughter of Brampton Gurdon of Assington Hall in Suffolk, who died in 1658 "at his house at Pel-a-Mel in St.
James's fields, Middlesex," leaving one son; and thirdly, in
1662, Abigail, daughter and co-heir of Thomas Barnes of
Alboro' Hatch, Essex. He was the third husband to this
lady, his third wife, who had been previously married to
John Lockey of Holms Hill, Herts, and to Josias Berners of
Clerkenwell Close, Middlesex.

Roger, his son by his second wife, was knighted by Charles II.
in 1668, and ultimately succeeded to the Poundsford estate,
which he afterwards sold to Dr. Simon Welman, and built
Denham Place about the year 1696.[2]

---

[1] Parl. Hist. iii. 1599.; Collinson's Somerset. iii. 233.
[2] From the Family Memorials, communicated by Albert Way, Esq.

JERMYN, PHILIP.

Just. U. B. 1649.

See under the Reign of Charles I.

THERE is not much probability that this judge was in any near relationship to the Suffolk family of that name, two of the members of which were ennobled by Charles I. and II. ; inasmuch as they adhered to the royal cause, while he took office under the parliament. He was admitted a member of the Middle Temple on February 15, 1604, was called to the bar on November 28, 1612, and became reader in autumn, 1629.[1] Before that date he had attained considerable practice in the courts, his name frequently occurring in the Reports of Croke, W. Jones, and Godbolt. He was called to the degree of the coif in Jannary, 1637 [2]; and was employed by the parliament in their prosecution of Judge Jenkins in 1647, and appointed by them on October 12 in the next year one of the judges of the King's Bench. The tragic destruction of the king made no change in his position, for he consented to act under the usurped power.[3] In the extraordinary trial of Lieutenant-Colonel Lilburne in October, 1649, at which the Lord Commissioner Keeble presided, Jermyn was one of the commissioners, and took a prominent and violent part against the prisoner, almost superseding the president.[4]

Peck dates his death on March 18, 1655. His daughter Mary married John Greene, recorder of London, in 1658.[5]

[1] Middle Temple Books.
[2] W. Jones's Reports, 390.
[3] Whitelocke, 255. 342. 378.
[4] State Trials, iv. 1269. et seq.
[5] Desid. Cur. B. xiv. 26.; Wotton's Baronet. iv. 600.; Morant's Essex, i. 183.

KEEBLE, RICHARD.

Com. G. S. 1649.

FROM Thomas Keeble, a native of Suffolk, who, as a learned serjeant, fills a large space in the Year Books of Henry VII., Richard Keeble of Newton of that county, traces his descent.[1] He became a member of Gray's Inn on August 7, 1609, and having been called to the bar on July 14, 1614, was elected an ancient in 1632, and attained the post of reader in Lent, 1639. His name appears in Croke's Reports in 1636.   Though he was never in parliament, his political sentiments were sufficiently known to induce that body to elect him for one of the judges of Wales in March, 1647, and to include him in the batch of serjeants appointed in October, 1648.   He was sent to Norwich in December to try the mutineers; and on the disposal of the Great Seal after the death of the king, he was the junior of the three commissioners to whose custody it was entrusted[2]; an office which he held for above five years. Soon after his appointment he presided at the curious trial of Colonel Lilburne, and he seems to have acted with less severity and unfairness than some of the judges who were joined in commission with him.   He was president also of the high court of justice on the trials of Christopher Love and John Gibbons in 1651.[3]   In April, 1654, Cromwell having been proclaimed protector, Keeble was displaced, and another commissioner named.   His salary of 1000l. a year was but irregularly paid; for there is a Privy Seal dated so late as April 6, 1658, for 1050l. due to him on that account.[4]

On the restoration of Charles II. the serjeant was excepted from the Act of Indemnity.[5]   How long he lived after that

---

[1] Wood's Athen. Oxon. iv. 575.; Gray's Inn Books.
[2] Whitelocke, 240. 342. 380.; Blomefield's Norwich, i. 396.
[3] State Trials, iv. 1269., v. 49. 268.   [4] 5 Rep. Pub. Rec. App. ii. 271.
[5] Parl. Hist. iv. 70.

period, or to what country he retired to avoid his trial, does not appear. His son, Joseph Keeble, became eminent as a lawyer, and published several law tracts, besides Reports of cases in the King's Bench from 1660 to 1678.[1]

KENT, EARL OF. *See* H. GREY.

LENTHALL, WILLIAM.

M. R. 1649.   COM. G. S. 1659, 1660.

See under the Reign of Charles I.

DERIVED from an ancient Herefordshire family, one member of which was a favourite of Henry IV., and shared with Henry V. the glories of Agincourt, the immediate ancestors of the master of the Rolls became possessed, by marriage with an heiress, of a large property in Oxfordshire, part of which was the manor of Latchford. He was the son of William Lenthall of that place, and Frances, daughter of Sir Thomas Southwell of St. Faith's in Norfolk; and was born in June, 1591. After receiving the rudiments of his education at Thame School, he was sent in 1606 to St. Alban's Hall, Oxford. Here he continued for three years, when, without taking a degree, he was removed to Lincoln's Inn.[2] Admitted a member of that society on October 6, 1609, he was called to the bar after the customary seven years' study on October 14, 1616; and in due course proceeding to the bench of the inn in 1633, he was elected reader in Lent, 1638.[3] Long before this date he had got into considerable practice; since, writing to Secretary Nicholas in 1641, he speaks of his previous labours of twenty-five years, the profits of the last years of which he subsequently states to have amounted to 2500*l.* a year.[4] Clarendon describes

---

[1] Legal Bibliography, 181
[2] A. Wood's Athen. Oxon. iii. 603.
[3] Linc. Inn Books; Dugdale.
[4] Notes and Queries, 1st S. xii. 358.

him, when elected speaker, as "a lawyer of no eminent account," but "of competent practice."[1]   He became recorder
of Woodstock, and was elected representative of that borough
in both the parliaments of 1640, over the latter of which he
was chosen to preside as speaker. It is curious to contrast
the fulsome compliments and humble professions of his opening and earlier addresses to the king, as the organ of the
Commons, with the proceedings against that sovereign which
he was soon to authenticate; and to watch the gradual
diminution of courtly expressions as those proceedings became more violent, and the adulatory and submissive strain
he adopted towards those who ultimately acquired the ascendancy. Clarendon says, with truth, that he was a weak
man, and unequal to the task; yet his answer to King
Charles on January 4, 1642, on his coming to the house to
demand the five members whom he had accused, bore some
semblance both of spirit and ingenuity. When the king asked
him "Whether any of these persons were in the house?
whether he saw any of them? and where they were?" the
speaker, falling on his knees, replied, "May it please your
majesty; I have neither eyes to see nor tongue to speak in
this place, but as the house is pleased to direct me, whose
servant I am here; and humbly beg your majesty's pardon
that I cannot give any other answer than this to what your
Majesty is pleased to demand of me."[2]

When the parliament set on foot the subscription for their
defence in June, 1642, the speaker, as his contribution, promised to maintain a horse and to give 50l. in money or plate.[3]
So well pleased were the Commons with his conduct in the
chair, that on their adopting a new Great Seal for themselves,
one of the first uses they made of it was to constitute him
master of the Rolls, taking no account of the king's previous

---

[1] Rebellion, i. 240. 297.   [2] Whitelocke, 52.
[3] Notes and Queries, ut suprà.

appointment of Sir John Colepeper. He was accordingly sworn into that office on November 22, 1643, and was continued by special votes in 1645, notwithstanding the self-denying ordinance.[1] In consequence of the difference of opinion in the two houses as to the persons to be named commissioners of the Great Seal in 1646, they placed it ad interim in the custody of the two speakers on October 30, to hold it for a week; but that period, by their continued irresolution, became nearly a year and a half, being extended to March 15, 1648, when new commissioners were agreed to.

In July, 1647, the London apprentices tumultuously presented petitions to parliament concerning the militia, and acted so insolently, threatening all manner of violence if their demands were not complied with, that both houses were from terror compelled to revoke the ordinances complained of. The speakers accordingly withdrew to the army, and put themselves under its protection; and though the Commons had in the meantime elected another speaker in Lenthall's place, he was, on his return with the army, after a week's absence, allowed to resume the chair. It was believed that the whole transaction was a plot to give power to the army, and that the speaker was compelled to join in it by a threat that he should be impeached for embezzlement if he did not comply. He was charged also, in the next year, with endeavouring to impede the treaty with the king in the Isle of Wight[2]; and in all the subsequent measures affecting the king's life he did not hesitate to preside. After the tragic scene of the 30th of Jannary, 1649, "the Parliament of England," or rather the House of Commons, assumed the government, Lenthall, as speaker, being nominally the head. The same honours were ordered to be paid to him when visiting the city of London as had been used to the king, by delivering to him the sword

[1] Whitelocke, 78. 146. 177.

[2] Clarendon, v. 461—469.; Parl. Hist. iii. 723—736. 1050.

on his reception, and by placing him above the lord mayor at the feast.[1]　But the real power was in a council of state, and that was constituted by the army, over which Cromwell, by his superior energy and his success in battle, soon acquired unlimited ascendancy.　In four years both the army and the nation got tired of the parliament, and on April 19, 1653, the speaker was compelled to vacate his chair by Cromwell's forcible expulsion of all the remaining members from the house.[2]

Retiring to the Rolls, he seems to have kept aloof from any public interference in politics till Cromwell summoned his second parliament on September 3, 1654, when Lenthall, being elected for Oxfordshire, was again chosen speaker.　It sat for nearly five months, and then, being too argumentative for the protector's purposes, was dissolved without passing a single act.[3]　The protector and his council, in the April following, proposed to the commissioners of the Seal and the master of the Rolls a new ordinance for the better regulation of the Chancery, and for limiting its jurisdiction, which all those officers (except L'Isle) strongly opposed.　Lenthall was most earnest against its adoption, protesting, " That he would be hanged before the Rolls Gate before he would execute it;" but no sooner did he see that the two opposing commissioners were dismissed than he " wheeled about," and gave in his adhesion.[4]　The next parliament, called by Cromwell in September, 1656, though Lenthall was again returned for Oxfordshire, was presided over by Sir Thomas Widdrington. In the farce that was enacted in it of offering to Cromwell the title of king, the master of the Rolls performed a leading part, using the most specious arguments to induce him to accept it.　Upon Cromwell's refusal and the establishment of a new constitution, Lenthall was not at first included in the number of lords which the protector was authorised to nomi-

[1] Whitelocke, 406.

[2] Parl. Hist. iii. 1481.

[3] Parl. Hist. iii. 1444. 1460.

[4] Whitelocke, 625, 626.

nate ; but on complaining of the omission, he received a summons to take his seat.   That parliament was dissolved within
a fortnight after the new Lords met, principally from the
hostility occasioned by their appointment; and Cromwell died
seven months after its dissolution.   In the parliament which
his son, the Protector Richard, called in January, 1659,
Lenthall again appeared as one of the Lords ; but on its
dismissal three months after, the Long Parliament having
resumed its sittings, he, after some hesitation, was induced
to forget his short-lived nobility, and again take his seat
as speaker.[1]   On May 23, he was voted keeper of the
Great Seal for eight days, at the end of which other commissioners were appointed, who, in turn, were superseded
by the Committee of Safety.   He again, for a third time,
held the Seal for a fortnight in January, 1660, by order of
the Long or Rump Parliament, which had again met, but
which in the following March was finally dissolved, having in
the interval conferred on him the chamberlainship of Chester.[2]

This and his other places the Restoration obliged him to
resign, though Ludlow says (p. 383) he offered 3000*l.* to be
continued master of the Rolls.   As he had been excepted by
name, together with Cromwell and Bradshaw, from the pardon offered by Charles's proclamation, dated Paris, May 3,.
1654, Lenthall no doubt trembled at his present position, till
he found that the extreme penalty was to be confined to those.
actually concerned in the king's death.[3]   During the discussions on the Act of Indemnity he found it necessary to
address a letter to the House of Commons, denying the reports of his "great gains" as speaker.   The Commons, notwithstanding, excepted him from the bill, to suffer such pains
and penalties, not extending to life, as should be proper to
inflict on him; but the Lords, probably through the influence,

---

[1] Parl. Hist. iii. 1488. 1519. 1546.; Ludlow, 252. 254.
[2] Whitelocke, 679. 698.   [3] Harris's Lives, iv. 129.

of Monk, moderated the vote, by directing that the exception should only take place if he accepted any office or public employment.[1] Eventually he received the king's pardon.

Thus preserving the wealth he had acquired in his various offices, he retired to Burford Priory, his seat in Oxfordshire, purchased of Lord Falkland, but not before he had offered another proof of his timeserving pusillanimity, by forgetting his famous reply to the king, and giving evidence of words spoken in parliament by Thomas Scott the regicide.[2] He died on September 3, 1662, and was buried at Burford. His confession or apology in his last illness, made to Dr. Brideoak, afterwards Bishop of Chester[3], confirms the impression universally formed of the weakness of his character, and the narrowness and timidity of his disposition.

By his wife Elizabeth, daughter of Ambrose Evans of Lodington in Northamptonshire, he left several children. His eldest son, John, whom Anthony Wood calls " the grand braggadocio and lyer of the age," was a member of the Long Parliament, and held several offices under Cromwell, who created him a baronet. After the Restoration, he was sheriff of Oxfordshire, and was knighted by Charles II. His son William had General Monk for a godfather[4], and his descendants still flourish in several branches, one of which resides at Bessels Leigh in Hertfordshire, a manor purchased by the speaker.

L'ISLE, JOHN.

Com. G. S. 1649.

JOHN L'ISLE was born about the year 1606 at Wootton in the Isle of Wight, the residence of his father, Sir William L'Isle, who was descended from a branch of the noble family of that name. After being educated at Magdalen Hall in

---

[1] Parl. Hist. iv. 68. 91.   [2] State Trials, v. 1063.
[3] Wood's Athen. Oxon. iii. 608.   [4] Mercurius Politicus, No. 611.

the university of Oxford, where he was admitted in 1622, and took the degree of bachelor of arts in February, 1625–6, he repaired, it is said, to one of the Temples as a student in law; but whether he was ever called to the bar is uncertain. He was chosen member for Winchester in both the parliaments of 1640 — that meeting on April 13 and dissolved on May 5, and that called for November 3, which afterwards voted itself perpetual. In the latter, he at once took the popular side, advocating the violent measures on the king's removal to the north, and obtaining some of the plunder arising from the sale of the crown property. On the eviction of Dr. William Lewis in November, 1644, he was made master of St. Cross, and retained that valuable preferment till it was given to Mr. Solicitor-General Cook in June, 1649.[1] In December, 1647, when the king was in duress at the Isle of Wight, L'Isle was selected as one of the commissioners to carry to him the four bills which were to divest him of all sovereignty, and to which they had to bring back the king's magnanimous refusal to consent. He showed his extreme inveteracy against his Majesty by his speech on September 28, 1648, in support of the motion that the vote which the Commons had come to two days before, that no one proposition in regard to the personal treaty should be binding, if the treaty broke off upon another, should be rescinded; and by his further speech, some days later, urging a discontinuance of the negotiation.[2]

He took a prominent part in the king's trial as one of the managers for conducting its details, being present during its whole continuance, and drawing up the form of the sentence.[3] The result of this activity was his receiving the appointment on February 8, 1648–9, little more than a week after the king's death, of one of the commissioners of the Great Seal,

---

[1] Wood's Fasti Oxon. i. 422. 437.; Whitelocke, 441.
[2] Parl. Hist. iii. 823. 828. 1025. 1038.   [3] State Trials, iv. 1053. et seq.

and being placed in the council of state.[1] He not only concurred in December, 1653, in nominating Cromwell protector, but administered the oath to him; and having been
reappointed lord commissioner, was elected member in the
new parliament for Southampton, of which town he was the
recorder.[2] In June he was constituted president of the high
court of justice, and in August he was appointed one of the
commissioners of the Exchequer. When the ordinance for
better regulating the Court of Chancery was submitted to
the keepers of the Seal, L'Isle alone was for the execution
of it, his colleagues pointing out the inconvenience of many
of the clauses. The consequence of his subserviency to Cromwell's wishes was that he was continued in the office on the
removal of his colleagues in June, 1655; and was again confirmed in it in October, 1556, by Cromwell's third parliament, to which he was again returned as member for Southampton.[3] In December, 1657, Cromwell having revived the
House of Lords, summoned L'Isle as one of his peers.[4] The
death of Oliver in September, 1658, made no difference in
L'Isle's position, Protector Richard preserving him in his
place; but when the Long Parliament met again in the following May, he was compelled to retire, and other commissioners were appointed.[5] The house, however, named him
on January 28, 1660, a commissioner of the Admiralty.[6]

In the changes that soon occurred, L'Isle, conscious that
he had taken such a part that he could not hope for pardon,
thought it most prudent to leave the kingdom, and escaping
to Switzerland, he established himself first at Vevay, and
afterwards at Lausanne. There he was shot dead on August
11, 1664, on his way to church, by an Irishman, who was
indignant at the respect and ceremony with which a regicide

[1] Parl. Hist. iii. 1287. 1290.   [2] Ibid. 1426. 1431.
[3] Whitelocke, 571. 584. 593. 621. 627. 653.   [4] Parl. Hist. iii 1518.
[5] Whitelocke, 666. 676. 678.   [6] Mercurius Politicus, No. 605.

was treated. The assassin escaped, and the murdered man was solemnly buried in the church of the city.

In the whole of his career he was a creature of Cromwell, and aided him in all his ambitious attempts. Several of his speeches delivered as president of the high court of justice have been published; and among the State Trials may be found those where he presided.

He married Alice, daughter and heiress of Sir White Beckcnshaw, of Moyle's Court in Hampshire, which was still in possession of the family as late as the present century. His widow lived long after him, and perished at last by a violent ·death; being beheaded in 1685 on a conviction, forced by the brutal Judge Jefferies from a jury who had twice returned a verdict of not guilty, for harbouring John Hicks, a preacher, who had been out with the Duke of Monmouth.[1]

MANCHESTER, EARL OF. *See* E. MONTAGU.

MONTAGU, EDWARD, EARL OF MANCHESTER.
COM. G. S. 1660.
See under the Reign of Charles I.

THE first Earl of Manchester, Sir Henry Montagu, lord chief justice of the court of King's Bench in the reign of James I., lived till November, 1642, and during his life his son Edward had been called up to the House of Peers by the title of Lord Kimbolton. At the meeting of the Long Parliament, Lord Kimbolton, having been for some time estranged from the court, took the popular side, and became a favourite organ of the party in the upper house, and the secret adviser of Pym, Hampden, and the other active spirits in the lower. In the attempt made by the king to draw off some of the leaders, Lord Kimbolton was designed to be keeper of the Privy Seal

---

[1] Wood's Athen. Oxon. iii. 665.; State Trials. xi. 297.

after his father's death; but the endeavour failing by the death of the Earl of Bedford, the plans of the opposition were urged on with greater violence and rapidity. The hasty resolution of the king to impeach Lord Kimbolton and the five members, and his unadvised appearance in the House of Commons to seize the latter, led to the most fatal results, and were among the signal causes of the civil war. Lord Kimbolton, on the charge being made by the attorney-general, stood forward, and pressed for immediate inquiry; and on the king's withdrawing the prosecution, the Commons, not satisfied, passed a bill " for clearing the Lord Kimbolton and the five members from the feigned charge;" and impeached Sir. Edward Herbert, the attorney-general, for the part he had taken in the proceeding. When the parliament resorted to arms his lordship accepted a colonelcy in their forces, and was present on October 12, 1642, at the indecisive battle of Edgehill. His father dying on the 7th of the following month, he became Earl of Manchester, and was entrusted with the independent command of a considerable army. He proved his capacity as a soldier by investing the town of Lynn, so that it fell into his hands; and by defeating the Earl of Newcastle's forces in Lincolnshire with great slaughter. In May, 1644, he took the city of Lincoln by storm, and in July, with Cromwell under him, was mainly instrumental in gaining the important victory of Marston Moor. The consequence of this battle was the fall of York. After several further successes, he was in the second battle of Newbury on October 27, where each party claimed the victory: and the king having subsequently been able to relieve Donnington Castle, Cromwell, who was jealous of the earl and disobeyed his commands, took the opportunity of making a complaint to the parliament that he was lukewarm and unfaithful to their interests, and wished to promote a peace with the king. This led to recrimination on the earl's part; but the mutual charges fell to the ground without investigation. The self-denying ordinance soon followed, in consequence of which the earl resigned his command in the following April; and the feelings between the two were anything but friendly. That Cromwell's dislike was not partaken by either house is evident from the Lords passing a complimentary vote in favour of him and the Earls of Essex and Denbigh, acknowledging their faithfulness and industry, and recommending their services for the consideration of parliament. The Lords also chose the earl for their speaker; and at the end of 1645, in the propositions to the king for peace, the parliament named him to be made a marquis.

On October 30, 1646, the Lords and Commons, not being able to agree upon the persons to be named commissioners of the Great Seal, determined to put it into the custody of the Earl of Manchester and William Lenthall, the speakers of the two houses, till they had decided, and limited their power for a week after the end of the then Michaelmas Term. When that period came, the same irresolution existed, and continued for near a year and a half, so that the earl and Lenthall remained keepers till March 15, 1648.

On the question of the king's death the opinion of the House of Lords was set aside; and a few days after the blow had fallen, that body was entirely abolished. Considering the relations that existed between the earl and Cromwell, it seems surprising that the latter, when he became protector, and instituted the " other house, " should have named the earl as one of his peers; a nomination which was of course declined.

When Cromwell was dead, the dismissal of his son Richard, and the restoration of the Long Parliament, seeming to open a prospect of the king's return, the earl concerted with Monk and others the means to effect it. The House of Lords being restored in the Convention Parliament which met on April 25, 1660, he was replaced in his former position as speaker, and on May 5 was added to three other commissioners of the Great Seal; which they continued to hold till the same was defaced on May 28, and the Seal of the kingdom came again into operation under Sir Edward Hyde as lord chancellor. The duty of conveying the Lords' congratulations on his Majesty's safe arrival devolved upon this earl, and his address was eloquent and dignified. He was rewarded with the Garter, and the office of lord chamberlain of the household, in which capacity he died at Whitehall on May 5, 1671.

Lord Clarendon's high character of him must be received with some allowance, influenced as he probably was by the latter phase of the earl's career. In many points, however, it is just. He was gentle and generous, and had a natural reverence and affection for the person of Charles I., upon whom he had attended in Spain when prince. When he saw the arbitrary acts of the government, he joined the popular party in resisting them, and by force of circumstances was led on to take part in the war, with a view of remedying what was wrong. But when he found that the object was likely to be attained without further bloodshed, he became a strenuous advocate for peace, and thus ensured the hostility of Cromwell and his party, whom he suspected of different views. The cruel fate awarded to the king convinced him he was right, and the efforts he made for the restoration of the legitimate monarch were dictated as much by abhorrence of the king's murder as by the conviction that the governments substituted were injurious to the happiness and liberties of the people.

George I. gave his grandson a dukedom in 1719, which has been enjoyed by his descendants till the present time.[1]

---

[1] Clarendon's Rebellion; Whitelocke's Memorials; Noble's Cromwell; Parl. Hist.; Collins's Peerage, ii. 57.

NEWDIGATE, RICHARD.

JUST. U. B. 1654. 1657.   CH. U. B. 1660.

THIS family, which is of extreme antiquity, derived its name from, or perhaps gave its name to the town of Newdigate in Surrey, where its property was situated as early as the reign of King John. A younger branch acquired the lordship of Harefield in Middlesex by marriage in the time of Edward III., and his descendant in the fourth generation was John Newdigate, serjeant at law to Henry VIII.[1] His great-grandson in the reign of Elizabeth exchanged a part of Harefield for the manor of Arbury in Warwickshire, where Chief Justice Sir Edmund Anderson had erected a mansion which thenceforward became the seat of the Newdigates. Sir John Newdigate, the son of this gentleman, married Anne the daughter of Sir Edward Fitton of Gawsworth in Cheshire, Bart., by whom he had, besides three daughters, two sons; John, who left no issue, and Richard, the judge, who thus became inheritor of the estate.

Richard Newdigate was born on September 17, 1602, and after receiving his education at Trinity College, Oxford, under the tutorage of Mr. (afterwards bishop) Skinner, was admitted a member of Gray's Inn.[2] Although he had considerable practice as an advocate in Chancery and on the circuits, none of his arguments in the courts at Westminster appear in the Reports. In 1644, he was engaged by the state with Prynne and Bradshaw in the prosecution of Lord Macguire and others for being concerned in the Irish massacres; but neither he nor Bradshaw are noticed as taking any part in the trial itself. The next occurrence of his name is in 1647, as one of the counsel assigned for the defence of the eleven members against the charges made by General Fairfax

---

[1] See Vol. V. p. 102.   [2] Athen. Oxon. iv. 842.

and the army[1]; which, however, having answered the purpose for which they were brought, were dropped without
trial. These employments, at least the former of them, Mr.
Newdigate probably owed in some measure to his relationship to John Hampden, who was his second cousin, and to
his connection with Oliver Cromwell, whose aunt had married
Hampden's father.

Seven years then elapse without his name being brought
forward; but on Jannary 25, 1554, soon after Cromwell
became protector, he was made a serjeant and sent the Home
spring circuit; and on May 30 he accepted a seat on the
Upper Bench in the place of Robert Nicholas. He is said to
have been one of those lawyers, who, when summoned before
Cromwell and offered judgeships, declined to act under his
commission; but on being answered by the protector, " If
you gentlemen of the long robe will not execute the law, my
red-coats shall," they, dreading such an alternative, consented
to serve. Newdigate soon showed that he would not be subservient to the ruling powers. On the trial of Colonel Halsey and others at York he directed the jury to acquit the
prisoner, saying that though it was high treason to levy war
against the king, no statute declared it to be so for levying
war against the protector. This mode of interpreting the
law was not likely to be satisfactory to Cromwell, and consequently Judge Newdigate was removed from the bench on
May 1, 1655, " for not observing the Protector's pleasure in
all his commands." Godwin gives a somewhat different account. He says that Newdigate and Thorpe, being appointed to try the prisoners in the north, requested Cromwell
not to call on them to discharge an office which they con-
scientiously disapproved; and that thereupon they received
their writs of ease.[2]

---

[1] Whitelocke, 106. 259.; State Trials, iv. 654. 858.

[2] Godwin, iv. 26. 179. 180.; Whitelocke, 591. 625.

By an entry in Burton's Diary (ii. 127.) it appears that Newdigate resumed his practice at the bar, but the date of his restoration to the bench has been generally misrepresented. Because Whitelocke does not mention him again till May 15, 1659, it has been supposed that he was not reappointed till that time; the fact being forgotten that Richard Cromwell had just then been removed from the protectorship, and that the Long Parliament had again seized the government. It thus became necessary to reappoint the judges whose commissions under Richard were of course void; and only one of the four then named by Whitelocke was a new judge, while the other three had probably nothing more than new patents. With respect to Newdigate, it is certain that he was reappointed before Michaelmas term, 1657, for his decisions are recorded in Siderfin's Reports from that date to the restoration of the king; and as these Reports commence with that term, he might have been replaced in his seat a long time before. Indeed, when Cromwell's reinvestiture in the office of Protector took place on the 26th of the previous June, Newdigate attended the ceremony as one of the judges of the Upper Bench.[1] It seems probable, therefore, that Cromwell's displeasure did not last long, and that either from his family connections, or from his anxiety to supply the bench with respectable and independent judges, he allowed but a short time to elapse after Newdigate's removal before he restored him to his place.

On the resignation of Chief Justice Glynne, the parliament advanced Newdigate to the presidency of the Upper Bench on January 17, 1660.[2] Siderfin reports some of the cases that were heard before him as chief justice; and among them is that of Sir Robert Pye and another, who applied for their Habeas Corpus, having been imprisoned some time on sus-

[1] Whitelocke, 678.; 2 Siderfin, 11.; Burton's Diary, ii. 512.
[2] Whitelocke, 629.

picion of treason without prosecution. The court said they could not be denied bail, if the counsel for the commonwealth would not proceed against them, " for it is the birthright of every subject to be tryed according to the law of the land." In direct contradiction to this apparently authentic report, Ludlow relates that Newdigate demanded of the counsel of the commonwealth what they had to say against the Habeas Corpus being granted, and on being answered that they had nothing to say against it, the judge, " though no enemy to monarchy, yet ashamed to see them so unfaithful to their trust, replied, that if they had nothing to say, he had; for that Sir Robert Pye being committed by an order of parliament, an inferior court could not discharge him."[1] A curious instance of the manner in which party prejudice will misrepresent a true narrative!

The Long Parliament being at last dissolved by its own act, preparations were made for the restoration of the monarchy; and the Convention Parliament was summoned for April 25, 1660. Chief Justice Newdigate was returned for Tamworth[2]—a plain proof of the sentiments he entertained, and that he felt that his judicial *status* no longer existed. Having only acted ministerially and never having exhibited any political hostility, no sooner had Charles returned, than a writ was issued to the late chief justice to take upon him in a regular manner the degree of serjeant; and he accordingly went through the accustomed ceremonies, with several others, on June 22, the first day of Trinity Term.[3]

Seventeen years after the restoration, they who had known the serjeant's worth and experienced his lenity, were anxious that he should receive some further honour from the king in recognition of his loyalty. With that view he was introduced to his majesty, who received him in the bedchamber, and

---

[1] 2 Siderfin, 179.; Ludlow, 356.   [2] Parl. Hist. iv. 6.
[3] 1 Siderfin, 3.

"gave him thanks for his kindness to his friends in the worst of times, and in particular to Colonel Halsey." His claims were supported by that gentleman, and by the Duke of Ormond and Lord Grandison; and his great desire was to be restored to the position he had previously filled of chief justice. That office, however, was then occupied by Sir Richard Rainsford, and had already been thrice filled since the restoration. It was evident, therefore, that, as he had been passed over on so many vacancies, the king was not likely, now that he was seventy-five years of age, to appoint him to so important and onerous a position. An Irish viscounty was suggested; but, the serjeant's son objecting, a baronetcy was substituted, which was conferred upon him on July 24, 1677, without fees. The good old man did not long enjoy the dignity, dying on October 14, 1678. He was buried under a splendid monument at Harefield; having repurchased that ancient patrimony of the family.

By his wife Juliana, daughter of Sir Francis Leigh of King's Newman, Warwickshire, and sister of the Earl of Chichester, he had a large family. The male line failed in 1806, by the death of the celebrated Sir Roger Newdigate, the fifth baronet, without issue; but the estates devolved on the representatives of a female descendant, who adopted the family name; and they are now possessed by Charles Newdigate Newdigate, Esq., M.P. for North Warwickshire.[1]

NICHOLAS, ROBERT.

Just. U. B. 1649.　B. E. 1654.　Just. U. B. 1660.

ANTHONY WOOD says that this friend of the commonwealth was of the same family with those two most loyal gen-

---

[1] To this gentleman I am greatly indebted for his kind communication of several details, and particularly for supplying me with the letters of Sir Nicholas Armore to the serjeant's son, describing the interview with the king and the attendant circumstances. Wotton's Baronet. iii. 618.

tlemen, Sir Edward Nicholas, Secretary of State to Charles I.
and Dr. Matthew Nicholas, Dean of St. Paul's, who were
both born at Winterbourn-Earles in Wiltshire.[1] Robert
Nicholas is described of Allcanning in that county in his admission to the Inner Temple on July 25, 1614. In 1640,
he was elected member of the Long Parliament for the
neighbouring borough of Devizes, and was an active mana-
ger of the impeachment against Archbishop Laud. He
treated the archbishop with most unseemly virulence and
insult, using such foul and gross language, and calling him
among other opprobrious names, "Pandar to the whore of
Babylon," that the archbishop desired the Lords, "if his
crimes were such as he might not be used like an archbishop,
yet that he might be used like a Christian;" and they accordingly checked the member in his harangue.[2] He gave another specimen of his harshness and intolerance in 1648 by
starting up, when a member objected to Lord Goring being
included among the delinquents, and saying, "What, Mr.
Speaker, shall we spare the man who raised a second war
more dangerous than the first and cudgelled us into a
treaty?"[3] Although his motion was negatived, the Commons showed their liking to the man by making him a serjeant at law on October 30, 1648; and they very appropri-
ately appointed him one of their assistants on the king's
trial.[4] But though his name is included in the act as one of
the king's judges, he appears to have abstained from attending at the trial.[5]

On June 1, 1649, he accepted the office of judge of the
Upper Bench, and in April of the following year he and Chief
Justice Rolle were much commended by the Commons for
settling the people's minds to the government by their charges

---

[1] Athen. Oxon. iii. 129. [2] State Trials, iv. 525, &c.
[3] Parl. Hist. iv. 1068. [4] Whitelocke, 346. 366. [5] State Trials, iv. 1052.

to the grand jury on the western circuit.[1]   When Oliver
Cromwell assumed the protectorate, Nicholas was removed
from the Upper Bench into the Exchequer, and was sworn a
baron in Hilary Term, 1653–4; an appointment which he still
held on the succession of Protector Richard in September,
1658, when he was resworn.[2]   His next change was made by
the Rump Parliament, who restored him to his former place
on the Upper Bench on January 17, 1659-60.[3]

There is no account of him after the return of King
Charles, and it is most probable that he was permitted
quietly to take advantage of the act of Indemnity.[4]   Being
of the Rump Parliament he was omitted from those serjeants
who were confirmed in their degree.

PARKER, JOHN.
B. E. 1655.

JOHN PARKER, in his admission to the society of Gray's
Inn on March 13, 1611, is described of Weylond Underwood
in Buckinghamshire.   He was called to the bar on June 26,
1617, became an ancient in 1638, a bencher in 1640, and in
autumn, 1642, arrived at the post of reader.

In March, 1647, he was appointed a judge of one of the
Welsh circuits; and in the next year was sent by the Commons with others to try the rioters in that country.   The
parliament included him in the serjeants they made on October 30, 1648; and on the death of the king confirmed him in
his office of Welsh judge.   On July 18 of the same year a
Mr. Parker had a patent with Mr. Oldsworth as Registrar of
the Prerogative Court; but whether it was the serjeant is
uncertain.   He was sent on the summer circuit of 1653,
either as a serjeant or a judge; for there is some doubt as to
the precise date of his being placed on the bench of the Exchequer; Hardres' Reports, which record his judgments as a

---

[1] Whitelocke, 405. 448.   [2] Exchequer Books.   [3] Whitelocke, 693.

baron, not commencing till Trinity Term, 1655. He was most probably appointed on the removal of Baron Thorpe in May, 1655, and he kept his seat till the Restoration, through all the changes occasioned by the accession of the Protector Richard and the return of the Long Parliament. In the parliaments of 1654 and 1656 he represented Rochester; and when Cromwell composed an upper house, he with the other judges was summoned as an assistant.[1]

Anthony Wood says that he was one of the assistant-committee men in Northamptonshire; that he was of the high court of justice which tried Lord Capell, the Earl of Holland, and the Duke of Hamilton, in 1649; that in the next year he published a remarkable book, called " The Government of the People of England, precedent and present," &c. ; and that on June 22, 1655, he was sworn serjeant at law, being a member of the Temple. The learned author seems, however, to have confounded two individuals; for besides the difference of the inn of court, it appears manifest that the John Parker who, according to Whitelocke, was made a serjeant in 1648, was the same man who by Hardres' Reports is proved to have been a baron in 1655.

At the Restoration he of course was removed from his place; but, instead of being subjected to any inquiry into his previous conduct, he was by a writ dated July 4, 1660, summoned to take the degree of serjeant at law: Anthony Wood says, " by the endeavours of Lord Chancellor Hyde." The same author describes him as father of Dr. Samuel Parker, made Bishop of Oxford by James II., and placed by that king as president of Magdalen College in opposition to the lawful elevation of Dr. Hough.[2]

---

[1] Godwin, ii. 235., iii. 527.; Whitelocke, 305. 346. 386. 414. 678. 693.; Hardres' Reports; Parl. Hist. iii. 1430. 1480. 1519. Noble, in his House of Cromwell, i. 433, mistakingly calls him Lord Chief Justice and Lord Chief Baron.

[2] Athen. Oxon. iv. 225.; 1 Siderfin, 4.; Dugdale's Chron. Ser.

PEPYS, RICHARD.

B. E. 1654.

IN the family of Pepys is illustrated every gradation of legal rank, from reader of an inn of court to lord high chancellor of England. The first who attained judicial honours was Richard Pepys, the son of John Pepys of Cottenham in Cambridgeshire, and the nephew of Talbot Pepys, who was a reader at the Middle Temple in 1623. His mother was Elizabeth, daughter of John Bendish of Steeple Bumpstead, in Essex. He was the second son, and, choosing the law for his profession, he studied at the Middle Temple. There he arrived at the post of reader in autumn, 1640, and was elected treasurer of the society in 1643. Beyond the notice of his name as a barrister in Style's Reports, there is no other trace of him till January, 1654, when he was called serjeant; immediately after which, he was named on the commission for the spring circuit through the midland counties; and on the 30th of the following May, he was made a baron of the Exchequer.[1]

Within a year, he was removed to the chief justiceship of the Upper Bench in Ireland; for though the date of his patent is not given, it appears that on the 14th of June, 1655, he was placed in that character as chief commissioner of the Great Seal of that country. He was relieved from this extra duty on August 20, 1656, by the nomination of William Steele, chief baron of the English Exchequer, to be lord chancellor of Ireland. Chief Justice Pepys, at the time of his death, in January, 1658, was the sole judge of his court; and it is much to his credit that in times like those in which he flourished, no touch of calumny sullies his name.[2]

The grandson of Richard, the judge's eldest son, was the

---

[1] Dugdale's Orig. 220. 222.; Godwin, iv. 26. 179.; Whitelocke, 591.
[2] Law Officers of Ireland, 31. 90.

father of two baronets; Sir Lucas Pepys, physician to George III., created in 1784; and Sir William Weller Pepys, a master in Chancery, created in 1801. The latter title, on the death of Sir William's eldest son without issue, devolved, in 1845, on his second son Charles Christopher, who, after filling the office of master of the Rolls, had been already elevated to the rank of lord chancellor of England, and raised to the peerage by the title of Baron Cottenham, to which Queen Victoria, in 1850, added an earldom of the same place.

Notwithstanding all these honours attaching to the family, the name of Pepys will be longer remembered through the literary reputation of Samuel Pepys, the fourth son of the chief justice, who was secretary of the Admiralty in the reigns of Charles II. and James II.

PHESANT, PETER.

Just. C. P. 1649.

See under the Reign of Charles I.

THE family of Phesant was established at Tottenham in Middlesex, and a daughter of Jasper Phesant of that place married Sir Stephen Slaney, lord mayor of London in 1595.[1] Jasper was probably the brother of Peter Phesant of Bletchworth in the county of Lincoln, an eminent lawyer and reader of Gray's Inn in 1582, and Queen Elizabeth's attorney "in partibus borealibus;" whose son and heir was Peter Phesant the judge.[2]

Following his father's steps, he was entered at Gray's Inn in 1602, became a barrister in 1608, and was chosen reader there in 1624. In May, 1640, he was honoured with the degree of the coif[3]; and, having been one of the common pleaders of the city of London, was elected recorder on May 2, 1643,

---

[1] Oldfield's Tottenham, 81.; Burke's Landed Gentry, 1246.
[2] Grandeur of the Law, (1684) 195.   [3] Gray's Inn Books; Dugdale.

on the removal of Sir Thomas Gardner, the solicitor-general, who was impeached by the Commons. Phesant, however, resigned the office on the 30th of the same month, on the plea of ill health [1], but probably in order to make room for John Glynne, the favourite of the parliament. Under the same plea, he had in the previous year excused himself from appearing in defence of Sir Edward Herbert, the attorney-general, on his impeachment.[2]

In February, 1643, the parliament proposed him to the king as one of the judges of the Common Pleas[3]; and, on their assumption of the government, voted him into that place on September 30, 1645.[4] Soon after he took a house in Boswell Court belonging to Sir John Bramston, late chief justice.[5] On the king's death, in January, 1649, he consented to act in his judicial capacity under " the keepers of the liberties of England ; " but in the following June he was allowed to stay at home from the circuit, " being sickly ; "[6] and dying three months after, on October 1, 1649, at Upwood in Huntingdonshire, a manor formerly belonging to the Cromwells, which he had purchased, he was buried in the church there. The inscription on his monument describes him as having been twice the only judge of his court. By his wife Mary, of the family of Bruges, of Gloucestershire, who was buried with him, he had several children.[7]

PULESTON, JOHN.

Just. C. P. 1649.

THE family of this judge is a very ancient one settled at Emral in Flintshire, as early as the reign of Edward I. John Puleston was the son of Richard Puleston, of the elder

---

[1] City List of Recorders. [2] Parl. Hist. ii. 1125. 1127.
[3] Clarendon, iii. 407. [4] Whitelocke, 174.
[5] Autobiog. of Bramston, 39. [6] Whitelocke, 378. 409.
[7] Hatfield's Hunts. (1854); Inscription in Upwood church.

branch, by Alice, daughter of David Lewis of Bulcot in Oxfordshire; and received his legal education at the Middle Temple, where he became autumn reader in 1634.[1] In February, 1643, he was recommended by the Commons as a baron of the Exchequer in the propositions they made to the king.[2] Failing in this application, they invested him with the dignity of the coif in October, 1648; and, after the king was beheaded, he was substituted for one of the judges who then refused to act, and took his place as justice of the Common Pleas on June 1, 1649.[3] His conduct in the following August at the assizes at York, when he and Baron Thorpe tried and condemned Lieut.-Colonel Morrice, the governor of Pomfret Castle, for high treason, speaks strongly against his justice and humanity.[4]

The want of Reports of the Common Pleas during this period renders it impossible to state with certainty how long Puleston sat as judge. From the state of the court it seems probable, though he did not die till September 5, 1659, that Cromwell, when he became protector in 1653, did not renew his patent; for then, by the appointment of Sir Matthew Hale, the court had its full complement.

The judge, by his marriage with Elizabeth, daughter of Sir John Woolrych, knight, had a son, the last of whose male descendants died, leaving an only daughter, who carried the estate of Emral to her husband, Richard Price, Esq. Their son took the name of Puleston, and was created a baronet in 1813.

RIGBY, ALEXANDER.

PARL. B. E. 1649.

" THAT Colonel Rigby be a Baron of the Exchequer," is the curious combination in the entry on June 1, 1649, of

---

[1] Dugdale's Orig. 220.　　　　　[2] Clarendon, iii. 407.
[3] Whitelocke, 342, 405.　　　　　[4] State Trials, iv. 1249.

Whitelocke's Memorials.[1] It appears, however, that he was bred a lawyer, and took up arms on behalf of the Parliament at the earliest stage of the troubles. He was of a Lancashire family seated at Middleton[2], and was elected member for Wigan in that county in the Long Parliament, which commenced its sittings in 1640. There he distinguished himself by moving, in a violent speech, plentifully interspersed with scraps of Latin and Biblical quotations, that Lord Keeper Finch should be accused of high treason.[3] Made a colonel by the Parliament, and entrusted with the command of the Lancashire forces, his first exploit was routing a party of the king's near Thurland Castle in 1643, and taking 400 prisoners and their commander-in-chief; which, says Whitelocke, " was the more discoursed of because Rigby was a lawyer." His next service is in the lengthened siege of Latham House, just before the battle of Marston Moor[4]; and immediately after he was appointed one of the commissioners for executing martial law. In the " Mystery of the Good Old Cause," he is said to have been governor of Boston.[5]

When the death of the king rendered the military assistance of Colonel Rigby no longer necessary, the Parliament determined to try his legal ability, and raised him to the bench on June 1, 1649, as a baron of the Exchequer[6], first in due form investing him with the coif. He retained his judicial dignity little more than a year, dying on August 18, 1650, of an infection taken at Croydon on the circuit, which was equally fatal to his learned colleague, Baron Gates, and to the sheriff of the county.[7]

He married Margaret, daughter of Sir Gilbert Hoghton, and had a large family.[8] The Alexander Rigby who was member for Lancashire in 1658-9, was probably his son.

---

[1] Whitelocke, 405.

[2] Wotton's Baronet. i. 152.

[3] Parl. Hist. ii. 611. 692.

[4] Whitelocke, 77. 93.

[5] Parl. Hist. iii. 286. 1607.

[6] Whitelocke, 405.

[7] Peck's Desid. Cur. B. xiv. p. 23.

[8] Wotton's Baronet. i. 20.

ROLLE, HENRY,

PARL. CH. U. B. 1649.

See under the Reign of Charles I.

THE founder of the opulent family of Rolle was a merchant in London, who acquired a large fortune in the reign of ·Henry VIII., and settled himself at Stevenstone in Devonshire, which, with other manors in that and the neighbouring counties, he acquired by purchase. To a descendant of his second son, George, the barony of Rolle of Stevenstone was granted by King George II. in 1748, but the first holder dying unmarried in 1759, it was regranted in 1796 to his nephew, on whose death without issue in 1839, the title again became extinct. The judge was the grandson of the merchant's fourth son, Henry, whose eldest son, Robert, married Joan, the daughter of Thomas Hele of Fleet in the same county, and left four sons, the second of whom is the subject of this memoir.

Henry Rolle was born at Heanton-Sachevil in Devonshire, about the year 1589, and at the age of seventeen was sent to Exeter College, Oxford, and from thence to the Inner Temple, where he was admitted a member on February 1, 1608–9. After serving the usual septennial period as a student he was called to the bar, and, practising in the King's Bench, his name is of frequent occurrence in the Reports after Michaelmas Term, 1629. An inference is not therefore to be drawn that he had before been unemployed in his profession, the leading cases only being given, and the arguments of the juniors being frequently omitted by the reporters. Mr. Rolle had used his time well in reporting the cases of James's reign, which were published after his death, and are still in considerable repute. That he had acquired too some eminence at an earlier period is manifest from his being selected as member of the last parliament of James I., representing Kellington, and of the first three parliaments of Charles I., in which he represented Truro. He took the popular side from the commencement of his political career: in the first parliament of Charles 'urging a redress of griev- ances; and in the second arguing in the case of the Duke of Buckingham that common fame was a sufficient ground for accusation.[1]

He subsequently devoted himself wholly to his profession, and was fully engaged in the courts. Four times appointed reader of his inn, he was prevented by the prevailing plague from performing the duties of that office till the last occasion in Lent, 1639; but during his leisure he employed himself in compiling that " Abridgment of Cases and Resolutions of the Law," which has been held up by some of the ablest lawyers as an example to be followed for its perspicuity and method. In May, 1640, he was made a serjeant-at-law.[2]

He contributed 100l. in 1642 for the defence of the parlia- ment against the king[3], and siding with the Puritans he took the covenant, and was in such esteem that he was recom- mended as a judge of the King's Bench on the propositions for peace which the two houses made to the king on February 1, 1642–3.[4] After they had assumed the govern- ment, one of their first legal appointments was of Mr. Ser- jeant Rolle to that office. The vote passed on September 30, 1645, and on October 28 he was sworn in. He filled this seat for three years, when on October 12, 1648, the Commons voted him to be chief justice of the same court, to which, after some demur, the Lords assented, and he took his seat on November 14. The king's decapitation soon followed, and Rolle was one of the six judges who accepted a renewal of their commission, on the condition that they should proceed

---

[1] Parl. Hist. ii. 35. 55.   [2] Dugdale's Orig. 168.; Chron. Ser.
[3] Notes and Queries, 1st Ser. xii. 358.   [4] Clarendon, iii. 407.

according to the fundamental laws of the kingdom. He was also nominated a member of the Council of State for that year, and again for the two subsequent years; and, in his charges to the grand jury on his different circuits, he endeavoured to settle the people's minds in regard to the existing government. When Cromwell was made protector, the chief justice was appointed in .1654 one of the commissioners of the Exchequer.[1]

In that year, being surprised at Salisbury by the party of royalists who had seized the town, he narrowly escaped being hanged, but was permitted to depart with the loss of his commission of assize. His refusal to assist in trying the deliuquents when taken, on the ground of his being a party concerned, offended Cromwell, who soon found further cause to be dissatisfied with his chief justice, as too honest a man to be relied upon in the impositions he attempted to raise without the consent of parliament. One Cony having refused to pay the customs charged on him, and being committed by Cromwell to prison, applied for his Habeas Corpus. His counsel were arbitrarily sent to the Tower for advocating his cause; and he was obliged to plead for himself. This he did so stoutly and with so much reason that the chief justice, afraid of resisting the ruling powers, yet too conscientious to give judgment against Cony, delayed his decision till the next term. In the meantime, fearing that this was only the beginning of similar illegal measures, he applied to the protector for his quietus, which was willingly granted on June 7, 1655; and Serjeant Glynne was put in his place.[2] Sir Matthew Hale, who edited his " Abridgment," in the preface to that work speaks in the highest terms of his character as a judge; enlarging on his great learning and experience, his profound judgment, his great moderation, justice, and integrity, his

[1] Whitelocke, 174. 342, 343. 378. 381. 448. 597.; Style's Rep. 140.
[2] Clarendon. vii. 144. 294. ; Godwin's Commonwealth, iv. 179.

patience in hearing and his readiness and despatch in deciding; and even royalists allowed his honesty on the judicial seat.

He survived his retirement little more than a year, and died on July 30, 1656. He was buried in the church of Shapwich, near Glastonbury, in Somersetshire, where he had a mansion.

His son Sir Francis Rolle of Tuderley in Hampshire represented that county in the parliament summoned to meet at Oxford in 1681; but the family of the chief justice failed in two other generations, his great-grandsons dying without issue, and leaving the estates to the father of the first Lord Rolle.[1]

ST. JOHN, OLIVER.

Ch. C. P. 1649.

See under the Reign of Charles I.

From the noble family of St. John of Stanton in Oxfordshire, a baron of which has been mentioned as a justice-itinerant in the reign of Henry III.[2], a direct descendant was created by Queen Elizabeth, Lord St. John of Bletsoe. His grandson was advanced in the peerage by James I., with the title of Earl of Bolingbroke, and was a commissioner of the Great Seal in the last reign.[3] Oliver, settled at Cayshoe in Bedfordshire, another grandson through Thomas, a younger son of the first Lord, was the father of the chief justice, by his wife Sarah, daughter of Edward Buckley, Esq., of Odell in the same county.[4] Clarendon calls him "a natural son of the house of Bullingbroke,"[5] and the writer of " The Mystery of the Good Old Cause " says, that his father " was supposed to be a bye-blow of one of the Earls of Bedford."[6] The

. [1] Wood's Athen. Oxon. iii. 416.; Collins's Peerage, viii. 519.
[2] See Vol. II. p. 462. [3] Vid. antè, p. 363. [4] Wotton's Baronet. iv. 178.
[5] Clarendon's Hist. i. 325. [6] In Parl. Hist. iii. 1600.

unpopularity of the man, and the circumstances of the times, will sufficiently account for these reports; but the above is the pedigree given by an unprejudiced genealogist, and confirmed by the description in his admission as a member of Lincoln's Inn.

Oliver St. John was born about the year 1598, and was educated in the university of Cambridge, being admitted a pensioner of Queen's College on August 16, 1615, under the tuition of Mr. Preston, afterwards master of Emmanuel.[1] He was then seventeen years of age, and Lord Campbell " supposes " that he had already " taken a trip to Holland," and by " seeing with his own eyes the respect for property, as well as personal liberty, ... he was first imbued with a taste for a republican form of government." His Lordship accordingly fathers upon him the " Letter to the Mayor of Marlborough " against a Benevolence then in collection, which was made the subject of prosecution in the Star Chamber in April of that very year.[2] To have formed such decided opinions, with reasons so clearly stated, and statutes and authorities so precisely quoted, as are found in the letter in question, would be an instance of most remarkable precocity in any youth who had not even commenced his college studies. But the statement will not bear the slightest investigation. There is absolutely nothing in the whole proceeding to lead to a suspicion that the writer of the letter could have been " a mere stripling ; " but, on the contrary, it is manifest from the letter itself, and from Bacon's well-prepared speech, who would scarcely have wasted his eloquence on a boy, that he was " a principal person, and a dweller in that town," and " a *man* likely to give both money and good example." [3] Instead of

---

[1] I am indebted for this and several other facts in this sketch to the kindness of William Durrant Cooper, Esq., F.S.A. The Queen's College Register, quoted in Baker's MS. xxv. 401—413, proves A. Wood's statement, that St. John was of Catherine Hall, to be erroneous.

[2] Lord Campbell's Ch. Justices, i. 450.   [3] State Trials, ii. 899.

the youth who was quietly preparing for his academical course, the person so described was Oliver St. John of Lydiard-Tregoze, a seat not far distant from Marlborough, who afterwards became Viscount Grandison and Lieutenant of Ireland.[1]

From the university our student proceeded to Lincoln's Inn, where he was admitted on April 22, 1619, and called to the bar on June 22, 1626. His name does not occur as an advocate in the Reports; but he received early employment in the law business of the Earl of Bedford, to whom he was distantly related. In consequence of this connection he was really brought before the Star Chamber in 1630; both he and the earl, with Selden, Sir Robert Cotton, and some others, being charged with publishing " A proposition for his Majesty's service to bridle the Impertinence of Parliaments; "— a piece of irony which was proved to be written by Sir Robert Dudley at Florence in the reign of James I. The government was glad to withdraw from this absurd prosecution, by availing itself of the birth of the king's son as a plea for extending mercy to the defendants.[2] They were consequently discharged; but Clarendon says, that St. John never forgave the court this "*first* assault." [3] This feeling of bitterness was no doubt increased by his study being searched, and his papers seized in 1637, in consequence of being suspected of having drawn the answer of Burton to the information filed against him in the Star Chamber for a libellous publication.[4]

About 1629 he had married his first wife, Johanna, sole child of Sir James Altham of Mark's Hall, Latton, Essex, the nephew of the baron of the Exchequer of that name.[5] The mother of this lady was Elizabeth, daughter of Sir Francis Barrington, by Joan, one of the daughters of Sir Henry Cromwell of Hinchinbroke, and aunt both to Oliver Cromwell the protector, and John Hampden the patriot.

---

[1] Harris's Lives, i. 236.　　　　　　　　[2] State Trials, iii. 387.
[3] Clarendon's Hist. i. 325.　[4] Harris's Lives, ii. 267.　[5] Vide antè, p. 49.

Bound thus more intimately to that party, who were dissatisfied with the unconstitutional measures of the court, this
connection made St. John the natural adviser of Hampden
in the celebrated resistance to the payment of ship-money.
His argument against the legality of that imposition was so
learned and so powerful, that not only was he complimented
at the time by the Solicitor-General Lyttelton [1], but, although
he had previously had little practice in Westminster Hall, he
acquired so much reputation, that "he was called into all
courts and to all causes where the king's prerogative was most
contested." [2]   The decision of the majority of judges was pronounced in June, 1638; and the consequences that ensued in
the Long Parliament have been already detailed.   His first
wife having died in childbed, he, on January 21, 1638,
strengthened the tie with the Cromwells by marrying Elizabeth, the first cousin of Oliver, and daughter of Henry Cromwell of Upwood. [3]

When the king, after a cessation of eleven years, was obliged
to call a parliament in April, 1640, St. John, whose notoriety ensured him a seat, made his first appearance in that
assembly as member for Totness. [4]   In the short period of
three weeks during which this parliament lasted, though he
does not appear to have put himself forward as a speaker, the
Journals show that he was named on all the committees connected with popular grievances, and that he was charged to
speak on one of them in the conferences with the Lords.
Finding that redress was insisted on before supplies would be
granted, the king dissolved the parliament, to the disappointment of the moderate, but to the joy of the extreme, party.
Clarendon relates, that within an hour after the dissolution
he met St. John, "who had naturally a great cloud on his

1 Rushworth, ii. 481.   2 Clarendon's Hist. i. 324.
3 Registry of Marriages in High Laver, Bucks.   4 Wood's Fasti Oxon. 453.

face, and very seldom was known to smile, but had then a most cheerful aspect;" and that after lamenting what had taken place, St. John answered him with a little warmth, "That it was well; but that it must be worse before it could be better; and that this parliament could never have done what was necessary to be done." [1]

In the new parliament, which met in the following November, St. John again represented Totness, and was immediately appointed on several committees, and chairman of that with regard to ship-money. On December 7 he brought up its reports, on which were founded the memorable resolutions, that not only the impost itself, but all the proceedings to enforce it, and the decision of the judges, were against law. These resolutions were adopted by the House of Lords, after hearing a luminous address from St. John, which is also remarkable for vindictive sternness towards the judges.[2] On January 29, 1640–1, within a fortnight after this speech was delivered, St. John was constituted solicitor-general[3], on the change occasioned by the flight of Lord Keeper Finch. He was thereupon called to the bench of Lincoln's Inn, and in the following year was elected treasurer of that society.[4]

St. Johu's promotion arose from a desire to gain over some of the popular party; among whom various places were to be distributed. The Earl of Bedford entered into the plan, and was to be treasurer, and Pym and others were to accept situations of trust. The king readily consented to St. John's appointment, " hoping that he would have been very useful in the House of Commons, where his authority was then great; at least that he would be ashamed ever to appear in anything that might prove prejudicial to the crown." But the Earl of Bedford's death three months after, and other circumstances, stopping these negotiations, the king found himself with a

---

[1] Clarendon's Hist. i. 246.   [2] State Trials, iii. 1262.
[3] Rymer, 20. 449.   [4] Black Book, Linc. Inn.

solicitor-general neither abating nor dissembling his enmity to the court, and who still retained the confidence of his party.[1]

The king soon had reason to see how much he had been mistaken in his expectations. The accusation of the Earl of Strafford by the Commons had been made in the previous November, but the trial did not begin till the 22nd of March; and St. John, though he was the king's officer, and well knew his royal master's anxiety to save the earl, used his utmost efforts to urge on the proceedings, and even dissuaded the Commons from hearing the argument of the earl's counsel on the matter of law. When the Commons found that the offences alleged against Strafford could not be touched by the existing laws, and that he was likely to be acquitted by the Lords, they brought in a bill of attainder, in the promotion of which unjustifiable course St. John was a prominent actor[2]; and in its support addressed the Lords in a speech betraying so much sophistry, brutality, and malice[3], as fully to justify Clarendon's condemnation of it[4], and the disgust of all unprejudiced men.

In all the violent measures that succeeded,—the bill for the continuance of the parliament, the bill against the bishops, the militia bill, &c.,—St. John took the same adversely active part. The king, naturally desirous of releasing himself from his obnoxious officer, offered the place to Hyde; but he prudently declined it, and dissuaded the king from removing St. John at that time, though agreeing that he might have filled it with a better man when the place was actually void.[5] But soon after, the breach with the Commons becoming complete, and no hope remaining of any alteration in St. John's conduct, the king revoked his appointment on October 30, 1643, and put Sir Thomas Gardner in his place.[6] The parliament, however,

[1] Clarendon's Hist. i. 370.   [2] Verney's Notes (Camd. Soc.), 49. 55.
[3] Rushworth, iv. 675.   [4] Clarendon's Hist. i. 407.
[5] Clarendon's Life, i. 100.   [6] Dugdale's Chron. Ser.

refused to recognise the new solicitor; and on providing a Great Seal for themselves, in lieu of that which had been taken to the king by Lord Lyttelton, and appointing on November 10 two Lords and four of the Commons for its custody, they named St. John as the first of the latter, with the title of "his Majesty's Solicitor-General;" and by this designation he was distinguished until he became chief justice. Whitelocke's statement, that in May, 1644, he was assigned to be attorney-general, is evidently a mistaken account of an ordinance of the Commons, enabling him to do all acts as effectually as the attorney-general, if present, might have done.[1]

St. John was one of the commissioners to treat for a peace at Uxbridge in January 1645, but, as neither party was sincere, the negotiation failed. In April of that year the self-denying ordinance, by which St. John and the other commissioners of the Great Seal would have been disqualified, was passed by both the houses: but before the forty days limited by it had expired, the parliament voted their continuance in office till the end of the following term: and this vote was repeated from time to time till October 30, 1646, when they delivered up the Seal to the speakers of the two houses, who were nominated its keepers.[2] St. John had, in the previous February, joined in the vote abolishing the Court of Wards; and now resuming his functions as solicitor-general, he was ordered to prosecute Judge Jenkins for exercising his judicial duties in defiance of the parliament. But before that sturdy royalist was brought to trial, the Commons had determined to fill up the vacancies on the bench. They accordingly appointed St. John chief justice of the Common Pleas on October 12, 1648, and, the Lords having concurred, he was sworn in on November 22.[3]

It was not then the custom, any more than it is now, for

---

[1] Journals; Whitelocke, 71. 88.   [2] Ibid. 124. 226.; Journals.
[3] Whitelocke, 194. 255. 342—356.

the judges to sit in the House of Commons.   St. John, therefore, on his elevation to the bench, though his seat for Totness
was not vacated, abstained from attending parliament, and
took no part in the tragic debates of the next two months,
which brought his sovereign to the block : and he asserts, in
the case which he published in 1660 [1], that so far from being
one of the advisers of the sanguinary proceedings, he was not
even consulted ; but " upon all occasions manifested his dislike and dissatisfaction."   In this he is confirmed by Thurloe,
who acted then as his secretary ; and by the vote which the
Commons passed when the Peers rejected the ordinance, that
the Lords, and the chief judges of each court, whom they
had named, should be left out of the commission for the trial.
But his denial that he favoured the alteration of the government to a commonwealth, and his assertion that he was ever
for King, Lords, and Commons, require more credit than
can be easily given to a man who had accepted a high judicial office from the opponents of the monarchy, and who,
within eight days after they had murdered their king, and
after their vote that the office of king was "unnecessary,"
and the House of Peers was " useless and dangerous," and that
both " ought to be abolished," consented, not only to remain
as a judge under the usurping government, but to be a member of its Council of State.   That he acted on that council
and was trusted by it, is apparent from his being one of the
committee in 1650 to confer with General Fairfax as to the
invasion of Scotland ; a conference which led to the appointment of Cromwell to be lord-general of the army.[2]

In March, 1551, he and Mr. Strickland were sent ambas-

---

[1] " Case of Oliver St. John ; " addressed by him to the House of Commons.
This curious pamphlet, which is very scarce, was lent to me by my liberal
friend William Durrant Cooper, who has since presented it to the Library of
the British Museum for historical reference.   I have adverted to all St. John's
material points of defence.

[2] Whitelocke, 366 377, 378. 381. 441. 460. 462.

sadors to the Dutch.   St. John says it was against his will;
but the assassination of Dorislaus, the former ambassador, and
the "losse of a good part of the profits of his place as judge
during his absence," seem to have been the only grounds of
his unwillingness.   It is curious that in speaking of this
embassy Clarendon calls him "the known confident of Cromwell," and Whitelocke designates him "Cromwell's creature;"
an agreement between writers of opposite parties, which goes
far to show the general impression at the time, and to warrant
the nickname he received of "The Dark Lanthorn," notwithstanding his denial of its justice.   In June he returned without having concluded the treaty he went to negotiate.   His
residence at the Hague was not unattended with danger.   He
was treated with indignity by the people, and with something
like indifference by the States; he received a gross insult
from Prince Edward, the Palgrave's brother; he was engaged
in a personal quarrel with the Duke of York, the details of
which do not tell to his credit; and he narrowly escaped an
attempt upon his life, similar to that lately practised by the
Thugs in India.   The parliament, indignant at the slight
endeavours made to punish the delinquents, and at the trifling
impediments that were every day thrown in the way of completing the treaty, recalled the ambassadors.   On their return
St. John took his seat in the House of Commons, and after
giving a detailed account of all their proceedings, they received thanks for their faithful services.[1]

A resolution, that the several judges who were members
should be discharged from their attendance in the house
whilst they executed their offices, which was passed in
October, 1649, was rescinded on June 27, 1651, no doubt
for the purpose of enabling St. John to resume his seat, and
make his diplomatic report on July 2.   From that time he

[1] Whitelocke, 487. 491, 492. 494. 496.; Parl. Hist. iii. 136ʔ

continued his attendance, and to his indignation at the treatment he received in Holland, and the failure of the negotiation, is to be attributed the adoption in the next month of the ordinance, upon which was founded the Navigation Act passed at the Restoration, prohibiting foreign ships from bringing any merchandise or commodities into England but such as were the proceeds and growth of their own country: an ordinance which was much more injurious to the Dutch, wholly suppressing their carrying trade, than to any other nation.[1] In September he was one of the four who were sent to compliment Cromwell on his victory at Worcester; and in October he was appointed a commissioner for the affairs of Scotland. In November he was re-elected on the Council of State, and was named by the committee for the reformation of the universities, chancellor of Cambridge, in the place of Edward Montagu, Earl of Manchester.

At the meeting called by Cromwell on the 10th of December to consider what was fit to be done for the settlement of the nation, in which the general agreed with Whitelocke that the question was whether a republic or a mixed monarchical government were the best, and gave his opinion that the latter would be most effectual, St. John declared that " the government, without something of monarchical power, would be very difficult to be so settled, as not to shake the foundation of our laws and the liberties of the people."[2]   Here is nothing to show that he was then opposed to Cromwell, who was feeling his way towards attaining that power which he afterwards assumed, and who, as soon as he found that some of the party suggested the selection of one of the late king's sons, put an end to the debate. On the 14th of the previous month St. John had been teller with Cromwell of the majority of two, which voted that a time should be declared beyond

---

[1] Journals; Clarendon's Hist. vi. 599.   [2] Whitelocke, 516.

which the parliament should not sit, which limit was on a subsequent day fixed for November 3, 1654.[1]

He then went to Scotland, where he was actively engaged with his colleagues in arranging the intended union with that country. After his return on May 6, 1652, he was ill for some time; but, in April, 1653, though it does not appear that he was a party to the violent mode adopted by Cromwell of dismissing the parliament, he strongly supported the general's determination to put an immediate period to its sittings[2]. Cromwell, however, did not summon him to the convention (called Barebone's Parliament) which met on July 4, and dissolved itself on the 12th of the following December, resigning its power to the lord general, who, four days after, was declared lord protector of the commonwealth of the three kingdoms. St. John alleges that he had nothing to do with this elevation of Cromwell, falling dangerously ill in the previous October, and not recovering till the May after the event; and so far from approving it, Thurloe testifies that he expressed himself strongly against it. In further proof of his dislike, he says that, though Cromwell named him on his council and appointed him a commissioner of the treasury[3], he never attended in either capacity, nor received any salary.

According to St. John's account, the cordiality between him and Cromwell had cooled since the latter had assumed arbitrary power, and their intercourse was limited to formal visits before or after the terms. But when the parliament of 1657 presented their "Humble Petition and Advice" to the protector, pressing him to take the title of king, St. John is found as one of the committee that waited upon him, and as a speaker contending against his scruples.[4] Cromwell's refusal to comply with this request led to a new arrangement of the government, by which he was confirmed as Lord Pro-

---

[1] Parl. Hist. iii. 1375.   [2] Whitelocke, 517, 532, 554.
[3] Ibid. 559, 571, 597.   [4] Parl. Hist. iii. 1498.

tector, with the additional power of naming his successor, and of calling not more than seventy nor less than forty persons to sit in what was designated "the other house." In the exercise of this power St. John was one of the *quasi* peers whom he selected. They had not, however, a long enjoyment of their honours, for within a fortnight after the parliament met the Commons showed so much hesitation in acknowledging this upper chamber, that Cromwell dissolved the parliament on February 4, 1658. Within seven. months after this Cromwell died, and his son Richard, who was immediately proclaimed his successor, continued St. John as chief justice, and summoned another parliament on January 27, 1659. This parliament did not last three months[1], during which the Commons were principally occupied in debates as to their intercourse with the "other house," manifesting all their former jealousy. St. John states that he never would sit as a peer; but it would seem that he had no great opportunity of doing so, for in the very limited period that either parliament sat after the first nomination of the new peers, little is recorded of their proceedings.

In the following month (May) the army recalled the remains of that parliament which Oliver Cromwell had expelled in 1653, and St. John not only took his place in it, but was named one of the council of state. The old government, "without a single person, kingship, or House of Peers," having been re-established, St. John and Sir John Pickering waited on Richard Cromwell, and obtained his written acquiescence in this arrangement, by which he was thus deprived of his short-lived dignity. The sittings of the Rump Parliament, as it was called, were violently interrupted in October by the same military power that had called them

---

[1] Whitelocke, 657. 666. 673—677. During the three months of Richard's parliament, it lost two of its speakers, Mr. Challoner Chute and Sir Lillisbone Long, by death.

together, and a Committee of Safety formed. They were again, however, by the aid of Monk, reinstated on December 26.[1]   St. John attended a meeting on February 17, 1659–60, at Monk's quarters, with reference to the members who were secluded in 1648, and was instrumental in restoring them to their places a few days after.[2]   The house dissolved itself on March 16, first passing an act for a new parliament to meet on the 25th of April.   Among the qualifications proposed for the members was an oath abjuring the title of Charles II., which St. John declares that he came out of the country on purpose to oppose; adding, that it was he that made the motion to put a period to the Long Parliament.

At the Restoration, which soon followed, St. John found himself in a difficult position.   His harsh and active proceedings at the commencement of the troubles; the lead he took against the king while holding an office under the crown; the inhumanity of his speech against Strafford; his partisanship in all Cromwell's earlier, if not later, measures; his recent adherence to the principle of a government without a single person, kingship or House of Peers; and even his relationship to the two protectors — setting aside his personal collision with the Duke of York at the Hague — could not but operate prejudicially against him.   In the discussions, therefore, in the House of Commons upon the Act of Indemnity, he was included among those reserved for such pains, penalties, and forfeitures, not extending to life, as by a future act should be imposed.   To counteract this vote he published the case before referred to, which is drawn up with a great deal of art and plausibility, but must be received with an equal degree of caution both as to its statements and its omissions.   With the strenuous aid of Thurloe, who had a grateful remembrance of his early patronage, it had its desired effect upon the Lords, who mitigated the clause against him

[1] Parl. Hist. iii. 1547—1571.   [2] Mercurius Politicus, No.

by the substitution of another (to which the Commons afterwards assented), declaring that if he accepted or exercised any offiee after September 1st (two days subsequent to the royal assent), he should stand as if excepted by name from the benefit of the act. The king, on hearing of his narrow escape, is said to have expressed a wish that he had been added to those excepted.[1]

St. John, after residing for a few years in privacy on his estate at Longthorpe, a hamlet near Peterborough, which he purchased about 1653, and where he had erected an elegant mansion under the direction of Webb, a nephew and pupil of Inigo Jones, retired to the continent under the assumed name of Montagu. It is uncertain whether he ever returned to England, authorities differing as to the place of his death, though all agree that it occurred on December 31, 1673, at the age of 75.

St. John's powers as an advocate were certainly great: of his qualities as a judge there are few means of forming an opinion, for there are no Reports of his court during the time that he presided in it. Of his private disposition all authorities concur in describing it as gloomy, reserved, and unamiable; but the charge which is made by some, that he was avaricious and died disgracefully rich, is not supported by sufficient evidence. He says himself that he not only refused the presents offered to him by the States on his embassy, and returned the plate, &c., with which he was supplied to the Wardrobe, but that the only reward he received was the compliance with his request on behalf of the citizens of Peterborough of the preservation of their cathedral from demolition. He asserts also that he never had one penny advantage, save from his place as a judge; and though the profits of that were considerable, he could not have accumulated largely, since he was obliged in 1657 to sell for the payment of his taxes an estate of 500

---

[1] Parl. Hist. iv. 70. 91. 114.; St. 12. Car. II. c. 11.; Ludlow, 393.

acres on the Bedford Level. That great undertaking was completed principally by his exertions; and his legal acumen is evidenced by the Act which he drew, and under which it is managed up to the present day. In commemoration of his services, his name is still connected with its greatest work, called " St. John's Eau."[1]

After the death of his second wife, St. John entered into a third marriage with Elizabeth, daughter of Daniel Oxenbridge, M. D., of Daventry and afterwards of London, and sister of John Oxenbridge, the well-known Nonconformist Fellow of Eton, and also of the wife of the parliamentary General Skippon. She was the widow of Caleb Crockcroft of London, merchant, and, having outlived St. John, she took for her third husband Sir Humphrey Sydenham of Chilworthy in Somersetshire, and died in 1680.

By her he had no issue; but by his first wife he had two sons and two daughters, and by the second, one son and one daughter. Of his first family his eldest son, Francis, served in the two parliaments of 1656 and 1658 for Peterborough, and was the father of another Francis who, in 1715, was made a baronet, but the title became extinct at his death in 1756. Joanna, one of the chief-justice's daughters, married Sir Walter St. John of Battersea, baronet, and was the grandmother of the celebrated Henry, first Viscount Bolingbroke, whose representative still enjoys the title.[2]

STEELE, WILLIAM.

Ch. B. E. 1655.

GIDDY HALL, a moated house at Sandbach in Cheshire, was the seat of the Steeles; and Richard, the father of the chief baron, is inserted in a pedigree in the British Museum

[1] Wells's Bedford Level, i. 199.
[2] Collins's Peerage, vi. 742 ; Wotton's Baronet. iv. 178.

as of that parish.[1]　While his son was pursuing his legal studies he probably removed nearer to London; for the books of Gray's Inn record that William Steele, the eldest son of Richard Steele of Finchley, in Middlesex, was admitted a member of that society on June 13, 1631, and that he became a barrister on June 23, 1637.[2]　He was one of the candidates for the judgeship of the Sheriffs' court in London in 1643, but was unsupported either by the Common Council or the Court of Aldermen, between whom there was a contest as to the right of election, and John Bradshaw, afterwards president of the High Court of Justice, was chosen.[3]　In 1647 he had the conduct of the prosecution of the unfortunate Captain Burley for his loyal but fruitless attempt to rescue the king in the Isle of Wight; and the zeal and energy he displayed so ingratiated him with the parliament, that when they were seeking a successor for Mr. Glynne in the recordership of London in January 1648, they recommended him to the city for the post.　The vacancy did not then take place; and, at the end of the year, the Commons found more active employment for him by appointing him attorney-general of the commonwealth, for the purpose of conducting the charges against the king.[4] But when the court sat on Jannary 18 to make arrangements for the trial, Steele was or pretended to be ill, and in sending a message announcing that he was " not like as yet to attend the service of the court," he signified that " he no way declined the service, out of any disaffection to it, but professed himself to be so clear in the business that if it should please God to restore him, he should manifest his good affection to the cause."　He thus escaped the odious office, which Solicitor-General Cook performed; but within ten days after the execution he was well enough to appear in the High Court

---

[1] Ormerod's Cheshire, iii. 449.; Harl. MSS. 2040. p. 240.
[2] Gray's Inn Books.　　　　　　[3] Com. Counc Books, xl. 74.
[4] Whitelocke, 290. 368.

of Justice on the prosecution of the Earl of Cambridge (Duke of Hamilton) against whom he delivered a long and laboured speech. So also against the Earls of Holland and Norwich, Lord Capel and Sir John Owen, who were tried about the same time.[1]

Mr. Serjeant Glynne being at last induced to resign his post of recorder of London, Steele was elected on August 25, 1649.[2] He had in the previous April been superseded in his temporary office of attorney-general by Mr. Prideaux, and the Commons were glad of this opportunity of rewarding his services, their sense of which they still further marked by giving him the privilege of pleading within the bar, and ordering that he should be freed from his reading at his inn of Court.[3]

He was one of the committee named in Jannary, 1652, to consider of the delays, the charges, and the irregularities in the proceedings of the law; and in May, 1654, was a commissioner to try the Portuguese ambassador's brother for murder. In the last case he is called Serjeant Steele[4], to which degree he had been admitted on January 25.[5]

Cromwell when he became protector in December, 1653, omitted Chief Baron Wilde from his reappointments, and left the offiee vacant for more than a year. He then bestowed it on Mr. Serjeant Steele, who was sworn in after a learned speech from Mr. Commissioner Whitelocke on May 28, 1655.[6] Three days after he resigned his recordership. On the 26th of August, in the following year, he was advanced to the Lord Chancellorship of Ireland[7]; and on December 10, 1657, he was nominated one of Cromwell's House of Lords.[8] He was continued in his office on the accession of the Protector Richard; on whose deposition and the second expulsion of

[1] State Trials, iv. 1064. 1167. 1209.
[2] City List of Recorders.
[3] Whitelocke, 394, 420.
[4] Whitelocke, 520. 590.
[5] Noble's Cromwell, i. 438.
[6] Wood's Ath. Oxon. iii. 1045.
[7] Smyth's Law Off. of Ireland, 33, 34.
[8] Parl. Hist. iii. 1518.

the Long Parliament he was named by Fleetwood in October, 1659, as one of the Committee of Safety. With this body, however, he refused to act, declaring his opinion to be that the parliament were the only proper judges as to the future establishment.[1]

At the restoration of Charles II. he of course lost his place, but is said to have secured his personal safety and made his peace with the government by betraying the secrets of Henry Cromwell to Clarendon and Ormond, and, what is worse, by giving up his former colleague in the prosecution of the king, Solicitor-General Cook.

He was a lawyer of ability and learning, but his character is described by the writers on one side as proud, crafty, insincere, and insolent[2], while, on the other, it is stated that he was generally esteemed to be a man of great prudence and uncorrupted integrity[3]; and nothing appears in his recorded history in contradiction to this, if confined to pecuniary transactions.

He married the widow of Michael Harvey, younger brother to the celebrated Dr. William Harvey.[4]

THORPE, FRANCIS.

B. E. 1649. 1660.

DESCENDED from the Yorkshire family of Thorpe of Thorpe, in Holderness, Francis Thorpe was the eldest son of Roger Thorpe of Birdshall, by Elizabeth, daughter of William Danyell of Beswick.[5] He was born in 1595, and was admitted on February 12, 1610, a member of Gray's Inn, where his father had studied before him. On May 11, 1621, he was called to the bar, and became reader in autumn, 1641. He held the post of recorder of Beverley from 1623 till he was

---

[1] Ludlow's Mem. 302. 313.   [2] Clarendon; Duhigge.   [3] Ludlow, 313.
[4] Noble's Cromwell, i. 396.   [5] Harl. MSS. 1487. 205. 503.; 1394. 122.

raised to the bench in 1649, receiving a fee of 10*l.* a year[1]; and was one of the witnesses examined against the Earl of Strafford, who had taken offence against him in Yorkshire for moving for prohibitions.[2] He obtained a seat in the Long Parliament in September, 1645, for the borough of Richmond, in the place of one of its expelled representatives.[3] Returned by the party then in the ascendant, he was made a serjeant on October 12, 1648, when the vacancies in the law were filled up.[4] After the king was beheaded (for the trial of whom Thorpe was named a commissioner, but never attended[5]), he was raised to a seat in the Exchequer on June 1, 1649, vacant by the refusal of one of the barons to act under the new government; being no doubt selected for this elevation on account of the " good service " done by him in the last northern circuit, on which, as was common with the serjeants, he rode as judge of assize.[6] In an elaborate charge to the grand jury at York (afterwards printed) he endeavoured to justify the murder of the king, and to vindicate the parliament in their proceedings, raking up all the invidious and scandalous invectives against kings and monarchy which the most celebrated republicans up to his time had ever written.[7] He was therefore again sent on that circuit for the summer assize, and was presented with 200*l.* for his zeal in the former.[8] He fully confirmed the opinion which the ruling powers had formed of him, by his condemnation of Lieut.-Colonel Morrice at York; though his conduct at the trial was more merciful than that of Judge Puleston.[9]

In the parliament called by Cromwell in September, 1654, and dissolved in the following January, Thorpe, though a judge, was returned for Beverley. He became disgusted with the Protector's proceedings, and, excusing himself from trying

---

[1] Poulson's Beverley, i. 377.　[2] Rushworth, iv. 116.　[3] Parl. Hist. ii. 625.
[4] Whitelocke, 342.　[5] State Trials, iv. 1051.　[6] Whitelocke, 405. 409.
[7] Drake's York, 171.　[8] Com. Journals, vi. 144.　[9] State Trials, iv. 1249.

the prisoners in the north as contrary to his conscience, he and Judge Newdigate, who had the same scruples, received their writs of ease on May 3, 1655. Whitelocke records that they "were put out of their places for not observing the Protector's pleasure in all his commands." Thorpe's disgrace at court made him so popular in his native county, that in the next parliament in 1656 he was elected for the West Riding: but not obtaining the council's, or rather Cromwell's certificate of approbation, he and above ninety others were excluded from its sittings. They thereupon published a spirited remonstrance, so violent in its language that it is surprising that the powers which had stirred up this resistance took no means to punish it.[1]

Thorpe was not returned to Protector Richard's parliament in January, 1659: but when the Long Parliament was restored he took his seat as a member.[2] On January 17, 1660, he was replaced on the bench as a baron of Exchequer[3], and was appointed to go to the Norfolk circuit.[4] His judicial career was of course closed by the return of Charles II.

In the "Mystery of the Good Old Cause," he is described as a bitter enemy to his prince, and as "receiver of the money in Yorkshire, charged by some of the country for detaining 25,000l."[5] This charge was probably alluded to when a motion was made that his name should be excepted from the Bill of Indemnity, which was seconded by Prynne, "who mentioned one Thorpe, a judge in Edward the II.nd's time, who for taking bribes and other misdemeanors was punished, and therefore desired that this Judge Thorpe might also suffer the same." He had a narrow escape; but, several members speaking in his behalf, he was acquitted.[6]

He married the daughter of . . . Oglethorpe, widow of . . . Denton; but it does not appear that he left any children.[7]

---

[1] Godwin, iv. 181.; Whitelocke, 625. 653.   [2] Parl. Hist. iii. 1548.
[3] Whitelocke, 693.   [4] Mercurius Politicus, Feb. 16. 1660.
[5] In Parl. Hist. iii. 1608. [6] Parl. Hist. v. 75. [7] Poulson's Beverley, i. 393.

TOMLINS, RICHARD.

CURSITOR B. E. 1649.

See under the Reign of Charles I.

RICHARD TOMLINS was the son and heir of Edward Tomlins of Todinton, in the county of Gloucester, as far as the writing of his admission as a member of the Inner Temple can be deciphered. The date of that admission is May 6, 1606 [1]; after which no more is recorded of him till he was assigned as counsel to assist Bastwick and Burton in their complaint of the cruel sentence pronounced against them in the Star Chamber.[2] Tomlins was not long in being rewarded for his exertions. In consequence of the illness of Baron Trevor, the only judge of the Court of Exchequer who adhered to the Parliament, and Cursitor Baron Leeke having joined the other barons at Oxford, a difficulty arose in September, 1645, as to who was to receive the customary presentation of the Sheriffs of London and to attend the other ceremonies usually performed on the 30th of that month. The Lords, therefore, on the day previous recommended Mr. Christopher Vernon as Leeke's successor, but, upon sending to the Commons for their concurrence, they unanimously substituted the name of Richard Tomlins, who was thereupon sworn into the place of Cursitor Baron quamdiu bene gesserit; and on December 27, an order was issued to the Middle [Inner?] Temple to call him to the bench of that society. He was resworn on the death of the king and kept his place through all the succeeding changes, his name being recorded in the Exchequer Books of Hilary Term, 1653-4, on the assumption of the protectorate by Oliver Cromwell, and of Michaelmas Term, 1658, on the succession of Protector Richard.[3]

---

[1] Inner Temple Books.　　　[2] State Trials, iii. 761. 763.
[3] Lords' Journ. vii. 606.; Commons', iv. 292. ; Whitclocke, 174. 185. 383.

He must have been a garrulous humorist, to judge from a speech printed as having been addressed by him to the sheriffs of London in 1659, on their coming to the Exchequer to be sworn. Its absurdity is too great to be supposed to be a faithful transcript of his words, but it is doubtless a true representation of his style and manner, taken by some auditor who was amused with the address, and who was so ignorant of his name as to call him Tomlinson.[1] He was then, as he says, a very old man; and he either died or was displaced at the Restoration, when Thomas Leeke, who was cursitor baron before him, resumed his office.

TYRRELL, THOMAS.

Com. G. S. 1659. 1660.

See under the Reign of Charles II.

WARBURTON, PETER.

Just. C. P. 1649. Just. U. B. 1656.

FROM one of five brothers who came over with the Conqueror, and who were all largely rewarded, the great family of Dutton was descended, which was endowed with extensive possessions in Cheshire. About the reign of Richard I. the township of Warburton was acquired by a younger son, by a grant from Roger Fitz-Alured, whose daughter he had married. One of his descendants, Peter, first assumed its name in the reign of Edward II., and it has been since borne by his posterity. The seat of Arley Hall in the same county was built in the time of Henry VII., and thenceforward became the residence of the family. Most of its members

---

[1] " Baron Tomlinson's learned Speech to the Sheriffs of London and Middle-sex, when they came to be sworn at the Chequer. London, printed in the year 1659."

received the honour of knighthood, and many were sheriffs of the county.

The second Peter Warburton, in legal biography, was a direct descendant from the family; being the grandson of Peter the purchaser of Hefferston Grange, who was the third son of Sir Peter Warburton of Arley, knight.[1] He acquired the rudiments of the law in Staple Inn, of which he was a member in 1618, and probably completed his studies at Lincoln's Inn, where several of his family had previously been educated.

The first account of him is that he was appointed by the Long Parliament in March, 1647, one of the judges in Wales, and that John Bradshaw and he were joined together on the Chester Circuit. His next advance was on June 1, 1649, when he was raised to the bench at Westminster as Justice of the Common Pleas[2]; in which character he was one of the commissioners for the trial of John Lilburn in October following; but he does not seem to have taken any active part in it. At a later period, apparently about June, 1655, he was removed to the Upper Bench, but the date is not precisely given. He is mentioned as sitting in that court in Style's and Siderfin's Reports, and on the trial in 1657 of Miles Sindercome for attempting to murder the Protector.[3] He probably died between Easter and Trinity, 1659, as his name does not appear in Siderfin's Reports after the former term, and as he is not among the judges who were named by the Rump Parliament in Jannary, 1660; nor among the serjeants re-made by Charles II.

The Grange remained in his family till the death of his grandson, also Peter, without issue in 1727, when it fell into possession of female representatives.[4]

---

[1] Ormerod's Cheshire, ii. 93.; and the information of the family.
[2] Report Pub. Rec., App. x. 252.; Whitelocke, 240. 405. 407.
[3] State Trials, iv. 1269.; v. 841.   [4] Ormerod, ut supra.

WHITELOCKE, BULSTRODE.

COM. G. S. 1649. 1659.

See under the Reign of Charles I.

To the industry of Bulstrode Whitelocke the historians of the Commonwealth are greatly indebted for the minuteness of his details of that stirring period : and from his Memorials may also be collected the principal incidents of his own life. His personal relations, however, must be received with those qualifications to which the story of an autobiographer is ever subject : and, when it is remembered that he lived for fifteen years after the Restoration, and that his work was published seven years after his death, in the reign of the restored king, it is perhaps not too much to suggest that some allowance must be made for certain modifications, not unnaturally introduced to suit the time in which the Memorials saw the light, and to avoid the risk of injuring the prospects of the family by whose permission they were issued from the press.

Bulstrode Whitelocke was the only son of Sir James Whitelocke, the judge of the King's Bench in the last two reigns. He was born on August 6, 1605, in Fleet Street, at the house of the eminent lawyer Sir George Croke, the uncle of his mother ; and was christened with his mother's maiden name, she being Elizabeth, daughter of Edward Bulstrode, Esq., and sister of the Reporter. He received his early education at Merchant Taylors' School, which he left at Michaelmas, 1620 ; and was then entered as a gentleman commoner at St. John's College, Cambridge. From Dr. (afterwards Archbishop) Land the then president, who was the intimate friend of his father, he received much kindness and attention. Soon after Land's promotion to the see of St. David's he left the university without taking a degree, and, having been previously admitted as a student at the Middle Temple in 1619, he proceeded with his legal studies there. His seven years' probation terminated, he was called to the bar in Michaelmas

Term, 1626. At Christmas, 1628, he was chosen Master of the Revels by his brother Templars; and was becomingly proud on receiving a frolicsome fee, and a prophecy of future greatness, from Attorney-general Noy, when he attended that officer on a matter arising out of these Christmas revels.[1] In his study of the law he had the advantage of his father's great experience and learning; besides the opportunity, of which he amply availed himself, of accompanying the judge and his colleagues on their different circuits.

Whitelocke is not mentioned by Dugdale as filling the office either of reader or treasurer of his house; but on the four inns of court joining together in 1633 in performing a masque before the king and queen, he was united with Mr. Edward Hyde (afterwards Earl of Clarendon) to act for the Middle Temple in the committee of preparation; and to him " in particular," he says, " was committed the whole care and charge of all the musick for this great masque, which was so performed that it excelled any musick that ever before that time had been heard in England." This masque (in the description of which Whitelocke revels with excessive delight) was performed before the court on Candlemas night, 1633–4, and was so well received that it was repeated by the desire of the queen at Merchant Taylors' Hall, on the invitation of the lord mayor. This probably was the commencement of the intimacy which Lord Clarendon records as existing between him and Whitelocke, of whom he always speaks with kindness: and to the reminiscences of that friendship Whitelocke was not improbably indebted for the impunity he experienced on the restoration of Charles II. The inclination of both of them at that time was to the popular party; each desiring to give what assistance he could to remove the grievances that pressed hard upon the people. Whitelocke relates several instances of the intimate footing of

[1] Athen. Oxon. iii. 1042.: Middle Temple Books; Memorials, 11.

their correspondence, and notes its close in 1643, when they took opposite sides in the civil conflict.[1]

Whitelocke's first public display in politics was at the Quarter Sessions at Oxford in 1635, when in his charge to the grand jury he ventured some allusions to the power of the temporal courts over ecclesiastical matters, which had begun to be questioned. He was engaged by the country gentlemen to defend their forest liberties and privileges, which were attacked; and he was advised with in the defence which Hampden so nobly maintained against ship money. These evidences of his opinions resulted in his being returned as member for Marlow to the Long Parliament, which commenced its sittings in November, 1640. In one of the earliest debates he took occasion to make a spirited defence of his father, who was charged as being one of the judges who had refused to bail Selden and his fellow-prisoners; and succeeded in exonerating his father's memory from the imputation. He was chosen chairman of the committee appointed to prepare the impeachment, and arrange the evidence, against the Earl of Strafford; and at the trial had the charge of the last seven articles. The unfortunate earl gave Whitelocke the credit of having used him like a gentleman; and Whitelocke seems evidently impressed, if not with the earl's innocence, with his eloquent defence, and his whole conduct before his accusers and judges.[2] In the debate on the militia Whitelocke made a compromising speech; but on the passing of the bill he accepted the deputy lieutenancy of two counties, Buckingham and Oxford: and in the great question of taking up arms he argued forcibly against commencing a civil war, but concluded by voting for its adoption. Actively engaged in his county for the parliament, and commanding a " gallant company of his neighbours," he experienced the

<hr/>

[1] Memorials, 19. 22. 25, 26. 81.; Clarendon's Life, i. 67.
[2] Memorials, 23—43.; State Trials, iii. 14. 38.

usual consequences. When the royal troops marched towards London, his house at Fawley Court became the quarters of a regiment of horse, who in the spirit of destruction despoiled it of all that was valuable. He was with the army opposed to the king at Brentford in November; and in the January following was one of the commissioners appointed to treat with his majesty for peace at Oxford. His declaration that at this period " he would never *appear* to be entirely of any faction, or party," and that he " industriously laboured to promote all overtures for peace," seems in curious contrast with his acting for the parliament against the king, and his consenting to be the bearer of proposals for reconciliation, which the latter could not be expected to accept.[1] Lord Clarendon, however, acquits the commissioners of any disloyal inclinations, acknowledging their sincere desire to make a peace, and their endeavours to induce his majesty so to qualify his counter-proposition that it might not be rejected by the parliament.[2]

This negotiation failing, Whitelocke in the next year repeated his endeavours, in a speech recommending a renewal of pacific overtures; which was followed in November, 1644, by a second commission to Oxford, partly English and partly Scotch, authorised merely to take certain propositions of the parliament and to obtain the king's answer, but not to treat with him concerning them. Whitelocke details an interesting conversation which the king had privately with him and Mr. Hollis at a complimentary visit they paid to the Earl of Lindsey, in which they were gratified with the royal acknowledgment of the sincerity of their wish to put an end to the unhappy dissensions. The propositions were such that the king could not with honour accede to them, but by his answer he suggested that persons should be named on both sides to discuss the various subjects and conclude a treaty. It was arranged that this conference should take place at Uxbridge,

---

[1] Memorials, 55. 58. 60. 63. 65—69.   [2] Clarendon's Life, i. 175.

where the commissioners, of whom Whitelocke was one, accordingly met on January 29, 1645 ; but the same fate attended it. After quarrelling, with obstinacy on both sides, upon subjects of church government and the settlement of the militia, the treaty was broken off on February 22.[1]

During the intervals between these several negotiations, Whitelocke had the courage to refuse to serve on the committee appointed to manage the charges against his early instructor and his friend, Archbishop Laud, and the house had the grace to admit his excuse. He was a member of the Assembly of Divines, and both there and in parliament he spoke, against the opinion that the government of the church by presbyteries was *Jure Divino.* In 1644 he was made attorney of the duchy of Lancaster by the parliament ; and in the next month he and Serjeant Maynard were placed in the awkward position of being called upon by the Lord General Essex and the Scots to advise whether Cromwell, of whom they began to be jealous, could be proceeded against as an incendiary. The counsel given by the two lawyers was such that the charge was deferred ; and Cromwell, to whom this incident was soon reported, was of course pleased with the two advisers ; and set himself to work to countercheck his enemies. This he effectually accomplished by the Self-Denying Ordinance, which resulted in the resignation of Essex. Whitelocke made a strong speech against the ordinance, but in the end, as his manner was, voted for it.[2]

In April, 1645, he was appointed governor of Henley on Thames and of the fort of Phillis Court, with a garrison of 300 foot and a troop of horse ; and in July he and Mr. Hollis had to defend themselves against a violent attempt of the independent party to fix a treasonable charge upon them for their communication with the king at Oxford. They suc-

[1] Memorials, 84. 113. 127. 133.
[2] Ibid. 71. 75. 99. 110. 115, 116. 119.; Clarendon, v. 90.

ceeded, however, in obtaining a full acquittal by the house, with a permission to prosecute their accuser, Lord Savile. On the termination of the civil war Whitelocke resumed his forensic duties; and was so successful, that on the circuit, he was retained in almost every cause. Nor was his practice confined to the Common Law Courts, but extended to the Chancery, the House of Lords, and also the Court of Wards till it was abolished in the beginning of 1646. To the suppression of that court he gave his aid in parliament; and was otherwise serviceable in that assembly, being commonly named on all committees on foreign affairs. In May, 1647, he advised and spoke against disbanding the army, though the party to which he was attached had proposed the measure. This of course disposed Cromwell more strongly in his favour, and saved him from being included in the attack made by General Fairfax and the officers against eleven of his colleagues; and from the consequences to which it led.[1]

To his high standing in his profession, to his industrious labours in parliament, and perhaps more than all to the favour of the general, and to the opinion which Cromwell had formed of his accommodating disposition, he owed his elevation to the important position to which he was next raised. On March 15, 1648, the two houses concurred in appointing him to be one of the four commissioners of the Great Seal for one year. In October of the same year he was elected a bencher of his society; and was named by the parliament a serjeant at law and king's serjeant. The latter appointments were, however, deferred in order that as lord commissioner he might swear in the other new serjeants. This he did on the 18th of the next month, having three days before sworn in Chief Baron Wilde. His speeches on both these occasions, which he has preserved in his memorials, are long and laborious dissertations on the antiquity of the two courts and the dig-

---

[1] Memorials, 137. 151—161. 181. 194. 234. 248. 253. 266. 293.

nity and duties of the officers. He was evidently fond of these antiquarian displays, for he reports two others in 1649; one on the appointment of new judges, and the other addressed to the House of Commons on a motion to exclude lawyers from parliament; and a third, still more elaborate, in 1650, historically vindicating the laws of England, in support of the act which directed all legal proceedings to be in the English tongue.[1]

The commissioners were soon interrupted in their judicial proceedings at Westminster by Pride's Purge; when, in order to avoid the tumult, they were obliged to sit in the Middle Temple Hall. This was followed by various conferences which Cromwell had with Whitelocke and his brother commissioner Widdrington, with the pretended object of settling the kingdom; while at the same time he was making active preparations in the House of Commons for bringing the king to trial. The two commissioners determined to refuse their countenance to the measure; and, on being sent for, escaped together to Whitelocke's house in the country, till the Commons had passed the ordinance for the trial without the concurrence of the Lords. They then returned to their duties, and shortly afterwards these two commissioners obeyed an ordinance, made by the same mutilated authority, to adjourn Hilary Term, that it might not interfere with the solemnity of the trial.[2]

The bloody deed accomplished, the functions of the four commissioners ceased. The House of Lords was next abolished, and Whitelocke, though he spoke against it, drew up the ordinance for the purpose. He says he "could not get excused;" but his pleading could not have been very earnest, since two days after, the same assembly, which would not excuse him, admitted Widdrington's "scruples of conscience," as a sufficient reason against his accepting the custody of the

[1] Memorials, 295. 342—355. 407. 431. 478.   [2] Ibid. 361—371.

Seal under the new government. Whitelocke justified his taking a contrary course when the same place was offered to him, by a speech in which, after the usual pretences of incapacity, &c., and acknowledging the parliament as the only existing authority, he maintained the absolute necessity that the place should be filled, in order that " Right and Justice " should be done to men. He was therefore sworn in, with L'Isle and Keeble for his colleagues. He accepted a seat in the Council of State also, and was appointed high steward and keeper of Greenwich Park, an office which he exchanged for that of constable of Windsor Castle, and keeper of the Forest. He also was made high steward and recorder of Oxford, and keeper of the library and medals at St. James's.[1]

Cromwell was named lord-general in June, 1650; and in September in that and the following year he won two great victories, the first over the Scots at Dunbar, and the second over the king's army at Worcester. On the latter occasion Whitelocke was one of the four members deputed by the house to convey its congratulations; and was rewarded by Cromwell with a horse and two prisoners, to whom Whitelocke immediately gave their liberty, and passed them home to Scotland. After this defeat of the royalists, Cromwell began to feel his way, how far he was likely to succeed in attaining absolute authority, the object of his present aspirations. To this end he called a conference, to consider the settlement of the kingdom. The general opinion was in favour of a mixture of monarchical government, which accorded with Cromwell's wishes; but when, on the question in whom the power should be placed, Whitelocke and others suggested one of the sons of the late king, the meeting was dissolved with no other result than a discovery of the inclinations of those who composed it. Some months afterwards (in November, 1652,) Cromwell again broached the subject, and in a curious con-

[1] Memorials, 377—381. 384. 415.; Evelyn, ii. 53.; Athen. Oxon. iii. 1043.

versation sounded Whitelocke as to his assuming the title of king; and on hearing the probable injurious consequences, pressed the lord commissioner for his opinion as to the best means to obviate the existing difficulties and dangers. The recommendation he received from Whitelocke,—that he should apply to Charles, and by a private treaty for his restoration, in which the rights and liberties of the people should be maintained, and proper limitations placed on the monarchical power, thus securing to the nation all they had been fighting for, and to himself, his family, and friends, not only impunity for the past, but riches and honours as his reward,—he professed to be worthy of consideration; and they parted. From this time Whitelocke says Cromwell altered his carriage towards him, and ceased to advise with him intimately. The general had before been displeased with Whitelocke for his " noncompliance with his pleasure in some things, and particularly in some Chancery causes; " and was suspected of an attempt to get him out of the way, by appointing him chief commissioner in Ireland; which he refused.[1]

Whitelocke's opposition to the dissolution of the parliament confirmed Cromwell's distrust in him, but did not prevent the violent dismissal of that assembly in April, 1653. In June, Cromwell, who now assumed the whole power, called a sort of council of 120 persons, afterwards nicknamed the Barebone's Parliament. To this assembly Whitelocke was not summoned; and by an early vote the Court of Chancery was ordered to be taken away. The ordinance was however suspended before completion, and never came into operation; so that the existing commissioners still preserved some influence in the State. The plans which Cromwell had formed he was aware were obnoxious to Whitelocke, whom therefore he was desirous of sending out of the way, in order that no obstacle might be raised to the attainment of his ulterior designs. This

---

[1] Memorials, 470. 507. 509. 516 536. 548. 551.

could only be safely effected by an appointment to some honourable trust which would temporarily exile Whitelocke from England. The pseudo parliament accordingly, by Cromwell's dictation, named him ambassador to the Queen of Sweden; an office which, however distasteful on many accounts, Whitelocke deemed it prudent not to refuse, conscious of the power of the general, and doubtful of the consequences of resistance.[1] He sailed on November 6, 1653, and began his voyage gracefully, by releasing a Dutch vessel which he took, with all her cargo, to the poor skipper, who would have been ruined by their detention and loss. He was absent from England till the 30th of the following June, and succeeded in effecting a treaty of amity with Queen Christina; the last public act that she transacted before her abdication. Both by her and Prince Charles Gustavus, who succeeded her, Whitelocke was treated with the greatest distinction and respect. He was honoured with her order of Amarantha, and on all occasions was admitted to private and familiar conferences. In his voyage out, as well as on his return, he had, as he describes them, miraculous escapes from the perils of the sea, and rather vauntingly attributes his safety from the latter to the orders that he issued to the ship's company in opposition to the naval captain. He moreover kept a daily journal, which is most interesting in reference to the description of the country through which he passed, his manner of travelling, and the detail of his receptions, the progress of his negotiations, and the conversations which he had with the queen and her ministers, particularly the Chancellor Oxenstiern; and his tenaciousness with the latter as to all forms of ceremony, lest the honour and dignity of the commonwealth should be compromised. This Journal is more minute as to personal matters than his Memorials, and, bating a rather copious sprinkling of vanity and ostentation, impresses the reader with a good opinion of his piety and

---

[1] Memorials, 554. 562. 568.; Burton's Diary, i., vi. l. xcvi.

judgment in the ordering of his household, and his abilities in diplomacy. He appears to have made himself agreeable to all those with whom he had intercourse, and, judging from the value and number of the presents and entertainments that were given and received, the friendly feeling and the liberality were reciprocal. His Journal was not published till near a century after the author's death.[1]

During Whitelocke's eight months' absence the little Parliament had resigned its power into the hands of Cromwell, who was immediately inaugurated Protector of the three kingdoms. A new commission for the custody of the Great Seal was issued in April 1654, in which Whitelocke (though absent) was the first named, with his old associate Widdrington and his late one L'Isle. On his return to England he gave an account of his embassy to Cromwell and his Council.[2] Consenting to act under the new government he was sworn into his office on July 14; and was soon after made one of the Commissioners of the Exchequer. Such was his popularity at that time that in the Parliament which was summoned by Cromwell, he was elected by three several constituencies, the county of Bucks, the town of Bedford, and the city of Oxford; while his son James was returned for the latter county.[3] The parliament was opened on September 4 in great state, when Whitelocke carried the Purse before the Protector, and two days after he made a second recital of his negotiation in Sweden to the assembly, and not only received public thanks from the Speaker but also a vote of 2000l. for his services. This sum was not however paid to him till the vote was renewed in February, 1657. Cromwell dissolved this Parliament on December 31, as not sufficiently compliant with his views. Looking with

---

[1] A new edition of this entertaining work has lately been published, under the able direction of Henry Reeve, Esq., F.S.A.

[2] Memorials, 584. 593.   [3] Embassy to Sweden, ii. 461—464.

jealousy upon Whitelocke, whose ascendancy in the House
he thought too great, and whose inclinations against his
government he suspected, he soon found an opportunity of
removing him from office.   He caused an ordinance to be
made by the council for new regulations of the Court of
Chancery; which were so objectionable both in matter and
form that Whitelocke and his colleague Widdrington declined
to adopt them.   They were accordingly deprived of the Seal
on June 6, 1655.[1]

Being thus dismissed from the office which he had held for
above six years, he resumed for a short time his practice at
the bar, but in the next month he was made Commissioner
of the Treasury with the same salary he had lost.   He was
subsequently appointed on the committee for trade; and
also one of the commissioners to negotiate with the Swedish
Ambassador, with whom a treaty was concluded on July 17,
1656.   In the next parliament, which met in the following
September, he was again chosen for the county of Bucks:
and, upon the illness of Sir Thomas Widdrington the Speaker,
he was elected to supply his place till his recovery, three
weeks after.   The important question of the settlement of
the nation soon after engaged the House, and considering the
sentiments professed by Whitelocke it is surprising that he
was named chairman of the committee appointed to confer
with Cromwell on the subject; and still more so that he
should endeavour to induce the Protector to take the title of
King, and urge arguments against his pretended scruples.
The army having remonstrated, Cromwell refused the monarchical title, but accepted a new instrument of government
confirming to him the title of Lord Protector, and empower-
ing him to declare his successor, and to nominate seventy
members of the "other house," that being the modest name
under which an intended House of Lords was designated.

---

[1] Memorials, 599. 601. 604. 610. 621. 626.; 5 Report Pub. Rec., App. 261.

A solemn inauguration followed in June, 1657,. in which Whitelocke took a prominent part, and new commissions were issued for all the offices of state. Dissatisfied with politics Whitelocke soon after sought for the Provostship of Eton, then vacant, but was disappointed in his application. He was however consoled by being created one of the Lords of Cromwell's "other house," in preparation for the meeting of parliament in January, 1658. The jealousy of the Commons of that "other house" caused a dissolution in the course of a fortnight; and no doubt had its effect in disinclining Whitelocke to accept the title of Viscount, with which Oliver wished in the following August to distinguish him. Cromwell's death took place on the 3rd of the next month, and his son Richard was proclaimed his successor.[1]

Whitelocke was confirmed in his place in the Treasury by the new Protector[2], who, on January 22, 1659, replaced him in his former position as first Commissioner of the Great Seal; which he retained for less than four months. At the termination of Richard's short reign, and the restoration of the Long Parliament, he was again deprived of it on May 14; and of course lost also his short-lived peerage, resuming his seat in the House of Commons. He was however placed on the Council of State and voted its President; and when the subsequent dispute with the army occurred and the Long Parliament was a second time dismissed, he was nominated one of the Committee of Safety, which, after some hesitation, he was induced to undertake. One of the first acts of that Committee was to appoint Whitelocke sole Keeper of the Great Seal on November 1; and on the 5th he received a commission to raise a new regiment of horse, to oppose General Monk who had declared himself in favour of the discarded parliament. When that parliament was again

---

[1] Memorials, 627. 630. 632. 649. 650. 656—661. 666. 673, 674.
[2] 4 Report Pub. Rec., App. 198.

restored at the end of December, Whitelocke, apprehensive of his being sent to the Tower for acting on the Committee of Safety, concealed himself in the country, leaving the Great Seal with his wife to be delivered to the Speaker.[1] He remained in retirement till the final dissolution of that parliament by its own act on March 16, 1660; nor did he venture to offer himself as a candidate for the Convention that succeeded it.   He does not again mention himself in his Memorials of the time, which terminate with Charles's solemn entry into London on May 29.

Great indeed must have been Whitelocke's perplexity in the various changes of the last year; and the conduct he pursued demonstrates by too conclusive evidence his utter want of principle.   The Protector Richard's entrusted keeper of the Seal, he became a member of the council of state of the party that dethroned him; and when that party was in turn dismissed by the army he again changed sides, and acted in the Committee of Safety and as keeper of the Seal: and to crown all, though the professed object throughout the various changes was the settlement of the Commonwealth "without a king," yet he proposed to General Fleetwood to go over to Charles and offer him the crown; not from any loyal feeling, but merely, as he himself acknowledged, to forestall Monk in his supposed intentions, and to secure impunity for the past.[2]

It is not surprising, therefore, that many who had seen him acting in high stations in every revolution since the king's death, always adhering to the side that was uppermost, should have deemed him a person so obnoxious as to be properly ex-cepted from the act of pardon and oblivion passed at the Restoration.   But, though his enemies were bitter, his friends were strong and numerous.   His undoubted merits and ability pleaded for him; and particularly his moderation when in

[1] Memorials, 676. 678. 682. 685. 692.   [2] Ibid. 691.

power stood him in great stead; and consideration for his numerous family united with the rest to preserve him, with some difficulty and by a small majority, from the ruin that threatened him.[1] He no doubt owed much to his old friend Hyde, now lord chancellor, whose kind feeling towards him is manifested in various passages in his Autobiography and his History of the Rebellion; in which he accounts for Whitelocke's fluctuating conduct by the weakness of his character. In his domestic relations he was kind, amiable, and good humoured, and was evidently much beloved by his family; as a lawyer, if not deep, he was well read and intelligent, his practice at the bar was consequently very extensive, and his decisions on the bench were uncomplained of; as a scholar the learned Selden's frequent letters to him would be sufficient, without other evidences from his speeches and writings, to prove him erudite in historical and classical literature; and the manner in which he performed the duties of the various employments in which he was engaged, shows that with whatever motive he entered on them, he exerted himself strenuously to effect their object. His real deficiency was the want of moral courage, and his great weakness was vanity. The sentiments of mankind with regard to him are a mixture of affection and contempt; acquitting him of all the harsh feelings attributed to the leading opponents of the monarchy, but convicting him of aiding, by his respectability, in their success. His character is ably summed up by Clarendon, who says, " he bowed his knees to Baal, and so swerved from his allegiance, but with less rancour and malice than other men; he never led, but followed; and was rather carried away with the torrent than swam with the stream; and failed through those infirmities, which less than a general defection and a prosperous rebellion could never have discovered."[2]

He is said to have had an interview with the king, when

[1] Parl. Hist. iv. 70. 74.   [2] Clarendon's Life, i. 67.

the merry monarch good-humouredly told him to go into the country, and not to trouble himself with state affairs, but to take care of his wife and sixteen children. He could not expect any better encouragement, and he wisely followed the advice. He lived fifteen years after the Restoration, and dying in his retirement at Chilton Park in Wiltshire on January 28, 1676, he was buried at Fawley in Bucks, where his family property was situate.

He was thrice married. His first wife was Rebecca, daughter of Thomas Bennet, Esq., an alderman of London; his second was Frances, daughter of Lord Willoughby of Parham; and his third, a widow named Wilson, the daughter of —— Carleton, Esq., who survived him. He had children by each, but none of his male descendants remain.

WIDDRINGTON, THOMAS.

Com. G. S. 1654, 1660.   Ch. B. E. 1658.

See under the Reign of Charles I.

THIS lord commissioner of the Great Seal belonged to a junior branch of the ancient and loyal family of Widdrington of Widdrington in Northumberland, one of whom was the gallant squire renowned in the ballad of "Chevy Chase." Thomas was the eldest son of Lewis Widdrington of Desbourne Grange in Norfolk, and, after spending some time at both universities, was admitted a member of Gray's Inn on February 14, 1618. In due time he became a barrister and bencher, and was elected reader there in Lent, 1640-1.[1]

Before the latter date he was known in the courts, his name being noticed by Croke in 1636. He was, even previous to that, recorder of Berwick, and addressed King Charles in a loyal speech when passing through that town on June 2, 1633, in his progress to Scotland, concluding with

[1] Wood's Athen. Oxon. iii. 661; Gray's Inn Books.

the affectionate wish "That the throne of King Charles, the great and wise son of our British Solomon, may be that of King David, the father of Solomon, established before the Lord for ever." Being elected in 1638 to the more important office of recorder of York, he had to perform the same duty on the king's arrival in that city on March 30, 1639, when his oration exceeded the former in fulsome adulation. The king is the "glorious sun," his "very royal aspect surmounts our (York's) former glory and scatters our later clouds." He is told that "the beams and lightning of those eminent virtues, sublime gifts and illuminations wherewith you are endowed, do cast so forcible reflections on the eyes of all men, that you fill not only this city, this kingdom, but the whole universe with splendor;" and the climax is, that "you have established your Throne upon two Columns of Diamonds, Piety and Justice; the one gives you to God, the other gives Men to you, and all your subjects are most happy in both." How lamentable to contrast this ardent speech with the different language soon to be common, and with the recorder's future career! Its immediate reward was the honour of knighthood.[1]

In the next year he was elected member for Berwick, and soon distinguished himself as a zealous Presbyterian by taking a prominent part in the violent proceedings of the times. He prepared the impeachment of Bishop Wren, and introduced it into the House of Lords with an intemperate and abusive speech[2]; the result of which was the bishop's imprisonment in the Tower for eighteen years. He was one of the commissioners sent by the parliament to the army in June, 1647, to know what would satisfy them; and, turning to the independent party, he received the appointment of a commissioner of the Great Seal on March 15, 1648[3], for which he was

---

[1] Rushworth, i. 179., ii. 887.; Drake's York, 368.
[2] Parl. Hist. ii. 861. 886.   [3] Whitelocke, 252. 293. 295.

probably indebted as much to his connection with the general, Lord Fairfax, whose sister he had married, as to his abilities in his profession.　In October following he was called to the degree of the coif, and by the parliament declared king's serjeant.　The duty devolved upon him of swearing in Chief Justice Rolle, who was nominated at the same time, when he delivered "a very learned speech" upon the occasion.　These formalities over, he and Whitelocke, the other commissioner of the Seal, had many conferences with Cromwell and others as to the settlement of the kingdom, without leaving all to the sword; and so determined were they against having anything to do with the trial of the king, that they both retired to Whitelocke's house in the country to "avoid the business."[1]

When the tragedy was over, Sir Thomas, though named as commissioner by the new government, declined to serve; and the Commons had so much respect for his scruples, as not only to excuse him but to order that he should practise within the bar, and have a quarter's wages more than were due to him.　He, however, was made serjeant for the Commonwealth on June 9, 1650, and became member of the Council of State in February, 1651; he was present at the meeting at the speaker's house in the following December when Cromwell discussed with those present what was fit to be done for a settlement of the nation after the battle of Worcester.　Widdrington on that occasion advocated a mixed monarchical government as the most suitable, and in answer to the objection that the late king's eldest son had been in arms against them, and his second son was their enemy, suggested that the third son, the Duke of Gloucester, was still among them, and was too young to be infected with the principles of their enemies.　This hint was not relished by Cromwell, who soon broke up the conference.　Nor had Widdrington's resistance to his proposal in April, 1653, to put a period to the

---

[1] Whitelocke, 342. 349. 360—365.

parliament any better effect, for the day after the general violently turned the members out of doors by his own authority.[1] Notwithstanding this opposition, Widdrington was reinstated in his former place of commissioner of the Great Seal on April 5, 1654, soon after Cromwell became protector. In July he was elected member for the city of York in Cromwell's second parliament, and in August he was placed on the commission for the Treasury[2]; for which he had an additional 1000*l.* a year.[3] He did not enjoy his office much above a year; for Cromwell and his council having made " an ordinance for the better regulating and limiting the jurisdiction of the High Court of Chancery," which Whitelocke and Widdrington considered injurious to the public and illegal in itself, both of them refused to put it into execution, and were consequently dismissed on June 6th, 1655.[4] Cromwell in discharging them expressed no displeasure at their scruples; and, before the end of the year, Widdrington was appointed chancellor for the county palatine of Durham with a salary of 50*l.* a year.[5]

In the new parliament of September, 1656, Widdrington was returned both for the city of York and for Northumberland. His residence being at Chisburn Grange in that county, he elected to sit for it, and having received the council's approval, was allowed to enter the house, and was chosen speaker. The first business that devolved upon him was the reception of the spirited remonstrance of those members who had been excluded for want of the council's certificate of approbation.[6] At the beginning of the next year, being so ill as to be unable to perform his duties as speaker, the parliament elected Whitelocke to act during his absence, which continued till February 18; when, Whitelocke says, the

[1] Whitelocke, 378. 488. 516. 554. [2] Ibid. 584. 597.
[3] 4 Report Pub. Rec. App. ii. 193. [4] Whitelocke, 621—627.
[5] 5 Report Pub. Rec. App. ii. 253. [6] Parl. Hist. iii. 1484. 1486.

speaker came back at the hazard of his life, in order that he might secure to himself the fee of 5*l.* each upon certain private bills about to be passed.[1] Besides these special fees, he had a salary of 5*l.* a day during the continuance of the parliament.[2]

It became his duty in March to present " The humble Petition and Advice " to the Protector, calling upon him to take the title of King; which he introduced in a speech showing the antiquity of the title, and the present convenience and necessity of its being assumed, very ingeniously but somewhat fancifully illustrated. When this was declined, and a new constitution established, Sir Thomas administered to Cromwell the new oath as Lord Protector, prefacing it by delivering to him the robe of purple, the bible, the sceptre, and the sword, with a pithy comment on each.[3] The parliament was dissolved on February 4, 1658, principally because the Commons wasted their time in debating the title to be given to the " other House; " and Widdrington, whose arbitrary conduct as speaker had been frequently complained of by the members, was rewarded with the vacant office of lord chief baron of the Exchequer on June 26.[4] The death of Cromwell, which occurred on September 3, made no difference in his position, the Protector Richard reappointing him; but, before Richard was deposed, Serjeant Wilde petitioned the parliament to be reinstated in his former place of lord chief baron.[5] The serjeant's application was not at that time successful; but when the Long Parliament reassumed the government, Widdrington, having been appointed one of the Council of State, was transferred on January 17, 1660, from the Court of Exchequer to be principal commissioner of the Great Seal[6]; in which place he continued till the return of the king.

[1] Whitelocke, 655.   [2] 5 Report Pub. Rec. App. ii. 255.
[3] Burton's Diary, i. 397. ; ii. 513.   [4] Siderfin, 106.
[5] Burton's Diary, iv. 390--468.   [6] Whitelocke, 693.

In the Healing or Convention Parliament of April, 1660, Sir Thomas was elected for two places, Berwick and York, and sat for the latter. On the restoration of Charles II., he had the benefit of the Act of Indemnity, and by interest, as some say, but more probably by his character for moderation, he was the first named of the reappointed serjeants on June 1.[1] A few days after he boldly opposed a proviso moved by Colonel Jones and Mr. Prynne, compelling all officers during the protectorate to refund their salaries, saying that if he was included in it, he had much better have been excluded from the act. The clause was rejected. In December he was confirmed in his previous appointment of chancellor of Durham; and in May, 1661, he was again returned for Berwick to the second parliament of the reign.[2] He lived three years after, dying on May 13, 1664; and was buried in the chancel of St. Giles in the Fields, with a handsome monument to his memory. Though evidently an accomplished man, and well versed in his own profession, there is much in his career to prove the truth of what was said of his character, that it had " more of the willow than the oak."

He married Frances, daughter of Ferdinand, Lord Fairfax of Cameron, the father of the parliamentary general, and had by her four surviving daughters, who all married well; one of them to Sir Robert Shaftoe, serjeant at law, whose descendant, R. D. Shaftoe, Esq., has lately been declared heir at law to Sir Thomas Widdrington, in a suit relative to the Free School at Stamfordham in Northumberland, founded by him in 1663.

He left behind him a " A Description or Survey of the City of York."

---

[1] Siderfin, 3.   [2] Parl. Hist. iv. 77. 195.; Noble, i. 428.

WILDE, JOHN.

Ch. B. E. 1649, 1660.

See under the Reign of Charles I.

THE father of John Wilde was George Wilde of Droitwich in Worcestershire, who was twice reader in the Inner Temple, and a serjeant at law in the reign of James I. He sent his son John to Balliol College, Oxford, where he took the degree of B.A. in ·October, 1607, and of M.A. in July, 1610.[1] Following his father's profession he went to the same inn of court, where he was called to the bar, and in due time to the bench; and was elected reader in Lent, 1631.[2] He is noticed in Croke's Reports in the Easter Term of the preceding year, and he was a member of Charles's second parliament in 1626; when he took part in the debate against the Duke of Buckingham, arguing from Bracton that common fame was a sufficient ground for accusation.[3] In 1636 he was called to the degree of serjeant.[4]

In the Long Parliament he was member for Worcestershire, and was a prominent actor in its proceedings. He was chairman of the committee appointed to prepare the impeachment against the thirteen bishops concerned in making the new canons, which, on August 3, 1641, he presented to the House of Lords. In December he presided over a committee of. inquiry as to a plot to bring in the army to overawe the parliament; and in January, 1642, he reported a conference with the lords as to the attorney-general (Sir Edward Herbert) having impeached the five members; and conducted the impeachment against that officer which the Commons ordered. In the same year he subscribed two horses and their mainte-

---

[1] A. Wood's Fasti, i. 321. 338.   [2] Dugdale's Orig. 168.
[3] Parl. Hist. ii. 53.   [4] Rymer, xx. 22.
[5] Parl. Hist. ii. 895. 1039. 1121.; Verney's Notes, 131. 161.

nance for the defence of the parliament [1]; and in February, 1643, he was recommended as chief baron of the Exchequer, in the unsuccessful propositions made by the Commons to the king.[2]

The parliament having ordered a new Great Seal in place of that which had been carried to the king by Lord Lyttelton, principally on the arguments of Mr. Serjeant Wilde showing its necessity, resolved to entrust it to six commissioners, two lords and four commoners; and on November 10, 1643, the serjeant was selected as one of the latter. By successive votes these commissioners, notwithstanding the Self-denying Ordinance, retained the custody of the Seal for three years, when on October 30, 1646, they surrendered it to the speakers of the two houses. During this time Serjeant Wilde still kept his seat in the Commons, and was one of the managers on their part in the impeachment of Archbishop Laud, whose trial commenced on March 12, 1644. His speeches against the primate were more conspicuous for political and religious rancour than for argument or good taste. When Mr. Herne, the archbishop's counsel, argued that none of the charges amounted to treason, the serjeant said it had not been alleged that they did so, " but we do say, that all the bishop's misdemeanours put together, do, by way of accumulation, make many grand Treasons." Herne immediately replied, " I crave your mercy, good Mr. Serjeant; I never understood before this time, that two hundred black rabbits would make a black horse." The trial was superseded, as in the Earl of Strafford's case, by a bill of attainder, under which the Archbishop suffered on January 10, 1644–5. Wilde was elected Recorder of Worcester in July, 1646.[3]

After the seal was taken from the serjeant, he was several times employed as judge of assize; and does not seem to have

---

[1] Notes and Queries, 1st Ser. xii. 338.   [2] Clarendon's Hist. iii. 407.
[3] Journals; Whitelocke, 77. 218.; State Trials, iv. 351. 453. 586. 598.

been very scrupulous in his proceedings. He is accused at one time of hanging Capt. John Burley at Winchester, for causing a drum to be beaten for God and King Charles at Newport in the Isle of Wight, in order to rescue his captive sovereign; and at another, of directing the grand jury to ignore the bill of indictment preferred against Major Edmund Rolph, for intending to murder the king. The Commons voted their thanks to him for his great and good service done to the parliament in that circuit; and Anthony Wood states that he received 1000*l.* for each of these transactions; adding that it " was all one to him whether he hung or hung not, so he got the beloved pelf." [1]

On October 12, 1648, the parliament took upon them to fill the vacancies on the judicial bench, and appointed Serjeant Wilde to be chief baron of the Exchequer, who was sworn into office on November 16, after a long speech from Lord Commissioner Whitelocke. He still retained his position when the king was beheaded, took the new oaths, and was placed on the Council of State.[2] When Cromwell assumed the protectorate in December, 1653, he did not, for some unrecorded reason, continue Wilde as chief baron, but appointed William Steele.[3] There is a letter from Wilde, dated July 12, 1654, complaining that after all his services he is removed, addressed to Whitelocke on his return from the Swedish embassy, who says that it was " a usual reward in such times for the best services; " and adds that he moved the protector on Wilde's behalf, " but to no effect, the protector having a dislike to the serjeant, but the ground thereof I could not learn." [4]

Wilde remained out of employment during the rest of Cromwell's life, but was elected member for Droitwich in

[1] Fasti, i. 336.; Parl. Hist. iii. 1043.; Clarendon, v. 511., vi. 198.
[2] Whitelocke, 343. 349. 378. 381.   [3] Hardres' Rep.; Rayner's Tithes.
[4] Emb. to Sweden (1855), ii. 461.

Protector Richard's parliament of 1558-9. He there pre-sented a petition from himself, praying a restoration to his former office, and for payment of the arrears of 1300*l.* due to him for his salary. The former was refused because the place was full and he had not applied for redress to previous parliaments, and because his patent determined by the death of the king; but the latter was granted. He was not satis-fied, and presented next day another petition, the precise object of which is not mentioned, but in the committee to which it was referred, it is stated that "he took occasion highly to magnify himself, but said not a word of the present Lord Chief Baron's merits;" and that what others said of him was "but by way of compliment, as being able to say little else in his case." The dissolution of the parliament, a few days after, put an end to the discussion.[1]

On the return of the Long Parliament Serjeant Wilde resumed his place as a member[2], and on Jannary 17, 1659-60, was restored to his judicial seat by the same power that had first appointed him.[3] Short, however, was his enjoyment of it. The return of the king in May, and the immediate nomination of Sir Orlando Bridgman as lord chief baron, terminated the serjeant's legal career. In consequence of his having assisted the Lords in several committees of the Con-vention Parliament, he escaped further question[4], and, ab-solved by the Act of Indemnity, he retired to his house at Hampstead. There he died about 1669, and was buried at Wherwill in Hampshire, the seat of Charles, Lord De la Warr, the husband of his only daughter and heir Anne.[5] His wife was Anne, daughter of Sir Thomas Harries of Tonge Castle, serjeant at law and baronet.

Whitelocke describes him as "learned in his profession, but of more reading than depth of judgment," and as exe-

---

[1] Burton's Diary, iv. 390. 421—438.   [2] Parl. Hist. iii. 1548.
[3] Whitelocke, 693.   [4] Collins's Peerage, i. 287., ii. 166.   [5] Ibid. v. 24.

cuting his place "with diligence and justice;" but the testimony of his other contemporaries is strongly against him.
Clarendon calls him "an infamous judge;" and Archbishop
Laud, in the account of his trial, says, "I had a character
given me before of this gentleman which I will forbear to
express, but in this speech of his, and his future proceedings
with me, I found it exactly true;" and Anthony Wood's
opinion of him has been already stated. Some later writers
have confounded him with Sir William Wilde, successively
judge of both benches in the reign of Charles II.[1]

WYNDHAM, HUGH.

Just. C. P. 1654.

See under the Reign of Charles II.

---

[1] Wood's Fasti, ut suprà; Chambers' Illust. of Worcestersh.

INDEX

TO THE SIXTH VOLUME.

$*^*$ *The names of the Judges whose Lives are given in this Volume are printed in* Small Capitals.

END OF THE SIXTH VOLUME.

LONDON:
Printed by SPOTTISWOODE & Co.
New-street Square.

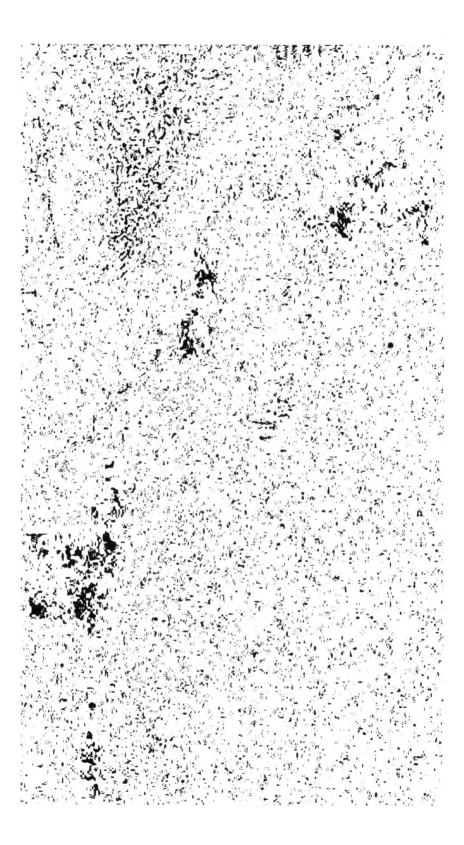

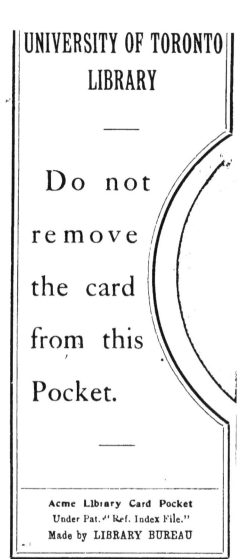

Lightning Source UK Ltd.
Milton Keynes UK
UKHW022018170119
335726UK00010B/693/P